DCU LIBRARY

030086574

WITHDRAWN

MAIN LENDING   **3 WEEK LOAN**   DCU LIBRARY

Fines are charged **PER DAY** if this item is overdue.
Check at www.dcu.ie/~library or telephone (01) 700 5183 for fine rates and
renewal regulations for this item type.
Item is subject to   .i.
Remember to   Book Bin when the library is closed.
The item is   turn on or before the latest date shown below.

KV-638-240

Complexity and Group Processes

The increasing intricacies of interdependence between people in modern life make it more important than ever to understand processes of human relating. In the West we tend to base our understanding of relating on a separation of the individual and the social. In *Complexity and Group Processes* Ralph Stacey explores an alternative way of understanding human interaction.

The key questions covered in this book are:

- Who am I and how have I come to be who I am?

- Who are we and how have we come to be who we are?

- How are we all changing, evolving and learning?

These are fundamental questions in the study of social relationships, and the exploration of these questions in *Complexity and Group Processes* is highly relevant not only for therapeutic groups but also those who are managing, leading and working in organizations.

Ralph Stacey is a member of the Institute of Group Analysis in London and works as a group therapist in the NHS. He is also Professor of Management and Director of the Complexity and Management Centre at the Business School of the University of Hertfordshire. He is co-editor of the Routledge series *Complexity Emergence in Organizations* and author of *Complex Responsive Processes in Organizations: Learning and Knowledge Creation*.

Complexity and Group Processes

A radically social understanding
of individuals

Ralph D. Stacey

Brunner-Routledge
Taylor & Francis Group

HOVE AND NEW YORK

First published 2003 by Brunner-Routledge
27 Church Road, Hove, East Sussex BN3 2FA

Simultaneously published in the USA and Canada
by Brunner-Routledge
29 West 35th Street, New York, NY 10001

Brunner-Routledge is an imprint of the Taylor & Francis Group

© 2003 Ralph D. Stacey

Typeset in Times by Mayhew Typesetting, Rhayader, Powys
Printed and bound in Great Britain by TJ International Ltd, Padstow,
Cornwall
Paperback cover design by Richard Massing

All rights reserved. No part of this book may be reprinted or
reproduced or utilised in any form or by any electronic, mechanical,
or other means, now known or hereafter invented, including
photocopying and recording, or in any information storage or
retrieval system, without permission in writing from the publishers.

British Library Cataloguing in Publication Data
A catalogue record for this book is available from the British Library

Library of Congress Cataloging-in-Publication Data

Stacey, Ralph D.
  Complexity and group processes : a radically social understanding
of individuals / Ralph D. Stacey.
       p. cm.
Includes bibliographical references and index.
  ISBN 1-58391-920-1 (alk. paper)
  1. Group psychoanalysis. I. Title.

RC510 .S73 2003
616.89'152–dc21

2002014300

ISBN 1-58391-920-1

616.89152 STA
030086574

Contents

Preface

This book has, of course, emerged from my own life experience in which, over the years, I have become increasingly interested in group processes and how individuals are involved in them. I was educated initially as a lawyer but before completing my law studies I moved to the area of economics. After a brief period teaching economics I spent many years working in commercial organizations before taking up a teaching post at the University of Hertfordshire where I taught strategic management. As part of this teaching I became involved, by chance, in group relations work with the Tavistock Institute, where I began to develop an interest in psychoanalysis. This involvement has exercised an important influence on my thinking. At much the same time, again by chance, I 'discovered' the sciences of chaos and complexity. This too has exercised a very important influence on my thinking. The combination of psychoanalysis, complexity sciences and organizational theory was reflected in various books I have written about life in organizations, where an understanding of group processes is of the greatest importance. Rather late in life, I undertook a training in group-analytic therapy and since then part of my work has been conducting clinical therapy groups. This encounter has also exercised a powerful influence on how I think.

My experience, therefore, has only relatively recently come to include work in mental health settings and my thinking about working in these settings displays the influence of a career in commercial organizations and teaching. As a consequence I have never come to feel committed to psychoanalytic ways of thinking. While psychoanalysis has certainly greatly influenced me, I have increasingly come to find problematic the fundamental assumptions on which it is built. I have also come to think that the heavy reliance group-analytic therapy places on psychoanalysis is restricting. I have, therefore, written this book in order to explore how one might think about groups in ways that draw on the important insights of psychoanalysis but do not rely on its meta psychological theories.

I want to express my gratitude to those many people who have formed my thinking and who have commented on drafts of this book. In particular

I want to thank Eliat Aram, Farhad Dalal, Doug Griffin, Morris Nitsun, Wil Pennycook-Greaves, Malcolm Pines, Chris Rance, Hansotto Reiber and Patricia Shaw.

Chapter 1

Introduction

> To be sure, criticism of self consciousness, the demand for a revision of the basic form of perceiving oneself and others prevalent in our own society, will meet understandable resistance. The basic structure of the idea we have of ourselves and other people is a fundamental precondition of our ability to deal successfully with other people and, at least within the confines of our own society, to communicate with them. If it is called into question, our own security is threatened. What was certain becomes uncertain. . . . But without throwing oneself for a time into the sea of uncertainty one cannot escape the contradictions and inadequacies of deceptive certainty.
>
> (Elias, 1991, pp92–93)

The central concern of this book is that of making sense, in general, of the phenomenon of human relating. It is an exploration of different ways of thinking about how individual and collective identities come about, how they are interrelated and how they change. The key questions are: Who am I and how have I come to be who I am? Who are we and how have we come to be who we are? How are we all changing, evolving, or to put it another way, learning? These are fundamental questions in any field of study to do with human action and interaction and they always raise issues to do with individuals and groups and the relationships between them. These questions also raise issues to do with what constitutes healthy and productive relating, as well as what constitutes failures of relating, what blocks change and what keeps us stuck in unproductive relationships. The arguments developed in this book are, therefore, relevant to those concerned with managing, leading and belonging to organizations, as well as those involved in education, training and development. However, I will be focusing my attention on thinking about therapeutic groups, leaving the reader to make translations to other areas of interest.

I am not setting out to provide an explicit set of prescriptions for group therapy or any other kind of activity in groups for that matter. My interest is, rather, in explanations of, or ways of thinking about, what we are doing in groups because I believe that it is in engaging with the contradictions between our various acts of thought that we begin to make more sense of what we are doing together. An emphasis on ways of thinking frequently seems to prompt the question: What difference does it make in practice? This question immediately reveals a key taken-for-granted feature of current Western thought. We have come to split ways of thinking as theory from action as practice. Such a split is, however, problematic. When one participates in a therapy group, one is thinking and acting, theorizing and practicing, at the same time. It follows that the kinds of theories one holds about individuals and groups inevitably affect what one says and does as an individual participant in groups in myriad small but potentially important ways. As one thinks differently so one practices differently. Implications for practicing emerge in exploring ways of thinking and immediate calls for 'what it means in practice' can easily close down the exploration.

Another position from which I start is that in coming to understand the differences between one way of thinking and another, it is essential to explore how they have evolved. I will, therefore, be exploring the historical evolution of two contradictory, indeed I would say incompatible, ways of thinking about the individual and the group in Western thought. The first is a stream of thought identified with Descartes, Leibniz, Kant, the neo-Kantians and Freud through to modern psychoanalysis. Basically, this is a way of thinking about mind as inside a person and social as a system outside a person. Individuals are then said to be social because they represent the social outside in the inside of their minds. I will argue that the result is a dualistic way of thinking in which paradox is eliminated. The second stream of thought runs from the reaction to Kant by the romantic idealists, particularly Hegel, to the dialectical process thinking of George Herbert Mead and Norbert Elias. Basically, this is a way of thinking in which both mind and society are the pattering activities of human bodies. For actions, there can be no inside or outside and so mind comes to be thought of as forming social interactions while being formed by them at the same time. Paradox, in the sense of simultaneously forming and being formed, is thus essential to this way of thinking. Individuals are then thought of as social not because of representations of social relations in their minds but because the processes of mind are the same processes as social relating. Individual and social are simply two aspects of one process – they are the singular and the plural of relating between human bodies.

Some traditions of group psychotherapy, particularly Foulkes' group-analytic one, try to hold the above two distinct streams of thought together in a form of 'both . . . and' or 'figure . . . ground' thinking in which one alternates between them. This book will present arguments against such 'both . . . and' thinking, primarily that the elimination of paradox in the alternation between two contradictory theories clouds our thinking.

Contradictory strands in thinking about group-analytic therapy

As a psychoanalyst, Foulkes introduced a major innovation in therapeutic practice when he began to work with patients in a group. However, he did more than conduct the psychoanalysis of individuals in a *group*. He moved away from a dyad to the group and developed distinctive ways of explaining what he was doing. In *Taking the Group Seriously* (1998), Dalal has teased apart two contradictory strands in Foulkes' thinking about the therapy group. The first strand is drawn from Freudian psychoanalytic theory, which focuses attention on the individual and understands individual psychology in terms of innate drives. Groups are thought of as being formed by individuals and so are to be understood in terms of individual psychology. Groups then act back on individuals to shape individual psyches in the clash between drive discharge and social constraints. The other strand in Foulkesian thought is derived from the process sociology of Elias ([1939] 2000, 1991), which fundamentally contests the notion of innate behaviors, holding that the manner in which individuals experience themselves is formed by social/group processes that they simultaneously form. For Elias, individual mind and social relations are simply two aspects of the same process. Foulkes reflects Elias when he claims that 'the individual is social to the core.'

As Dalal cogently explains, these two theories are contradictory. Freud's psychoanalytic theory grants primacy to the individual, understanding group functioning in terms of intrapsychic agencies and innate, universal drives. Elias' process sociology grants primacy to neither the individual nor the group but considers both as aspects of basically the same social processes evolving over long time periods. Neither of these two theories presents a dichotomy requiring one to think in terms of either the individual or the group. Both are theories about the relationship between the individual and the group but one locates the explanation of this relationship in innate universals and the other locates the explanation in the detailed specifics of particular histories of social evolution. The two explanations are, therefore, mutually incompatible, a contention that I will justify in some detail in Part II.

As group-analytic thinking has developed over the last half century, it has retained both of Foulkes' contradictory ways of thinking, largely without noticing the internal inconsistency. However, it is clear that the psychoanalytic strand has predominated, while the process view drawn from Elias has been accorded relatively little attention. My purpose in writing this book is to explore how we might develop a way of understanding what we are doing in a therapy group if we keep these two contradictory strands of thought apart and focus entirely on a process theory of the relationship between the individual and the group. The purpose of developing such a perspective is to move toward an internally consistent way of explaining what we, therapists and patients, are doing together in a therapy group, one which avoids trying to hold two incompatible ways of thinking together. In order to clarify what I mean by a 'process perspective', I will be exploring, in some detail, the differences between such a perspective and theories of individual and group drawn from a combination of psychoanalysis and systems thinking. I will be exploring how one might think of therapy groups without drawing in any way on psychoanalytic meta psychological theory, on the one hand, or altogether abandoning a meta theory, on the other.

Toward a process theory of the individual and the group

The chapters that follow explore Norbert Elias' view of social processes, bringing his view together with George Herbert Mead's theory of symbolic interactionism (1934). Both Elias and Mead were concerned with human relating and the relationship between individual and social, which they understood in process terms. I will be arguing that their theories, in their similarities and their differences, can be understood within a wider general framework provided by the natural sciences of complexity. Over the last few decades, biologists, chemists, physicists, mathematicians, computer scientists and other natural scientists have been developing general theories of iterative nonlinear interaction between entities that have relevance in many fields of enquiry. More recently, these ideas have been taken up in medicine, psychology, sociology, political science and organizational theory. I will be arguing that the complexity sciences provide analogies for human interaction that can be interpreted in human action terms using the theories of Elias and Mead.

In drawing together the work of Elias, Mead and the complexity scientists, I will be presenting a theory of human interaction, which colleagues and I have been calling complex responsive processes of relating (Fonseca, 2001; Griffin, 2001; Shaw, 2002; Stacey, 2000; Stacey, 2001a; Stacey, Griffin & Shaw, 2000; Streatfield 2001). We developed this perspective as a way of understanding organizational life and what we are doing together as managers and consultants. In this book, I will be arguing that the perspective of complex responsive processes also provides a way of explaining what we are doing together in a therapy group. Most of the book will be concerned with the theory of complex responsive processes and how it differs from psychoanalytic theory but there is one chapter (Chapter 8) which provides pointers to the implications for participating as therapists in group therapy. My main concern in this book, therefore, is to develop an explanation of what we are doing together in a therapy group that draws fundamentally on dialectical process thinking and does not draw at all on the meta psychology of psychoanalysis or upon the notion of a system.

A key question may help to point to one of the main distinctions I will be trying to make in this book. What do you think human interaction accomplishes in psychological–sociological terms? One answer is that human interaction provides objects for drive discharge but also constrains that discharge, so shaping the individual psyche. Freud and most object relations theorists provide an answer along these lines. Another answer is that human interaction produces systems we call groups, organizations, cultures and societies in which individuals are parts of the systems they form. Systems thinking, including its incorporation into relational and intersubjectivity psychoanalytic theories, provides an answer along these lines. A third answer is that in interacting, humans pattern further interaction between them. This is the answer provided by the kind of process theory I will be exploring.

The first two answers to the question are in no way contradictory and so can be combined to provide a single explanation of human interaction. They are not contradictory because both are built on the spatial metaphor of an inside and an outside. Both understand individual minds to be systems called 'internal worlds' and both understand the social to be a system formed by individuals but external to them. Within the internal world of mind, process is understood as interaction between internal objects, or agencies producing a 'whole' called 'mind' and this 'whole' is often thought of as an illusion. Beneath this interaction it is assumed that there is a causal agency, namely 'the unconscious'. Outside of the internal world in the social sphere, process is understood as interaction between people to produce a system, which then affects them. This means that there is a causal agency above human interaction called social structure, culture, group mind, matrix, collective unconscious, and so on.

The third answer to the question posed above is incompatible with the other two because here interaction produces nothing above or below it, acting as a causal agency on it. Interaction produces only further interaction and is its own reflexive, self-referential cause. There is only process, no system at all. In fact there is no inside and outside. There is no 'internal world' and there is no social system.

It is at this point that some who have read preliminary drafts of this chapter have protested. Surely, even as we read these sentences we experience an 'internal world'. Surely we are experiencing this 'internal world' in the context of a social system of which we are parts. First, let me explain that I am in no way questioning our experience of individuality or our experience of social relations. Instead I am suggesting that it is possible to think about this experience in a different way. When I consider what I directly experience as my mind while I write these sentences, walk down the street, drive my car or engage in a conversation with others, what strikes me is this: all I can identify as my mind is an endless, silent conversation with myself. I experience my unique, individual mind not only as an endless stream of chatter but also as melodies I silently hum, images I privately view and rhythmic bodily feelings I am sometimes aware of. It seems that silent words, intertwined with other silent sounds, private images and feelings, all trigger each other in endless succession. Furthermore I am aware that I am only aware of some aspects of this endless activity while being unconscious of most aspects of it. I certainly do have very individual experiences and they certainly do seem to be unique to me in many respects. And what is striking about all this activity is precisely that it is activity, namely the activities of my body directed toward itself. When I think, I am talking to myself and when I feel, it is my body that is *doing* the feeling. The important point about an action, however, is that it is not inside anything. Talking is not inside the throat just as walking is not inside the legs. I can understand my experience of myself, then, as the activities of my body directed to itself and this in no way requires me to think of myself in an abstract way as *having* an 'internal world.'

However, we have clearly come to believe that thinking is in the mind and that the mind is an 'internal world', which is somehow inside us. So how has this happened? Elias argued ([1939] 2000) that we came to experience ourselves as having a mind inside us in response to the slowly growing social pressures to hide particular affects such as aggression and sexuality and conceal certain bodily functions such as sex and discharging waste material. In other words, the sense of an internal world grew out of a need to hide what we really experience. The evolution of this way of experiencing ourselves was closely tied up with the need for greater individual self-control required by the evolution of increasingly complex and differentiated webs of relationships between people and the monopolization of violence by the state. The feeling we have of a mind inside ourselves is thus an illusion produced by social evolution. In Chapter 2 I will be exploring in more detail how this way of thinking and experiencing ourselves has evolved but here I simply want to make the point that it is possible to explain our experience of unique individual minds in terms of the direct, phenomenological experience of the activities of our bodies without any recourse to the abstract notion of an 'internal world'. As soon as one does this, it becomes clear that individual mind and social relating are the same processes of bodily action. While mind is silent, private interactions of a body with itself, social relating is vocal, public interactions of bodies with each other. Social is then understood as processes of bodily interaction and such an understanding has no need for the concept of system. I will be suggesting, then, an explanation that runs in terms of direct bodily experience without appealing to *abstractions* from that direct experience such as 'system' and 'internal world.'

It might be said that we have to continue thinking in terms of mind inside and society outside because this is how people of our time experience themselves. I am not arguing against ever using notions of inside and outside as metaphors when talking to people in a therapy group. What I am suggesting is that in seriously discussing what we are doing in a therapy group it may not be appropriate to carry on talking in metaphoric ways that are problematic. In the ensuing chapters I will be explaining why I think that talking in this way is problematic and I will be arguing that talking in terms of an inside and an outside is an abstraction from our direct experience of interacting with each other. I will be offering alternative ways of explaining what we are doing together in a therapy group without continuing to use the metaphor of inside and outside simply because it is so widespread.

At first it may appear that I am laboring a rather minor point. Does it really matter whether we start off explaining our experience of mind in terms of an 'internal world' or in terms of 'processes of bodily activity'? This book argues that it is profoundly important. Knowing and explaining is path-dependent. It matters greatly where one starts and which routes one takes because each step we take affects subsequent ones. What seems to be a minor fork in the path rapidly leads to a very different journey. I suggest that if you take the route of 'internal world,' you easily move to explanations of mind and social that abstract from direct experience and can become increasingly elaborate and implausible. The route of 'processes of bodily activity,' however, avoids abstracting from direct experience of interaction between people and so develops different explanations. It is the purpose of this book to explore these differences through developing a process perspective.

The process perspective I will be taking is a temporal not a spatial one. From a temporal perspective, process means something quite different to its spatial meaning in psychoanalysis and systems thinking. In the spatial sense interaction is a process producing a system inside and a system outside as the 'wholes' of mind and society. In the temporal sense, however, process is not producing anything other than itself. Here, participation means the direct interaction between people, which is self-organizing processes in which pattern emerges, a central concept in the complexity sciences. People are participating with each other in their own interaction – they are not participating as parts in something outside of their direct interaction. The temporal notion of process is, therefore, completely incompatible with the spatial notions of psychoanalysis and systems thinking simply because in it there is no inside or outside at all. As members of Western society, we have indeed come to experience ourselves as individuals with psyches that are 'internal worlds' and as parts of systems that make decisions and oppress us. However, as Elias argued, this is a consequence of the evolution of Western society. Our experience of having minds inside of us and systems outside of us is a social construction which we have come to universalize and this potentially clouds our thinking about individuals and groups.

Why the move to process thinking matters

Why does this distinction between psychoanalysis/systems thinking and temporal process thinking matter as far as group therapy is concerned? It matters because it points to two quite different foci of attention. If one assumes that the mind is an 'internal world' inside a person, then one focuses attention on internal objects and universal patterns of interaction between those objects. One thinks of individual and group processes in terms of innate universals such as infantile sexuality, the Oedipus complex, unconscious fantasies, and so on. As soon as one sees the notion of 'internal world' as simply a social construction produced in the last few hundred years of social evolution in the West, this way of thinking about therapy and therapy groups becomes problematic. If one assumes that mind and social are aspects of the same process of relating then one focuses attention on the direct, ordinary experience of relating to each other. A shift to the kind of process view I am suggesting then calls for a very different way of explaining what we are doing in a therapy group or in a therapy dyad for that matter. Shifts in thinking affect what we do together in ways that we cannot know in advance.

But why do we have to choose between the process and psychoanalytic ways of thinking? Why can we not have both? This is, of course, what Foulkes and most subsequent group analysts have tried to do by alternating between one and the other in a figure–ground manner. Indeed, this has come to be claimed by some group analysts to be a merit because the consequent lack of internal coherence has prevented the kind of thought censorship found in some other institutions. This seems to me to be a rationalization of the confusion in thought that a group-analytic training simply acclimatizes one to. While it may have some merit in avoiding rigidity, continuing to work with a way of thinking that is fundamentally contradictory displays a lack of rigor that would be unacceptable in most disciplines. For example, basic theoretical contradictions in physics trigger active searches for new theories – they are not seen as a laudable condition simply to be accepted. It is also a matter of theoretical aesthetics to seek to develop theories which are internally consistent and parsimonious in that they do not rely on unnecessary or mysterious constructs to yield an explanation. Some justify the retention of two inconsistent theories by claiming that it leads to a dialectic, by which they mean a discussion or dialogue, or a Kantian notion of synthesizing two opposites. However, in the Hegelian dialectic, which is the basis of the process view I will be arguing for, thought moves by opposites negating each other and it is in this tension that new meaning emerges. This provides another argument against the 'both . . .

and' retention of two inconsistent theories, namely that such a way of thinking obliterates difference and eliminates paradox, so obstructing the evolution of new meaning.

For me, these reasons are enough on their own for exploring the move from one theoretical position to another, but there is also the important matter of the impact of ways of thinking on power relations and resource allocation in institutions dealing with mental health. The currently dominant ways of thinking about mental health are clearly those of cognitive psychology and to a lesser extent humanistic psychology and psychoanalysis. All of them are individual-centered theories of human psychology. This individual-centered view is so widespread and taken-for-granted that it feels quite natural to therapists and patients alike to regard individual treatment as the treatment of choice. Treatment in groups has to be justified using reasons such as lower cost and this simply perpetuates the popular view that it is second-best. From the process perspective to be developed in Part I of this book, the opposite is true. As soon as one adopts a radically social understanding of individuals, it follows that treatment in groups is the treatment of choice and it is individual treatment that needs to be justified for special cases. A shift in thinking along the lines I am proposing would, therefore, have major implications for how resources are allocated for treatment.

The relevance of psychoanalysis to group therapy

What I am suggesting, then, is a move away from the heavy reliance group analysis and other forms of group therapy have placed on psychoanalysis and systems thinking. To replace them, I am suggesting that a great deal more attention be paid to the process theories that Elias and Mead developed. My reasons for wanting to move away from psychoanalytic thinking in some respects are as follows. The universalizing tendency of psychoanalytic thinking is based on a particular view of evolution that greatly downplays social evolution and the effects it has on our experience of ourselves. Although psychoanalysis has been making significant moves toward a more social perspective, this has been restricted, in my view, by the dyadic nature of psychoanalytic practice and the retention of key notions, such as the internal world of mind. While relational and intersubjective theories of psychoanalysis have taken account of the social, they do so by understanding it as a field, a third, or a system. Psychoanalytic theorizing, including Foulkes when he relies on it, therefore posits something outside direct interaction as a causal power explaining social relations. Furthermore, psychoanalytic thinking is based on socially specific assumptions about the desirability of individual autonomy and problematic assumptions to do with inside–outside, psychic contents that take the form of representations, particularly those representations of instincts called drives, and sender–

receiver modes of communication in which mental contents are transmitted from one mind to another. Although there has been a significant move in psychoanalysis away from the innate drives to the social and relational, the notion of inside and outside has, nevertheless, been retained. This book challenges the notion of inside and outside, of mind as an internal world containing representations and the social as system.

The process view I am talking about also implies a different notion of time to that of psychoanalysis and systems thinking. The latter are built on linear notions of time. Psychoanalysis focuses attention on the past, on early childhood and the repressed wishes that continue to govern behavior in later life. The direction of the therapeutic inquiry is then into the past in order to uncover what has been repressed in the belief that this insight frees the person from rigid defenses. Modern psychoanalysis has moved away from the notion of the past as accurately represented and stored in the memory to a view of memory as reconstructed in the present. However, the notion of the present is still that of the 'here-and-now' as a point in time that excludes the past and anything happening outside of the immediate encounter. The process perspective takes a prospective view in which the future is being perpetually created in the living present on the basis of present reconstructions of the past. In the living present, expectations of the future greatly influence present reconstructions of the past, while those reconstructions are affecting expectations. Time in the present, therefore, has a circular structure. It is this circular interaction between future and past in the present that is perpetually creating the future as both continuity and potential transformation at the same time.

In this book, I will be trying to show how one could explain group processes, including group therapy, without recourse to psychoanalytic meta psychology or other psychoanalytic ideas having to do with the relationship between the individual and the group. This does not mean that I am suggesting that psychoanalysis be completely abandoned as a source of understanding human behavior. What psychoanalysis brings is a rich exploration of human fantasy, emotion, distress, destructiveness and pathology. However, it seems to me that these insights need to be understood afresh in terms of process theory. I want to stress this point. I am not suggesting a wholesale abandonment of psychoanalysis or psychoanalytic thought in every area, nor am I seeking to denigrate psychoanalytic thinkers. In my view, when one makes a move in thought from one position to another by critiquing the first, this is not a rejection but a compliment. If thought moves in this critical process, then what is being critiqued is just as important as what is suggested as a replacement. I am arguing that the meta psychological foundations of psychoanalytic thought are incompatible with the dialectical process view I will be taking on group processes and the relationship with the individual. In developing the complex responsive processes perspective outlined in Part I, certain key notions have been drawn from the psychoanalytic literature. However, in doing this they often come to have different meanings. These key notions are:

- Attachment and separation as key to understanding the development of mental and social functioning, and the identification of early traumatic disturbances in attachment behavior as the key to understanding later psychological and social difficulties. The names of Bion, Winnicott, Fairbairn, Balint and Bowlby immediately come to mind as does the work of Daniel Stern on the emergence of infant selves.
- Anxiety and the defensive and other responses to it.
- The repetition or iteration of motivational and behavioral patterns throughout life and the tendency to get stuck in unhelpful patterns for defensive reasons. Here, of course, Freud's work is of the greatest importance but this concept features in the work of all psychoanalysts.
- The role that feelings play in our understanding of each other as indicated by concepts such as transference and countertransference, projection and identification, empathy and attunement. Again, these notions are central to most psychoanalytic writing and it is particularly here that they come to have different meanings in the theory of complex responsive processes.
- The patterning of emotional and fantasy life and how fantasy can distort perception and communication.
- The notion of variant in invariant principles organizing experience taken from the writings of Daniel Stern and from Stolorow.
- Finally, the concept of unconscious processes. While the perspective I will be developing in Part I does not rely on the notion of 'the unconscious,' it places central importance on the notion of unconscious processes. Here it is the writing of relational and intersubjective psychoanalysts, such as Donnel Stern and Robert Stolorow, who provide important insights taken up in the perspective of complex responsive processes.

One might argue that the key points listed above are what psychoanalysis is all about and if one regards them as central then one is thinking in the psychoanalytic tradition. However, I want to draw a distinction between psychoanalysis in the broadest sense and the specific, fundamental assumptions of the theory through which these key notions are understood. The term meta psychology seems to me to be too narrow to encompass what I mean by these assumptions. In the chapters that follow, therefore, I will use the term *psychoanalysis* in a rather narrow sense to mean *the fundamental assumptions upon which psychoanalytic thinking is built.* Most of these assumptions have been challenged from within psychoanalysis and this has not led to the wholesale rejection of psychoanalysis. However, it has called for thorough re-interpretation. This is what I am attempting in relation to individuals and groups.

There are matters that this book does not propose to deal with. The book focuses on thinking about the relationship between the individual and the group, giving some pointers to what this might mean for what we do in groups. It is not concerned with the details of, or implications for, psychosis, neurosis, diagnosis and treatment. It does not attempt to deal with ways of understanding personality disorders or other mental illnesses, which are well developed in the psychoanalytic literature. The critique of psychoanalysis I present in this book does not, therefore, relate directly to the issues of diagnosis and treatment, although I would be surprised if there were no implications for how they are thought about. The provocation of the perspective I will be developing is to look at these issues afresh.

What I am challenging in psychoanalysis is some of its more extravagant developments in, for example, object relations theory. Many of these developments seem to have acquired the status of dogma, which it feels difficult to challenge. However, this means acquiescing to a way of talking which feels so far from my experience that it clouds how I think about what is going on. Let me give some examples. When people talk about someone acting on behalf of the group, or holding something for the group, or of the group talking through one of its members, I find myself having difficulty in believing this. More and more it sounds to me like reification, anthropomorphism and a mystification of the group. I respond similarly to the notion that some individual is holding the group's anxiety or that people in the group are projecting mental contents into each other. I also find it meaningless when I hear people talk about something being 'in the matrix' or when they talk about the group being unconsciously experienced as a 'womb' or an 'avenging mother'. Talking about 'the unconscious' as if it were a particularly cunning and powerfully intentional agency is mystifying to me, and it also expresses an ideology establishing the basis of a particular configuration of power in which the therapist is the expert who knows what this unconscious is up to. The complex responsive processes perspective developed in Part I does not lead one to think and talk in this way.

I have also found that expressing this kind of skepticism, indeed any fundamental challenge to psychoanalysis, can provoke outrage. I am trying to lessen this response right at the start of the book by pointing to what I find valuable in psychoanalysis, but I also want to argue that the tendency to resist any major questioning of psychoanalysis has the effect of shutting down further thought.

Some questions

Before proceeding to Part I and the main argument of the book, I would like to respond to some of the comments made by the people who very helpfully commented on a draft of this book.

One argument against fundamental challenges to psychoanalysis is that psychoanalysis provides a holding framework for practitioners in terms of diagnosis and treatment. It provides ways of thinking about psychosis and neurosis that practitioners need in order to function. The implication seems to be that to criticize psychoanalysis without offering any immediate replacement for its diagnostic framework would be irresponsible. I am not offering a replacement because I am not able to, but what I am offering is a provocation to further thinking. I do not believe that we need to hold off challenging some fundamental assumptions until we have developed a complete replacement for all of them.

There is another clarification that I think it might be useful to make in this introduction. One commentator on an early draft asked why the book pays so much attention to Freud's views on the group when few psycho-analysts now heed them. The argument is that later psychoanalytic thinkers, object relations theorists and then relational and intersubjectivity theorists, have now fully taken account of the social. My response to these comments is twofold. First, I regard it as important to look in some detail again at Freud's thinking on the individual and the group in order to justify my argument that his thought continues in the tradition of Leibniz and Kant and that this tradition continues to influence all later psychoanalytic thought. Part II of the book provides examples of what I mean. Second, in Part II of the book, I will be looking in some detail at the work of relational and intersubjective psychoanalysts and arguing that they do not take account of the social in the way that the complex responsive processes perspective proposes. The reason for the rather lengthy Part II of the book is precisely to present in detail my argument against the swift dismissals of the challenge I am proposing by claiming that psychoanalysis has already moved to the position I am suggesting. I hope Part II makes it clear why I hold the view that psychoanalytic thought remains in the tradition of Kant, with its problems of dualistic causality, whereas the process thinking I am proposing lies in the tradition of Hegel. Other differences are that while later object relations theory did move toward the importance of actual rather than fantasized relations between people, it always retained the notion of mind as an internal world of representations and the later development of relational and intersubjective psychoanalysis utilized the notion of society as system. The complex responsive process view does not utilize the notion of internal representations and it does not use the notion of external systems.

Another claim is that psychoanalytic practice has moved ahead of psychoanalytic theorizing and that psychoanalysts are already practicing in the way that the perspective of complex responsive processes might suggest. The implication is that since I am not proposing anything new as far as practice is concerned there is not much need for the theoretical perspective I am suggesting. If this is true then it means that psychoanalysts are writing one thing and doing another. For me, this is a powerful argument for developing a different explanation. If we are not doing what we are writing, the scope for confusion is immense. I suggest that we need to write about what we are doing.

This brings me to the advantages of appealing to the complexity sciences for analogies with human action. First, consider the importance of analogies. Some may argue that we ought to stay with actual explanations of human behavior rather than appealing to mere analogies coming from some other discipline. However, I will be arguing that human explaining always involves metaphor and analogy. In Chapter 11, for example, I will be exploring the origins in thought of the notion of an 'internal world' and showing how they lie in analogies with the camera obscura. What we now think of as a solid, direct explanation of human behavior turns out to have originated long ago in an analogy. The problem lies not in using analogy but in our losing sight of the fact that is what we are doing. In this spirit, a key insight from the complexity sciences is that interaction between entities has the intrinsic capacity to produce emergent coherence in the absence of any blueprint or program. In other words, local interaction between entities can pattern itself into local and widespread coherence without any causal agency above or below it. I will be explaining this in Chapter 3. I think this is extremely important because it means that we do not need to postulate some boundaried whole to explain coherent patterns in human interaction. For example, we often explain coherence or order in human interactions in terms of a culture, or a matrix, or a group mind, or the unconscious. This is completely unnecessary if interaction can pattern itself. If we abandon the notion of wholes as an explanatory device, then we abandon the notion of system and of boundaries, and if we do this then there is no need for notions of inside and outside. The virtue of this from the perspectives of theory and practice is that we avoid explanations which abstract from our direct experience of interaction with each other. A second insight from the complexity sciences is that nonlinear iteration of interaction between diverse entities explains how novelty emerges. I will explain this in Chapter 3 as well. What this is suggesting is that change occurs in the perpetual construction of the future not in the uncovering of the past or in making conscious that which is unconscious. Third, the complexity sciences, at least on one reading, point to the fundamental importance of paradox and uncertainty and link such aspects of complexity with health and vitality.

Analogies from the complexity sciences, therefore, call for a re-evaluation of how we are making sense. It is in this kind of re-evaluation that change emerges. The question then posed is whether the move from one theory to another would make us better off. I find this an odd question in that it suggests that we can know in advance whether we are going to like a shift in our thinking. If someone proposing a shift can show us that it is good for us we will have it and if they cannot we will ignore it. This turns thought into a kind of commodity that we can choose to buy or not. However, in this book I am not trying to sell such a commodity but seeking to differentiate between two strands of thinking as a provocation to further thought.

Part 1

Social selves and group processes

Taking the perspective of complex responsive processes

The chapters in Part I outline the perspective of complex responsive processes. This is a process theory of the continuing evolution of individual minds and social relationships. Essentially, the individual is understood to be social to the core because the processes of mind are the same as social processes. Both are processes of communicative interacting and power relating between human bodies in which individual minds form and are formed by social relations at the same time. Individual mind is the actions of a body directed toward itself while social is the actions of bodies directed toward each other in paradoxical processes of continuity and potential transformation at the same time. This is, therefore, an action theory that makes no appeal to notions of inside and outside. Mind is not regarded as an internal world inside a person and social is not regarded as a system, field, matrix, or third, outside a person. The theory of complex responsive processes, therefore, is a theory of experience understood as direct interaction between bodies. In their interaction bodies do not create any system above them and they are not driven by any system, such as 'the unconscious', acting as a causal power beneath or behind their interaction. Instead, interaction is understood to construct further interaction in processes that pattern themselves. The patterns that emerge in these self-organizing processes are patterns of collective and individual identity at the same time.

The theory of complex responsive processes draws together Elias' process sociology and Mead's symbolic interactionism as ways of translating analogies from the complexity sciences into a theory of human action. Chapter 2 reviews Elias' understanding of the relationship between the individual and the social and Chapter 3 makes the connection between Elias' long term social process and complexity theories. Mead's theory of meaning as the social act of gesture and response is linked to complexity theory in Chapter 4 and Chapter 5 draws attention to Stern's work on infant development, understood in terms of Mead's conversation of gestures. Since the theory of complex responsive processes is a theory of interaction between bodies, Chapter 6 reviews recent studies of brain functioning and argues that they provide support for the theory of complex responsive processes. Chapter 7 further develops the theory in terms of processes of shame and power and Chapter 8 explores the implications for group therapy.

Chapter 2

The social evolution of the person

> . . . concepts such as 'individual' and 'society' do not relate to two objects separately but to two different yet inseparable aspects of the same human beings, . . . Both have the character of processes, and there is not the slightest necessity, in forming theories about human beings, to abstract from this process character.
>
> (Elias, 1991, p45)

In moving from the psychoanalysis of an individual in a dyadic setting to therapy in a group, Foulkes placed belonging, socialization and support at the center of the therapeutic process:

> The first and foremost aspect with which group psychotherapists are usually concerned, and according to which they form their concepts, is that of belonging, of participation. . . . the need for psychotherapy arises when this participation and sharing are disturbed.
>
> (Foulkes, 1966, pp155–156)

Foulkes' shift to emphasizing the social nature of therapy represented a major change at a time when psychoanalysts were focusing on interpretation of the intrapsychic in terms of transference, repressed wishes, defensive mechanisms and unconscious fantasies. However, although he was departing from psychoanalysis in significant respects, Foulkes always regarded himself as a psychoanalyst and thought in dualistic terms, moving between Freudian spatial models and the temporal processes of Elias without ever pointing to any contradiction between them (see Chapter 15). While continuing to use the intrapsychic language of Freud, Foulkes also argued against the spatial notion of mind inside a person and the social outside, which is fundamental to psychoanalytic thought. He held that the individual and the social could never be separated and in this he drew on Elias, whose central contention was that our experience of ourselves changes as the social structure evolves over long time periods. This is a completely different argument to the notion of innate universals to be found in Freud's thought.

This chapter reviews Elias' argument and explores its differences from Freud. It concludes that Elias and Freud provide completely different and quite incompatible accounts of the relationship between the individual and the group. This incompatibility is not founded simply on the differing emphasis the two accounts place on nature compared to nurture. It is true that they do account for the influence of biological and social evolution in very different ways but the key distinction relates to the use of the spatial metaphor of mind inside and social outside a person. This distinction is fundamental to Freudian thought and that of almost all subsequent psychoanalysts but it is completely rejected by Elias in his process theory of mind and society. I will be arguing throughout the chapters in Part I of this book that this difference between Elias and Freud has significant implications for how we think about what we are doing in a therapy group, or any other group for that matter.

The biological evolution of the human species

Elias referred to the evolution of human behavior as civilizing processes. The word 'civilizing' did not have, for him, the connotations it has for many to do with progress and the superiority of some cultures over others. By 'civilizing' he meant a particular pattern of evolution characterized by greater and greater self-control on the part of individuals. He did not regard the process as necessarily progressive because he also understood human evolution in terms of spurts of de-civilizing processes. He distinguished between three evolutionary processes (Mennell, 1992). First, there is the civilizing process of every person from infancy to adulthood, linked to the process of biological maturation through the capacities for learning. Second, there is the development of social standards and codes of acting, which is also a learning process, but one that takes place over long time periods across generations and continues to evolve in every person's lifetime. The third process encompasses humanity as a whole and it too is a learning process in which humans have learned to talk, use fire, make tools, and so on. For Elias, all humans are one species who have continued to evolve not biologically but culturally.

> In short, the structure of societies composed of non-human creatures can change when the biological structure of those creatures alters. Animals of the same species always form societies of the same type, except for very slight local variations. This is because their behavior towards each other is prescribed by inherited structural characteristics peculiar to each species, which allow only more or less limited scope for

modifications. Human societies on the other hand can change without any change occurring in the species – that is, in the biological constitution of man.

(Elias, 1991, p108)

Although humans are similar to other animals in some respects, Elias argued against making inferences about humans from other animals because humans embody unique biological innovations. Most importantly, human evolution has produced a distinctive biological organization in which humans are fundamentally directed toward others and also have greatly enhanced capacities for learning, which enables adaptation to very different conditions without further biological evolution.

It is the greater freedom of human relations from the control of inherited automatic mechanisms that really clears the way for the free play of social network mechanisms.

(Elias, 1991, p37)

Elias draws attention to the connection and the difference between natural and social orders:

Human beings are part of a natural order and a social order. . . . the social order, although quite unlike a natural order such as the order of the organs within an individual body, owes its very existence to a peculiarity of human nature. This peculiarity is the special mobility and malleability by which human behavior-control differs from that of animals.

(Elais, 1991, p41)

For Elias, then, humans are part of nature and so subject to its laws, but subject in a different way to other animals because of the high degree of malleability produced by human biological evolution. This malleability enables continuing social evolution independently of biological evolution, which means that innate and species specific means of orientation have virtually disappeared in humans.

By nature – the hereditary constitution of the human organism – human behavior is directed less by inborn drives and more by impulses shaped by individual experience and learning than is the behavior of any other living creature. Thanks to their biological constitution, not only is it true that people are better *able* to learn to control their behavior than any other creature, but also that their behavior *must* bear the imprint of what they have learned. The behavior patterns of a human infant not only can but must develop extensively through learning if the infant is to survive.

(Elias, 1991, p109)

For example, a human has to learn what is edible and what is inedible, while most other animals know this instinctively. Another distinctive human biological innovation is the simultaneous evolution of hands and brains capable of making and using tools. However, tool making could not have been due to biological evolution alone – it had to be due to the intertwining of social, or learning process, and biological evolution. Furthermore, humans cannot communicate without having *learned* a language and although emotions have a biological bodily basis, no emotion of an adult person is ever entirely instinctual. In other words, there are no fixed genetic reaction patterns. For example, the smile is innate but it is molded in different ways in different societies. Humans *learn* to control instincts because they have no innate control mechanisms, only learned ones. People have learned to control fire but an important part of this process was learning to control the fear of fire.

> In other animals self-regulation in relation to other creatures and things is restricted in advance by reflex mechanisms to fairly narrow paths. Even in those animals closest to man in the sequence of organisms, a certain relaxation in this respect can be observed, a somewhat greater adaptability to changing relations, a slight widening of the paths of their self-regulation. But only in man is the loosening and malleability of relations–functions so great that for the individual human being a period of years is needed for the molding of self-regulation by other people, a social molding, in order for it to take on a specifically human form. What man lacks in inherited predetermination in his dealings with other beings must be replaced by social determination, a socio-genic shaping of the psychical functions.
>
> (Elias, 1991, pp35–36)

Elias is arguing, therefore, that biological evolution has produced a human body having a physiological need to attach to other human beings and belong to groups. Elias argues against the idea of genetically determined instincts, or their mental representation as drives, having a major impact on human behavior. Biological evolution has produced a biological organism that can only survive in relation to others and continues to evolve in interaction with those others through social processes of learning. Even at a physiological level, then, humans are social through and through. Chapter 6 will find backing for Elias' view in recent research on the biochemistry of the human brain, which concludes that the human body cannot regulate itself in isolation but requires contact with other bodies.

Elias' view of biological evolution is clearly different to that of Freud. Elias stresses the malleability of human behavior and the manner in which it has evolved and continues to evolve in social processes so that the universal and the innate play a very small part in behavior. Even emotions have to be understood in terms of social processes of interaction between bodies. The emphasis here is very different indeed to Freud's emphasis on inherited, innate drives and to object relations theory notions of inherited unconscious fantasies. Elias moves a considerable distance from Freudian reliance on the biological determination of human action:

> But because of this biologically determined relative dissociation from biological mechanisms, and because of the dependence of growing human beings on learning from others, human societies constitute a field of investigation with a type of order and forms of organization different from those which concern biologists.
>
> (Elais, 1991, p110)

Consider now what Elias had to say about social evolution.

The civilizing process and personality structure

In *The Civilizing Process*, first published in 1939, Elias argued that as Western society evolved, social functions became more and more differentiated under the pressure of competition. This differentiation meant that the number of social functions increased so that any individual had to depend more and more upon others to do anything. As this interdependence rose, more and more people had to attune their actions to each other, making it necessary for them to regulate their conduct in increasingly differentiated, more even and more stable ways. This requirement for more complex control had to be instilled into each individual from infancy if society was to function. The more complex forms of control became increasingly automatic, taking the form of unconscious self-compulsion that individuals could not resist even if they consciously desired to do so.

> The web of actions grows so complex and extensive, the effort required to behave 'correctly' within it becomes so great, that beside the individual's conscious self-control an automatic, blindly functioning apparatus of self-control is firmly established. This seeks to prevent offences to socially acceptable behavior by a wall of deep-rooted fears, but, just because it operates blindly and by habit, it frequently produces such collisions with social reality. But whether consciously or unconsciously,

the direction of this transformation of conduct in the form of increasingly differentiated regulation of impulses is determined by the direction of the process of social differentiation, by the progressive divisions of functions and the growth of the interdependency chains into which, directly or indirectly, every impulse, every move of an individual becomes integrated.

(Elias, [1939] 2000, pp367–368)

Self-restraint became habitual, or unconscious, through the evolution of societies. Without this people could not operate in increasingly differentiated societies and without such societies such self-restraint would not be required. Note here how Elias is introducing a notion of unconscious processes, which is simultaneously individual and social. This is very different to Freud's notion of 'the unconscious' arising in the individual through repression of innate drives.

Elias also linked the growth of self-control to the growth of centralized organs of society and the monopolization of force by those organs. In societies in which force is not monopolized, individuals are thrown more directly and more frequently between pleasure and pain. The relationships between individuals are more volatile as people engage more frequently in physical violence against each other, swinging between victory and defeat. Life is uncertain and risks cannot be calculated so that people live more impulsively in the present. As society develops in the direction of the monopolization of physical force, the individual is no longer engaging in feuds but rather in the more permanent compulsions of peaceful functions like economic exchange and the pursuit of prestige.

The monopolization of force created pacified social spaces that were normally free from acts of violence so that the free use of physical violence by the physically strong was no longer possible. Non-physical forms of violence became more frequent, for example, from economic monopolies and from the loss of self-control by individuals when driving cars. Both danger and control, therefore, came less frequently from physical force and more frequently from the very nature of self-control.

Here the individual is largely protected from sudden attack, the irruption of physical violence in his life. But at the same time he is himself forced to suppress in himself any passionate impulse urging him to attack another physically. And the other forms of compulsion which now prevail in the pacified social spaces pattern the individual's conduct and affective impulses in the same direction. The closer the web of interdependence becomes in which the individual is enmeshed with the advancing division of functions, the larger the social spaces over which this network extends and which become integrated into functional or institutional units – the more threatened is the social existence of the individual who gives way to spontaneous impulses and emotions, the greater is the social advantage of those able to moderate their affects, and the more strongly is each individual constrained to take account of the effects of his own or other people's actions on a whole series of links in the social chain. The moderation of spontaneous emotions, the tempering of affects, the extension of mental space beyond the moment into the past and the future, the habit of connecting events in terms of chains of cause and effect – all these are different aspects of the same transformation of conduct which necessarily takes place with the monopolization of physical violence, and the lengthening of the chains of social interdependence.

(Elias, [1939] 2000, p370)

However, the more moderate swings of emotion, the extension of time horizons, less impulse acting and more internal control all bring pressures for individuals:

. . . physical violence and the threat emanating from it have a determining influence on individuals in society, whether they know it or not. It is, however, no longer perpetual insecurity that it brings into the life of the individual, but a peculiar form of security. It no longer throws him, in the swaying fortunes of battle, as the physical victor or vanquished, between mighty outbursts of pleasure and terror; a continuous, uniform pressure is exerted in individual life by the physical violence stored behind the scenes of everyday life, a pressure totally familiar and hardly perceived . . . A strongly mediated compulsion or pressure mediated in a variety of ways is constantly exerted on the individual. This operates to a considerable extent through the medium of his own reflection. . . . The monopoly organization of physical violence does not usually constrain the individual by a direct threat . . . the actual compulsion is one that the individual exerts on himself either as a result of his knowledge of the possible consequences of his moves in the game in intertwining activities, or as a result of corresponding gestures of adults which have helped to pattern his own behavior as a child.

(Elias, [1939] 2000, p373)

Elias is arguing here that social evolution results in fears to do with socially correct behavior. These fears are banished to an individual's own personality and to interactions with others that are shielded from public visibility 'behind the scenes,' for example, in the bedroom. Self-control encompasses an individual's whole conduct and many impulses and affects no longer reach the level of consciousness. Although life becomes less dangerous, it also becomes less emotional and this is compensated for in

dreams, fantasies, books and pictures. The consequence of growing interdependence in larger groups and the exclusion of physical violence lead to
social constraints that are transformed into unconscious self constraints as
'habitus.' Perpetual hindsight and foresight is instilled from childhood,
becoming conscious self-control and unconscious automatic habit. However, these constraints also produce tensions and disturbances for individuals, taking the form of restlessness and dissatisfaction because impulses
can only partially be gratified.

Elias talks about how the stresses of self-control can so block people that
they are no longer capable of expressing even modified affects. People may
become so surrounded by unconscious automatic fears that they remain
deaf or unresponsive to emotion throughout life. Energy may be released in
compulsive actions or flow into uncontrollable and eccentric attachments,
or predilections for peculiar things, or repulsions, all permitting no real
satisfaction. Elias talks about how unplanned this all is and how there is no
end to it because although the malleable person is shaped to some extent in
childhood, with patterns formed and then solidifying afterwards, the process of formation never ceases throughout life. Unresolved conflicts are
repeated throughout life in situations reminiscent of childhood and this can
lead to contradictions between alternative self-control modes. Elias points
out how the increasingly complexity of Western society makes it harder and
harder to develop and sustain a good enough capacity for self-control. It is
not clear why some form a good enough capacity for self-control and
others do not.

This view of the development of individual restraint presents a very
different explanation to that of Freud. Elias argued that socially developed
self-restraint required people to control the spontaneous expression of body
action and conceal much of it if they were not to be seen to behave
inappropriately and so feel shamed. This kind of self-restraint easily leads
to a feeling of being isolated in which people come to think that they have
an inner core, a natural self which society restricts, so preventing them from
being their true selves. Hiding instinctual expression is thus a social process.
For Freud, this process is explained in terms of intrapsychic repression.
Here there is an inner core of drives seeking expression but encountering
social prohibition. Such wishes are repressed and become unconscious as,
for example, in the Oedipus complex. The result is a very different view of
what is unconscious or repressed and how this comes about. For Elias,
unconscious refers to aspects of human interaction, whereas for Freud there
is 'the unconscious' as a fundamentally individual phenomenon.

Shame and unconscious self-control

Elias attaches particular importance to shame, embarrassment and repugnance in the formation of 'habitus', that is, individual-social habits.

The feeling of shame is a specific excitation, a kind of anxiety which is automatically reproduced in the individual on certain occasions by force of habit. Considered superficially it is fear of social degradation or, more generally, of other people's gestures of superiority. But it is a form of displeasure or fear which arises characteristically on those occasions when a person who fears lapsing into inferiority can avert this danger neither by direct physical means nor by any other form of attack.

(Elias, [1939] 2000, pp414–415)

Elias puts rising levels of shame an embarrassment, that is, conscience formation, at the centre of the evolution of a society of individuals. Conscience is thus not a matter of an individual in a family developing a universal in the form of the father's voice (intrapsychic) but a social process. He talks about second nature, habitus, and the social make up of the individual.

. . . people of a later generation entered the civilizing process in a later phase. In growing up as individuals they had to adapt to a later standard of shame and embarrassment, of the whole social process of conscience-formation, than people of preceding generations. The entire stock of social patterns of self-regulation which the individual has to develop within himself or herself in growing up into a unique individual, is generation-specific and thus, in the broader sense, society-specific. . . . people are influenced in their development by the position at which they enter the flow of the social process.

(Elias, 1991, pviii)

In *The Civilizing Process*, Elias argued that there had been a gradual removal of sexuality behind the scenes of social life, reflecting the advancing threshold of shame and embarrassment and the shift in the balance of external and internal controls, accompanied by the increasing psychological difference between childhood and adulthood (Mennell, 1992). In the Middle Ages, the sight of the naked body was not unusual and copulation was probably frequently stumbled upon, as depicted by artists in their scenes of everyday life. There would not have been excessively traumatic embarrassment in witnessing copulation because the sight of it did not excite or gratify a wish-fulfillment denied in life. Marital sexuality was ordinary, as evidenced by the public practice of laying bridal couples out naked in the bridal bed and it was common until very recent times for parents and children to sleep in the same room. Only gradually did sexuality come to be associated with shame and embarrassment as people began to sleep in their own private bedrooms. Elias argued that it was the growing division of labor, the market and competition, together with changing power figurations, particularly between men and women, that imposed restraint and control on impulses and emotions. The gradual concealment of sexual life behind the scenes was not merely spatial but involved the development of a view of childhood which entailed people spending first twelve, fifteen and then almost twenty years of their lives as 'children'. Growing up became a problem and the increasing sense of shame about sex made it more difficult for parents to talk about it to their children. This difficulty around sex has come to seem natural and biological but it was the personality structure of adults, with their highly developed self constraints, that made sex so difficult to speak about.

The same process applied to aggressiveness and cruelty. In the early Middle Ages strife was normal and people experienced joy and exultation in the clash of arms. Warriors derived sheer pleasure from cruelty and prisoners were mutilated with relish. Gradually, these military pleasures were subjected to increasingly strong social control exercised by the increasingly powerful state organizations. It was not just the military who enjoyed cruelty; ordinary people enjoyed the spectacle of burning heretics, public torture and execution. People were also cruel to animals on a wide scale. All of these behaviors were subjected to long-term molding and taming and came to be impeded by shame as the impulses of aggression and cruelty were transformed from direct experience to spectator forms of sport. In this way, what had before aroused pleasure now came to arouse repugnance and disgust, and socially undesirable expressions of pleasure were threatened and punished by measures that generated shame and anxiety. For Elias, anxiety, shame, repression and self-control are all social processes.

> . . . the 'privatization' or exclusion of certain spheres of life from social intercourse, their association with socially instilled fear in the form of shame and embarrassment, for example, . . . cause the individual to feel that 'inside' himself he is something that exists quite alone, without relations to other people, and that he only becomes related 'afterwards' to others 'outside'.
>
> (Elias, 1991, p28)

Elias also describes the civilizing process in terms of the dynamics between the established and the outsiders. As one grouping emerges as established and privileged, others press for emancipation from their outsider status. Initially, the larger group of outsiders, who are poorer 'lower classes' oppressed by the established 'upper classes', tend to follow their drives and affects more spontaneously. Their conduct is characterized by less self-control than the established upper classes. In the evolution of Western society this contrast between the behavior of the upper and lower classes decreased considerably due to the growing necessity of all people to earn their living in regulated work. As the upper classes came to have to 'work' in similar ways to the lower classes and as the manners of the upper classes spread to the lower, the differences in conduct between them diminished. And here again we see a very different notion of what is unconscious to that found in psychoanalytic theory.

> The habituation to foresight, and the stricter control of behavior and affects to which the upper classes are constrained through their situation and functions, are important instruments of their dominance, as in the case of European colonialism, for example. . . . For just this reason, such a society regards offences against the prevailing pattern of drive and affect control, any 'letting go' by their members, with greater or lesser disapproval. . . . The effort and foresight which it requires to maintain the position of the upper class is expressed in . . . the degree of reciprocal supervision they practice on one another, by the severe stigmatization and penalties they impose on these members who breach the common distinguishing code. . . . And it is this fear of the loss of prestige in the eyes of others, instilled as a self compulsion, whether in the form of shame or a sense of honor, which assures the habitual reproduction of distinctive conduct, and the strict drive control underlying it, in individual people.
>
> (Elias, [1939] 2000, pp384–385)

Elias then argues that although the contrast in conduct between the upper and lower groups diminishes as society evolves, the varieties or nuances of conduct increase. It is important to note how Elias understands the simultaneous evolution of society and individuals in terms of power relations, in terms of competition and cooperation. He talks about the characters and attitudes of people who form power figurations being formed by these figurations.

Consider now the implications of Elias' perspective for the way in which we might understand how we experience ourselves.

Changing ways of experiencing ourselves

In *The Society of Individuals*, Elias (1991) makes the point that the way one thinks about questions such as the relationship between individual and group depends very much on the society one lives in. Ways of thinking evolve and as such are contingent upon history, a matter we usually tend to forget because it feels natural and unquestionable to think as we do. Elias illustrates the point with reference to the transition, some 350 years ago, from the religion-based conception people in the West had of themselves and their world to a secularized way of thinking. The transition took a long time and cannot be said to be the work of an individual or a number of individuals but was, rather, connected to specific changes in power relations in society. The religion-based view had been taken for granted for centuries and it provided people with a picture of themselves and their world that gave them considerable security. People thought of themselves as part of a divinely created universe and the questions that mattered to them then had to do, for example, with the purpose of all creatures in the divine creation and the destination of human souls. These questions had to do with matters that could not be directly observed and individual thought or reflection was not likely to be of much help so answers to questions like these had to depend upon authoritative revelation. Around 350 years ago, however, the major social institutions sustaining this view began to lose power, creating the conditions in which the religious view of life became a target for doubt and began to lose its self-evident status. There was a growing awareness that people could decipher natural phenomena using their own observations and reasoning powers. People began to think of themselves in terms of their own powers of observation and reason, without necessary recourse to authority and revelation, in a way that we now take for granted.

Although we now take it for granted that individual observation and thought is the route to unraveling the operation of nature and of ourselves, this is not some 'truth' that exists a priori. This perspective evolved slowly over more than 200 hundred years as part of the evolution of social situations. What was evolving was the position of individuals in social structures, the social structures themselves and the relation of social human beings to the non-human world. The transition from a largely authoritarian mode of thinking to a more autonomous one was bound up with a transition from a more 'external' conscience dependent on authorities to a more 'autonomous individual' one. This new form of self consciousness was closely linked to commercialization, the emergence of nation states and the increasing power of humans over the non-human world. As they discovered new things about the non-human world, people's images of themselves changed. They became more and more 'individualized' in the sense of seeing themselves as seemingly independent of, and apart from, their group, even as persons in opposition to their group. Individuals came to examine themselves in the mirror of their consciousness just as they were examining objects in the non-human world. In other words, they came to understand themselves in both subjective and objective ways.

Elias illustrates the transition in relation to the thought of Descartes who wrote some 350 years ago:

> Thus Descartes' reflections, for example, express the experience of a person who on the one hand began to experience himself as a thinker and observer independent of authorities and reliant only on himself in his thinking, and on the other as part of what he observed, a body among others. . . . As an observer the individual person confronted the world as a fairly free and detached being; he distanced himself to a

certain extent from the world of inanimate things as from that of human beings, and therefore of himself. In his capacity as the observed, the human being perceived himself as part of a natural process and, in keeping with the state reached by thought in Descartes' time, as a part of the world of physical phenomena. . . . Accordingly, Descartes in his intellectual experiments posited his own existence in his capacity as a body as something that was just as uncertain, just as exposed to radical doubt, as all the other objects that we know through the mediation of the senses. The only thing he saw as indubitably existing was himself in his capacity as thinker and doubter. . . . he attributed each of the different ways in which he perceived himself to a different and separate plane of existence.

(Elias, 1991, pp103–105)

Previously, people had experienced themselves as members of family groups and other associations embedded in a spiritual realm ruled by God. They now increasingly experienced themselves as individuals, and changes in society imposed a growing restraint on feelings and a greater need to think before acting. This made more valuable the consciousness of oneself as an individual detached from other people and things. The detachment in observing others and oneself became a permanent attitude generating in the observer an idea of himself as a detached being who existed independently of others. This became an idea of universal detachment of the individual who possessed an insubstantial capacity located inside him called mind, reason or intelligence. So body and mind became separate and eventually this became reflected in the existential loneliness of the individual and in the idea of an absolute divide between the knowing subject and the object. Elias summarized this whole perception with the term *homo clausus*, closed man.

The self-perception of the person as observer and thinker was reified in speech and thought, giving rise to a notion of an entity within the human being which was cut off from everything going on outside itself by the walls of its bodily container, and which could gain information about outside events only through the windows of the body, the sense organs. How reliable this information was, whether the senses presented a distorted picture of what went on 'outside', whether, indeed, there was anything 'outside', whether and how far the 'thinking thing' inside us, the *res cogitans* as Descartes called it, influenced and changed what came to us though the senses in its own way – all these were questions that had to be discussed over and over again, given the presuppositions that have been described.

(Elias, 1991, p107)

People thus came to think of an inside or 'internal world' and an 'outside' or external world. The 'inside' was thought of as a kind of container that came to be filled up with knowledge of the 'outside' through the sense organs. This led to the problem of explaining how an individual mind could build up relationships between the different perceptions of the sense organs, particularly relationships of a regular kind involving cause and effect. The answer provided by some philosophers was that the capacity to form relationships was an innate capacity of the human mind. This innate capacity took the form of pre-existing ideas such as Kant's categories, which were primal ideas or pre-existing forms of consciousness, or Hume's habituation in which relationships were perceived simply as the result of experienced association. The big question was whether the mind operated by processing sense signals through an innate mechanism functioning according to mental laws common to all people at all times, existing prior to experience, or whether these signals simply reflected reality independent of any prior ideas. Either way, people thought that the mind resided in the person and was different to the body.

In talking about an internal world or about an inner life, people ascribed spatial qualities to mental activity that they simply do not posses. Elias pointed out that just as we cannot say that something takes place inside walking or speaking so it does not make any sense to say that something happens inside an activity such as thinking or being conscious. He said that no one suggests that speech is inside the throat or that walking is inside the legs but as a result of social evolution people came to believe that thinking took place inside the mind or the brain. This belief is still central today and it is expressed in the notion of 'mental models' constituting mind according to cognitivist psychology and in the notion of the psyche as 'internal world' in psychoanalysis.

> . . . the human characteristic discovered by Freud in people of our own time and conceptualized by him as a strict division between unconscious and conscious mental functions, far from being part of humans' unchanged nature is a result of a long civilizing process . . . Thus the form and structure of the more conscious and more unconscious psychological self-steering functions can never be grasped if they are imagined as something in any sense existing or functioning in isolation from one another. Both are equally fundamental to the exercise of human being; both together form a single great functional continuum. Nor can their structure and changes be understood if observation is confined to individual human beings. They can only be comprehended in connection with the structure of relationships *between* people, and with the long-term changes in that structure.
>
> (Elias, [1939] 2000, pp410–411)

Here, Elias is arguing that the way we have come to experience ourselves actually stands in the way of our understanding both mental and social phenomena. He is also arguing against theories of psychology that explain mental functioning in terms of 'internal worlds' and the social as an external system. In doing this he is identifying the completely different intellectual path he takes to that of Freud and psychoanalysis ever since. Psychoanalytic theory is firmly built on the notion of the psyche as an 'internal world' and the social as an external reality. Elias' conception of the relationship between the individual and the social is completely different and logically contradictory to the Freudian position.

Elias' approach to the individual and the group

Elias did not think about the relationship between individual and society in terms of any spatial distinction between inside and outside, nor did he adopt any kind of systemic formulation that abstracts from direct experience. Instead, he understood both individual and social purely in process terms. As he pointed out, for some people,

> . . . the relation between the 'individual' and the 'society' is an 'interpenetration' of the individual and the social system. However, such an 'interpenetration' is conceived, what else can this metaphor mean than that we are concerned with two different entities which first exist and then subsequently 'interpenetrate'. . . .
>
> (Elias, 1991, pp45–46)

He argues against this metaphor of interpenetration because it obscures our understanding of the relationship between individual and social and suggests that we can discern the connection between individual structures and social structures more precisely if we refuse to abstract from the processes of their development. For him, 'structures of personality and of society evolve in an indissoluble interrelationship' (Elias, 1991, pp45–46).

Elias developed an activity theory of human psychology and sociology and argued against the spatial notions of containers and contained, which feature so prominently in some psychoanalytic thinking, for example, in the work of Bion.

> If we ask once again what really gives rise to this concept of the individual as contained 'inside' himself, severed from everything existing outside him, and what the container and the contained actually stand for in human terms, we can see the direction in which the answer must be sought. The firmer, more comprehensive and uniform restraint of the affects characteristic of this spurt in the civilizing process, together with the increased internal compulsions that, more implacably

than before, prevent all spontaneous impulses from manifesting themselves directly and motorically in action, without the intervention of
control mechanisms – these are what is experienced as the container,
the invisible wall dividing the 'inner world' of the individual from the
'external world' or, in different versions, the subject of cognition from
its object, the 'ego' from the 'other', the 'individual' from 'society'.
What is contained are the restrained instinctual and affective impulses
denied direct access to the motor apparatus. They appear in self perception as what is hidden from all others, and often as the true self, the
core of individuality. The term 'the inner man' is a convenient metaphor, but it is a misleading one.

(Elias, 1991, p479)

He was very clear in his rejection of any metaphor of 'inside' and 'outside'.

There is good reason for saying that the human brain is situated within
the skull and the human heart within the rib cage. In these cases we can
clearly say what is the container and what is contained, what is located
within the walls and what outside, and of what the dividing wall consists. But if the same figures of speech are applied to personality structures they become inappropriate. The relation of instinct controls to
instinct impulses, to mention only one example, is not a spatial relationship. The former do not have the form of a vessel containing the
latter within them. . . . there is no structural feature of human beings
that justifies our calling one thing the human core and another the
shell. Strictly speaking, the whole complex of tensions, such as feeling
and thought, or spontaneous behavior and controlled behavior,
consists of activities. If instead of the usual substance-concepts like
'feeling' and 'reason' we use activity-concepts, it is easier to understand
that while the image of 'outside' and 'inside', of the shell of a receptacle
containing something inside it, is applicable to the physical aspects of a
human being mentioned above, it cannot apply to the structure of the
personality, to the living human being as a whole. On this level there is
nothing that resembles a container – nothing that could justify the
metaphors like that of the 'inside' of the human being.

(Elias, 1991, p480)

In rejecting the notion of the individual mind as an 'internal world,' Elias
also argues against thinking of the social as an organic unity or supra
individual by taking models

. . . primarily from the natural sciences, particularly biology. But here,
as so often, the scientific modes of thought easily and imperceptibly
merge with religious and metaphysical ones to form a perfect unity. A

society is conceived, for example, as a supra-individual organic entity which advances ineluctably towards death through the stages of youth, maturity and age. . . . Sometimes the members of this latter camp . . . ascribe to whole social formations or to a mass of people a soul of their own beyond the individual souls, an *anima collectiva* or a 'group mind.'

(Elias, 1991, pp5–6)

In arguing against such notions, Elias is arguing against both Freud, who thought of the social as a supra individual (see Chapter 9) and also against Foulkes' formulations when he talked about the group matrix as a group mind and a supra personal system (see Chapter 15). Elias had much the same view of concepts of society as some kind of whole:

By a 'whole' we generally mean something more or less harmonious. But the social life of human beings is full of contradictions, tensions and explosions. Decline alternates with rise, war with peace, crises with booms. The communal life of human beings certainly is not harmonious. But if not harmonious, at least the word 'whole' evokes in us the idea of something complete in itself, a formation with clear contours, a perceptible form and a discernible, more or less visible structure. But societies have no such perceptible form. They do not possess structures that can be seen, heard or touched directly in space. Considered as whole, they are always more or less incomplete: from wherever they are viewed they remain open in the sphere of time, towards the past and the future. . . . it is in reality a continuous flow, a faster or slower change of living forms; in it the eye can find a fixed point only with difficulty.

(Elias, 1991, p12)

He also dismissed attempts to retain the concepts of inside and outside by postulating an interaction between them and in so doing challenges the way in which psychoanalysts deal with relationships between people.

Others again favor a kind of compromise; they imagine an interaction between 'inside' and 'outside', between 'psychical' and 'social' factors, though they tend to give one or the other greater emphasis. . . . in adopting a wider, dynamic viewpoint instead of a static one . . . the vision of an irreducible wall between one human being and all others, between inner and outer words, evaporates to be replaced by a vision of incessant and irreducible intertwining of individual beings, in which everything that gives their animal substance the quality of a human being, primarily their psychical self-control, their individual character, takes on its specific shape in and through relationships to others.

(Elias, 1991, pp31–32)

Elias and Freud: two incompatible perspectives

Elias developed a comprehensive explanation of how individual personality structure and social processes are inextricably intertwined so that one cannot talk about one without also talking about the other. What is most important for understanding personality structures and social interactions is the evolution of 'habitus.' He identified the particular kind of habitus that emerged in the West over the past 350 years as one of increasing self-control of affects.

On the face of it, Elias adopted a similar approach to Freud. He even used the same terminology of drive, id, ego and superego but as Mennell notes:

> Elias uses Freudian vocabulary – ego and superego, drives, libido, unconscious, repression and so on – in discussing psychological changes in the course of the civilizing process. This vocabulary is more prominent in his early work than later. Yet Elias never accepted Freudian doctrines uncritically. He accused Freud of an ahistoric view of human psychology . . . Freud, having observed certain striking characteristics of the personality structure of people in his own time, jumped to the conclusion that these had always existed as parts of an unchanging human nature, true for all time. In particular, he assumed that there had always been the same quite strict division between unconscious and conscious mental functions that he could diagnose in his own contemporaries. On the contrary, Elias contended that this division was one result of the long-term civilizing process, . . . Freudians had tended to conceive the most important element in the whole psychological structure as an 'unconscious,' an 'id' without a history.
>
> (Mennell, 1992, p100)

So, despite using some of the same terms, Elias' approach is completely different to that of Freud; in fact it contradicts Freud. Freud presented a particular view of the psyche as an 'internal world' inside an individual and identified a psychic structure, part of which was the controlling superego or conscience, as universal to all humankind. Elias, on the other hand, described how a particular form of self-control had emerged in the personality structures of some humans in some parts of the world during a particular period in history. At other times, and in other cultures, forms of self-control and personality structure are different. What Elias presented are personality structures that are historically and geographically relative, not universal and determined in primeval times as Freud held.

For Elias, the personality of an individual is patterned by social developments. The patterning of personality becomes automatic, formed by habit and elaborated by fantasy. He emphasized human 'habitus' and argued that biological evolution had produced an organism that is malleable and not limited by instincts. Emotions are shaped by social evolution, as is sexual and aggressive behavior. Human attitudes towards body functions and body parts are not at all innate and what psychoanalysis refers to as the 'primal scene' and the Oedipus complex are rather specific social formations not at all universal to humankind. Freud goes down another route altogether in that in his theory the mental apparatus is structured from within by innate instincts. The male infant is born with sexual desire directed toward the mother and the social enters through the prohibition of the father. The Oedipus complex is regarded as a universal, experienced not only by all individuals but also by humankind as a whole in the form of the primal horde (see Chapter 9). The later development of psychoanalysis in the form of object relations theory elaborates on inherited fantasies of the primal scene and aggression. The even later development of self psychology continues to adopt the perspective of the individual mind as an 'internal world' structured by representations of self objects. The focus is on intrapsychic processes of repression and regression to primitive mental states. The thrust of psychoanalytic thinking is back into the past, particularly to early childhood experiences as overwhelmingly formative of the personality structure. Elias, however, stays with social processes and links habituation to wider and longer term social evolution, which is reflected in early relationships with the parents and in all subsequent relationships. From the perspective Elias developed, the psychoanalytic focus on infantile sexuality, primal scenes of parental intercourse and Oedipal complexes become dubious or at the very least rather recent social constructions in one part of the world.

Elias also explains repression and other unconscious aspects of human action in terms of socialization processes. He talks about automatic processes and habit linked to social processes of shame. While Elias explains patterns of individual self-control in terms of wider, evolving social processes, Freud posits an inherited universal Oedipus complex to explain why the individual mental apparatus suppresses wishes and defends against their exposure. The Elias approach relies on evolving social configurations of power to explain particular patterns of self-control without any need to appeal to inherited complexes or innate unconscious fantasies.

There are major differences for understanding the therapy process from these two perspectives. From one, the therapist looks for the effects of intrapsychic Oedipal conflict and primal scenes, while in the other the therapist tries to understand the emergence of patterns of experience that are simultaneously individual and social and related to particular unique histories of experience. Instead of innate drives and universals such as the pleasure principle, Elias talks about social processes molding people psychologically. There is a social form of repression but it is not simply repression of some urge that stays the same because urges themselves evolve in the social process. Instead of an innate Oedipus complex, there are social processes of gradually removing marital sex to behind the closed doors of the bedroom and the inevitable fantasy this provokes. What is important here is historical social processes of the evolution of shame. Particular feelings about shame and sex then get ascribed by thinkers like Freud to children and held to be innate universals.

What for Freud was innate and universal was for Elias the product of social evolution and he was clear that this product in its Western form of mind inside and social outside clouds our thinking about mind and society. It was, perhaps, his main project to develop a process way of thinking about the relationship between individuals and society that was not clouded in this way.

Chapter 3

Complexity and group processes

> Though it is unplanned and not immediately controllable, the overall process of development of a society is not in the least incomprehensible. There are no 'mysterious' social forces behind it. It is a question of the consequences flowing from the intermeshing of the actions of numerous people . . . As the moves of interdependent players intertwine, no single player nor any group of players acting alone can determine the course of the game no matter how powerful they may be. . . . It involves a partly self-regulating change in a partly self-organizing and self-reproducing figuration of interdependent people, whole processes tending in a certain direction.
>
> (Elias, 1970, pp146–147)

Chapter 2 described the principal conclusions that Elias reached from his detailed research on changes in behavior in Western society. One of his most important conclusions was that social and personality structures evolve together. This provides the basis of Elias' process theory of the evolution of Western society and the way in which people in the West have come to experience themselves. This chapter turns to the nature of this process and the question of just how social and personal evolution occurs. The chapter starts with Elias' explanation of social and personal evolution and then suggests that his explanation finds support in key ideas from the complexity sciences to do with self-organization and emergence.

The emergence of social order

Elias argued that what we now call Western civilization is not the result of any kind of calculated long-term planning. Individual people did not form an intention to change civilization and then gradually realize this intention through rational, purposive measures. It is not conceivable that the evolution of society could have been planned because that would suppose that 'modern' rational, calculating individuals with a degree of self-mastery already existed centuries ago, whereas Elias' research shows that such individuals did not exist then but were, rather, themselves the products of social evolution. Societal changes produced rational, planning kinds of individuals, not the other way around. In mediaeval times, people experienced their self consciousness in a completely different way, in a completely different kind of society, compared to the way we experience our self consciousness in modern society. Elias argued that the change in society occurred in an unplanned manner but nevertheless displayed a specific type of order. His research demonstrated:

> . . . how constraints through others from a variety of angles are converted into self-restraints, how the more animalic human activities are progressively thrust behind the scenes of men's communal social life and invested with feelings of shame, how the regulation of the whole instinctual and affective life by steady self-control becomes more and more stable, more even and more all-embracing. All this certainly does not spring from a rational idea conceived centuries ago by individual people and then implanted in one generation after another as the purpose of action and the desired state, until it was fully realized in the 'centuries of progress'. And yet, though not planned and intended, this transformation is not merely a sequence of unstructured and chaotic changes.
>
> (Elias, [1939] 2000, p365)

Elias said that this is the general process of historical change and asked how it is possible that orderly formations, which no human being has intended, arise in the human world. He answers the question in the following way:

> It is simple enough: plans and actions, the emotional and rational impulses of individual people, constantly interweave in a friendly or hostile way. *This basic tissue resulting from many single plans and actions of men can give rise to changes and patterns that no individual person has planned or created. From this interdependence of people arise an order sui generis, an order more compelling and stronger than the will and reason of the individual people composing it.* It is the order of interweaving human impulses and strivings, the social order, which determines the course of historical change . . .
>
> (Elias, [1939] 2000, p366)

Although it is highly unlikely that Elias was ever aware of the complexity sciences, what he is describing here is what complexity scientists call self-organization and emergence, concepts to be explored more fully later on in this chapter. Elias is arguing that individuals and groups are interacting with each other, in their local situations, in intentional, planned ways. However, the widespread, global consequences of the intermeshing of these intentions and plans cannot be foreseen by any of them – long-term global consequences emerge. Elias goes on to explain why long-term consequences cannot be foreseen.

> And this fact, that each 'I' is irrevocably embedded in a 'we', finally makes it clear why the intermeshing of the actions, plans and purposes of many 'I's constantly gives rise to something which has not been planned, intended or created by any individual. As is known, this permanent feature of social life was given its first historical inter- pretation by Hegel. He explains it as a 'ruse of reason'. But what is involved is neither a ruse nor a product of reason. . . . The interplay of the actions, purposes and plans of many people is not itself something intended or planned, and is ultimately immune to planning. The 'ruse of reason' is a tentative attempt, still swathed in day-dreaming, to express the fact that the autonomy of what a person calls 'we' is more powerful than the plans and purposes of an individual 'I'.
>
> (Elias, 1991, p62)

Here I understand Elias to be pointing to the important fact that indi- viduals pursuing their plans are always in relationship with each other in a group or power figuration. While individuals can plan their own actions, they cannot plan the actions of others and so cannot plan the interplay of plans and actions. The fact that each person depends on others means that none can simply realize their plans. However, this does not mean that anarchy, or disorder, results. Elias talks about a trend or direction in the evolution of the consequences of the interweaving of individual plans and intentions. In other words, he is talking about self-organization and emergence and this immediately suggests to me the potential for greater insight into the process that may be found in the complexity sciences, which are concerned with the same kind of process.

Elias also argued that the order, which emerges without individuals planning it, is neither rational, that is, resulting from the purposive deliberation of individuals, nor irrational, that is, arising in an incompre- hensible way.

> Civilization is not 'reasonable'; not 'rational' any more than it is 'irrational'. It is set in motion blindly, and kept in motion by the autonomous dynamics of a web or relationships, by specific changes in the way people are bound to live together.
>
> (Elias, [1939] 2000, p367)

Elias described how particular kinds of interdependence between people had set in motion processes of feudalization and how the competition between feudal lords had led to the emergence of absolutist states. He showed how these reorganizations of human relationships went hand in hand with changes in manners and personality structures. He quite explicitly talked about personality structures forming the social while being formed by it at the same time. For example, in his analysis of the bedchamber ceremonies of Louis XIV he says:

> Our intention here is to bring them alive step by step so that we can understand through them the structure and functioning of the court figuration of which they are a segment, and so understand the character and attitudes of the people who form this figuration and are formed by it.
>
> (Elias, [1969] 1983, p82)

Here, Elias is talking about an essentially paradoxical process in which individuals are forming groups while being formed by them at the same time. This is a fundamentally different way of thinking to the dualism of individual and social to be found in psychoanalytic thought (see Part II). Freud argued that groups were to be understood in terms of individual psychological processes. In effect, the group was understood as a supra individual. The group then constrained individuals, even destroyed their thinking capacity. There is a relationship between individual and group, with each affecting the other, but in the interpenetrating way that Elias was so critical of in the last chapter. Later psychoanalytic thought (see Chapter 12) developed systemic notions of individual and group, which continued the dualistic mode of thought. There is a major difference in the nature of causality underlying Eliasian and psychoanalytic thinking. Elias' process theory is one in which change occurs in paradoxical transformative processes – change is self-organizing, emergent processes of perpetually constructing the future as continuity and transformation. For Freud, development is the unfolding of innate, enfolded archetypes such as the primal horde/Oedipus complex (see Chapter 9) and for later psychoanalytic thinking, change is the unfolding of a system's purpose (see Chapter 12). Elias argued that we cannot identify self-organizing social order with the order of nature, or with some kind of supra individual, or spirit. Instead order arises in specific dynamics of social interweaving in particular places at particular times.

> Our thinking today is still extensively governed by ideas of causality which are inadequate to the process under discussion: we are strongly inclined to explain any change in a particular formation by a cause outside that formation.
>
> (Elias, 1991, pp45–46)

To summarize, Elias argued that social evolution could not be understood in terms of social forces, cultural systems, supra individuals, supra systems, spirit, élan vital, or any other kind of whole outside of experience. Instead he argued for a way of understanding that stayed with the direct experience of interaction between people. He suggested a kind of circular, paradoxical causality in which individuals form social relationships while being formed by them at the same time and he acknowledged the link between this view and the philosophy of Hegel (see Chapter 10), shorn of its metaphysics of spirit. Elias held that there is nothing mysterious about the simultaneous evolution of social order and individual personality structures. He posits processes of interweaving intentional actions of people that produce transformation, which is not unstructured or chaotic change even though none of the interacting people planned or intended the change. He talked about self-regulating change in self-organizing and self-producing figurations of interdependent people. He described this as the autonomous dynamics of a web of relationships in particular places at particular times. But how plausible is the process he posits? How plausible is it to claim that order arises in the interaction of interdependent people?

Elias developed his process sociology during the 1930s and 1940s well before the emergence of the new sciences of nonlinear dynamics, which include far-from-equilibrium thermodynamics, mathematical chaos theory and theories of complex adaptive systems. He continued to develop his theories until his death in 1990 but it is unlikely that he knew anything about the developments in the natural sciences just referred to. However, these developments provide considerable support for what Elias was arguing. What these sciences are pointing to is the ubiquitous presence in nature of the unpredictable emergence of order in disorder through processes of spontaneous self-organization. The next section describes some developments in what can be loosely called the complexity sciences and explores the connection with the thought of Elias.

The complexity sciences

Over the last decade or so, there has been a growing awareness amongst psychologists, sociologists, economists, political scientists and organizational theorists of what has come to be known as the natural sciences of complexity, or more technically, nonlinear dynamics. Complexity scientists are concerned with complex, apparently disorderly and sometimes turbulent systems in nature, for example, the weather, the human brain, ant colonies, convection in thermodynamics, urban evolution and the evolution of life itself. Their experiments and models demonstrate the possibility of order emerging from disorder through processes of spontaneous self-organization in the absence of any blueprint. The development of these new sciences is now widespread with notable centers of work at the Santa Fe Institute in the United States; centers in Brussels and Austin, Texas, headed by Prigogine; one headed by Häken in Stuttgart; and another by Scott

Kelso in Florida. Gleick (1988), Lewin (1993) and Waldorp (1992) have popularized their work, hailing it as a 'new science,' even a new worldview. There is as yet no single science of complexity but, rather, a number of different strands, the most prominent being chaos theory dissipative structure theory and the theory of complex adaptive systems. The first two strands are concerned with natural phenomena at a macro level, that is, with mathematical models of whole systems, populations, or ensembles, of entities. The third strand adopts an agent-based approach to modeling much the same phenomena. Instead of consisting of rules or laws for whole populations, these models consist of rules of interaction between the individual entities comprising a population or system.

Chaos theory

Chaos theory (Gleick, 1998; Stewart, 1989) provides an explanation of the behavior of a system that can be modeled by deterministic nonlinear equations in which the output of one calculation is taken as the input of the next. In other words, the equations are recursive, or iterative. Chaos theory shows how particular control parameters, determined outside the system, cause its behavior to move according to a particular pattern called an attractor. In other words, such systems have the potential to move according to one of a number of different attractors, depending upon the parameter values. Attractors are global patterns of behavior displayed by a system. For example, the control parameter might be the speed of energy or information flow through a system. At low rates of energy or information flow, the system moves according to a point attractor in which it displays only one form of behavior, namely, a stable, equilibrium pattern. At higher rates of energy or information flow, the system may switch to a periodic attractor. This too is a stable equilibrium state in which behavior cycles between two states. Then, at very high rates of energy or information flow, the system displays patterns of explosive growth or even random patterns of behavior. In other words, behavior takes on a highly unstable form in which the system may disintegrate. Furthermore, at some critical level of the control parameter, between levels that lead to equilibrium attractors and those that lead to unstable attractors, behavior displays patterns called a strange attractor.

In precise mathematical terms, a strange attractor may be depicted as a spatial pattern abstracted from time, or in process terms, as rhythmic variations over time. Strange attractors are reflected in patterns of behavior, that is, shapes in space or movements over time, which are never exactly repeated but are always similar to each other. A strange attractor has a distinctive shape, or cyclical movement, but that shape or movement is much more complicated than a single point or a regular cycle. A strange attractor displays a recognizable pattern in space or over time but that pattern is irregular. In other words, strange attractors are paradoxically regular and irregular, stable and unstable, at the same time. They are neither equilibrium nor random states but, rather, an intertwining of both at the same time: within any stable space or time sequence there is instability and within any unstable space or time sequence there is stability. Another term used to describe patterns of this kind is 'fractal.' It is the identification of strange attractors, or fractals, which distinguishes chaos theory from all other systems theories. Strange attractors, fractals and mathematical chaos are not simply combinations or syntheses of the dynamics of stability and instability. They are terms for a completely different kind of dynamic in which there is always stability in instability and instability in stability so that the very meanings of the terms are transformed. Or to put it another way, the terms fractal and chaos describe a dynamic that is quite different to a synthesis of order and disorder. This different dynamic is orderly disorder or disorderly order, a paradox in which the very meanings of order and disorder are transformed (see Chapter 10 on Hegel's dialectic).

The weather is usually used as an example of a system that displays patterns typical of a strange attractor. The abstract representation of the weather system's attractor has a shape rather like a butterfly, in which patterns of air pressure, temperature, and so on, swirl around one wing and then shift abruptly to the other wing, never ever exactly repeating the same movement. The heartbeat of a healthy human also follows a strange attractor reflected in temporal rhythms (Goldberger, 1997). Although heartbeats are regular when averaged over a particular period of time, movements within that average display a regular irregularity. A failing heart is characterized by a loss of complexity in which it moves to a periodic attractor.

The precise parametric conditions required to produce a strange attractor for a given mathematical model are predictable. Once revealed by iteration, the spatial shapes and time contours of the strange attractor are also predictable because a given equation, or set of equations, can produce one and only one strange attractor for given parametric conditions. It is as if the equation enfolds an implicit order that is revealed by iteration. For example, the strange attractor followed by the weather system has the characteristic shape already referred to and any deviation from it is soon drawn back into it. The shape of the attractor bounds the movement of the system in space and time, that is, it establishes the limits of the behavior that it is possible for the system to produce. The overall shape of weather movements can therefore be predicted. It is possible to predict the limits within which temperature will vary over a particular season in a particular geographical area, for example. Furthermore, the specific behavior displayed by the system within these limits is reasonably predictable over short ranges in space and short periods of time.

However, over long ranges in space and long periods of time the specific behavior of a system displaying the dynamics of a strange attractor cannot be predicted. This is due to the system's sensitivity to initial conditions, more popularly known as the butterfly effect, which means that the long-term trajectory of the system is highly sensitive to its starting point. The usual example is that of a butterfly flapping its wings in São Paulo. The flapping will alter air pressure by a minute amount and this small change could be escalated up by nonlinear iteration into a major change in specific behavior. Long-term predictability would then require the detection of every tiny change and the measurement of each to an infinite degree of precision. Since this is a human impossibility, the specific long-term pathway is unpredictable for all practical purpose. The long-term behavior of such a system, therefore, is as much determined by small chance changes as it is by the deterministic laws governing it. Deterministic laws can therefore produce indeterminate outcomes, at least as far as any possible human experience is concerned.

Chaos theory, then, produces a rather clear conclusion. Any system governed by iterative, recursive nonlinear laws may display behavior of the strange attractor type at certain parameter values. When it follows a strange attractor, its behavior is predictable at global, macro, levels of description but only in qualitative terms. At the specific micro level, predictability is confined to short term, local occurrences, leaving the specific long-term trajectory unpredictable due to the inability of humans to measure with infinite accuracy. What is distinctive about chaos theory, compared to other systems theories is the clear identification of the limits to predictability. From a chaos perspective, the move toward the simplicity of equilibrium could be interpreted as a move toward failure, where health and success are strange attractors in which long-term predictability of specific trajectories is impossible.

However, chaos theory cannot be applied directly to human action because human interaction is not deterministic. But its insights to do with strange attractors and unpredictability do present a challenge to taken for granted views and it could serve as a source of metaphor for human action. Elias, for example, was talking about social evolution as processes of interaction between many people and their plans, which have unpredictable long-term consequences and so cannot be controlled by anyone, and yet have pattern, or order. What seems implausible from traditional equilibrium perspectives, namely, that order emerges in apparent disorder of numerous interactions, is completely plausible in the theory of mathematical chaos. Indeed this is how nature seems to operate.

Dissipative structures

The discovery of a distinctive kind of dynamic characterized by the paradoxical intertwining of stability and instability is not restricted to chaos theory. The same phenomenon is also revealed in the theory of dissipative structures (Nicolis & Prigogine, 1989; Prigogine, 1997; Prigogine & Stengers, 1984) and it too points to the potential that deterministic iterative nonlinear relationships have for producing unpredictable behavior.

At the beginning of his book called *The End of Certainty*, the Nobel prize-winning chemist Prigogine poses what he sees as a central question: 'Is the future given, or is it under perpetual construction?' (1997). His answer to the question is clear: he sees the future for every level of the universe as under perpetual construction and he suggests that the process of perpetual construction, at all levels, can be understood in nonlinear, non equilibrium terms, where instabilities, or fluctuations, break symmetries, particularly the symmetry of time. He says that nature is about the creation of unpredictable novelty where the possible is richer than the real. He sees life as an unstable system with an unknowable future in which the irreversibility of time plays a constitutive role. He sees evolution as encountering bifurcation points and taking paths at these points that depend on the micro details of interaction at those points. Prigogine sees evolution at all levels in terms of instabilities with humans and their creativity as a part of it. For him, human creativity is essentially the same process as nature's creativity and this is the basis for his call for 'a new dialogue with nature.' These features, unknowable futures emerging in local interactions in the present, are essentially the same as those that Elias has identified in the transformative process of social evolution.

Central to Prigogine's approach, at all levels, is the distinction between individual entities and populations, or ensembles, consisting of those entities. He points to how classical physics, within which he includes relativity and quantum mechanics, takes the trajectories of individual entities as the fundamental unit of analysis. He then argues that individual trajectories cannot be specified for complex systems, not simply because humans are unable to measure with infinite precision, as in chaos theory, but for intrinsic reasons. Poincaré identified two kinds of energy for dynamical systems, the first being the kinetic energy of a particle itself and the second being the potential energy arising in the interaction between particles. When potential energy is zero, the world is static and when it is positive, the world is dynamic, the reason being the existence of resonance. Resonance occurs when the frequencies of particles are coupled, so increasing the amplitude of their motion. Resonance, therefore, makes it impossible to identity individual trajectories because the individual trajectory depends not only on the individual particle (kinetic energy) but also on the resonance with frequencies of other particles (potential energy). Resonances tend to be unimportant for transient interactions but become dominant for persistent ones and resonances drive instabilities. Resonance, an intrinsic property of matter, therefore, introduces uncertainty and breaks time symmetry, making the future unknowable.

Since individual trajectories cannot be identified for intrinsic reasons, Prigogine takes the ensemble as fundamental and argues that change in whole ensembles emerges over long periods through the amplification of slight variations in individual entities, that is, the variability of individuals in the case of organisms or microscopic collisions in the case of matter. It is this variability that is amplified to reach bifurcation points where a system spontaneously self-organizes to take completely unpredictably paths into the future. He sees whole populations, or ensembles, changing at bifurcation points where symmetry is broken by intrinsic differences between parts of a system and between the system and its environment. Self-organization is the process in which a system chooses a path at a bifurcation point as a result of individual variability, or fluctuations. Prigogine is arguing, therefore, that at the most fundamental levels of matter, it is the individual variability of entities and the interactions between them that lead to change in populations or ensembles. He sees this process as extending to every level including that of human action. There is, for me, a strong resonance between Prigogine's arguments and those of Elias. Elias argues for social processes that form and are formed by individuals and Prigogine is saying much the same about physical processes in nature.

The possibility of the evolution of novelty, therefore, depends critically on the presence of microscopic diversity (Allen, 1998a & b). When individual entities are the same, that is, when they do not have any incentive to alter their strategies for interacting with each other, the model displays stability. When individual entities are different and thus do have incentives to change their strategies of interaction with each other, the model displays rapid change of a genuinely novel kind. The 'openness' of the individual entities to the possible, through some 'error-making' or search process, leads to a continuing dialogue between novel individual 'experiments' and (almost certainly) unanticipated collective effects.

Models representing a critical degree of micro diversity, therefore, take on a life of their own, in which their future is under perpetual construction through the micro interactions of the diverse entities comprising them. The 'final' form towards which it moves is not given in the model itself, nor is it being chosen from outside the model. The forms continually emerge in an unpredictable way in the interaction of the entities comprising the system. However, there is nothing mysterious or esoteric about this. What emerges does so because of the transformative cause of the processes of micro interactions, the fluctuations themselves. Prigogine and Stengers write as follows:

> Order through 'fluctuations' models introduce an unstable world where small causes can have large effects, but this world is not arbitrary. On the contrary, the reasons for the amplification of small events are a legitimate matter for rational enquiry. . . . Moreover, the fact that

fluctuations evade control does not mean that we cannot locate the reasons for the instability its amplification causes.

(Prigogine & Stengers, 1984, pp206–207)

The origins of change and novelty do not lie in chance or accident, as in neo-Darwinian evolutionary theory but rather, in differences between individual entities that are amplified. These differences and their amplification can be understood and explained.

> We believe that models inspired by the concept of 'order through fluctuations' will help . . . to give more precise formulation to the complex interplay between individual and collective aspects of behavior. . . . This involves a distinction between states of the system in which individual initiative is doomed to insignificance on the one hand, and on the other, bifurcation regions in which an individual, idea or behavior can upset the global state. Even in those regions, amplification obviously does not occur with just any individual, idea, or behavior, but only those that are 'dangerous' – that is, those that can exploit to their advantage the nonlinear relations guaranteeing the stability of the preceding regime. Thus we are led to conclude *the same* nonlinearities may produce an order out of the chaos of elementary processes and still, under different circumstances, be responsible for the destruction of this same order, eventually producing a new coherence beyond another bifurcation.
>
> (Prigogine & Stengers, 1984, p206)

What emerges, then, is always potentially transformed identity: the identities of the whole and of the entities constituting it at the same time. And therefore, the differences between the entities themselves, and their collective difference from other wholes, also emerge at the same time. Micro interactions transform global patterns and themselves in a paradox of forming while being formed and an explanation of what is happening requires an understanding of these micro interactions. Again, the resonance with Elias' theory of social evolution is striking.

Complex adaptive systems

Consider now the agent based modeling of scientists at the Santa Fe Institute, who have developed the notion of complex adaptive systems. A complex adaptive system consists of a large number of agents, each of which behaves according to its own principles of local interaction. No individual agent, or group of agents, determines the patterns of behavior that the system as a whole displays, or how those patterns evolve, and neither does anything outside of the system. Here self-organization means agents interacting locally according to their own principles, or 'intentions,' in the absence of an overall blueprint for the movement of the system. These adaptive systems, just as with the chaos and dissipative structure models discussed above, display broad categories of dynamic that include stable equilibrium, random chaos and a distinctive dynamic of stability and instability at the same time, known as 'the edge of chaos.'

One type of simulation of a complex adaptive system assumes that each agent follows the same small number of simple local rules. Here the agents are homogeneous. For example, three simple rules are sufficient to simulate the flocking behavior of birds (Reynolds, 1987). Here, each agent is the same as every other agent and there is no variation in the way that they interact with each other. Emergence is therefore not the consequence of non-average behavior, as was the case with dissipative structures. Instead, emergence is the consequence of local interaction between agents. Unlike dissipative structures, and because of the postulated uniformity of behavior, these simulations do not display the capacity to move spontaneously, of their own accord, from one attractor to another (Allen, 1998a & b). Instead, they always stay within one attractor and do not evolve. The process of interacting according to simple rules forms the behavior of the system, a form that is already there, enfolded in the simple rules. However, other simulations of complex adaptive systems do take account of differences amongst agents, or classes of agents, and different ways of interacting (for example, Ray, 1992). Here the agents are heterogeneous and they do, therefore, display the capacity to move spontaneously from one attractor to another. Even more than that, such systems display the capacity for evolving new attractors as the local rules of interaction between agents and the system as a whole evolve at the same time. These models therefore produce much the same evolutionary possibilities as those of Prigogine (1997) and Allen (1998a & b) discussed above. They too are models that take on a life of their own.

Some complexity scientists, therefore, are seeking to model phenomena that display the internal capacity to spontaneously produce coherence, as continuity and transformation, in the absence of any blueprint or external designer. Their work demonstrates the possibility that both continuity and transformation can emerge spontaneously and that the process of interaction has the intrinsic capacity for patterning interaction in coherent ways. Again, there is a clear connection with Elias' theory of social process.

Most systems theories envisage the systemic unfolding of that which is already enfolded, usually by a designer, in the system itself. They offer the prospect of control from outside the system, by a designer, and any transformation of the system must also be determined from outside by a designer. The interaction of entities comprising such a system is then determined by the nature of the whole system. The complexity approach I am interested in, however, is one that is trying to simulate the process of evolution as a dynamic internal to evolution that expresses identity and difference at the same time. When this process of evolution is modeled as a 'system' of interacting entities, that 'system' has a life of its own, rendering it much less susceptible to control from outside, if at all. This kind of systems modeling points towards processes of perpetually constructing the future as continuity and transformation. However, the modeling only points toward this kind of causality because it is all too easy to focus attention on the 'system' and lose sight of the process of interaction.

Complexity as source domain for analogies of human action

Earlier on in this chapter, I argued that the complexity sciences provide a source domain for analogies with human action. To conclude this chapter, I want to explore the nature of such analogies in greater detail.

The action of complex adaptive systems is explored using computer simulations in which each agent is a computer program, that is, a set of interaction rules expressed as computer instructions. Since each instruction is a bit string, a sequence of symbols taking the form of 0s and 1s, it follows that an agent is a sequence of symbols, arranged in a particular pattern specifying a number of algorithms. These algorithms determine how the agent will interact with other agents, which are also arrangements of symbols. In other words, the model is simply a large number of symbol patterns arranged so that they interact with each other. It is this local interaction between symbols patterns that organizes the pattern of inter-action itself since there is no set of instructions organizing the global pattern of interaction across the system. The programmer specifies the initial rules, that is, symbol patterns, and then the computer program is run, or iterated, and the patterns of interaction across the system, the attractors, are observed. Simulations of this kind repeatedly produce patterns of behavior that are coherent and sometimes novel. In other words, the models are a demonstration of the possibility of interaction patterning itself. They provide a 'proof' of existence in the medium of digital symbols arranged as algorithmic rules.

For example, in his Tierra simulation, Ray (1992) designed one bit string, one symbol pattern, consisting of eighty instructions specifying how the bit string was to copy itself. He introduced random mutation into the bit string replication and limited computer time available for replicating as a selection criterion. In this way, he introduced chance, or instability, into the repli-cating process and imposed conditions that both enable and constrain that process. This instability within constraints made it possible for the system to generate novel attractors. The first attractor was that of exponentially increasing numbers, which eventually imposed a constraint on further replication. The overall pattern was a move from sparse occupation of the computer memory to overcrowding. However, during this process, the bit strings were gradually changing through random bit flipping, so coming to differ from each other. Eventually, distinctively different kinds of bit strings emerged, namely, long ones and short ones. The constraints on computer time favored smaller ones so that the global pattern shifted from one of exponential increase, to one of stable numbers of long bit strings, to one of decline in long strings accompanied by an increase in short ones. The model spontaneously produced a new attractor, one that had not been pro-grammed in. In other words, new forms of individual bit strings and new overall global patterns emerged at the same time for there can be no global pattern of increase and decline without simultaneous change in the length of individual bit strings and no sustained change in individual bit string lengths without the overall pattern of increase and decline. Individual bit string patterns, and the overall pattern of the system, are forming and being formed by each other, at the same time. To repeat, the new attractor is evident both at the level of the whole population and at the level of the individual bit strings themselves at the same time.

Furthermore, the new attractors are not designed but emerge as self-organization, where it is not individual agents that are organizing them-selves but, rather, the pattern of interaction and it is doing so simul-taneously at the level of the individual agents and the population as a whole. It is problematic to separate them out as levels, since they are emerging simultaneously. No individual bit string can change in a coherent fashion on its own since random mutation in an isolated bit string would eventually lead to a completely random one. In interaction with other bit strings, however, advantageous mutations are selected and the others are weeded out. What is organizing itself, through interaction between symbol patterns, is then changes in the symbol patterns themselves. Patterns of interacting are turning back on themselves, imperfectly replicating them-selves, to yield changes in those patterns of interaction.

Ray, the objective observer external to this system, then interpreted the changes in symbol patterns in his simulation in terms of biology, in par-ticular, the evolution of life. Using the model as an analogy he argued that life has evolved in a similar, self-organizing and emergent manner. Other simulations have been used to suggest that this kind of emerging new attractor occurs only at the edge of chaos where there is a critical combi-nation of both stability and instability.

The computer simulations thus demonstrate the possibility that inter-action between digital symbols arranged as algorithmic rules can pattern itself in novel ways. Digital symbols can quite clearly self-organize in the dynamics at the edge of chaos to produce emergent attractors of a novel kind, provided that those symbol patterns are richly connected and diverse enough. Natural scientists at the Santa Fe institute and elsewhere then used this demonstration of possibility in the medium of digital symbols as a source of analogy to provide explanations of phenomena in particular areas of interest such as biology. The purpose of this chapter has been to point to how the abstract nonlinear, iterative relationships of complexity models are analogous to the interactive process of social evolution proposed by Elias. Furthermore, these analogies also point to other work in the social sciences. The abstract relationships I have just been talking about take place in the medium of symbols – digital symbols. Human interaction also takes place in the medium of symbols, admittedly more complex than digital symbols. In the next chapter, I will argue that the interaction between patterns of digital symbols described above provides an abstract analogy for human interaction, if that interaction is understood from the perspective of Mead's thought on mind, self and society.

The modeling of abstract interactive processes, such as those described above, cannot directly say anything about human acting and knowing. Such models can only be used as a source of analogy for understanding human action and the use of analogy requires caution. First, the very act of modeling requires an external modeler and the specification of the model requires the initial design of a system, even though what is being modeled is an evolutionary process that is supposed not to depend upon any outside design and even may not be usefully thought of as a system. It requires an act of imagination, then, to avoid thinking about the model from an external perspective as a system and to think, instead, about what the modeling of interaction might be saying *from a perspective within that interaction.* There is no analogy, then for the modeler or the design when it comes to human behavior. Also, *the 'system' provides no analogy for human action but the process of interaction does.* Furthermore, the models of complex adaptive systems are nothing more than abstract sets of relationships that demonstrate possible properties of those relationships. These are relationships completely devoid of the attributes of any real processes and, therefore, their use as analogies requires imaginative acts of translation if they are to say anything about real processes. Elias provides one such translation and I will come to another, that of Mead, in the next chapter.

To emphasize, then, the complexity sciences can never simply be applied to human action; they can only serve as a source domain for analogies with it. Complexity scientists think in terms of models and systems, which are spatial concepts. Process in systemic terms means the process of entities interacting to create a system, that is, a whole. However, when a system takes on a life of its own, the idea of a whole breaks down because any whole cannot be given. Instead it is in the process of perpetual construction. It follows that the whole can never be complete – there is no end to it and the whole is never there. This means that one has to talk about absent wholes, which sounds rather mysterious. It is this mystification that Elias rejects and this is why he did not think in terms of wholes or systems. In Elias' theory, there is no system, only the process of interaction producing further interaction, without any notion of a whole. In complex adaptive system theory there is a programmer defining the initial system and within that system there is the process of interaction. Taking this a source domain for human action, I would argue that there is no analogy for the programmer and there is no analogy for the system. However, the process of transformative interaction and its properties does provide a useful analogy for human action. Taking this analogy, there is a strong resonance with Elias' theory of the evolution of Western civilization, providing that one avoids taking literally the spatial metaphors, such as the 'edge of chaos.' This resonance is explored further in the following section.

Games and social processes

Elias argues in *What is Sociology?* ([1970] 1978), that sociology cannot be reduced to the psychology of individuals because the figurations of human interdependence cannot be reduced to the actions of individual people. On the contrary, the actions of individuals can only be understood in terms of their patterns of interdependence, that is, in terms of the figurations they form with each other.

> Some people tend to shrink from this insight. They confuse it with a metaphysical assumption of long standing which is often summed up in the saying 'the whole is more than the sum of its parts.' Using the term 'whole' or 'wholeness' creates a mystery in order to solve a mystery. This aberration must be mentioned because many people appear to believe that one can only be one or the other – either an atomist or a holist.
>
> (Elias, [1970] 1978, p72)

Elias contests this either–or position and explores how people, because of their interdependence and the way their actions intermesh, form figurations while those figurations form them. To illustrate this he uses a number of game models to demonstrate the relational character of power in a simplified form. These are game contests in which the relative power of the contestants is explored to bring out the features of various power figurations. He starts with a game in which antagonists face each other in an all out struggle in which there are no rules.

> Here, as in other similar cases, a fairly enduring antagonism reveals itself as a form of functional interdependence. The two groups are rivals for shrinking food resources. They are dependent on each other: . . . each move of one group determines each move of the other and *vice versa*. The internal arrangements in each group are determined to a greater or lesser extent by what each group thinks the other might do

next. Fierce antagonists, in other words, perform a function for each other, because the interdependence of human beings due to their hostility is no less a functional relationship than that due to their position as friends, allies and specialists bonded to each other through the division of labor. Their function for each other is in the last resort based on the compulsion they exert over each other by reason of their interdependence. It is not possible to explain the actions, plans and aims of either of the two groups if they are conceptualized as the freely chosen decisions, plans and aims of each group considered on its own, independently of the other group.

(Elias, [1970] 1978, p77)

The central question for Elias is how people have come to be able to regulate their interdependence so that they need not resort to all out struggle. He explores this by comparing a number of games in which the strength differential between two playing individuals diminishes. In other words the power ratio declines. As this happens the possibility of any one of them controlling both the other and the course of the game, the figuration of power between them, diminishes. This game becomes more like social processes.

The more the game comes to resemble a social process, the less it comes to resemble the implementation of an individual plan. In other words, to the extent that the inequality in the strengths of the two players diminishes, there will result from the interweaving of moves of two individual people a game process *which neither of them has planned.*

(Elias, [1970] 1978, p82)

He is showing here how you cannot reduce the social to the individual. He is beginning to develop his explanation of why no one in the game can control its evolution. The explanation has to do with the constraints they place on each other and the unpredictability of their responses to each other. He then moves on to games with multiple players on several levels and concludes that:

An increase in the number of players can cause the group of players to disintegrate, splintering into a number of smaller groups. Their relationship to each other can take two possible forms. The split groups can either move further apart and then continue to play the game quite independently of every other group. Or they can make up a new figuration of interdependent groups, each playing more or less autonomously, although all remain rivals for certain chances, equally sought after by all groups. A third possibility is that the group of

> players . . . remains integrated, turning, however, into a highly complex figuration; a two-tier group can develop out of a one-tier group.
>
> (Elias, [1970] 1978, p85)

Elias then goes on to explore the two-tier game. Whereas all played on the same level before, now a specialization develops. Special functionaries now coordinate the game; representatives, delegates, leaders, governments, and so on. Together they form a smaller group and they play directly with and against each other but are also bound together in some way with the mass of players, the second tier. Both levels depend on each other but the distribution of power between them can vary. Elias then explores what happens when the power differentials decline.

> Even in a game with no more than two tiers, the figuration of game and players already possesses a degree of complexity which prevents any one individual from using his superiority to guide the game in the direction of his own goals and wishes. He makes his moves both *out* of the network and *into* the network of interdependent players, where there are alliances and enmities, cooperation and rivalry at different levels.
>
> (Elias, [1970] 1978, p86)

Elias uses this game analogy to explain the process in which the functions of upper and lower classes in Western Europe change as the power differential diminishes. He emphasizes that these games are didactic models illustrating the evolving effects of interdependence on power figuration and ability to control the game.

> Metaphors are used which oscillate constantly between the idea that the course of the game can be reduced to the actions of the individual players and the other idea that it is of a supra-personal nature. Because the game cannot be controlled by the players, it is easily perceived as a kind of superhuman entity. For a long time it is especially difficult for the players to comprehend that their inability to control the game derives from their mutual dependence and positioning as players, and from the tension and conflicts inherent in this interweaving network.
>
> (Elias, [1970] 1978, p92)

Once again, Elias is arguing that social evolution is a self-organizing process of emergent change in patterns of relationship. He is pointing to how this insight is clouded by the persistent tendency to either locate the cause of change in an individual or in some 'whole' outside of the direct experience of interaction. Note how Elias is explaining the evolution of figurations of relationships using parameters to do with power differences and numbers of players. A key part of his argument about the civilizing process is the increasingly elaborate chain of connections between people. He shows how this increase in connectivity, as a feature of social structure, also brings with it changes in the way people experience themselves as requiring more foresight and greater self-control.

> The network of human activities tends to become increasingly complex, far-flung and closely knit. More and more groups, and with them more and more individuals, tend to become dependent on each other for their security and for the satisfaction of their needs in ways which for the greater part, surpass the comprehension of those involved. It is as if first thousands, then millions, then more and more millions walked through this world with their hands and feet chained by invisible ties. No one is in charge. No one stands outside. . . . No one can regulate the movement of the whole unless a great part of them are able to understand, to see, as it were, the whole patterns they form together. And they are not able to visualize themselves as part of larger patterns because, being hemmed in and moved uncomprehendingly hither and thither in ways which none of them intended, they cannot help being preoccupied with the urgent, narrow and parochial problems which each of them has to face. . . . Thus what is formed of nothing but human beings acts upon each of them, and is experienced by many as an alien external force not unlike the forces of nature.
>
> (Elias, 1987, p9)

I now want to link Elias' conceptual games and their insights into social processes with the complex adaptive systems models developed by Kauffman and their insights into biological evolution.

Evolutionary processes

Kauffman (1995) demonstrates in his computer simulations of the evolution of life that a large number of entities, or agents, interacting randomly with each other, are highly likely to evolve into a connected, autocatalytic network in a relatively short period of time. In other words, as entities, such as chemicals in the primordial soup before life emerged, interact randomly with each other, some entities are highly likely to come to play a part in the construction of others, the process of catalysis. Sooner or later, the strings of catalytic interaction that emerge will bend back on themselves and form autocatalytic networks. This means that entity A plays a part in the construction of B, which plays a part in the construction of C, which plays a part in the construction of A. There is no design or blueprint for this network. It emerges and sustains itself in a self-referential manner that can be thought of as self-organizing. Here, then, self-organization is an inevitable cooperative, participative dynamic, which is an intrinsic property of inter-action and causes the emergence of pattern. Causality here is of a trans-formative kind because it is interaction, or relationship, that causes emergent form.

Kauffman also shows how the dynamics of a self-organizing network, consisting of a number of entities, are determined by the number and strength of the connections between those entities. When the number of connections is low, the dynamics are characterized by stable attractors and when the number is high the attractors have properties similar to mathe-matical chaos, or they may be completely random. In an intermediate state, between stability and instability, the dynamic known as 'the edge of chaos' occurs, namely, the paradox of stable instability. When the strength of connection between agents is lowered then the number of connections producing stability is higher. At the edge of chaos, novelty emerges in a radically unpredictable way. In his work, Kauffman is developing a notion of causality in which numbers and strengths of connection between entities in a system cause the patterns of behavior of that system. The patterns of behavior are not, initially anyway, caused by chance and competitive selection, on the one hand, or by an agent's choice, on the other. No agent within the system is choosing the pattern of behavior across the system and neither is Kauffman, the simulator. Instead, that pattern emerges in the interaction between the agents, neither by chance nor by choice, but through the capacity to produce coherence that is intrinsic to interaction itself. The connection between Kauffman's computer models and Elias' didactic games is clear. Just as Kauffman does, so Elias draws attention to how increasing connectivity and variety changes the dynamics of inter-action. The changed dynamics he was referring to have the characteristics of 'the edge of chaos' in which novel patterns emerge that no one intended, and over which no one has control, and yet there is coherence in what emerges.

Chapter 4

The fundamental importance of communicative interaction

> Group-analytic theory and practice has almost from its beginning paid special attention to the communication process and has considered it of central importance.
>
> (Foulkes, 1964, pp68–69)

The last chapter linked insights from the sciences of complexity with the process sociology of Elias, which explains how patterns of social interaction evolve simultaneously with individual personality structures over long periods of time in a process of interweaving individual human intentions and plans that no one engaging in them can control. Social and individual personality patterns emerge in the local interactions between people, analogous to the emergence of patterns in the local interaction of entities in nature according to complexity theories. Elias presented a theory of process and argued against understanding social and personality patterns in terms of systems. The notion of 'system' brings a spatial metaphor to what is a temporal process and, furthermore, the notion of 'system' unjustifiably reifies that process. A central concept in systems thinking is that of a whole, often thought of as a 'supra individual.' In relation to human action, this amounts to an abstraction from, and a mystification of, direct human experience. Elias held that there was nothing mysterious about the process of social evolution and argued against looking for any cause outside the process of interaction itself. In other words, the cause of social/personality evolution lies is the process of interaction itself, an idea that seems to me to be quite consistent with insights coming from the sciences of complexity.

The last chapter briefly reviewed the central concepts in theories of complexity to be found in the natural sciences. I argued that these sciences provide a source domain for analogies with the kind of social process Elias was describing. In a theoretically rigorous manner, supported by models and simulations, theories of complexity demonstrate the possibility of local interactive relationships in the medium digital symbols producing widespread emergent coherence. The complexity sciences model the dynamics of abstract relationships in order to demonstrate their inherent properties. The central insight is that iterative nonlinear local interaction in the medium of digital symbols has the capacity to pattern itself in such a way that both global and individual entity patterns emerge simultaneously. When one reasons by analogy, one takes abstract relationships from one domain and clothes them in the attributes of another. One cannot simply apply the insights about abstract relationships in the complexity sciences to human behavior. Some kind of translation is required and while Elias' process theory provides such a translation in terms of social evolution over long time periods, the purpose of this chapter is to explore a translation in terms of the detail of human interaction in local situations in the living present.

Humans interact with each other in the medium of symbols, importantly in the medium of symbols called language. In other words, human interaction is communicative interaction. Perhaps the most important characteristic distinguishing humans from other animals is their ability to communicate with each other using sophisticated symbols and this communication is the basis of the sophisticated forms of cooperative and competitive activities, often using tools, which constitute society. Elias was concerned with the evolution of patterns of communicative interaction across large groupings of people over long time periods. This chapter turns to a more detailed understanding of the nature of communicative interaction in smaller groupings of people in the present for it is in such interaction that the wider and longer-term social/personality patterns emerge. The concern of this chapter, therefore, is ordinary communicative interaction between people in groups and Mead's symbolic interactionist theory provides an insightful way of understanding this.

Mead and the 'conversation of gestures'

Mead (1934) held that mind was not suddenly there at some point in evolution and it neither preceded society nor did society precede it. Human societies are not possible without human minds and human minds are not possible in the absence of human societies. Mead therefore sought an explanation of how mind and society, that is cooperative interaction, evolved together.

Mead's explanation starts with the interactive behavior of the higher mammals. For example, dogs relate to each other in a responsive manner, with the act of one fitting into the act of the other so as to constitute, for example, aggressive or playful interaction in a rudimentary form of social behavior. Mead defined a social act as a gesture by one animal that calls forth a response from another, which together constitute meaning for both. Immediately, meaning becomes a property of interaction, or relationship. For example, one dog makes the gesture of a snarl and this may call forth a counter snarl, which means fight; or the gesture could call forth flight, which means victory; or the response to the gesture could be crouching, which means submission. Meaning, therefore, does not lie in the gesture alone but in the whole social act. In other words, meaning arises in the responsive interaction between actors and gesture and response can never be separated but must be understood as moments in one act. Meaning does not arise first in each individual, to be subsequently expressed in action, nor is it transmitted from one individual to another but, rather, it arises in the interaction between them. Meaning is not attached to an object, formed as a representation, or stored, but is created in the interaction.

Mead described the gesture–response as a symbol in the sense that it is an action that has meaning. Here meaning is emerging in the action of the living present in which the immediate future (response) acts back on the past (gesture) to change its meaning. Meaning is not simply located in the past (gesture) or the future (response) but in the circular interaction between the two in the living present. In this way the present is not simply a point but has a time structure. Mead talked about a *continuous process* of gesture and response. Every gesture is a response to some previous gesture, which is a response to an even earlier one, thereby constructing history. This is analogous to the iterative, history dependent interaction between entities that the complexity sciences deal with. Both Mead and at least some of the complexity scientists are talking about processes in the living present, iteratively reconstructing the past while perpetually constructing the future.

The question that Mead then poses is this: what is required for the interacting mammals to be aware of the meaning of their gesture? In other words, the question relates to the prerequisite of consciousness, that is, the capacity to know the meaning of, to point to the potential responses to, the gesture. Mead's answer is that our mammal ancestors must have evolved central nervous systems that enabled them to gesture to others in a manner that was capable of calling forth in themselves the same range of responses as in those to whom they were gesturing. This would happen if, for example, the snarl of one called forth in itself the fleeting feelings associated with counter snarl, flight or submissive posture, just as they did in the one to whom the gesture was being made. The gesture–response, as symbol, now has a substantially different role because it makes it possible for the gesturer to 'know' what he or she is doing. Mead described such a gesture–response as a significant symbol, where a significant symbol is action that calls forth the same response in the gesturer as in the one to whom it is directed. Significant symbols make it possible to intuit something about the range of likely responses from the other. The body, with its nervous system, therefore, becomes central to understanding how we 'know' anything.

Chapter 6 will review research on the brain that provides support for Mead's insight. That chapter will argue that feelings are rhythmic patterns in a body, which make it possible for the gesture of one body to call forth in itself similar responses, similar feeling rhythms, to that called forth in another body to whom the gesture is made. In other words, there is some kind of resonance between the body rhythms of the two interacting individuals. Possessing this capacity, the maker of a gesture can predict the consequences of that gesture. In other words, he or she can know what he or she is doing, as the other responds. The whole social act, that is, meaning, can be experienced in advance of carrying out the whole act, opening up the possibility of reflection and choice in making a gesture. Furthermore, the one responding has the same opportunity for reflecting upon, and so choosing from, the range of possible responses. The first part of a gesture can be taken by the other as an indication of how further parts of the gesture will unfold from the response. In this way, the two can indicate to each other how they might respond to each other in the continuous circle in which a gesture by one calls forth a response from another, which is itself a gesture back to the first. Obviously, this capacity makes more sophisticated forms of cooperation possible.

Mead said that humans are fundamentally role-playing animals, by which he meant that *rudimentary forms of thinking take the form of private role-playing*, that is, gestures made by a body to itself, calling forth responses in itself. It is this private role-play that constitutes mind. Social relationships are, therefore, gestures made by bodies to other bodies and mind is the gesturing and responding of a body to itself. The process is the same in both cases, namely a 'conversation of gestures' in significant symbols, that is, the body rhythms of feelings, and they both proceed at the same time.

Mead then argued that the gesture which is particularly useful in calling forth the same attitude in oneself as in the other is the vocal gesture. This is because we can hear the sounds we make in much the same way as others hear them, while we cannot see the facial gestures we make as others see them, for example. The development of more sophisticated patterns of vocal gesturing, that is, of the language form of significant symbols, is thus of major importance in the development of consciousness and of sophisticated forms of society. Mind and society emerge together in the medium of language, where mind is private, silent conversation and social is public, vocal conversation. However, since speaking and listening are actions of bodies, and since bodies are never without feelings, the medium of language is also always the medium of feelings.

Taking the attitude of the group and the society

Mead takes his argument further when he suggests how the private role-play evolves in increasingly complex ways. As more and more interactions are experienced with others, so increasingly, more roles and wider ranges of possible responses are taken up in the role-playing activity that is continuously intertwined with public gesturing and responding. In this way, the capacity to take the attitude of many others evolves and this becomes generalized. Each engaged in the conversation of gestures can now take the attitude of what Mead calls the generalized other. This is reflected in the familiar experience of being concerned about 'what *others* will say about our conduct.' Eventually, individuals develop the capacity to take the attitude of the whole group, or what Mead calls the game. In other words, creatures have now evolved who are capable of taking the social attitude to their actions as they gesture and respond. The result is much more sophisticated processes of cooperative interaction. There is now mindful social behavior with increasingly sophisticated meaning and an increasing capacity to use tools more and more effectively to transform the context within which the interacting creatures live.

The next step in this evolutionary process is the linking of the attitude of specific and generalized others, even of the whole group, with a 'me.' In other words, there evolves a capacity to take the attitude of others not just towards one's gestures but also towards one's self. The 'me' is the configuration of the gestures–responses of the others/society to one as a subject, or an 'I'. What has evolved here is the capacity to be an object to oneself, a 'me'. A self, as the relationship between 'me' and 'I,' has therefore emerged, as well as an awareness of that self, that is, self consciousness. In this interaction, the 'I' is the response to the gesture of the group/society to oneself, that is, the 'me'. Mead argues, very importantly, that this 'I's response to one's perception of the attitude of the group to oneself (the 'me') is not a given but is always potentially unpredictable in that there is no predetermined way in which the 'I' might respond to the 'me.' In other words, each of us may respond in many different ways to our perception of the views others have of us and there is always some spontaneity or choice. Here, Mead is pointing to the importance of difference, or diversity, in the emergence of the new, that is, in the potential for transformation. Language plays a major role at this stage of evolution and Mead argues that without it, the emergence of human mind, self and society, as we know it would be impossible.

Throughout this explanation, human society is emerging simultaneously with human minds, including selves. Mead consistently argued that one is not more fundamental than the other; that one could not exist without the other. The social, in human terms, is a highly sophisticated process of cooperative interaction between people in the medium of symbols in order to undertake joint action. Such sophisticated interaction could not take place without self conscious minds but neither could those self conscious minds exist without that sophisticated form of cooperation. In other words there could be no private role-play, including silent conversation, by a body with itself, if there was no public interaction of the same form. Mind/self and society are all logically equivalent processes of a conversational kind. Social interaction is a public conversation of gestures, particularly gestures of a vocal kind, while mind is a conversation of gestures between 'I,' 'me,' 'other' and 'group' in a silent, private role-play of public, social interaction. The result is self-referential, reflexive processes of sophisticated cooperation in the medium of symbols that constitute meaning. These processes, always involving the body and its feelings, both enable and constrain human actions. Individual selves/minds emerge between people, in the relationship between them, and cannot be simply 'located' within an individual. In this way of thinking, individual minds/selves certainly exist, and very importantly so, but they emerge in relationships between people rather than arising within an individual. It is important to note here how in the gesture–response, individual and collective identities are emerging. In this process, identities are iterated as both continuity and transformation at the same time. Individual identities are forming and being formed by social identities just as in the process sociology of Elias.

The symbolic processes of mind/self are always actions, experienced within a body as rhythmic variations, that is, feeling states. Mind is an action of the body, rather like walking is an action of the body. One would not talk about walking emerging from the body and it is no more appropriate to talk about mind emerging from the brain. Note how the private role-play, including the silent conversation of mind/self, is not stored as representations of a pre-given reality. It is, rather, continuous spontaneous action in which patterns of action are continuously reproduced in repetitive forms as continuity, sameness and identity, and simultaneously as potential transformation of that identity. In other words, as with interaction between bodies, the social, so with interaction of a body with itself, mind, there is the experience of both familiar repetition of habit and the potential for spontaneous change. The process is not representing or storing but continuously reproducing and creating new meaningful experience. In this way, the fundamental importance of individual self and identity is retained, along with the fundamental importance of social relationships. In this way too, both continuity and potential transformation are always simultaneously present.

Note that Mead never claims that one person can grasp another's state of mind, nor is there any notion of one mind putting anything into the mind of another. What he does argue is that one person can call forth in himself or herself a similar response to a gesture to that called forth in another. This is possible because one body can experience similar feeling rhythms to another's. This is not the same as grasping another's state of mind. Instead it is saying that one human body can empathize with, can be attuned to, another. The response is simultaneously called forth by the gesture of the other and selected or enacted by the responder on the basis of past history reconstructed in the present, always with the possibility of spontaneous variation. In other words, the response of the 'I' is both being called forth by the other and being enacted, or selected by the history, biological, individual and social of the responder. The process is one of emergence in which the future is being perpetually constructed and it does not ultimately locate the source of change in the individual alone.

Social structure is shared, repetitive and enduring values, beliefs, traditions, habits, routines and procedures. These are all social acts of a particular kind. They are couplings of gesture and response of a predictable, highly repetitive kind. They do not exist in any meaningful way in a store anywhere but, rather, they are continually reproduced in the interaction between people. However, even habits are rarely exactly the same. They may often vary as those with whom one interacts changes and as the context of that interaction changes. Habits here are understood not as shared mental contents but as history-based, repetitive actions, both private and public, reproduced in the present with relatively little variation.

Complex responsive processes of relating

What I have been describing in the previous section is a process of interaction between people in which their actions of gesturing and responding are understood as significant symbols. Complexity scientists (see Chapter 3) explore the properties of abstract models of interaction between symbols of a different kind, namely, digital symbols. It is possible that certain properties of interaction demonstrated in the abstract models might offer analogies for human interaction, interpreted through Mead's thought. But why would one be looking for analogies in the first place? The reason, I think, is that Mead's powerful insights do not take us far enough. As one imagines the process of gesturing and responding between larger and larger numbers of individuals, the complexity of it all becomes mind-boggling. How could continuous circular processes of gesturing and responding between thousands, even millions of people produce the kind of long-term, widespread coherence that Elias talks about? This is not an issue that either Mead or Elias dealt with, but it is one where the complexity sciences offer important insights.

The intrinsic ordering properties of interaction

Chapter 3 drew attention to a key insight from the complexity sciences, namely, the intrinsic property of interaction to form pattern in itself. The modeling of complex systems demonstrates the possibility that interactions between large numbers of entities, each entity responding to others on the basis of its own local organizing principles, will produce widespread coherent patterns with the potential for novelty in certain conditions, namely, the paradoxical dynamics of stability and instability at the same time. In other words, the very process of self-organizing interaction, when richly connected enough, has the inherent capacity to spontaneously produce coherent pattern in itself, without any blueprint or program. Furthermore, when the interacting entities are different enough from each other, that capacity is one of spontaneously producing novel patterns in itself. In other words, abstract systems can pattern themselves where those patterns have the paradoxical feature of continuity and novelty, identity and difference, at the same time. By analogy, I understand the circular process of gesturing and responding between people in the medium of symbols to have the same kind of intrinsic patterning capacity.

What Mead presents in his theory of symbolic interactionism is complex, nonlinear, iterative processes of communicative interaction between people in which mind, self, and society all emerge simultaneously in the living present. Elias' theory of process sociology presents processes of power relating in which social structures (habits, routines, beliefs) emerge at the same time as personality structures (ways of experiencing ourselves). Both Mead and Elias are concerned with local interaction in the present in which widespread, global patterns emerge as social and personality structures, as identity and difference, as human 'habitus.' I have been pointing to how the complexity sciences model complex adaptive systems as generalized, abstract interactions that demonstrate the possibility and plausibility of the theories that Mead and Elias present. In the rest of this book, I will refer to a combination of these theories as the theory of complex responsive processes of relating. This terminology comes by way of the complexity sciences that utilize the notion of complex adaptive systems. I have already given reasons in this and previous chapters why it is inappropriate to think of human action as a system and this argument will be developed further in Chapter 13. With regard to human action, the useful concept is process rather than system. Also, the notion of adaptation has a particular meaning associated with neo-Darwinian evolutionary theory, which I also argue is an inappropriate way to understand human action (see Chapter 14). With regard to human action, responsive is a more useful notion than adaptation because humans do not always fit in with each other but they usually respond to each other in some way. In using the analogy of complex adaptive systems, therefore, the shift to human interaction is indicated by the terminology of complex responsive processes.

If one takes the complex responsive processes view then one thinks of the emergence of long-term, widespread coherent patterns of relating in the process of local relating. It follows that there is no need to look for the causes of coherent human action in concepts such as deep structures, archetypes, the collective unconscious, transcendental wholes, common pools of meaning, group minds, the group-as-a-whole, transpersonal processes, foundation matrix, the personal dynamic unconscious, internal worlds, mental models, and so on. Instead, one understands local human relating to be inherently pattern forming.

Communicative interaction always takes place in specific local situations in the living present. People interact with each other locally in the absence of any global blueprint or program and these local interactions are iterative, that is, they are perpetually reproduced. Furthermore, these iterative interactions are nonlinear, which means that differences, even very small ones, from one iteration to the next are both dampened and potentially amplified. One consequence of thinking in these terms is that *time* is immediately of the essence because one is thinking of iteration or reproduction from one period to the next in which the patterns of interactions in the present depend upon the history of interactions in the past and expectations of the future.

The complex responsive processes perspective, therefore, is based on a particular understanding of time in relation to human action. First, there is the question of the arrow of time. Clearly human experience is experience of the arrow of time in the sense that we all know that what has been said cannot be unsaid, what has been done cannot be undone. We cannot go back in time and unsay or undo. We can only go forward in time and elaborate on what we have said or done. It is also our experience that interacting with each other in one way immediately precludes all alternative ways of interacting and that what happens next will be different to what might have been if we had interacted in one of these alternative ways. This is analogous to the bifurcations of nonlinear dynamics. Such path dependency means that the viewpoint from which we act changes as we move from the past through the present into the future. It is only the present viewpoint that is relevant to action because action is always in the present and the arrow of time means that we can never go back from the present viewpoint to a past one. We can only understand the past in terms of our present viewpoint. As soon as one understands human interaction as iterative, one understands that the past is being reproduced in the present. And as soon as one understands the implications of the arrow of time in relation to human interaction, it follows that the reproduction of the past in the present is from the viewpoint of the present. In other words human action explicitly and implicitly reconstructs or reinterprets the past as the basis of present action. This means that human action is forming the past and being formed by it at the same time in the present. The same point applies to expectations about the future. Human action is always in the present but it also is always explicitly or implicitly taken on the basis of expectations about the future. These expectations cannot be from the viewpoint of the future, only from that of the present. So, human action in the present is, at the same time, forming and being formed by expectations about the future.

I now want to turn to a more detailed examination of the nature of the symbols that are the medium of human communicative interaction and power relating. This will lead into a discussion of how human communicative interaction and power relating is patterned.

Symbols: the medium of human communicative interaction

The meaning of the word 'symbol' is now most commonly taken to be a thing that represents something other than itself, such as the word 'table' representing a wooden object upon which some other object is placed. The word itself is derived from the Greek words *symbolon* meaning a mark or a token and *sym-ballein*, which means to throw together. Mead's use of the word is very different to common usage and more in line with the origins of the word in the sense that he takes symbols to be actions. For him, a gesture made by one animal that is responded to by another is a symbol. I understand this to mean that a gesture is thrown together with a response and together they 'stand for,' or better still constitute, a meaning. Mead rejected the notion that symbols are independent of their meaning and said that they could not lie outside of interaction. He focused his attention on significant symbols but here I want to make a distinction between three kinds of symbol:

- protosymbols;
- significant symbols;
- reified symbols.

The importance of feelings: protosymbols

Earlier in this chapter, I referred to the importance of the rhythmical patterning of bodily experience (see also Chapter 6). The body is characterized by the millisecond rhythms of neuronal firing in the brain; the second by second rhythms of the heart; the slower rhythms of the metabolic and endocrine systems; the hourly dynamics of the digestive system; and the daily, weekly, monthly and yearly rhythms of body energy. The suggestion is that these temporal dynamics, located in parts of the body, mesh into a symphony of rhythms having particular time contours marked by beat, duration and variations in intensity, constituting what Stern (1985, 1995) calls vitality affects, and Damasio (1994, 1999) calls background feelings (see Chapters 5 and 6). In other words, feelings are rhythmic variations of the body, its spatial and temporal dynamics. While all humans share these physiological characteristics in general, individuals seem to have their own unique pattern of bodily time contours (with reference to the heart, see Golberger, 1997). These unique bodily time contours constitute a person's feelings as unique experiences of self, or identity. A bodily sense of self, an identity, is actualized through the way in which others respond to that person's unique bodily time contours and the way in which such responses are experienced (see Chapter 6). People's experience of being with each other has to do with their bodily resonance with each other's feeling dynamics through perceptions of timing, intensity and shape in posture and movement.

It seems, therefore, that it is the equivalence between the time/space contours of the stimuli and the time/space contours of feeling in the body that make possible the emergence of meaning. I would argue that this linking between qualitative aspects of perceived experience and similar qualitative aspects of felt bodily experience is the basis of human knowing. I refer to this linking, this throwing together of a stimulus with a bodily response, as a protosymbol and protosymbols provide humans with the means for protomental processes. It is important, I think, to note that these protomental processes are not mysterious inner essences, but rather, actions of the whole body. This is how I understand the process of communication that Mead proposes. A protosymbol is a gesture, which in relation to the response constitutes meaning for both of those involved but does not call forth a similar response in the one making the gesture as in the one responding to it. In other words, the communication is unconscious.

This form of communication amounts to protoconversation but it is in no way rudimentary or primitive. It does not underlie other forms of conversation as some lower layer but is, rather, simultaneously present in all other forms of conversation because all conversation involves a body and all bodies always have feeling dynamics. Protoconversation is the unconscious communication of feelings as bodily resonance, expressing the need to be met and understood. It seems to me that it is in the rhythmic, protoconversational exchange between us that a felt sense of reality, of existing, continually emerges. Protoconversations take a theme-and-variation format, with patterns of beat, rhythm, duration and intensity. Through them, we directly express, in our looking, vocalizing and touching, the rhythms and intensities of our bodily experience, our own temporal feeling dynamic, thereby evoking responses in terms of feeling rhythms from others. In essence, what we are doing is mirroring, echoing and resonating with each other's temporal feeling dynamic and thereby empathically attuning ourselves to each other in ways of which we are not normally conscious. Furthermore, repeated experience of events of this kind are organized and integrated into protonarratives, which then organize and integrate further experiences of this kind. Protoconversations are constructing protonarratives and this is the unconscious mental process of organizing and integrating experience into meaning, the ongoing construction of knowledge in the act of living together.

What I have been describing is a continuous process of action and interaction that cannot be stored anywhere. It is a process in the living present and does not exist as a 'thing' anywhere. However, this does not mean that what arises is completely new at each moment, arising from nothing, as it were. Interaction in the medium of protosymbols at any one moment takes place in a context of place and time, including the past history of interaction. Interaction in the living present is an extension of the historical experience of interaction, in which protosymbols trigger other protosymbols in a process of continuous reproduction that always has the potential for transformation.

In other words, habitual feeling dynamics of a repetitive kind are intertwined with spontaneous variations in them, in that even habits are rarely reproduced in exactly the same form. It is in this way that individuals amplify what is probably the inherited uniqueness of their bodily rhythm. Small variations in the experience of interaction and in the context of that interaction may be amplified into different patterns of bodily experienced identity, an example of the sensitive dependence on initial conditions typical of complex phenomena. This may well be the bodily basis of the unique sense of self that people experience. Notice that this way of thinking about mind, self and communication does not require any notion of sharing. Each individual is bodily resonating in their own unique ways without sharing mental contents or putting feelings into each other. The possibility of bodily resonance is sufficient to explain empathy and attunement without anything being shared or transmitted from one to another.

Communicative interaction between people in the medium of protosymbols is, however, not conscious interaction. Conscious interaction occurs in the medium of significant symbols.

The importance of reflection-in-action: significant symbols

While protosymbols are bodily gestures that call forth a bodily response in another to produce meaning for both, significant symbols have an additional feature: the bodily gesture of one calls forth a similar response in the maker of the gesture to the one called forth in the other. This enables the maker of the gesture to be aware, or mindful, of the meaning of the gesture he or she is making. A significant symbol could be a facial gesture or some other movement of the body, one that produces in the body of the maker a similar feeling dynamic to that produced in the body to which it is directed. However, it is the vocal gesture that opens up the greatest possibilities for communication in significant symbols because the maker of the vocal gesture can hear it in the same way as the one to whom it is directed. The most elaborated use of significant symbols, therefore, takes place in the action of speaking, that is, in the use of language. The action of speaking throws together a vocal gesture by one person with a similar response in that person as in the other. The meaning is in the dual nature of this response.

Significant symbols are usually expressed in the medium of ordinary, everyday conversation, in which people relate to each other, not as objects, but as each having their own subjectivity, that is, their own private role-plays or silent conversations. The vocalized and the silent conversations simultaneously taking place in significant symbols form themselves into stories and narratives that organize the experience of being together. Both the vocalized and the silent conversations that are taking place simultaneously are, of course, the actions of bodies. It follows that interaction will be taking place in both significant symbols and protosymbols at the same time. Protosymbols are not more fundamental and they do not underlie significant symbols, nor are they earlier and so more primitive. Protosymbols have a different structure to significant symbols and communication between bodies takes place in both throughout human life.

The importance of abstract thinking: reified symbols

I want to distinguish protosymbols and significant symbols from another kind of symbol. Protosymbols and significant symbols are both actions of bodies having a gesture–response structure in a context. The context for both is the living present and the historical background from which the gesture–response action evolves. The gesture–response action is shaped and given meaning by this context even though the actions themselves do not directly make reference to it. However, the use of language opens up another very important possibility for human communication, namely, the use of abstractions. Humans have developed abstract, systematic frameworks within which to talk about their worlds. For example, there is the framework of physics within which some talk about the material environment we live in and there is the framework of medical sciences within which others talk about the functioning of the human body. The historical development of abstract-systematic explanatory frameworks of all kinds has created a context additional to the kinds of current and historical contexts discussed in relation to protosymbols and significant symbols. That additional context is the abstract-systematic frameworks themselves. When one takes account of this aspect of context, I think it so substantially shifts the nature of gesture–response that it calls for the distinguishing of an additional category of symbol. I will call these reified symbols for the following reasons.

When people talk to each other with reference to an abstract explanatory framework, such as physics or meta psychological theory, the gesture of one takes the form of words or mathematical symbols that represent and directly refer to the abstract-systematic framework and so do the responding words. If two people are talking about physics and one uses the words 'gravity' and 'relativity', those words immediately refer to a whole abstract-systematic framework and the responses those words call forth in each must also refer to that framework if they are to continue to discuss physics. The meaning of these words does not lie in those words, those gestures, themselves. It lies in the responses that they call forth, just as for any other symbol, but those responses are indirectly linked to the gesture through the framework. Furthermore, we seem to have developed a strong tendency, particularly in communication conditioned by abstract-systematic frameworks, to locate meaning in the word, in the gesture alone, and then proceed as if that word were the reality it stands for. We come easily to talk about words 'gravity' and 'relativity' as if they were things. This becomes even more prevalent when the words are written and the text replaces the conversation. It is for this reason that I am calling them reified symbols. A reified symbol throws together the gesture with an aspect of the context, that is, an abstract-systematic framework, and in the process comes to represent and refer to it in a way that is identified or fused with the phenomenon being explained as though it were that phenomenon.

Using symbols in this reified form can cut people off from their lived experience. They can be used to defend against feelings and the anxiety of changes in meaning and thus identity, commonly expressed as the duality of feeling and intellect. But they can also be used to transform the context of human action in highly creative and also very destructive ways. However, communication in reified symbols on their own is impossible because even when they discuss matters within abstract-systematic framework, people will still be communicating in significant and protosymbols as well, simply because they are human bodies.

Communicative action as patterning processes

In this section I will be arguing that communication between people in the medium of symbols is patterned in processes in which people account to each other and negotiate with each other, in collaborative and competitive ways in order to 'go on' together (Shotter, 1993). Coherence and order is reproduced and potentially transformed in self-organizing processes that are the meshing together of individual actions in the way Elias outlined.

First, whenever people communicate with each other they quite clearly display, in the very act of that communication, some kind of expectation of each other. People expect those whom they are addressing to reply to what they are saying in some way that is associated with what they are saying. If people do not comply, more or less, with this expectation, there is no communication, and thus no meaning. Associative responding is the very basis of communicative action. Furthermore, people generally expect others to be more or less competent, compliant and reasonable in communicating, just as those others expect them to display these qualities too (Boden, 1994). People hold each other morally accountable for their communicative and other actions. Or, they may expect others to be incompetent, rebellious, unreasonable and immoral. These expectations have a profound impact on how people proceed together. They undertake very different kinds of communicative action depending upon the expectations they have and if they expect completely uncooperative responses from each other they will try to avoid communication altogether. Even if this is not possible, the meaning arising in communicative action will be completely different in different contexts of expectation.

People do not refer to some set of rules, conscious or unconscious, in order to form those expectations. Instead, they form them in the very action of communication with each other. In that interaction, they may draw on, or point to, local or global sets of rules that have previously been formulated. However, they are not referring to those rules in order to form their expectations, but rather, as resources or tools to be employed in their negotiations with each other. They are patterns of reified symbols forming abstract-systematic frameworks. They point to external rules to justify their current actions or persuade others to change theirs. They are not simply applying the regularities of rules but referring to them in order to explain, justify or condemn their own, or others', deviations from them. They may refer to rules to guide their joint action together but since rules can never cover every contingency, what they will be doing in their communication is negotiating how any rules are to be employed in the current context they find themselves in. They are functionalizing abstract, generalized idealizations. Here action, rather than being rule driven, is employing rules as tools, from time to time. This action-based approach emphasizes the social, or collaborative nature of the action of communicating in which people make sense of their actions together, taking account of each other's sensibilities, spontaneously sustaining and repairing their unceasing flow of speech entwined activity in an unreflective, unforced, unplanned and unintended way (Shotter & Katz, 1996).

The second, strikingly observable feature that imparts coherent pattern to communicative interaction is the turn-taking sequence that creates the rhythms of daily life (Boden, 1994; Garfinkel, 1967; Goffman, 1981; Sacks, 1992; Shotter, 1993). The basis of this turn-taking sequence is the expectations people have of each other, as described above. People value turns to speak. They compete for them, abandon them and construct them, so making, as well as taking, turns to speak. People make turns for themselves and others by asking questions, soliciting advice, clarifying issues, expressing opinions, and so on. They negotiate rights and obligations in this turn-taking process and it is this negotiating that structures the action of talking and, therefore most other human actions, because they are accomplished in talking. Everyday turn taking and turn making in conversation is simultaneously stable and unstable, predictable and unpredictable. Here, communicating, as iterative, recursive nonlinear processes, structures itself from within itself.

Third, turn taking/turn making in communicative interaction imparts structure to that communication by actions of sequencing, segmenting and categorizing. One of the most important of these categorization devices is that to do with membership (Boden, 1994): who may talk and who may not, who is 'in' and who is 'out.' These are matters that I will return to in Chapter 7. Another important aspect of the turn-taking/turn-making process is referred to as 'adjacent pairs' (Boden, 1994), which urge forward turns and topics. For example, turn-taking/turn-making exchanges tend to be organized in distinct matching pairs of question and answer, request and response, invitation and acceptance, announcement and acknowledgement, complaint and response, and so on.

Fourth, people employ rhetorical devices such as 'directive' and 'instructive' forms of talk in which they are 'arrested,' 'moved,' 'struck' and 'feel called upon to respond' (Shotter, 1993; Shotter & Katz, 1996). In this way, people negotiate with each other, responding to each other's utterances in an attempt to link in their practical activities. They notice and point to the content of each other's speech, including their references to the context; they agree and disagree with each other; they sympathize and fail to sympathize with each other. In doing this, they are constructing living social relationships as they connect, link and orient themselves to each other and to their surroundings in their turn-taking/turn-making communicative interaction.

The patterning effect of communicative interaction

Now consider the patterning effect of communicative interaction in which people take and make conversational turns, categorizing, using adjacent pairing and rhetorical devices, all influenced by expectations that arise as they do so. In this responsive process people gesture and respond in the form of utterances of one kind or another. Incomplete sentences, stories, propositions, and so on, mutually shape the evolution of their exchanges. The local, situated use of words by one produces responses in others, making momentary, practical differences. People resonate with each other and they may grasp something new, unseen but sensed in the emerging interaction. They are not transmitting information about things but, rather, they are going on with each other in a responsive expression and potential understanding that grows from their very interaction. If they share anything, it is certainly not rules, but sensibilities and responses that are refined and elaborated (Shotter, 1993). It is the very features of the process of interaction, namely, taking turns, using rhetorical devices, categorizing, and so on, in the context of mutual expectations, that patterns people's ongoing communicative interactions.

However, while this patterning produces coherence and stability, it also has within it the possibility of change. That possibility exists because the beginnings of understanding arise in the moments that strike people and these are often small details that may seem at first to be trivial, but which may amplify into new patterns of relating (Shotter, 2000). It is in the unique variations in each other's expressions, as opposed to the exact regularities of rules, that people have their living understanding of each other. Living moments of the unique variations strike people and so arrest the ongoing routine flow of spontaneously responsive activity. As these variations are articulated, elaborated and refined, people change. Complex mixtures of unique influences occurring both within and around people shape their actions in this way as reciprocally responsive movement between them points beyond the present moment to other possible connections. These movements of dialogue are both repetitive and potentially transformative and it is in the minute variations that the possibility of the novel arises. Given the local unrepeatable nature of context, these moments are inevitably unique, where thought, feeling, perception, memory, impulse and imagination are so tightly interwoven that they cannot be separated (Shotter, 2000). As a result people's actions are never fully orderly nor fully disorderly.

As individual bodies interact communicatively with each other, each simultaneously acts communicatively toward him or herself. In other words, as individuals engage in public, vocal conversation with each other, they simultaneously engage in private, silent conversations with themselves. These silent private conversations that are individual mind have exactly the same features as public vocal conversations described above: they mirror each other. Minds are associative, with one thought or voice silently triggering another thought or voice. One voice seeks to persuade or negotiate with some other voice, in a silent role-play, always involving the bodily rhythms of feelings just as in the public vocal conversations. One has expectations of oneself as one has of others, namely, that one should be competent and reasonable and morally accountable to oneself as well as to others. One seeks to justify oneself to oneself, to account for oneself to oneself for both one's public and private communicative and other actions. The same sequencing of turn taking is evident as first one aspect of oneself and then another takes turns, makes turns, to participate in role-plays. The same kind of membership categorization occurs in which some thoughts have a voice and others are denied or repressed. An individual asks questions of him or herself and gives replies, complains and responds, compliments and denigrates oneself, and so on. Furthermore, the same kinds of rhetorical devices are in evidence in one's silent conversation with oneself. One is struck by some aspects of this conversation with oneself and such striking moments call forth responses from oneself. Private role-plays and the public interactions proceed simultaneously in the same modes and they make each other possible.

Although a beginning and an end might be ascribed to a particular sequence of communicative interactions, that description is purely arbitrary, for even before a particular episode begins, even between total strangers, each has a history of experience. That history has patterned the private role-playing of each individual in particular ways that enact (selectively enable and constrain) what the individual responds to both privately and publicly. That history establishes what aspects of the gesturing of the other will be striking, will call forth, or evoke, a response and what kind of response it will evoke. This dance of enactment and evocation is made possible, and at the same time limited, by previous history. And when they are not strangers, the history of their own personal relating to each other, and the histories of the groups they are part of, also become relevant. However, this history is not some kind of 'true' factual account but a reproduction in the living present that always leaves room for potential transformation.

Furthermore, those collective and individual histories reproduced in the living present of communicative action are extending those histories into the future. This points to the narrative-like structuring of human experience. It is not simply that people are telling each other stories or that narrative is simply an alternative type of knowledge. The turn-taking, responsive relating of people may be thought of as forming narrative at the same time as that narrative patterns moral responsibility and turn taking. In other words, the experience of the living present, like the past, is structured in narrative-like ways. It is in the micro interaction of their turn-taking conversations that people are perpetually constructing the narrative pattern of the living present and thus the future. This perpetual construction has the paradoxical characteristics of repetition and transformation at the same time. And what is being constructed is nothing less than the individual and collective identities of those involved, identities always open to potential transformation.

I use the term narrative-like, rather than narrative, in order to make an important distinction. A narrative or story is normally thought of in its 'told' sense. A narrative is normally someone's narrative, told from the perspective of a narrator. It normally has a beginning, an end and a plot that moves the listener/reader from the beginning to the end in a more or less linear sequence. This kind of 'narrative told' must be distinguished from the narrative-like processes that are narrative-in-its-making. Interaction in the manner described above evolves as narrative-like themes that normally have no single narrator's perspective. Beginnings and endings are rather arbitrary and there are many plots emerging simultaneously. The narrative told is retrospective while narrative-in-its-making is currently emerging in the living present. The former is inevitably linear while the latter is intrinsically nonlinear. Despite these differences, there is a connection and it is, I think, useful to think of experience as being patterned in a narrative-like way. This idea is explored in the following section, which looks at how one might think about the pattern, both private and public, that people spin together as they interact communicatively in the manner described in this section.

The narrative-like patterning of experience

Bruner (1990) suggests that humans are born with a predisposition to organize experience in narrative form and that the self is an autobiographical narrative that is continually retold, with variations. He is concerned with the manner in which narrative organizes experience.

First, the sequential order of narrative provides structure, one that is internal to itself. It is this internal structure, or plot, that gives the narrative its meaning, one that has nothing to do with a reality, true or false, outside of itself. The meaning of the narrative lies in its overall configuration or plot and each event, happening or mental state takes its meaning from the overall configuration. In order to make sense of the constituent aspects of the narrative one must grasp the overall plot. Narratives are inextricably interwoven truth and possibility. Second, narratives display sensitivity to what is ordinary and what is exceptional in human interaction. The negotiation of meaning between people is made possible by this feature of narrative. Narrative achieves its meaning by identifying deviations from the ordinary in a comprehensible form. As they interact with each other in a group, each person takes it for granted that others will behave appropriately in a given situation, the norms for such appropriateness having been established by their history of interacting with each other. In other words, the habits, or practices, developed in the past create expectations for current and future action. When people behave in what is taken to be the normal, ordinary way, there is no need for further explanation. It is simply taken for granted and if pressed for an explanation, people normally reply that such actions are what everybody does or is supposed to do. However, deviations from these expected actions, or ways of speaking, trigger a search for meaning that is usually provided by a story giving an account of an alternative world in which the unexpected action makes sense, that is, provides reasons for the behavior. Narrative, therefore, mediates between cultural norms and unique individual beliefs, desires and hopes. It renders the exceptional comprehensible. It provides a means of constructing a world and identifying its flow as well as regulating the affects of people.

The thematic patterning of experience

I am arguing, then, that human relating is human communicating and that human communicating is the action of human bodies in the medium of symbols. Through communicative interaction with each other, and with themselves, humans are able to cooperate in sophisticated ways in joint action using tools to operate within their human and non-human surroundings. It is communicative interaction that enables people to construct significant features of the nonhuman environment they live in: they breed cattle; they build physical structures; they design equipment that extends the range of communication, for example. However, communicative action in the medium of symbols does much more than this in that it constructs both individual mental and social realities. In communicative interaction, people actively respond to each other and in so doing their experiences are patterned in narrative-like forms. Human experience is story-like. In their relational communication people are constructing intricate narratives and abstract-systematic frameworks. When they reflect on what they have been doing, on what they are doing and on what they hope to do, they select aspects of these dense narratives/abstract frameworks to tell stories or extend their abstract-systematic frameworks of propositions in order to account for what they are doing and make sense of their worlds. In the process their very identities, individually and collectively, emerge.

Life, on this view, is an ongoing, richly connected multiplicity of stories and propositional frameworks. In this sense the process is nonlinear, although stories told select a theme in all of this and give it a linear structure. My proposition, then, is that all human relationships, including the communicative action of a body with itself, that is mind, and the communicative actions between bodies, that is the social, are story lines and propositions constructed by those relationships at the same time as those story lines and propositions construct the relationships. They are all complex responsive processes of relating that can be thought of as themes and variations that recursively form themselves in bodily interaction.

The private role-play, the silent conversation, of each individual and their public interactions can be thought of as themes and variations reproducing history that melds with evocations triggered by the gestures of others in the transformative process of the living present. It is these themes and variations that organize individual and collective experience in the living present. However, what those particular themes are at particular moment will depend just as much on the cues being presented by others as upon the personal history of a particular individual. Each individual is simultaneously evoking and provoking responses from others, so that the particular personal organizing themes emerging for any one of them will depend as much on the others as on the individual concerned. Put like this, it becomes clear that no one individual can be organizing his or her experience in isolation because they are all simultaneously evoking and provoking responses in each other. Together they immediately constitute complex responsive processes of an iterative nonlinear, recursive, reflexive, self-referential kind. And as they do so themes emerge that organize their experience of being together out of which further themes continuously emerge.

Furthermore, this notion of themes organizing the experience of being together does not mean that all interacting individuals share the same theme. Each member is responding differently around emerging themes. There is no need to postulate the sharing of any kind of mental content. Nothing is being shared at all as people resonate individually around common themes to do with being together. They are responding to each other in a meaningful way, not sharing something.

The dynamics of conversational life

Conversation is that form of communicative interaction conducted in the medium of vocal symbols, language. Human futures are perpetually constructed in these conversational exchanges. How those conversations pattern while being patterned by communication is thus a matter of great importance. I argue that an analogy from the complexity sciences, that of stable, unstable and 'edge of chaos' dynamics, illuminates the dynamics of conversation in the living present.

Some conversational processes display the dynamics of stability when patterned by habitual, highly repetitive themes. In this dynamic, people are 'stuck' and their conversation loses the potential for transformation. Identity arising in 'stuck' conversation is continuity with little variation. One might characterize such conversational dynamics as neurotic. The quality is lifeless, depressing, even obsessive and compulsive. Other conversational processes display the dynamics of instability in which coherent pattern is lost as fragments of conversation trigger other fragments with little thematic structure. One might characterize such conversation as disintegrative, approaching the psychotic. The quality is manic confusion and distress with a fragmenting of identity. Yet other conversational processes display the dynamic analogous to the 'edge of chaos,' where patterning themes have the paradoxical characteristics of continuity and spontaneity at the same time. The felt qualities of such conversations are liveliness, fluidity and energy but also a feeling of grasping at meaning and coherence. There is excitement but also, at the same time, tension and anxiety. When conversational processes are characterized by this kind of dynamic, they have the potential for transformation. For example, in describing the quality of therapeutic conversation, Foulkes (1948, 1964) referred to 'free floating conversation' and he contrasted this with the location of neurotic symptoms in individual members of a group which lead to stereotypical patterns of conversation that have no therapeutic, that is, transformational potential.

We now come to the important mode of communication in such a group. Manifestly this assumes the character of what I have described as 'free-floating discussion.' Not only the content of what is said is important, but also the form of speech, its expressive qualities, its transactional directions, silences and other non-verbal communications, facial and other expressions, appearance, attitudes, gestures, actions.

(Foulkes, [1968] 1990, p180)

The characteristics of fluid conversation with transformative potential are thus of great importance. A further analogy from the complexity sciences is helpful here. Allen (1998a & b) has used abstract models to demonstrate a possibility, namely, that it is only interaction between diverse entities that gives rise to the potential for transformation. With regard to human conversation, this analogy suggests that transformative potential arises in conversations when participants are diverse, that is, sufficiently different to each other. In these conditions interaction may amplify small differences into major discontinuous changes in understanding. It is in their struggling to understand each other in fluid, spontaneous conversational exchanges that people change. However, this is by no means an easy communicative process. First, it entails misunderstanding, which is usually experienced as frustrating, even distressing, as well as stimulating and exciting. However, the pressure to relieve the frustration may well lead to the closing down of conversational exploration, making transformation a highly precarious process. This connection between misunderstanding and change is an important and provoking insight.

Second, conversational processes having transformative potential, by their very nature threaten the continuity of identity. If a group of people have spent the past decades thinking and talking in terms of particular meta psychological theories, for example, their individual and collective identities are inevitably closely tied up with that way of thinking. Conversations that challenge these theories hold out the potential for transformation but at the same time they threaten identity. In other words, conversations with transformative potential inevitably arouse anxiety at a deep existential level. Such anxiety provokes defenses such as denial. In other words, themes emerge in conversations that counter themes with transformative potential and so shut down further exploratory conversation. The questions of how people deal with the anxiety, almost always unconsciously, and how they might find ways of living with it, are therefore central.

Third, conversation with transformative potential inevitably threatens current power relations, which are also an important aspect of identity. The sensed undermining of existing power relations provokes reactions that once again seek to shut down exploratory conversations with their transformative potential. Conversations that threaten current power relations raise the real fear of exclusion or smothering inclusion and so also prompt moves to shut them down.

The complex responsive process perspective, then, presents a different meta psychology and a different meta sociology to that of psychoanalysis. Instead of internal worlds of innate forms and representations of experience, there are the processes of a body interacting with itself and instead of wholes and systems outside the internal world of mind, there are self-organizing processes of thematically patterned interaction between bodies. Instead of understanding human action in the regressive, archaeological terms of the past being repeated, one understands human action in prospective terms in which the past and the future are being perpetually constructed. The different concept of time involved here focuses the therapist's attention in a different way. The therapist pays attention to the conversational dynamics of the group and the manner in which the experience of being together is thematically and narratively patterned as the construction of the past and the future in the present. The next chapter explores in more detail the thematic patterning of interactive experience.

Chapter 5

The emergence of self in the 'conversation of gestures'

> Even though the nature of self may forever elude the behavioral sciences, the sense of self stands as an important subjective reality, a reliable, evident phenomenon that the sciences cannot dismiss. How we experience ourselves in relation to others provides a basic organizing perspective for all inter-personal events.
>
> (Stern, 1985, p6)

The last chapter drew on the thought of Elias and Mead to explore the nature of human communicative interaction and suggested the perspective of complex responsive processes of relating. This chapter interprets, from a complex responsive process perspective, the work of Stern (1985, 1995) on child development and the emergence of self. Stern's two influential books present detailed findings on infant development, partly interpreted from a psychoanalytic perspective and partly from a social perspective. However, his findings also provide considerable support for the complex responsive processes perspective, describing in detail as they do the 'conversation of gestures' in which an infant's identity emerges.

Stern's studies of infant development

All reasonably healthy infants have similar sensori-motor capacities in that very soon after birth they can see within a certain range of focus; they can hear; and they can move their heads. These capacities enable researchers to 'ask questions' of newly born infants. For example, it is possible to deter-mine whether infants prefer one shape to another by the frequency with which they move their heads to look at one shape rather than another. Stern (1985, 1995) provides a detailed review of this kind of observation and experimentation and reaches the following conclusions about the inherited, innate motivations and cognitive-affective capacities of infants.

Infants are born with the capacity to directly experience and signal to others basic emotions or what Stern calls categorical affects: for example, happiness, sadness, fear, anger, disgust, surprise, interest, shame. Each of these is signaled to others through discrete facial displays present at birth and subject to little change throughout life. This is what Elias (1989) identified as species-specific symbols and they are the basis of Mead's conversation of gestures. Each of these affects is generally thought to be experienced in differing degrees of intensity (activation) and differing degrees of pleasure or nonpleasure (hedonic tone). Stern also draws attention to other qualities of these categorical affects. For example, a 'rush' of anger might be experienced, as might a 'surge' of joy. He maintains that infants also directly experience these vitality affects, the rush and the surge, for example, which can occur as part of the categorical affects or in their absence. Vitality affects, then, are qualities of feeling such as surging, fading away, fleeting, exploding, bursting, floating, rushing, and so on. Stern points out how these vitality affects are temporal contours which he sometimes calls temporal feeling shapes, in that they have the characteristics of beat, rhythm, duration and intensity. To quote:

> These qualities of experience are most certainly sensible to infants and are of great daily, even momentary, importance. It is these feelings that will be elicited by changes in motivational states, appetites, and tensions. The philosopher Suzanne Langer (1967) insisted that in any experience-near psychology, close attention must be paid to the many 'forms of feeling' inextricably involved with all the vital processes of life such as breathing, getting hungry, eliminating, falling asleep and emerging out of sleep, or feeling the coming and going of emotions and thoughts. The different forms of feeling elicited by these vital processes impinge on the organism most of the time. We are never without their presence, whether or not we are conscious of them, while 'regular' affects come and go.
>
> (Stern, 1985, p54)

Infants are born seeking sensory stimulation and opportunities to engage in learning activities that widen and integrate experience, and in these learning activities there is no separation between cognitive and affective experience, conforming to Damasio's (1994, 1999) research on the brain (Chapter 6). In other words, infants are innately curious. This seems to me to be the basic motivation in mental development – it is the urge to relate to others, to survive, to live and grow.

Infants are born with distinct biases with regard to the sensations they seek, having a tendency to be attentive to specific features of a stimulus array and ignore others. This is much the same as saying that infants are born with a capacity for selecting, enacting or 'calling forth a world,' rather than a capacity for faithfully representing and then responding to their environment (Varela et al, 1995). According to Stern, infants have an innate tendency to categorize sensations, events and experiences. Stern believes that one of the innate criteria they use is the distinction between the variant and invariant features of a pattern of sensations, events and experiences. Infants are innate pattern recognizers, capable of distinguishing between the persistent and novel aspects of different patterns.

Stern also believes that infants have an innate tendency to order their subjective worlds. According to Stern, this means that they seek the invariant or persistent features in the patterns of their experience. However, I would argue that it is not simply the invariants that matter in coming to know anything. This focus on invariants, or regularities, flows very much from a representational perspective on mental phenomena. From the enactive, constructionist perspective it is the variances that matter, but of course a variance only has any meaning in relation to an invariant and vice versa. It is by recognizing and working interactively with others around the variations on themes that experience unfolds. Anyway, the point is that infants arrive in the world with the capacity to work with invariants in perception and the variances around them.

Stern argues that infants are also born with a capacity for integrating sensations across modes of sensing. There are certain common qualitative features in all of the modes of sensing: seeing, hearing, touching, smelling and tasting. All sensing, no matter what the mode, takes place in time and thus has time contours marked by variations in beat and rhythm, intensity and duration and they all have some kind of locational or spatial referent. Stern suggests, on the basis of experimental evidence, that it is these time/space contours that are directly perceived no matter what the sensing modality and that it is this capacity that enables infants to yoke together sight, sound, touch, smell and taste of some experiences, so integrating them into the experience of some person or thing.

> The translation, then, from perception to feeling in the case of style in art involves the transmutation from 'veridical' perceptions (color, harmonies, linear resolutions and the like) into such virtual forms of feeling as calmness. The analogous translation from perceptions of another person's behavior to feelings involves the transmutation from the perception of timing, intensity and shape via cross-modal fluency into felt vitality affects in ourselves.
>
> (Stern, 1985, p159)

The key point is this: an infant is physiologically capable of selecting from an array of stimuli (images, sounds, touches, smells and tastes) impinging on the body, directly perceiving the amodal time/space qualities of that selection and combining, matching, or even fusing these qualities with the time/space qualities experienced in the body. It seems, therefore, that it is the equivalence between the time/space contours of the stimuli and the time/

space contours of feeling in the body that make possible the emergence of any sense of meaning for the infant in the stimuli that are being integrated. Indeed, it may not be going too far to say that the very possibility of mental development is based upon this temporal/spatial contour equivalence between inner physiologically-based feeling dynamics and externally presented stimuli. I would argue that it is the linking between qualitative aspects of perceived experience and closely similar qualitative aspects of felt bodily experience that is the fundamental, basic way of human knowing – protomental processes.

Protomental processes are obviously central to 'knowing' in infancy. However, when adult development is the focus of attention, there is a tendency to place almost all the importance on linguistic ways of knowing and so lose sight of the extremely important protomental processes, often categorizing them as primary, primitive, infantile or regressed. From a complex responsive process perspective, they are not at all infantile or primitive but fundamental to all mental processes. Just as protoplasm is the viscous, translucent substance forming the basis of life in plants and animals, so the protomental are fundamental processes from which all mental life is continuously emerging.

The infant is born, then, with quite comprehensive innate capacities for relating and knowing but they present no more than a potential for development. Development itself depends upon the unfolding experience of relationship with others, that is, upon the detailed development of the conversation of gestures between mother and infant as well as between each of them and others in the family.

The importance of relationship in the development of mind

The web of family relationships is affected as soon as a woman is aware that she has conceived. Her partner, her parents and other members of the family all respond in some way and relationships between all of them shift in ways that have effects, large and small, on the developing fetus. Relationships are important from conception on and the fetus takes part in these relationships right from the beginning. Observational studies (Chamberlin, 1987; Piontelli, 1989, 1992) show that the fetus has perceptual capacities as early as the seventh week of gestation and by nine to twelve weeks there are facial gestures indicating approach–avoidance reactions. By the latter half of gestation, the fetus registers and responds to experiences within the womb and it shows temperamental characteristics. Fetus and mother affect each other. The construction of an infant self and the further evolution of a maternal self, as well as the selves around her, gets underway right from the point of conception. These experiences, these first relationships, will be aspects of an individual's life history.

> Thus the first relationship in life may not be with the mother, but with the affective and physiological context that her inner body provides.
>
> (Rucker, 1998, p79)

> Most remarkable here, as with all of Piontelli's twin observations, was the opportunity to observe physical interactions between fetuses. Luca, in his activity, characteristically would reach out through the dividing membrane to stroke Alice's cheek, to which she would respond by moving closer to him, head to head or cheek to cheek.
>
> (Lombardi, 1998, p98)

So, infants have the physiology that both motivates and enables them to relate to others and to a place even before they are born. By the time that they are born, they have the impulse and the ability to evoke from care-givers what they need, both physically and emotionally, and at the same time respond to those caregivers. Stern departs from the assumption widely made in psychoanalysis that the infant begins life in a subjective state of symbiosis with the mother. In this state there is no sense of self and other, only undifferentiated, omnipotent subjective experience. Stern finds no evidence for this and argues that the infant has a sense of separateness right from the beginning and the various aspects of the infant's self emerge in relationships with the mother and others. This perspective stresses the centrality of social relationships from even before birth:

> The tasks of eating, getting to sleep, and general homeostasis are generally accompanied by social behaviors by the parents: rocking, touching, soothing, talking, singing, and making noises and faces. These occur in response to infant behaviors that are also mainly social, such as crying, fretting, smiling and gazing.
>
> (Stern, 1985, p43)

The activity of looking is of particular importance in these interactions between parents and infant. Newborn infants do not have much limb co-ordination but they do see reasonably well at the right focal distance and their eye reflexes are well developed. Their looking patterns are, therefore, a form of communication through which they can express preferences – for example tests with infants only a few days old show that they prefer faces to other visual patterns. Looking and gazing rapidly become more sophis-ticated modes of communication so that by two to three months reciprocal looking and gazing between mother and infant amounts to what Mead called a 'conversation of gestures':

> ... mothers give the infant control – or rather the infant takes control – over the initiations and terminations of direct visual engagement in

social activities . . . In gazing behavior the infant is a remarkably able interactive partner. And gazing is a potent form of social communication . . . In this light it becomes obvious that infants exert major control over initiation, maintenance, terminations, and avoidance of social contact with mother; in other words they help to regulate engagement. Furthermore, by controlling their own direction of gaze, they self-regulate the level and amount of social stimulation to which they are subject.

(Stern, 1985, p21)

It is important to emphasize that right from the beginning there is a full relationship between infant and caregivers. It is not a one-way provision from caregivers to infant but a two-way traffic, in which both are developing. Mothers, fathers, siblings and the relationships between them all change when a new infant arrives and they continue to change as the infant interacts with them. From conception on, then, an individual emerges in what Elias called a figuration, in this case a pattern of family relationships with its own distinctive power relations, supported by its own distinctive ideologies, all reflecting the larger figurations of the communities and societies of which they are a part. The participation of the family in these wider figurations, particularly the command the family can exert over resources, plays an important role in the emergence of the infant mind and identity.

Protoconversation

Mutual touching, looking and vocalizing between infant and caregivers amounts to what we might call a protoconversation. It is important, I think, not to regard this form of communication as somehow rudimentary or primitive, later to be supplanted by the much more sophisticated conversation that will take place in language once the infant can speak. Protoconversation is fundamental in the sense that it continues throughout life to form the basis of all conversations.

In protoconversations the manifest communication is concerned with meeting the infant's physiological needs to be fed, to be warm and to be comfortable. More profoundly, however, the communication is about feelings. I am not talking here about the caregivers responding to, or understanding some inner essence of an individual 'true' self. I am talking about caregivers who intuitively respond to an infant with gestures that, in their rhythm, recognize the bodily rhythms of the infant. It seems to me that it is out of the rhythmic exchange between caregivers and infants that a felt sense of reality, of existing, emerges for the infant.

Stern (1985, 1995) emphasizes the pattern that can so easily be observed in these protoconversations – the beat and rhythm to them, the variations in duration and the fluctuations in intensity. In the protoconversation the infant is directly expressing, in his looking, vocalizing and soon touching, the rhythms and intensities of his own bodily experience, his own temporal feeling dynamic, thereby evoking a response from others in their gazing, vocalizing and touching. This is a two-way protoconversation and the mother too is directly expressing her bodily rhythms, her temporal feeling dynamic, which in turn evokes responses from her infant.

In essence, what the participants in this protoconversation are doing is mirroring, echoing and resonating with each other's temporal feeling dynamic. Stern has called this attunement:

> . . . the mother must go beyond true imitations, which have been an enormous and important part of her social repertoire during the first six months or so of the infant's life . . . Caregivers and infants mutually create the chains and sequences of reciprocal behaviors that make up social dialogues during the infant's first nine months. . . . And in the leadings, followings, highlightings and elaborations that make up her turn in the dialogue, she is generally performing close or loose imitations of the infant's immediate behavior. However, the dialogue does not remain a stereotypic boring sequence of repeats, back and forth, because the mother is constantly introducing modifying imitations . . . or providing a theme-and-variation format with slight changes in her contribution at each dialogic turn; . . .
>
> (Stern, 1985, p139)

A key process in the protoconversation is the mother's empathic response to her infant. Empathy is more than attunement in that it involves not only resonance with the internal feeling dynamic of the infant but also the abstraction of some empathic knowledge and the integration of that knowledge into a response. It is thus more than a direct feeling-to-feeling response and involves some cognitive elements. Once again, it is important to emphasize that all these processes involved in protoconversation continue to feature in relationships between adults to the end of their lives. It is in this way that we are able to sense something of each other's subjective states and so give meaning to our verbal conversations.

Stern argues that it is in these protoconversations that an infant's sense of self and other emerges. If the mother is sufficiently attuned to the feeling dynamic, in a way affirming the validity of what the infant feels, he experiences a growing sense of his own agency. He develops a sense that he can evoke the response he needs in the other and experiences an ability to have evoked in himself a response that affects the other. There are consequences for the mother too, taking the form of a sense of fulfillment in her maternal role, the basis of her agency as a mother. Between them, in their protoconversation, they develop an emotional atmosphere of trust and love, a culture. For both the mother and the infant then, agency, the capacity to do what needs to be done to live in a fulfilling way, lies both in their individual senses of self and in their relating to each other, at the same time. They form and are formed by each other at the same time.

The attunement and empathy may, however, not be good enough – there may be under attunement and there may also be over attunement. The result is some disjuncture in the emergence of a sense of self and damage to both aspects of human agency. In the studies he is quoting, Stern is describing the process from which there either emerges a sense of self that is effective in the world, or some lack that might be experienced throughout later life. Winnicott (1965) wrote about a good enough maternal holding environment. Bion, Fairbairn, Balint, Bowlby, Kohut and others wrote in a similar vein about the consequences of early failures in the infant–caregiver relationship.

Some psychoanalysts write as if this process in which a reasonably effective sense of self emerges in the relationship with others is a once-for-all experience that one either passes and is then an effective agent, or fails and then requires some form of treatment. People's capacities for coping with poor early environments differ considerably, so that some develop adequate self-confidence in very difficult situations. Furthermore, this self-esteem is not a 'thing' that is possessed but a continually arising process that always depends upon, and emerges from, supportive relationships. Most people rapidly lose their self-esteem in social figurations in which they are not valued and are excluded by the pattern of power relations. An individual sense of agency, the capacity to affect one's context, continuously emerges and re-emerges in social relationships throughout life. Individual self-esteem is, thus, a social construction.

Protosymbols, protonarratives and organizing themes

Most psychoanalytic theories of development postulate an initial mental state for the infant of merger with the mother. A central developmental task then becomes the successful achievement of separation from the mother. This is held to be finally achieved, with the assistance of the father, in the resolution of the Oedipal complex at around the age of four. The psychological journey is from complete merger and utter dependence to autonomy and independence. Stern's research challenges this view by showing that infants are capable of relating to others at birth, if not before. The above discussion of protoconversations points to how an increasingly sharp subjective experience of a difference between self and other emerges so that by about six months of age this sense of self and other is established. This is not a picture of a valiant individual infant struggling to negotiate the terrifying stage of separation. It is, rather, a picture of an infant in a web of relationships out of which a distinction, present from the beginning, emerges more and more clearly. The process may well be accompanied by anxiety but this will be arising, not from some innate and unavoidable propensity in the individual, but from the nature of the relationship. Where the relationship is not good enough, a terrifyingly fragile sense of self may well emerge as a consequence of that social relationship.

Stern goes even further than this, employing the results of detailed observations of infants and others engaged in protoconversation, to make inferences about the infant's subjective world. Stern thinks in spatial terms of internal worlds consisting of representations. The theory of complex responsive processes avoids such spatial metaphors and the whole idea of inside and outside. However, Stern's findings can be re-interpreted in purely process terms. I will use his constructs to talk about psyche as intersubjective organizing and integrating processes rather than a subjective world of representations. While Stern writes about the infant representing his interpersonal relationships, it is quite simple to take his notions and cast them in purely process terms that involve no representations. The question to be considered now is that of how the subjective experiences of sensations, perceptions, thoughts, emotions and feeling quality are organized and integrated.

Stern emphasizes that all experience is 'in time' in which changes unfolding in the present create experience. The mind, at this stage, is the process of organizing and integrating the subjective experience of time in terms of beat, rhythm, duration and intensity:

> . . . whenever a motive is enacted (whether initiated internally or externally, as in drinking when thirsty or receiving and adjusting to bad news), there is necessarily a shift in pleasure, arousal, level of motivation or goal attainment, and so on, that accompanies the enactment. These shifts unfold in time and each describes a temporal contour. The temporal contours, although neurophysiologically separate, act in concert and seem to be subjectively experienced as one single complex feeling, which is a combination (an 'emergent property') of the individual temporal contours of hedonics, arousal and motivation. This is the *temporal feeling shape*, which I will call the *feeling shape* for short. The feeling shape will also include the particular quality of feeling that gets temporally contoured. And that will depend on which affects and motivations are involved.
>
> (Stern, 1995, p84)

Stern gives examples of what he means by a feeling contour. One example is of a game a father might play with his infant that involves rhythmically walking his fingers across the infant's body while making some noise and pulling a face. The father then pauses, repeats what he has just done a number of times, each time with some variation in speed, vocalization and facial changes, and then unexpectedly tickles the child under the chin, whereupon the child explodes with laughter:

> In this case the baby's affective experience is the subjective contour of his cresting waves and troughs of excitement, suspense, and pleasure. A kind of meaning in the form of a feeling shape has been added to the pure temporal beat.
>
> (Stern, 1995, p85)

What Stern is suggesting here seems to me to be very important. I think that he is indicating how a sense of meaning (say, loving, engaged excitement and happiness) is emerging for the infant, and the father, out of the 'throwing together' of temporal beat/intensity in the stimuli (touch, sound, facial shapes) and the temporal beat/intensity of feelings arising in the bodies of both. These fusions of temporal/spatial contours perceived in stimuli and time/space contours felt in the body form what I have called protosymbols in Chapter 4. This is not Mead's significant symbol, which has the quality of consciousness in that it is a gesture calling forth the same response in the one making it as in the one to whom it is directed. The kind of bodily and stimulus time/space contours that I am talking about do not have this conscious quality. It is, rather, an unconscious fusion and that is why it seems useful to refer to it as a protosymbol rather than a symbol. It is then also clear that protosymbols must always be woven into significant symbols, the unconscious weaving through the conscious. This is because vocal symbols are sound stimuli that have temporal/spatial contours and in speaking these contours fuse with feeling states, or bodily time/space contours, at the same time as the conscious aspect of the vocal symbols is called forth. Protosymbols, then, are the context within which significant symbols emerge throughout life just as, by analogy, protoplasm is the transparent medium within which living forms emerge.

Stern then goes on to point out that subjective experiences have a beginning and an end as well as some motive. He gives the example of a hungry baby crying for his mother to come and feed him and suggests that this baby's subjective experience takes a narrative form which he calls a protonarrative – the enactment of a local motive with its attendant affects which has a beginning and an end. The nature of this protonarrative can be seen by following carefully what happens to the crying baby. Before his mother enters the room he is experiencing a rising wave of hunger and increasingly unpleasant feelings while moving his arms and legs about in a jerky manner. As the mother enters the room the sight of her leads to some diminishment in the subjective sense of hunger and the unpleasant feelings associated with it, and his limb movements diminish too. The initial image of the mother is here combined with a particular feeling contour, namely, a feeling of diminishing. As she approaches, however, the sense of hunger and the unpleasant feelings rise rapidly once more, as do the limb movement. Once again, an image, that of the approaching mother, is combined with a feeling shape, namely feelings rising. Then the nipple is placed in his mouth and the edge comes off the baby's hunger. Now a tactile sensation is combined with a feeling contour, once again a feeling of diminishing. Together these three feeling shapes constitute a protonarrative.

The point, then, is that repeated experience of an event, like waiting to be fed and then being fed, are organized and integrated into a protonarrative which then organizes and integrates further experiences of this kind. Proto-conversations are constructing protonarratives and this is the unconscious mental process of organizing and integrating experience into meaning. And the individual mental processes are inseparable from relating to others, the social.

What is being suggested, therefore, is this: infants have the physiological capacity to select stimuli according to physiological preferences, categorize them, integrate them transmodally, and in so doing select invariant repetitions of stimuli. This is what enables infants to participate fully in the continual protoconversations with others that take place in their sensuous, day-to-day lived experience of events to do with feeding, being cleaned and playing. Furthermore, because of the physiological ability to select the invariant features of the stimuli they encounter, they are able to participate in organizing their subjective experience through their relating to others. They repeatedly encounter similar themes in the continual theme and variations of protoconversational life and from this there emerge proto-symbols taking the form of images, sounds and tactile experiences closely combined with feeling contours rooted in bodily rhythms. These proto-symbols link together into protonarratives that become increasingly complex as the infant develops. The protonarratives are themes that organize and integrate experience. When talking about protonarratives, Stern emphasizes how the infant selects the invariant aspects of experience, but in other places he stresses how the protoconversation between infant and caregivers is not simple imitation. He describes how a mother, for example, varies the back and forth play with her baby and how the response is continued attention rather than boredom. What this means is that the infant is responding not simply to invariant themes but also, and very importantly, to variations, often very subtle, around the theme. It is both the invariance and the variance that are important in emergent experience.

So, protonarratives and protosymbols emerge in protoconversations and are simultaneously experienced in the body of the infant as feeling contours, those of short duration nesting within others of longer duration, in turn nesting within others of even longer duration. This is a continuous process that is not stored anywhere – it is a process in the moment and does not exist as a 'thing' anywhere. One protosymbol can trigger others as can one protonarrative. This triggering means that protosymbols, and the protonarratives they combine into, are continuously recreated – a replicating or reproducing process in which they are rarely exactly the same. Note how this discussion of infant development focuses throughout on real observable relating, not speculations about unconscious fantasies.

The organization of experience

Stern (1985, 1995) explains how an infant's self emerges in the mutual relationships between him and his family members and how they relate to each other in accordance with principles that organize their experience. Stern calls these organizing principles *schemas-of-being-with*:

1. A *schema-of-being-with* is based on the interactive experience of being-with a particular person in a specific way, such as being hungry and awaiting the breast or bottle or soliciting a smile and getting no response. . . . a way that is repetitive in ordinary life.
2. A *representation-of-being-with* is a network of many specific schemas-of-being-with that are tied together by a common theme or feature. Activities that are organized by one motivational system are frequently the common theme – for example, feeding, playing, or separation. Other representations are organized around affect experiences: they might be networks of schemas-of-being-sad-with or happy-with, for example. Yet other representations are assemblies made up of many representations that share a commonality such as person (all the networks that go with a specific person) or place or role.

(Stern, 1995, pp19–20)

Stern is here using the terminology of 'representations' but this terminology is not essential to his description of individual mind. I have argued against thinking of mind as an 'internal world' of representations and stressed how mind is silent conversation and private role-playing having narrative structures. I have also stressed how this narrative structure enacts or organizes experience. So, for 'schema' and 'representation' substitute the notion of a 'narrative theme that organizes' and Stern's description is quite consistent with the complex responsive processes perspective. From this perspective, then, mind is a process of interacting narrative themes, rather than some mental apparatus. Stern's descriptions show how an infant's narrative themes that organize the experience-of-being-with evolve in the interactive experience with the mother and the father and other family members and how an infant self emerges in this evolution. The mother's many narrative themes that organize the experience-of-being-with, for example, her infant, mother, husband, herself, interact with her infant's narrative themes that organize the experience-of-being-with her. Both normal and pathological developments of personality emerge in the continuous interaction between all of these narrative themes and, indeed, the infant's arrival contributes to their further evolution. The process that Stern has identified can quite easily be described as complex responsive processes in which each individual's narrative themes are interacting with those of others to produce emergent patterns of family relationship that constitute the further evolution of their narrative themes. These relational, responsive narrative themes are continuously replicated, or recreated, and as this happens there is the possibility of novel emergent relational patterns.

Those writing from an intersubjective psychoanalytic perspective adopt a similar formulation:

> . . . recurring patterns of intersubjective interaction within the developmental system result in the establishment of invariant principles that unconsciously organize the child's subsequent experiences . . . It is these unconscious ordering principles, crystallized within the matrix of the child–caregiver system, that form the essential building blocks of personality development . . .
>
> (Stolorow, Atwood & Brandchaft, 1994, p5)

> Thus the basic units of analysis for our investigations of personality are *structures of experience* – the distinctive configurations of self and other that shape and organize a person's subjective world. These psychological structures are not to be viewed simply as 'internalizations' or mental replicas of interpersonal events. Nor should they be regarded as having an objective existence in physical space or somewhere in a 'mental apparatus.' Instead, we conceptualize these [as] . . . ordering or organizing principles . . . through which a person's experiences of self and other assume their characteristic forms and meanings.
>
> (Stolorow, Atwood & Brandchaft, 1994, pp23–24)

Communicative interaction can then be defined as complex responsive processes continuously replicating patterns of *intersubjective themes that organize the experience of being together*. These themes emerge, in variant and invariant forms, out of the interaction between people as they organize that very interaction. The themes organizing the experience of being together emerge in the interaction. In that sense they are between people and therefore cannot be located 'inside' any individual. However, the experience that is being so organized is always a bodily experience.

The role of language

Stern's research focuses on the period of infancy up to the age of around eighteen months when the infant acquires the ability to talk. Stern says that this opens up a new domain of relatedness for the infant.

But in fact language is a double-edged sword. . . . It drives a wedge between two simultaneous forms of interpersonal experience: as it is lived and as it is verbally represented. . . . Language, then, causes a split in the experience of the self. It also moves relatedness onto the impersonal, abstract level intrinsic to language and away from the personal, immediate level intrinsic to other domains of relatedness.

(Stern, 1995, p163)

Wright (1991) develops, in considerable detail, this view of language as alienating. Language is symbolic, and for Wright, a symbol does not refer directly to an event or object but to a concept of that event or object. In other words, for him, a symbol points to a meaning and symbolization, therefore, requires consciousness. He says that although a symbol may be an object, it is not psychically related to as an object. Instead, in order to operate in language it is necessary to give up the object (word) as something related to in the physical mode, that is, as a sound or noise, and instead, it is necessary to relate to it in an another mode so that it conveys meaning. By holding off from possessing the object and seeing through it, one acquires the capacity to use symbols. For him, using symbols involves detaching meaning from one object and uniting it with another, that is, detaching a personal meaning from one object and throwing it together with another. Wright says:

Meaning emerges from the word, from language, in the same way that the expression emerges from the face: the face suddenly *means* 'I love you' or 'I recognize you' or 'I'm pleased with you.' The expression that shines through the face is the prototype of emergent meaning, occurring before language begins to draw the child into a cultural world of symbols.

(Wright, 1991, p107)

For Stern and Wright, language is alienating and involves some kind of sacrifice or separation. Mead, however, regarded language as significant symbols and emphatically rejected the notion that symbols are independent of their meaning. He argued that language is not vocal gestures randomly assigned to objects and that symbol and action cannot be separated and assigned in some other way. What needs to be stressed, then, in this view of the nature of symbols is how they are actions (vocal gestures) that select, or call forth meaning in the form of responding actions, where those actions can be taken either by another or by oneself in silent conversation. Elias used the notion of symbol in a similar way. For him people do not put thought into language because thought is language and can be nothing else. Meaning and symbol are thus undetachable for him too.

Wright argues that people have to give up relating to the vocal object in the physical mode, hold off possessing it and see through it. Stern says using language entails separation from lived experience. None of this makes any sense from a complex responsive processes point of view. Language is lived experience and since it is a gesture made by a body it is at one and the same time a protosymbol and significant symbol. There is nothing to see through or hold off from. Any alienation from lived experience will be due not to language itself but to the themes that are organizing the experience of being together, in other words, to the culture of the group. The problem with the Stern and Wright approach is that they see no link between social interaction and symbols because they assume the primacy of the individual and they seem to have a notion of experience as something apart from what bodies are actually doing; something they have to 'translate.' Meaning then becomes some kind of free floating, disembodied transcendent, which is then said to emerge from the word, the gesture, with no part for the response to play. Meanings become absolutes, representations of a pre-given world, rather than completely context dependent phenomena.

For me, the problems with Wright's approach are compounded the more he develops them. He argues that it is the Oedipal father who brings language as an already existing system and gives it to the child. The father gives the word from the outside world by requiring the child to look but not touch. This is a theory of language acquisition that is heavily based in myth and stereotype. Rather like Lacan's notion of 'in the name of the father,' Wright's father is the bringer of the community's law, the one whose duty it is to assist the valiant son to separate from mother, the reward being the ability to use language, the gift of the community. These views, unlike the developments Stern reports for infants up to eighteen months old, are theoretical assertions not based on careful observation.

Fathers are there, involved or not, right from the birth of the infant. They are playing and talking, or not, very early on. The infant hears language from birth from the mother, the father and everyone else he is in contact with. Language is a part of the total communication in the family. No one is bringing language as a gift from the community. Language is the very atmosphere in which the infant develops, through which and in which he develops. The infant's use of language is not given as a gift and does not require any sacrifice. It gradually emerges, as the conversation of gestures becomes more and more complex. The community enters into the relationships that all of the members have with the infant through the very first contacts. It is a myth to regard the infant as entirely taken up with the mother, divorced from the wider culture until it is nearly eighteen months old. Infants imbibe the wider culture as soon as they are born, if not before, through the manner in which others relate to them. A child is not given the capacity for silent conversation; it is a process that emerges in the relationships with family members. The basis of Wright's theory of development is a socially constructed notion of a sentimentalized mother–infant dyad and a stereotypical father.

The point I have been making in this section is this. The further development of the infant is a continuing social process in which this infant's self, identity and capacities are emerging as relationships with others are continually iterated and the infant is participating fully in these relationships. This participation is communicative interaction/power relations. This is very different to the notion of an individual developing according to a pre-given pattern such as the Oedipus complex.

Transitional phenomena and secrets

At around the same time as infants begin to talk, at roughly eighteen months of age, they take up a particularly important form of play. It was Winnicott (1965) who pointed to the importance of the small child's intense attachment to a particular object such as a piece of blanket, a teddy bear or some other toy. Approaching this from an object relations point of view he suggested that the child uses the special toy as a way of coping with the anxiety aroused by separation from the mother. He argued that during the first phase of life, the infant had no sense of separation from the mother and when that sense did emerge, it gave rise to intense anxiety. The infant copes with this in a highly creative manner by using the piece of blanket as if it were the mother. Winnicott pointed to this as the first use of a symbol and the beginning of learning and creativity. He called it a transitional object because it was an object quite clearly outside the infant's body, but it was used in the infant's inner life to stand for something else. The transitional object is thus part reality and part illusion constituting the creative use of fantasy and imagination in play, a process that continues as the basis of creative, cultural and religious experiences. Wright (1991) also emphasizes the importance of transitional phenomena but sees the transitional object as the precursor to a symbol because it does not separate the object from its meaning in that the infant fuses the object with the mother, treating it as if it really were the mother.

In the light of Stern's evidence there seems to be little justification for believing that an infant is merged with its mother until about eighteen months of age. By this time, Stern's observations suggest, there is already a well-developed differentiation between some sense of self and other. Furthermore, Winnicott's transitional object is not a symbol in Mead's definition. Both Winnicott and Wright define a symbol as an object that stands for something else; the blanket stands for the mother. The difference between them is that Wright holds that the separation between the blanket and the mother in the infant's mind is not distinct enough to qualify it as a symbol. In Mead's sense, however, the blanket is not a symbol at all because it is not a gesture made by the child calling forth a response in another or in himself. The symbol is the child's gesture to the object and the imagined response to that gesture. This view of symbol in no way detracts from the creative nature of the transitional as process. In the frame of reference I am using here, the infant already experiences a self that is separate from the mother but not yet in a way that can be said to be self conscious. The transitional process is an important step toward that self consciousness, in which the infant imaginatively creates the absent mother and comes to take the attitude of the mother to himself. The child constructs the illusion of another, to which he then gestures and imagines a response, the response that the infant wants. The transitional object is thus not a symbol but rather an object employed in a private role-play. In this kind of role-play, the child is taking an important step toward the ability to engage in silent conversation, which is itself a form of role-play. The child at first talks aloud to himself and to the transitional object and gradually switches, at least partially, to silent conversation with the transitional object as a step toward silent conversation. Winnicott emphasized that this use of fantasy and illusion continues throughout life in the form of creative imagination. The object is transitional not in the sense that it is superseded by anything more sophisticated but, rather, transitional in the sense that it is a paradoxical process embracing reality and fantasy at the same time, that is, imagination. The object is not a symbol. It is the child's gesture–response that is symbol.

Meares (1992) draws attention to the work of Janet to argue that the small child is fully self conscious at around the age of four years.

> Amongst his [Janet's] ideas was the notion that the child's discovery of the concept of secrecy is an event of enormous significance since it heralds the birth of an inner world. When the child learns that thought and ideas can be kept within him/her and are not accessible to others, he/she realizes that there is some kind of demarcation between his/her world, and that which is outer.
>
> (Meares, 1992, p7)

I have argued above that the child already has a sense of separation so that the knowledge that secrets are possible does not 'herald the birth of an inner world.' Nevertheless, the realization that it is possible to conduct a silent conversation with oneself, in a private, secret way, does seem to be of enormous importance in developing self-awareness. Awareness of this secret is a social event because, as Meares shows, it is in playing with others that the child discovers that he or she can 'hide' something from others. In the years to come, given a supportive enough family network, this child will develop what Winnicott called the capacity to be alone in the presence of others. In this way, the unique individual continually emerges in social relationships which he or she is forming and being formed by at the same time. The emergence of the capacity to be alone, the capacity for taking comfort in the secret, private, silent conversation, itself continually emerges in the social sphere.

School and work

By the age of four, then, a child is conscious and also self conscious in the sense that this child has acquired the awareness of a capacity to be alone in the presence of others and converse privately and silently with himself. He knows he has a choice as to whether he will disclose the nature of this silent conversation. He knows that if he is skilful enough he can falsify the nature of this private conversation if he is pressed to disclose what he is saying to himself. They may not believe him but they can never know. He has his own unique, individual mind but this is continuously emerging in his interactions with his family and others and it continues to evolve in those interactions. Indeed, his mind is the same processes as social relating, continuously arising processes of symbolization forming narrative themes that organize his experience. These significant symbols, woven into narrative themes, are not objects separate from their meaning, but rather, gestures calling forth responses which are their meaning.

When one thinks about the development of the group and the individual in this way, as complex responsive processes of symbolization, private and public, conscious and unconscious, simultaneously forming and being formed by each other, it is evident that group and individual evolution never ends. So, when the young child goes to school, further important developments occur in the nature of mind and social relations. This comes about, it seems to me, because the child is then systematically introduced to symbols of a kind that have probably played a relatively minor part in his or her development up to this time. In learning to read and write, the child encounters bodies of propositional knowledge claiming to represent reality. A different kind of conversation develops in the groups known as school classes and this must be reflected in the kind of conversations individuals have with themselves. In other words, minds, the very selves, of individuals change as they take part in school education. One of the key developments in this evolution lies in the use of reified symbols. These are symbols that are used to represent and model phenomena. In Western culture, they are employed in a manner that objectifies the world and they raise the possibility of the kind of alienation from sensuous lived experience that Stern and Wright ascribe to language itself. My argument is that it is not language itself that alienates but the use of reified symbols.

Chapter 6

The physiological basis of mind, self and society

> In my view, if you develop a theory about human action, let us say, you also have to know how the organism is built and functions. If you are working out theories of knowledge and know nothing about brain structures, something is wrong.
>
> (Elias, 1994, p31)

So far, in the chapters in this part of the book, I have been developing a theory of mind and social relations as complex responsive processes of relating between human bodies. In this theory, mind and social relations form and are formed by each other at the same time in the iterative, nonlinear processes of interaction between human bodies. It is the actions of bodies that are iterated from one moment to the next, where that iteration is understood as the perpetual repetition of patterns of interaction, always with the simultaneous potential for transformation because of the possible amplification of small differences from one repetition to the next. This is a bodily action theory of mind and social relating and it makes no sense to talk about an action being inside or outside of anything. So, unlike cognitivist, constructivist and psychoanalytic psychological theories, there is no notion of mind being inside an individual or of society being outside of an individual. Since mind is not thought of as being inside a person, it is not thought of as consisting of internal representations of external stimuli or objects. In the theory of complex responsive processes, then, the notion of representations does not feature at all. It follows that memory is not thought of as the retrieval of representations of past experience that have been stored somewhere. Instead of containing representations, in the theory of complex responsive processes mind is thought of as the pattering of bodily actions in the form of narrative-like themes of silent conversation and private role-play. Instead of thinking of memory as retrieval from a store, the complex responsive processes perspective regards memory as the associative repetition of habitual thematic patterns of bodily action, always with the potential for transformation. This is a view in which memories are perpetually reconstructed in the living present and they are potentially transformed in this reconstruction simply because reconstruction is always affected by current context, including expectations of the future. From this perspective, memories of the past are changed in their reconstruction in the living present. These are major features distinguishing the theory of complex responsive processes from cognitivism, constructivism and psychoanalysis, all of which think of mind as consisting of representations and memory as retrieval from a store.

There is also another major distinction. Because of their perpetual reconstruction and potential transformation, mind and social relations are thought of as continually evolving. Human action in the form of processes of mind and social relating are not thought of as genetically determined or as reflecting instinctual patterns of behavior. Instead, both mind and social relating are thought of as ongoing processes of human learning.

This complex responsive processes perspective is built upon insights from the complexity sciences understood in relation to humans in terms of the thought of Mead and Elias. Both of these thinkers emphasized the embodiment of human action and claimed that their theories of mind and society implied something about the functioning of the central nervous system, as in the quote at the start of this chapter. Neither Mead nor Elias, however, were suggesting that human action could be reduced to the functioning of the brain. As I understand them, they were suggesting that their theories had to be consistent with our knowledge of brain functioning in some way. This seems an important point to me and is the reason for this chapter. The theory of complex responsive processes holds that mind is not inside a person, does not contain representations, does not involve the retrieval of memories from a store somewhere and is not genetically programmed or determined by instincts. Other psychological theories hold the opposite view on these matters. It follows that the theory of complex responsive processes would be rather implausible if human brains do indeed form representations of a given reality, if memory is retrieval from a store in long term memory banks and if the actions of a body are the expressions of genetic programs or instincts encoded in the brain.

In this chapter, I want to point to the way in which a number of neuroscientists are moving away from textbook views of brains forming and storing representations to views of brain functioning that are quite consistent with the theory of complex responsive processes. I am not presenting this move as some kind of proof in favor of the theory of complex responsive processes quite simply because too little is known at present about brain functioning to claim that any one theory is 'true.' I am suggesting, however, that it is both relevant and interesting to note how a similar shift in thinking seems to be occurring in neuroscience to that being proposed in this book in relation to thinking about mind and society and the implications for group therapy.

Put simply, the human brain consists of 10 billion neurons, each of which is connected through synapses to others by many thousands of axons and dendrites. Neurons trigger each other by firing in response to each other, that is, by discharging electric pulses generated by biochemical changes, particularly at the synaptic connections. Brain functioning, therefore, may be thought of as patterns of electro-chemical change. Brain components, that is, neurons, axons, dendrites and synapses, are organized into local assemblies and networks, such as areas of the cortex, sensory systems and motor systems. The physiological processes involved in mental functioning and bodily action, therefore, take the form of patterns of electro-chemical change in the brain, which is organized into highly interconnected, networks of neurons and highly complex chemical changes. Thinking about brain functioning has moved on from simple notions of neural networks, parts of which can be isolated and linked to particular functions. For example, it is now realized that it is not just interaction between neurons that is important but also interaction between neurons, dendrites, and non-neuronal glyal cells.

This chapter first explores the connection between attachment–separation behavior and the brain. It then reviews the assumptions made about the brain by today's most popular theory of human behavior, namely cognitivism, and considers the criticisms made of these assumptions. An alternative to the cognitivist view is presented in the form of a dynamical process perspective.

Attachment and separation

The brains of many animals are highly undifferentiated organs at birth and this is particularly so of humans. Some neuroscientists argue that it is experience that primarily shapes connections in the brain, not genetically pre-planned hard-wiring. Furthermore, this shaping and re-shaping by experience continues throughout life. In other words, the human brain is highly plastic.

> In experimental animals, enriched environments have been shown to lead to increased density of synaptic connections and actual volume of the hippocampus, a region important for learning and memory. Experiences lead to an increased activity of neurons, which enhances the creation of new synaptic connections. This experience dependent brain growth and differentiation is thus referred to as an 'activity-dependent' process.
>
> (Siegel, 1999, p14)

Schore (1994) has explored research leading to the conclusion that child–caregiver interaction shapes the development of the brain just as the developing brain is implicated in the shaping of child–caregiver interaction. He argues that interaction itself alters the genetic expression that creates behavior. Studies suggest that the structure of the brain is unique to each individual as a result of brain plasticity and each individual's unique experiential history. Genes create only biological potentials, while inter-active experiences, that is, the social, shape the individual brain. Through-out life, new brain connections are made and old ones pruned. It seems that traumatic experiences and emotional disturbances result in over-pruning of brain connections, so affecting subsequent experience.

> The lessons from attachment research can guide our understanding of the powerful effect interpersonal relationships can have on the develop-ment and ongoing functioning of self regulation. Studies suggest that the orbitofrontal cortex remains plastic throughout life; that is, is able to develop beyond childhood. The orbitofrontal cortex mediates neuro-physiological mechanisms integrating several domains of experience: social relationships, the evaluation of meaning, autonoetic conscious-ness, response flexibility, and emotion regulation.
>
> (Siegel, 1999, p285)

Smith and Stevens (Smith & Stevens, 1999; Smith, 2001) quote a number of researchers (McGuire et al, 1984; Reite & Field, 1985; Wise & Rompre, 1989) who have identified a specific group of neurochemicals and receptors in the brain identified as opioid processes. These involve endogenous neuro-peptides such as endorphins and enkephalins, mainly functioning in the limbic regions of the brain. Opioids are morphine-like and an example is the endorphins released by exercise. They give rise to physiological changes associated with feelings of comfort, control and calm. Other neurochemicals, however, are involved in arousal processes, which are also centered in the limbic regions of the brain and consist of hormones such as neurotrans-mitters (for example, norepinephrine), which produce feelings of excitement, fear and anxiety. Taken together, opioids produce a soothing effect partly through inhibiting the release of arousal hormones and vice versa. The linked opioid and arousal processes, therefore, constitute iterative, nonlinear physiological processes of body regulation. Too much opioid leads to passive bodies and this triggers the release of arousal hormones, which could lead to hyperactivity, triggering opioid release in an inevitably cyclical process.

Smith and Stevens then point to research indicating that the human body cannot accomplish this chemical regulation in isolation from other bodies. Researchers suggest that attachment behavior may trigger opioid release while separation behavior may trigger the release of arousal hormones. It seems that the human body, therefore, requires attachment to, and separa-tion from, other bodies in order to regulate itself. Brain processes and social processes seem to be interlinked in the form of what Smith calls a hyper-structure. Smith thinks of this hyperstructure as a complex adaptive system in which attachment behavior triggers opioids, which inhibit arousal hormones so that the body experiences calming, which then reduces attachment needs. The consequent separation triggers the release of arousal hormones, which inhibit opioid releases so that the body experiences excitement and anxiety. This could trigger attachment behavior. What Smith is describing is complex, iterative, nonlinear processes in which patterns of brain chemical release are shaping behavior, which is simultaneously shaping brain chemical releases. Smith uses complex adaptive system simulations to explore the patterning of attachment and separation behaviors emerging in self-organizing ways. This is a view of brain functioning in which the brain is spontaneously seeking responses from other bodies, which may or may not materialize. The body, it seems, is spontaneously gesturing to others in search of responses.

The conclusion seems to be that the body requires, and will therefore provoke, attachment and separation actions for the purpose of physiological regulation and it is in this sense that we can say that attachment and separation are innate. They are innate in the sense that genetic actions may play a significant part in the development of the opioid and arousal processes in each body. Genes interacting in a medium produce brains that require interaction. This makes it unnecessary to talk about attachment instincts and urges determined by genes. It is the physiological functioning of the body that is produced by the interaction of genes, not specific patterns in the body's actions. The relevance of human biological evolution, which has not changed much for 100,000 years, is that evolution had produced social humans that operated biologically and socially in the way indicated by the hyperstructure. However, there is nothing specific about this hyperstructure except for the particular kind of brain processes involved in the social processes of attachment and separation. How particular patterns of interaction materialize in the operation of the hyperstructure depends upon human interaction in the living present as that interaction reconstructs the past and perpetually creates the future. As Elias, argued, social/cultural evolution has become much more important for humans than biological evolution. The biological process has not changed but the social process has. Social behavior is physiologically constrained into certain patterns and we depend upon social life to maintain requisite physiological states.

Smith (2001) attaches considerable importance to anxiety, which he understands as a signal of the downward fluctuation in the level of opioid activity in the brain. Anxiety is usually thought of as pathological but for him it helps to explain healthy behavior. He argues that social life ceases when people cease to feel the milder forms of anxiety, such as uneasiness, discomfort, boredom and listlessness. Anxiety communicates the ways in which we are uncomfortable, such as pain, disease, fear, suffering and boredom. We respond to anxiety, falling opioid levels, by seeking attachment, which raises them. The infant cries and the mother responds with attachment. This produces opioids in the infant's brain and so he/she is soothed. The infant's cries raise anxiety levels in the mother and she responds with attachment because it increases her opioid release. The effect of opioids is to constrain the mother–infant relationally into a process of attachment, rather like an addiction. Both the infant's and the mother's neurochemistry are involved and interaction spreads and modulates anxiety.

This connection between neurochemical processes and social interaction is postulated to change as both parties increasingly develop the capacity to modulate their feelings of anxiety apart from each other. Affective regulation can then be carried out much more within the body than just through social pathways. The kinds of behavior to do with attachment and separation increase and diversify with psychological growth and the higher a person's cognitive development, the less their anxiety spills over into social interaction. However, one person always influences and is influenced by the opioid/arousal of another and when internal mechanisms fail there is pressure to reassert attachment behaviors.

Smith argues that hyperstructures become active in social interaction under conditions of increasing anxiety and are fuelled by distress signals eliciting responsive and comfort enhancing behaviors. Central to this are the behaviors of reciprocity and altruism. Because anxiety and arousal are automatically communicated, one person's feelings establish a kind of biological claim on another to enable the other to control feelings. This constrains behavior to appear as reciprocity, which is not a calculation but a physiological process. If one does not reciprocate he/she is left with the subjective burden of the other's anxiety, now his/her own, so that ignoring the needs of the other turns out to be ignoring one's own. This explanation does not rely on the normative, the calculating or on kinship. The pooling of emotional and cognitive resources raises the stress buffering capacity of a whole group and altruism is an outcome of comfort management.

Although based to some extent on what is known about neurochemicals, Smith's development of the notion of the hyperstructure is speculative and it is based on a simple correlation between brain chemical change and patterns of attachment and separation. The correlation is not sufficient to prove causal links. Nevertheless, I think that Smith's work imparts some plausibility to the emphasis that Foulkes, Elias and Mead place on social processes of attachment–separation, belonging and communicative interaction. It also supports those psychoanalysts, notably Winnicott, Fairbairn, Balint and Bowlby, who have placed so much importance on attachment behavior. However, the concept of the hyperstructure does not require one to postulate an attachment instinct or look for genetic causes of particular forms of attachment behavior. Instead, the hyperstructure presents a perspective from which one can understand brain processes and social interaction forming and being formed by each other at the same time, just as in the theory of complex responsive processes.

The next section turns to the assumptions made about the brain in the cognitive sciences and the section after that looks at an alternative explanation.

Cognitivist assumptions about brain functioning

The essence of the cognitivist view of human behavior is that of a mind that processes symbols of the stimuli presented to it according to logical rules governing the throughput and transformation of those symbols. The mind is thought to computationally transform symbols into representations of the pre-given, real world of stimuli into which a human being acts. Through experience, these representations are formed into maps, or models, of the world and of the person acting into that world. A person then attaches meaning to these symbols, representations, maps and models, which are posited to be stable representations of the pre-given world. It is postulated that the maps and models are stored in the long term memory from which they are retrieved when a person is presented with a familiar stimulus. Most of the maps and models are said to sink below the level of awareness as a person repeatedly encounters similar experiences and develops a skilled, or automatic, response to them. Deep learning is supposed to occur when these implicit, tacit or unconscious mental models are brought to awareness, made explicit and then changed. Humans are thought to share mental models either through mimicry or through making them explicit so that they can be acquired by others, a notion of one human transmitting knowledge to others.

For this cognitivist explanation to be acceptable, it is necessary to identify the physiological processes involved in:

- symbol processing and the logical laws governing that processing;
- the formation and storing of representations;
- the formation of representations into stable maps and models;
- the attachment of meaning to symbols, representations and models;
- the processes of transmitting them to others so that they may be shared.

What evidence is there to support the view that brains function in this way? There is, to date, no universally acceptable, factually confirmed explanation of how the brain functions but, rather, a number of different theories, supported to varying degrees by evidence. Freeman (1994) classifies these theories into those proposing that the brain is a computational system and those suggesting that it is dynamical. The computational models provide the foundations of cognitivism, while the dynamical approach presents cognitivism with a serious challenge.

Brains as computational systems

Two strands of thinking about the brain as a computational system can be distinguished, both of them being entirely consistent with a cognitivist approach to mental functioning. The first strand uses a computing mode of the brain, while the second adopts a connectionist model.

Computing models

In the early forms of the computing model, the physiological basis of mental functioning is located at the level of individual neurons. It is proposed that a stimulus triggers an individual neuron, which shows up as the most active when presented with the stimulus. Experimental work, however, showed that a number of neurons become active when a body is presented with a stimulus and that they are organized in a geometric arrangement, that is, a kind of map created by a pattern of neuronal firing. The task was to show how complex features were synthesized in the pattern of on–off neurons. From this perspective, the physiological correlates of mental symbols were thought to be the on–off positions of neurons and the correlates of logical rules governing symbol processing were the laws governing a neuron's responses to the firing of others. Other neuroscientists within this tradition were concerned with lasting chemical changes at the level of the synapse, arguing that permanent biochemical changes at the synapses were the correlate of learning and memory. In other words, repeated exposure to a stimulus caused lasting biochemical changes at the synaptic connections and it was this that constituted learning and enabled recall. Representations of stimuli, therefore, were recorded in the brain as fixed patterns of biochemical change. Meaning is then attached to these representations and transmitted from the brain of one person to that of another through the senses.

This extremely reductionist approach was criticized on the grounds that cellular and molecular changes in response to a stimulus were more spatially widespread than the focus on individual neurons, or small group of them, would suggest. The alternative was to understand these cellular and molecular changes at the level of neural networks. This is the connectionist model.

The connectionist model

The basis of the connectionist model is the proposition that the biological correlates of learned behavior are distributed processes of gradual variations in the strengths of connections between components of neural networks. It is postulated that these connections form and dissolve following Hebb's (1949) rule according to which the connection between two neurons is strengthened if they happen to be active together and weakened if they are not. When a new stimulus is presented to the brain, some neurons happen to be active together and the link between them is strengthened, while links with other inactive neurons are weakened. On the next occasion that the stimulus is presented, the network of neurons again follows the rule of strengthening links between those that are active together. Strengthening and weakening take the form of lasting biochemical changes at synaptic connections. The more the same stimulus is presented, the stronger some particular links become and the firing of this particular pattern of links becomes associated with that particular stimulus forming stable patterns that are distributed across networks of neurons.

In this way, the network of neurons learns to recognize a stimulus so that ultimately when it is presented with this stimulus it falls into an internal configuration, a strengthened neural pathway, which produces a distinctive global pattern of electro-chemical activity in the brain. This global state is said to represent the stimulus and, in a sense, the strengthened neural pathway may be said to be storing a template of the stimulus for later comparison with other stimuli so that learned stimuli are recognized utilizing stored memories. The biological correlate of a symbol or representation then becomes a pattern of neuronal activity across a sub network in the brain. The correlate of learning is the strengthening of synaptic connections, through biochemical changes, required to produce the pattern and the correlate of memory is the triggering of a particular pattern of firing that reproduces the same stable distributed pattern as previous encounters with the stimulus. Memories are stored as particular pathways connecting a network of neurons. Meaning is then attached to these representations and mental models are transmitted from one person to another and so shared.

Work with artificial neural networks (ANN), that is, computer programs following the procedures outlined above, does demonstrate the capacity of such networks to learn to recognize patterns in the manner just described. In the computer simulations, the weights of connections between symbols in the form of computer code are increased by repeated use, simulating the increased strength of synaptic connection in the brain. ANN are presented with some recognition task and repeated presentations result in a pattern of greater weight between some connections than others so that the presented stimulus is recognized with increasing rapidity. In this way, symbols are manipulated to convey information. This work also demonstrates how such networks can accurately recognize complex patterns even in the presence of noise and when they are partially damaged. Because a neural network is characterized by distributed connections, damage to one part of it can be compensated for by operations in other parts of the network. When some connections are damaged, the rules about strengthening and weakening connections soon lead to other links replacing the damaged ones. In other words, a neural network is not designed so that portions of it exclusively specialize in specific parts of the recognizing task. Rather, the connections, and thus the work of recognition, tend to be spread across the network. The pattern of network activity that represents the stimulus is thus not localized but takes the form of a global pattern across the network. Some connectionist perspectives suggest that brains are self-organizing systems in the sense that neurons are following rules about strengthening and weakening their connections with others but there is no blueprint producing the global patterns across the network. Global patterns emerge from the local self-organizing activity of the neurons.

Alternatively neural networks can be studied in the laboratory examination of anaesthetized, paralyzed or surgically prepared animals where parts of the brain are disconnected or destroyed. Freeman (1994) argues that laboratory experiments of this kind are equivalent to ANN in that the animals so studied are incapable of goal directed behavior. They can only perform reflex actions on being presented with an input, just as in the case of ANN.

As with the computing model, the connectionist perspective postulates that brains represent stimuli but instead of doing so in a straightforward, linear, localized manner, they do so in a distributed self-organizing and emergent way. However, brains are still assumed to be representing a pre-given reality and they are still assumed to be storing templates that represent reality. Perception is the processing of incoming stimuli by comparing them with templates or maps in memory. Learning is the building up of large stores of ever more accurate templates, mental models or cognitive maps to which meaning is attached and then transmitted to others. It can be seen, therefore, that the connectionist perspective is thoroughly cybernetic (see Chapter 13) in that there is a fixed reality outside the system that is compared with a template and if the gap is small enough, the stimulus is recognized. This is perfectly compatible with the cognitivist view of human behavior.

When the connectionist and computer models are compared it becomes clear that the only real difference in assumptions relates to how representations are formed and stored. In the connectionist model they emerge from the self-organizing strengthening of neuronal connections and in the computer model they are registered in particular neurons or groupings of them.

Criticisms of the connectionist model

It has proved difficult to confirm connectionist theory with experimental evidence in that no one has yet been able to demonstrate long term biochemical and morphological changes in nerve cells. It has been demonstrated that a cascade of biochemical reactions and cellular responses, or traces, last for 0.5 to 1.5 hours in the learning process and this is taken to be the basis of short term memory. A subsequent wave of change in bio-chemistry and cell morphology has been detected for periods ranging from 4 to 8 hours (Rose, 1995). However, biochemical changes for periods longer than this have not yet been detected. Changes at synaptic connections are temporary and easily affected by other activity across them. Indeed, bio-chemicals are continuously decaying and being replaced. As a result, the connectionist model cannot explain long term memory any more than the earlier computational models could. At best, the connectionist perspective provides an explanation of only a part, perhaps only the first step, of the processes of recognition, learning and long term memory.

Freeman (1994) presents detailed criticisms of the connectionist model, arguing that biological neural networks (BNN) in the normal waking state are fundamentally different to ANN or equivalent laboratory experiments in the following important respects:

- ANN are silent until addressed from outside by the scientist. They are passive and capable only of homeostatic reflexes. BNN, however, are ceaselessly and spontaneously active, even in the absence of external stimuli. This activity takes the form of unstable, even random, waves and pulses across time and space within the brain. This is a very important point because it means that the brain is creating its own activity. It is dynamical processes that have the internal capacity to change spontaneously of their own accord.

- In ANN, the succession of states of the network is carefully controlled by rules governing throughput and transformation, operating by way of conditioned reflex. BNN, on the other hand, induce self modification using the environment as input. They actively seek input through sniffing, touching, looking and listening. They are oriented to the achievement of intentionally formulated goals. Instead of stable patterns, the patterns constructed in the sensory cortex destabilize and drive motor systems to search for new stimuli and construct meaning. BNN are continually changing state globally and this property is destroyed by surgery or anaesthetizing. This is also a very important point because it means that the human brain selects what it attends to by reference back to itself. It does not simply process information presented to it from outside but actively selects, or enacts, the world into which it acts. The body/brain calls forth, in a sense creates, the world into which it acts, rather than acting in response to whatever is presented to it.

- ANN retrieve fixed patterns stored in memory banks as strengthened connections, where these patterns are images, or representations, of the stimulus. BNN, however, construct neural activity and, Freeman argues, do not retrieve fixed patterns stored in memory banks. The patterns of neural activity are not images, or representations, of the stimulus. The pattern is the expression of the meaning of the stimulus in a particular context in the light of previous experience of the stimulus in that context. Freeman's work shows that altering the context within which a stimulus is presented alters the pattern of brain activity corresponding to it. Furthermore, when a new stimulus is encountered in a motivating context it not only leads to a corresponding new pattern but, in the process, alters all other patterns slightly. The patterns are unique for each individual. The patterns are thus not fixed representations and cannot be said to be stored in any simple way. They are continually being reproduced.

- Manipulation of ANN symbols conveys information rather than meaning, which is attached later. In BNN, there is no computation of symbols but rather the construction of spatio-temporal patterns across populations of neurons and this macroscopic activity, Freeman argues, reflects the meaning of, not information about, the stimulus.
- ANN produce stable patterns. BNN, however, are characterized by unstable patterns and Freeman argues that the dynamic is chaotic (see Chapter 2), not merely noisy, and that chaotic dynamics are crucial to the memory process.

Freeman's basic criticism is that the computational and connectionist models of the brain are reductionist in that they seek to explain the functioning of the brain in terms of the parts, such as neurons and synaptic connections. Because of this, they cannot explain the global patterning activity of the brain. They assume that the only mechanism of brain functioning is synaptic change and they assume passive reflex reaction that does not take account of the active selection and creation of brain patterning that is observed. He extends this criticism to those who think of the brain as a dynamical self-organizing system when they concentrate on synaptic change as the only mechanism of brain functioning. Freeman claims that all of these traditional explanations make it difficult to understand the rapidity of perceptual recognition and its meaning.

So, it seems that the brain is not processing in a sequential manner, nor is it acting as a passive mirror of reality to form more or less accurate pictures of the world. Instead, it is being perturbed, or triggered, by external stimuli into actively constructing global patterns of electro-chemical activity. Furthermore, these patterns are not stored in any simple way in specific parts of the brain because each time a stimulus is presented to the body, the brain is constructing a pattern on the basis of past experience, which involves whole ensembles of neurons in many different parts of the brain.

> . . . memory . . . retrieval will lead to the formation of new memories made on the background of a retrieved prior experience . . . Moreover, decoding or retrieval will change the information content of the 'trace'

> such that memory can be viewed from a neurobiological point of view as an emergent, dynamic, adaptive property of the nervous system.
>
> (Sara, 2000, p73)

If the brain functions in this more complex manner then it becomes problematic to talk about representation and memory in terms of pathways of connections between neurons. Patterns of brain activity can hardly be described as representations if:

- initial patterns of brain activity in response to a stimulus are rapidly washed away and replaced by constructions of the brain itself;
- these new constructions are unique to each individual;
- they change when the contexts and the motivations to act change; and
- they alter when other stimuli are learned.

The cognitivist case is thus seriously challenged by the above perspectives since it seems that brains do not process symbols, nor do they represent a pre-given reality or store templates or models. Instead, it seems that brains select, call forth or enact a sensed world that perturbs, or triggers, brain activity, which constructs the world called forth.

I have so far been talking about cognitivist assumptions about brain functioning in terms of representing, storing and processing. Psychoanalytic theory is nowhere near as explicit in its assumptions about brain functioning but implicitly the assumptions are the same as those of cognitivism. The basic assumption of almost all psychoanalytic thinking is the existence of the mind as the internal world of the individual. This internal world consists of representations of objects and object relationships. There is a clear assumption that these are stored memories. The implicit assumption is that the brain is capable of representing and storing so that the criticism of cognitivism can also be made of the implicit assumptions of brain functioning in psychoanalytic theory.

Brains as dynamical processes

What is the alternative to the cognitivist view of brain functioning? Any alternative, it seems is at least as speculative as the cognitivist view.

> . . . virtually nothing is known about the physiological processes underlying the act of remembering. The initial process must involve some orientation to a particular stimulus or ensemble of stimuli. How these particular stimuli are recognized as 'meaningful' or how they activate the specific distributed network presumed to be the neuronal substrate of the memory still remains unknown.
>
> (Sara, 2000, pp76–77)

However, a number of neuroscientists are arguing for a dynamical perspective of the brain. Rose (1995) suggests that:

> . . . simple memories . . . are not confined to a single set of synapses in a defined brain locale, but, as long term memory is formed, become widely distributed across several brain regions. In each region, there will be synaptic plasticity to encode the information within an appropriate ensemble of neurons, but the mechanism of such encoding will no longer be Hebbian, and it ceases to be possible to ask where in the brain a particular memory resides; rather, it has become a distributed property of the system.
>
> (Rose, 1995, pp252–253)

Freeman argues that the neuronal correlates of recognition and memory recall are patterns of activity taking the form of oscillatory bursts or pulses across large cortical areas. The correlates are spatially extended patterns of activity over a short time period. Learning results in a new pattern of neuronal activity and this pattern is highly sensitive to small changes in the context within which the learning takes place. Chance fluctuations play an important part in the emergence of new patterns.

According to Kelso,

> . . . the brain is *fundamentally* a pattern-forming, self-organized, dynamical system poised on the brink of instability. By operating near instability, the brain is able to switch flexibly and quickly among a large repertoire of spatio temporal patterns. It is, I like to say, a 'twinkling' system, creating and annihilating patterns according to the demands placed on it.
>
> (Kelso, 1995, pxvii)

The body and feelings

We frequently make a sharp distinction between intellectual activity and rational decision making, on the one hand, and emotionally charged behavior, on the other. Rational thinking is thought to be disrupted by the feelings and emotions that are inevitably aroused in personal relationships in groups. This was certainly Freud's view (see Chapter 9). However, this separation between the rational and the emotional is challenged by Damasio's (1994) studies. He has found that severe damage to certain areas of the brain (ventromedial prefrontal and somatosensory cortices, amygdala in the limbic system, anterior cingulate) leads to a profound change in behavior.

When these areas of the brain are damaged, perfectly competent, normally functioning people lose the capacity to make rational, ethical choices and also the capacity to experience emotional variability. Damasio concludes that the damaged brain subsystems are the primary areas dealing with both rational decision making and emotional experience. The rational and the emotional are physiologically intertwined and the one cannot arise without the other, except in the most restricted of situations. Damasio points out how people suffering from this particular form of brain damage may well continue to function very well at an intellectual level in the sense that they can rationally generate sensible ranges of options for action. In simple laboratory situations they may even be able to take the next step and make rational decisions about which option to act upon. However, in the uncertainty and complexity of ordinary, everyday life they may continue to generate rational options for action but prove incapable of selecting and acting upon an option that is sensible in the circumstance. They display no emotion and at the same time they are incapable of acting either ethically or rationally, in their own best interests. Their lives fall apart.

Damasio concludes that emotionally flat experience makes rational choice impossible and he suggests that this connection between emotions and feelings is not a chance one. He argues that feelings are an essential part of the process of selecting actions that are sensible in the circumstances. Feelings orient the decision-maker in a useful direction, acting as a means of screening out some options when they do not 'feel right.' Damasio connects this function with the capacity for ethical and moral judgment, pointing out how those with the brain damage referred to above also lose all moral capacity.

Damasio goes on to propose that feelings are not an elusive quality attached to an object. He argues that the brain continuously monitors and integrates the rhythmical activity of the heart, lungs, gut, muscles and other organs, as well as the immune, visceral and other systems in the body. At each moment, then, the brain is registering the internal state of the body and Damasio argues that these body states constitute background feeling states. This continuous monitoring activity, that is, registration of feeling states, is taking place as a person selectively perceives external objects, such as a face or an aroma, and experience then forms an association between the two. Every perception of an object outside the body is associated, through acting into the world, that is, through learning, with particular body states or background patterns of feeling. When a person encounters situations similar to previous ones, he or she experiences similar feeling states, or body rhythms, which orient that person to act into the situation. In this way, human worlds become affect laden and the feeling states unconsciously narrow down the options to be considered in a situation. In other words, feelings unconsciously guide choice and when the capacity to feel is damaged so is the capacity to rapidly select sensible action options. Damasio suggests that, from a neurological standpoint, the body's monitoring of its own rhythmic patterns is both the ground for its construction of the world it acts into and its unique sense of subjectivity.

In Damasio's scheme, feelings are distinguished from emotions. Emotions arise when a background feeling state is associated with a mental image. These emotions then play a role in communicating meaning to others and they guide cognition and choice. When we have to choose an action in a context, the features of that context stimulate the brain and options for response rapidly arise. Some of these options will have good associations based on past experience and others will have bad associations. The body will fleetingly respond with a feeling in the gut. This fleeting feeling can be thought of as a somatic marker, in the sense that feelings generated by previous emotional experience lead to instantaneous selection and de-selection of options. Rational choice can then be made from fewer alternatives.

For Damasio, the self is a repeatedly reconstructed physiological state based on activities throughout the body. This is the subjective sense of self and it is not a central knower or inspector of all that goes on in the mind. He holds that mind arises when bodies interact with each other and that changes in body rhythms continually affect mental states and the sense of self. It is not a great step to suggest that when people are relating to each other, in the presence of each other, their body rhythms might resonate with each other. An intuitive sense of how another is feeling could well be conveyed in this way. A process of resonance, rather than any form of transmission or mimicry, might then be the basis of empathy between people, that is, a deep way of knowing each other.

Damasio (1999) also suggests that human bodies construct consciousness and knowledge in interaction with each other in a process in which the biological correlates of this activity take a narrative-like form. Damasio says that consciousness:

> . . . consists of constructing an account of what happens within the organism when the organism interacts with an object, be it actually perceived or recalled, be it within the body boundaries (e.g., pain) or outside of them (e.g., a landscape). This account is a simple narrative without words. It does have characters (the organism, the object). It unfolds in time. And it has a beginning, middle, and an end. The beginning corresponds to the initial state of the organism. The middle is the arrival of the object. The end is made up of reactions that result in a modified state of the organism.
>
> (Damasio, 1999, p168)

Damasio is suggesting that humans become conscious, they develop a feeling of knowing, when their bodies construct and present a 'specific kind of wordless knowledge' to do with being changed by contact with others and he describes in detail how this might happen.

As far as the brain is concerned, the organism in the hypothesis is . . . the state of the internal milieu, viscera, vestibular system, and musculoskeletal frame. The account describes the relationship between the changing . . . [state] . . . and the sensorimotor maps of the object that causes those changes. . . . As the brain forms images of an object – such as a face, a melody, a toothache, the memory of an event – and as images of the object *affect* the state of the organism, yet another level of brain structure creates a swift nonverbal account of events that are taking place in the varied brain regions activated as a consequence of the object–organism interaction. . . . Looking back, with the license of metaphor, one might say that the swift, second order non-verbal account narrates a story: that of the organism caught in the act of representing its own changing state as it goes about representing something else. But the astonishing fact is that the knowable entity of the catcher has just been created in the narrative of the catching process.

(Damasio, 1999, p170)

The resonance with Mead's description of the 'I-me' dialectic described in Chapter 4 is striking. Mead talks about interactions between organisms while Damasio focuses on the physiological correlates, that is, interactions between neural patterns in different brain regions. In doing so, he in effect provides an explanation of Mead's contention that the mind and self arise in interaction and that the central nervous system is such as to enable this to happen.

The implications for thinking about human action

According to a dynamical process perspective, the brain does not passively process information arising from stimuli. Its activity is not the sum of reflex responses to whatever stimuli hit the sense receptors. Instead, the brain is highly plastic, forming and reforming connections and emergent patterns throughout life in self-organizing, internally generated neural processes. Perception does not begin with the causal impact of a stimulus on a receptor but with internally self-organized neural activity that lays the ground for responding to future receptor input. The brain itself creates the conditions for perceptual responses by generating activity patterns determining what receptor activity will be accepted and responded to. Perception is a dynamic process inaugurated by the motivated brain, which does not respond to the irrelevant. The brain opens itself to the input it accepts, reorganizes itself, reaches out to change the input, and in doing so gives biological 'meaning' to the stimulus. Perception does not copy objects as representations, but rather, creates meaning for the organism. Perception is a process that destabilizes and re-stabilizes, reaching back to the stimuli and giving them form, while creating meaning and reaching forward in action. This is not representing, processing and retrieval from a store but the iterative reproduction of patterns as continuity and potential transformation.

This view of brain functioning challenges the cognitivist and psychoanalytic theories of mind in that it denies biological correlates for processing, representation and simple storing. A theory of mind that is consistent with the dynamical process perspective on brain functioning would have to center on:

- Processes that are selectively enacting, and so creating, the world into which people act. These are, self-organizing, internally spontaneous processes of emergent reproduction and transformation rather than information processing.
- The importance of instabilities and the high degree of sensitivity to small changes in the contexts of stimuli rather than the production of stable patterns.
- Memory as an associative process of reproduction and potential transformation rather than simply representing and storing.
- Meaning and sense-making as dynamical processes arising in behavior rather than computation and later attachment of meaning.

I would argue that these are all features of the complex responsive processes way of understanding human action and interaction outlined in previous chapters. The kind of thinking about the brain that has been presented here is antithetical to notions coming from evolutionary psychology (Pinker, 1997) or socio-biology (Wilson, 1992), which will be discussed in Chapter 14. From these perspectives, the genetic program largely determines the patterns of connections in the brain. Organisms take the action they take because of the way that genes have programmed their brains to act. The notion of the brain as dynamical processes, however, would view the genes as setting the physiological enabling constraints of brain functioning. Genetics create particular potentials but it is the organism's selective action into its world that shapes the brain connections through self-organizing processes forming emergent patterns. Action shapes while it is at the same time being shaped by brain processes.

Furthermore, a theory of mind consistent with this view of brain functioning could not locate the mind in brain functioning alone. Although there must always be physiological correlates of mental functioning, it is clear that nowhere in the body is there to be found a mind, a self, consciousness or self consciousness. Additionally, the view of the brain as a self contained closed system raises particular questions around how human beings share mental constructs. One response might be to deny the existence of mind, self and consciousness but this would be to deny what most of us experience as very real. The alternative is to look for an understanding of mind and self as emerging in relationships between people while being experienced in their bodies. Mind and self are then located not inside people but take the form of actions of their bodies.

This view of a knowing, acting body, that does not form and act upon representations of an objective external reality has a number of important implications.

First, the brain does not store memories in the sense of some kind of memory bank from which memories can be retrieved. Instead, some stimulus, selected by the brain itself, triggers an associative sequence of patterns across whole subsystems of the brain, or across the whole brain, in which past events are actively reconstructed in the living present. Memories are not representations of a past reality that are found. Each time they are recalled, they are new creations of the past in anticipation of the future. Each new experience subtly changes past memories. Memories, then, display the hallmarks to be expected of complex responsive processes, namely, a combination of stability and instability in recall. Far from being a weakness, this fluidity in recall enables new patterns and thus understandings to emerge. Those new understandings involve physiological processes taking the form of new patterns.

Second, the cognitive and the emotional aspects of body/brain functioning cannot be separated in terms of effectively living an ordinary, everyday life. Damasio has shown how the subsystems of the brain that are primarily involved in feelings and emotions are also involved in the later stages of reasoning, namely, the capacity to select an appropriate course of action. Emotion plays a very important part in the rational selection of action and feelings are an essential part of the motivated selection of stimuli for response.

Third, the human brain is highly plastic in the sense that most of the connections between neurons are forged by experience after birth and these connections continue to change throughout life as old ones dissolve and new ones form. The specific experiences of a human being thus physically affect the structure of the brain, which affects enacted experience, yet another reflexive feature. The process of learning and knowledge creation is a cycle of action.

Fourth, it is hard to see what it could be that individual brains could share with each other when individuals interact in a social setting. Instead of thinking about sharing something going on in a brain one might think of bodies resonating with each other, yielding empathic understanding and of bodies jointly acting into the physical world they inhabit and understanding through that joint action. This immediately focuses attention on relationships between active bodies as the source of common understanding, rather than anything being transmitted between and then shared by them.

Chapter 7

The importance of belonging: vicissitudes of attachment and separation

> [Society] . . . is not an originally harmonious whole into which – as if by the ill-will or incomprehension of particular people – conflicts are accidentally introduced. Rather tensions and struggles – as much as the mutual dependencies of people – are an integral part of its structure; they decisively affect the direction in which it changes. . . . habituation to a higher degree of foresight and greater restraint of momentary affect . . . can give one group a significant advantage over another. But a higher degree of rationality and drive inhibition can also, in certain situations, have a debilitating and adverse effect.
>
> (Elias, [1939] 2000, p408)

In previous chapters I have been drawing on the thought of Elias and Mead, as well as work done in the natural complexity sciences, to suggest a theory of complex responsive processes in which individual minds and social relations emerge simultaneously. The processes being referred to are those of communicative interaction and power relating between human bodies, where those processes of interaction have the intrinsic capacity for coherently patterning themselves. Communicative interaction between human bodies patterns itself as coherent narrative-like themes fundamentally to do with being, doing and becoming together. From this perspective, the patterning of communicative interaction patterns further communicative interaction. Interacting humans are not thought of as producing anything outside of this direct interaction, such as a social or cultural system, a group mind, a matrix or a common pool of meaning. Direct interaction leads to more direct interaction and nothing else. We produce artifacts and tools in that interaction to use in further interaction but we do not produce mysterious wholes outside our direct experience. Furthermore there is no underlying deep structure or innate, internal world of representations in which subsequent experience is stored in conscious and unconscious memory.

The theory of complex responsive processes takes a particular perspective on time, thought of as the living present. The time structure of the living present is paradoxical in that the interaction takes place in a present which reproduces the past in expectation of the future and that expectation changes the reproduction of the past. In other words, this is a perspective of continuous iteration in the present in which the past is reproduced, always with the potential for transformation. The potential for transformation lies in the intrinsic capacity of nonlinear iteration to amplify small differences. What is being iterated in human interaction is simultaneously individual and collective identity, always with the potential for transformation.

The last chapter turned to recent research and speculation about the human body and brain, asking whether this provides a plausible physiological basis for the perspective of complex responsive processes. That chapter suggested that there is good reason to believe that the human brain does not process information, form representations of external reality or store memories in any simple way. Indeed, the views presented in that chapter see the human brain in terms of iterative processes of much the same kind as those just described in relation to interaction between human bodies. Furthermore, that chapter described the physiological characteristics that make attachment and separation behavior absolutely fundamental to bodily functioning. In biological and physiological terms, therefore, it is plausible to argue for a complex responsive processes perspective in which individual mind is social to the core because mind and social are the same processes of communicative interaction. This is a completely different view to arguing that the individual mind is social through and through because it internalizes representations of the social, is impregnated with the social or intersects with the social. Such views are based on the assumption, the spatial metaphor, of an inside and an outside. While there clearly is an outside to the body and an inside to the body in physiological terms, one cannot think of the actions of the body occurring inside or outside of anything. The complex responsive processes perspective is an action theory, a temporal process theory, in which it makes no sense to talk about mind and society in terms of inside or outside, above or below, in front or behind. In the complex responsive process perspective, the only distinction between individual and social is that the former is the action of a body privately and silently directed towards itself, while the social is the actions of bodies publicly and vocally directed towards each other. One is impossible without the other.

In this chapter, I want to pick up on the points made in Chapters 4 and 5 about the nature of communicative interaction and explore in more detail the implications for inevitable power relating between people. Complex responsive processes of relating are simultaneously communicative and formative of figurations of power relations. Power relations between people inevitably involve the dynamics of inclusion and exclusion. This chapter will link these dynamics to the fundamental human dynamics of attachment and separation and that will lead in to a discussion of the role of shame, panic, envy and other emotions in complex responsive processes of human relating. The chapter will conclude with an exploration of unconscious human communication and power relating.

Power, ideology and inclusion–exclusion

From the complex responsive processes perspective, humans are fundamentally social animals, that is, they are human bodies undertaking joint action, using tools in sophisticated cooperative and competitive ways in order to transform their environment in the interest of their survival and development. This joint action is accomplished through continuous communicative interaction in the medium of proto, significant and reified symbols and in that interaction emerges the very identity of humans, both individual and collective: the 'I' and 'we' identities that Elias refers to. Of particular importance is the emergent reproduction of themes and variations that organize communicative actions into membership categories. These tend to be themes of an ideological kind that establish who may take a turn, as well as when and how they may do so. It is the ideological thematic patterning of turn taking/turn making that enables some to take a turn while constraining others from doing so and inevitably the process is one of inclusion and exclusion. In addition, in order to go on together, people have to account to each other for what they do. In other words, the maintenance of relationship imposes constraint. Power is constraint that excludes some communicative actions and includes others. However, at the same time, power enables.

In *What is Sociology?* ([1970] 1978), Elias says:

> We say that a person possesses great power, as if power were a thing he carried about in his pocket. This use of the word is a relic of magico-mythical ideas. Power is not an amulet possessed by one person and not by another; it is a structural characteristic of human relationships – of *all* human relationships.
>
> (Elias, [1970] 1978, p74)

He argues that we need to understand power as a structural characteristic of relationship, which can be good or bad. It reflects the fact that we depend on each other.

> In so far as we are more dependent on others than they are on us, more reliant on others than they are on us, they have power over us, whether we have become dependent on them by their use of naked force or by our need to be loved, our need for money, healing, status, career, or simply for excitement.
>
> (Elias, [1970] 1978, p93)

However, the dependency of one is always linked to the dependency of the other.

> The mythology dictated by linguistic usage urges us to believe that there must be 'someone' who 'has power.' So, because we feel the pressure of 'power,' we always invent a person who exercises it, or a kind of superhuman entity like 'nature' or 'society' in which we say power resides.
>
> (Elias, [1970] 1978, p94)

Elias expresses his relational view of power as ongoing processes of configuring power relations between people.

> This concept of figuration . . . expresses what we call 'society' more clearly and unambiguously than the existing conceptual tools of sociology, as neither an abstraction of attributes of individuals existing without society, nor a 'system' or 'totality' beyond individuals, but the network of interdependences formed by individuals.
>
> (Elias, 1993, p214)

A key feature of communicative interaction, one upon which the whole patterning effect of turn taking/turn making depends, is that of association. Expectations emerge from past experience that people will link their communicative actions together in an associative manner. Communicative cooperation arises in the process of people holding each other accountable for their actions in some way. They act towards each other in a manner that recognizes their interdependence and so negotiate their actions with each other. Without this, relating breaks down.

The immediate consequence of such interdependence is that the behavior of every individual is both enabled and constrained by the expectations and demands of both others and themselves. To carry on participating in the communicative interaction upon which an individual's very life depends, that individual has to rely on the enabling cooperation of others. At the same time that individual has to respect the wishes of others and those wishes will frequently conflict with his or her own. Communicative interaction is, thus, the patterning of enabling and conflicting constraints, a central feature of any complex process. Broadly defined, power describes interpersonal relationships of just this kind.

Power enables one to do what one could not otherwise have done and it also constrains one from doing what one might autonomously like to do. Communicative interaction is a process in which people account for their actions and negotiate their next actions. This is a political process, the exercise of power. Because all relationships have these characteristics, all relationships are simultaneously power relations (Elias, [1970] 1978, 1989) and communicative interaction. If one accepts that an individual mind is the private role-play of communicative interaction, taking the same form, as the public, it follows that an individual mind is also a role-play in power, a private political process. What is being suggested, then, is a self-referential, reflexive process in which individual minds are formed by power relationships while they are, at the same time, forming those power relationships in both private relations with themselves and public forms of power relations with others.

The dynamics of inclusion and exclusion

Turn taking/turn making is both enabling and constraining at the same time and it therefore immediately establishes power differences in which some people are 'included' and others are 'excluded.' This process of power relating, with its dynamic of inclusion and exclusion, is ubiquitous in all human communicative interaction, that is, in all human relating. The very process of turn taking/turn making makes the dynamics of inclusion and exclusion an inevitable and irremovable property of human communicative interaction quite simply because when one person takes a turn, others are at that moment excluded from doing so. These dynamics feature prominently in Elias' process sociology.

Elias and Scotson ([1965] 1994) studied events following the influx of a working class group into a new housing estate in the UK, adjacent to an older estate that was also occupied by working class people. Although there was no recognizable difference between the two groups, hostility soon appeared, and persisted for a very long time, in which the older inhabitants denigrated the newer ones.

> . . . oldness of association, with all that it implied, was, on its own, able to create the degree of group cohesion, the collective identification, the commonality of norms, which are apt to introduce the gratifying euphoria that goes with the consciousness of belonging to a group of higher value and with the complementary contempt for other groups.
>
> (Elias & Scotson, [1965] 1994, pxviii)

Elias and Scotson point to the importance of the cohesion that had emerged over time in the already-established group of inhabitants. They had come to think of themselves as a 'we,' a group with common attachments, likes, dislikes and attributes that had emerged simply because of their being together over a period of time. They had developed an identity. The new arrivals lacked this cohesive identity because they had no history of being together and this made them more vulnerable. The more cohesive group therefore found it easy to 'name' the newcomers and ascribe to them hateful attributes such as being dirty or liable to commit crimes.

> . . . structural characteristics of the developing community of Winston Parva bound two groups to each other in such a way that the members of one of them felt impelled, and had sufficient power resources, to treat those of another group collectively with a measure of contempt, . . .
>
> (Elias & Scotson, [1965] 1994, pxxi)

So, although there was no obvious difference between the two groups, one group used the fact that the other was newly arrived to generate hatred and so maintain a power difference. Furthermore, this was, in a sense, 'accepted' by the newcomers who took up the role of the disadvantaged.

> . . . an established group tends to attribute to its outsider group as a whole the 'bad' characteristics of that group's 'worst' section – of its anomic minority. In contrast, the self-image of the established group tends to be modeled on its exemplary, most 'nomic' or norm-setting section, on the minority of its 'best' members.
>
> (Elias & Scotson, [1965] 1994, pxix)

I would describe what happened here as follows. Patterning themes of an ideological nature had emerged in the communicative interaction within and between both the established and the newcomer groups. That ideology established, and continued to reinforce, membership categories and differences between those categories.

One of the principal ways that power differentials are preserved, then, is the use of even trivial differences to establish different membership categories (Elias & Scotson, [1965] 1994). This suggests that it is not that a racial or religious difference generates hatred of itself, but rather that such differences are given an ideological form and then used to stir up hatred in the interests of sustaining power positions in a dynamic of inclusion and exclusion. Dalal (1998) points out how this as an unconscious process in that the hatred between the groups emerges in an essentially self-organizing process that no one is really aware of or actually intends.

> Thus one misses the key to the problem usually discussed under headings such as 'social prejudice,' if one looks for it solely in the personality structure of individual people. One can find it only if one considers the figuration formed by two (or more) groups concerned or, in other words, the nature of their interdependence.
>
> (Elias & Scotson, [1965] 1994, pxx)

Note how the very differences that are essential to the emergence of the new are, at the same time, generators of destructive processes of hatred. It should also be noted that what I have been describing is an everyday occurrence in less dramatic ways. For example when we debate differences in our theories, or when we talk in particular ways in ordinary, everyday life we are often using differences to sustain power relations.

There are other aspects of ideological themes that also serve to preserve power differentials in essentially unconscious, self-organizing ways. A key aspect of ideology is the binary oppositions that characterize it and the most basic of these is the distinction between 'them' and 'us.' Ideology is thus a form of communication that preserves the current order by making that current order seem natural. In this way, ideological themes organize the communicative interactions of individuals and groups. As a form of communication, as an aspect of the power relations in the group, ideology is taken up in that private role-play, that silent conversation, which is mind in individuals.

Note that ideology here is thought of as mutually reproduced in ongoing communicative action rather than anything shared or stored. Here, ideology is not some fundamental hidden cause located somewhere. It is not stored anywhere, transmitted and then shared. Rather, it is patterning processes, that is, narrative themes of inclusion and exclusion organizing themselves in perpetual reproduction and potential transformation. Ideology exists only in the speaking and acting of it.

Gossip

Elias and Scotson point to how ideology emerges in a self-organizing process of gossip. Streams of gossip stigmatize and blame the outsider group while similar streams of gossip praise the insider group. The gossip builds layers upon layer of value-laden binary pairs such as clean–dirty, good–bad, honest–dishonest, energetic–lazy, and so on.

> Exclusion and stigmatization of the outsiders by the established group were thus powerful weapons used by the latter to maintain their identity, to assert their superiority, keeping others firmly in their place.
> (Elias & Scotson, 1994, pxviii)

In less obvious form, the same point applies to the 'inclusion–exclusion' dynamics created by particular ways of talking, for example, talking in terms of complexity, in terms of psychoanalysis, and so on. Such gossip and other ways of talking attribute 'charisma' to the powerful and 'stigma' to the weak, so reinforcing power differences. In established, cohesive groups, streams of gossip flow along well-established channels that are lacking for newly arrived groups. The stigmatization, however, only sticks where there is already a sufficiently large power difference. Again these are social relations that are reflected in the private role-play of individual minds, conferring feelings of superiority on the powerful and feelings of inferiority on the weak. Eventually, however, the weak or marginalized groups will probably retaliate with what may be thought by others to be unreasonable vigor.

Any change in the process of communicative interaction must at the same time constitute a shift in power relations and, therefore, a change in the pattern of who is 'included' and who is 'excluded'. Such shifts generate intense anxiety and communicative interaction is recruited in some way to deal with this anxiety. These ways may be highly destructive of effective joint action and may even completely disrupt the reproduction and creative transformation of coherent communication.

Family patterns

The inclusion–exclusion dynamics discussed above are also reflected in family structures. Elias and Scotson show that family structures differ between the outsider and the established. Family structure and the wider social inclusion–exclusion dynamics form and are formed by each other at the same time. This renders problematic ways of thinking about the family as a universal human phenomenon instead of understanding how family and social processes form and are formed by each other.

In commenting on family-centered views Elias and Scotson say:

> It suggests that one moves outward from the married couple or the family which appears at the centre of the social universe in a number of stages to what appears as the shell called the 'outside world.' It is a family-centered theoretical framework, . . . which bears some resemblance to early geocentric conceptions of the universe according to which the earth was the kernel and the heavens the outer shell. . . . Because one confines one's attention to the selection of data about 'the family,' the structure of families stands out clearly while that of other aspects are summarily conceived as the world 'outside' and remain rather dim.
>
> (Elias & Scotson, [1965] 1994, p183)

They are critical of:

> . . . the belief that 'the family' has a structure of its own which is basic and more or less independent of that of the surrounding world . . . it is a belief which, as one can see, persists in spite of all the evidence that the structure of 'the family' changes with changes in society at large, . . .
>
> (Elias & Scotson, [1965] 1994, p185)

In their study of Winston Parva, Elias and Scotson show how different family structures characterize the 'village' and the 'Estate.' In the village, as a result of a long history of living together, there are extended families which are mother-centered, in two-or-three-generation kinship networks. In the Estate, even though the influx of displaced persons from London had occurred during the War some twenty years before the study, there was a very different family structure in that the families were not so mother-centered and consisted of small families of parents and two children. The limited kinship networks resulted in less visiting and gossip. The close-knit families of the village had more power, occupied more important communal positions, and had more satisfying leisure activities.

As a consequence, the experience of growing up in the two different kinds of family was very different; the collective, or 'we' identities in the two groups stood in stark contrast to each other. Since individual and group are but two aspects of the same process, it followed that individual, or 'I' identities were also very different. People experienced themselves as they did as much because of the social process of inclusion and exclusion as any intra-family processes. To understand individuals from families in either group one has to understand the wider social processes. For the therapist this is as important as family relating. Psychoanalytic theory, on the other hand, does not take account of this interaction between the family and the social but, rather, proposes to understand the individual in terms of universal family and developmental dynamics such as the Oedipus complex, sibling rivalry, envy and other intrapsychic processes. Obviously, the orientation of the therapist operating from this perspective is going to be different to one who is continually aware of the wider social processes involved. Furthermore, the distinction between complex responsive processes and psychoanalytic perspectives points to different understandings of unconscious process, a matter to be taken up later in this chapter. Briefly, the psychoanalyst makes sense of the patient's narrative in terms of 'the unconscious' understood as an individual 'internal world' of fantasy, repressed wishes and defenses. From the complex responsive processes perspective, the therapist thinks of unconscious processes in terms of the impact of social dynamics on family processes and the personal identities of family members, where what is unconscious is the inclusion–exclusion process and its consequences. And one of the principal consequences is power differentials.

Psychoanalysis places the individual in a family context at the centre of its theorizing and posits universal family dynamics in just the way that Elias and Scotson are critical of. In relying on Eliasian thought, the complex responsive processes perspective focuses attention on how family interactions form and are formed by wider social processes.

Elias and Scotson argue that inclusion–exclusion processes are expressed as differentials of cohesion and integration, which are sources of power differentials. There is a complementarity between one group's charisma and another's disgrace and this sets up emotional barriers on the part of the former to any contact with the latter, as well as processes within each group, as follows. All belonging to an established group participate in its charisma in return for which they have to conform or else suffer the humiliation of exclusion. The charismatic group uses language that deeply hurts the members of the disgraced group and this has a paralyzing effect on the latter's members. Stigmatization is an interaction between a person's image of his group's standing amongst others and therefore of his own standing. The silent voices of members of the disgraced operate as the ally of the dominant group because the disgraced have come to believe what is said about them. The processes that keep the disgraced in place are those of humiliation and shame. The power differential with which the disgraced comply, even agree, is essential to enable the stigma to be driven in. The disgraced often act out the aspersion cast upon them, such as being dirty and noisy, because they know they can annoy the established in this way.

> It is symptomatic of the high degree of control that a cohesive group is able to exercise upon its members that not once during the investigation did we hear of a case in which a member of the 'old' group broke the taboo of the group against non-occupational personal contact with members of the 'new' group. The internal opinion of any group with a high degree of cohesion has a profound influence upon its members as a regulating force of their sentiments and their conduct. . . . Approval of group opinion . . . requires compliance with group norms. The penalty for group deviance is loss of power and a lowering of one's status. However, the impact of the group's internal opinion upon each of its members goes further than that. Group opinion has in some respects the function and character of a person's own conscience. In fact the latter, forming itself in a group process, remains attached to the former by an elastic, if invisible cord. . . . A member's self-image and self-respect are linked to what other members of the group think of him or her. . . . The view, widespread today, that a sane individual may become totally independent of the opinion of all his or her we-groups and, in that sense, absolutely autonomous, is as misleading as the opposite view that his or her autonomy may disappear within a collective of robots. . . .
>
> (Elias & Scotson, [1965] 1994, ppxxxix–xli)

Power confers on a group much more than economic advantage because the struggle is about the satisfaction of needs to do with esteem and identity. The outsiders suffer deprivation of identity and of meaning. Elias talks about the peculiar helplessness of groups unconsciously bound together in these dynamics of inclusion and exclusion. Growing up in a stigmatized group can result in specific intellectual and emotional deficiencies.

Elias stresses the importance of streams of gossip in sustaining the group fantasy, showing how closely praise–gossip and blame–gossip are interlinked. A closely knit group, with its high power ratio, has more opportunities for effective gossip and the more people feel threatened or insecure, the more gossip becomes fantasy of a rigid kind. Thus gossip of praise for the charismatic and blame for the disgraced becomes part of the individual personality structures of both groups. In trying to understand patients in a therapy group, therefore, it is very limiting to focus on universal family patterns and ignore the specific impact of particular wider social processes.

> The collective identity, and as part of it the collective pride and the charismatic group claims, help to fashion his individual identity in his own as well as other people's experience. No individual grows up without this anchorage of his personal identity in the identification with a group or groups even though it may remain tenuous and may be forgotten in later life, and without some knowledge of the terms of praise and abuse, of the praise gossip and the blame gossip, of the group superiority and group inferiority which go with it.
>
> (Elias & Scotson, [1965] 1994, p105)

I would like to add that these dynamics of power relations and inclusion–exclusion, with their concomitant charisma and disgrace sustained by praise and blame gossip can also be detected within families. This may be evidenced in sub-groups within the family where a parent, child or other relative, or grouping of them, come to be experienced as charismatic and others as disgraced. This may well mirror what is going on in the wider social process and be just as unconscious. This could well provide a more insightful way of understanding patients than a focus on speculations about universal Oedipal patterns and intrapsychic defenses.

Attachment, separation and anxiety

Inclusion and exclusion are processes that are at the heart of power relations. Since inclusion is a form of attachment and exclusion a form of separation, it follows that attachment–separation behaviors are closely linked with power relating. Chapter 6 drew attention to the direct connection between attachment–separation behavior and opioid-arousal mechanisms in the brain. Together they constitute a process of bodily regulation. It seems that biological evolution has produced a human body that is fundamentally social requiring interaction with other bodies to regulate itself. Communicative interaction/power relating is fundamentally linked to attachment and separation between bodies and opioid-arousal within bodies. This is what ensures the social behavior required for survival. This biologically evolved universal characteristic of human physiology is expressed as communicative interaction/power relating/inclusion–exclusion and the specific patterns formed by this activity is what social/mind means. The patterns of interaction are not universal even though the physiological processes are. Rather, the patterns of mind/social are historically specific and social evolution is the evolution of these patterns as narrative themes that are experience.

The experience of inclusion, of a 'we' identity, therefore, is the experience of attachment and physiological calming. On the other hand, the experience of exclusion is the experience of separation, indeed of a threat to 'we' identity, linked to physiological arousal felt as anxiety. An individual's experience of the social process of exclusion can then be understood as a particular thematic patterning of the action of a body directed towards itself, where the theme is the feeling of anxiety. This is the same process as the thematic patterning of interaction between people in a group of the excluded and in their interactions with members of the group of the established, the 'included.' Again, individual mind and social are seen to be the same process.

This argument suggests that it is the vicissitudes of attachment–separation that pattern the processes of mind and society, not the vicissitudes of instincts. The inevitable dynamics of inclusion and exclusion have very important consequences. If communicative interaction is essential, not only for the survival of every individual, but also for the continued reproduction and transformation of their very selves, or identities, then any exclusion must be felt as very threatening. For a being for whom the social is essential to life itself, the deepest existential anxiety must be aroused by any threat of separation or exclusion since it means the potential loss or fragmentation of identity, even death. Also, categorizing people into this or that kind, with this or that kind of view, may be experienced as threatening. This is because it creates potential misrepresentation of identity and potential exclusion from communication.

The process of turn taking/turn making that reproduces and transforms themes of emergent patterns of collaboration, at the same time reproduces and transforms themes to do with inclusion and exclusion, or power, and these arouse feelings of existential anxiety, which trigger themes to deal with that anxiety in some way. The themes triggered by anxiety may well have to do with re-patterning the dynamic of inclusion and exclusion, that is, with shifting the relations of power. These and other themes triggered by anxiety may well disrupt collaboration and they may also be highly destructive. However, without such disruptions to current patterns of collaboration and power relations there could be no emergent novelty in communicative interaction and hence no novelty in any form of human action. The reason for saying this is that disruptions generate diversity. One of the central insights of the complexity sciences is how the spontaneous emergence of novelty depends upon diversity (Allen, 1998a & b).

Furthermore, there is a link between anxiety and the use of fantasy to cope with it. By this I mean that an individual who experiences, not necessarily consciously, the anxiety aroused by exclusion, may well elaborate on his or her own actions and those of others in the private role-play/silent conversation of mind, in a way that has little to do with what they are actually doing. The result can be fantasy and misunderstanding to varying degrees, even serious breakdowns in the whole process of communicative interaction. Again, however, there is a close relationship between fantasy and misunderstanding, on the one hand, and the emergence of novelty, on the other. Fantasy is close to imaginative elaboration and misunderstanding triggers a search for understanding thereby provoking continued imaginative elaboration and communication. It is in such continued struggles for meaning, and the imaginative elaboration going with it, that the novel emerges and with it the potential for therapeutic change.

> Elias is aware that the individual civilizing process undergone by all members of society is frequently a painful experience which inevitably leaves its scars. This process, like that at the social level, is still largely blind. Some people may become permanently restless and dissatisfied because the gratification of their impulses can only come about indirectly through fantasy; so they experience a numbing of affects as the inhibition over-extends itself and an all-pervading feeling of boredom, may predominate; unwanted compulsive forms of behavior may predominate; or the transformation of energies may flow in an uncontrolled manner in eccentric attachments and repulsions.
>
> (Fletcher, 1997, p27)

These interrelated matters of power and anxiety, fantasy, imagination and misunderstanding, therefore, are central to an understanding of the communicative interaction that is human relating. They provide a way of understanding individual distress, depression, neurosis, disruption to identity, personality disorders, and so on, that is essentially social rather than intrapsychic.

Shame and panic

According to Elias (Smith, 2001) the roots of civilization are firmly planted in the soil of shame, which includes self-disgust, inhibition, isolation and fear. Shame is produced by any kind of transgression against the rules of society. As people become more self-disciplined and self-aware, their thresholds of repugnance rise. Shame is in turn rooted in the body and because human metabolism cannot be easily controlled (blushing, sweating, breaking wind) people feel vulnerable in a civilized society, which pushes such bodily expressions behind the scenes of social life so that when the body plays its tricks the person gets blamed for infringing norms. Ironically feelings of shame trigger many of the bodily responses that cause shame in the first place.

Mennell and Goudsblom (1998) write:

> Elias's remarks about the 'advance of thresholds of shame and embarrassment' go to the heart of this theory. Shame and embarrassment are personal emotions, deeply affecting the individual's state of mind; at the same time they are socially induced emotions par excellence. If a person feels that he or she has been observed committing an offence against good manners, that is reason for shame; seeing someone else commit a similar offence is a cause for embarrassment. As the written and unwritten rules of etiquette became more encompassing and subtle, the range of occasions for transgressing those rules and, therefore, for shame and embarrassment increased. Erving Goffman described with great accuracy how people in contemporary society experience and cope with embarrassment and shame; Elias's theory provides a framework for explaining the *sociogenesis* of such situations.
>
> (Mennell & Goudsblom, 1998, p19)

Aram (2001) links shame with panic, which is a response to the fear of potential embarrassment or shame. She argues that panic is simultaneously relationally constructed and individually experienced, and may be thought of as a response to anxiety that serves the purpose of not dealing with the situations provoking that anxiety. The fear of the fear is translated into panic. She also links panic to waiting for something to happen, dreading it and avoiding it until it 'arrives.' Panic is, then, an investment of energy into not feeling and not knowing that leads to exactly that which is being avoided. The physical symptoms of panic include not breathing, irritable bowel, stomach pain, feeling sick, feeling weak, near fainting, and problems with sleeping. Panic is associated with strong desires to be with others, with avoiding being alone and ascribing great importance to what others think, so that withdrawing from interaction with others is experienced as particularly difficult. The fear of being on one's own, out of control and in constant need of support makes it extremely difficult to relax. It is not necessarily any change itself that leads to panic because when that which is being unconsciously avoided does happen, the panic symptoms diminish and the capacity to manage is found. It is the phase before a change, namely, the waiting period, which is experienced as panic. This waiting is felt to be an unconscious immobilizing fear that past experiences are about to reoccur. People who suffer panic usually end up feeling exactly that which they are actively trying to avoid. They are highly invested in trying to maintain a strong, 'in control' sense of self and they feel humiliated when they realize how affected they are by others and how important others are in helping them maintain a sense of self. They fear dependency, yet are highly dependent. They long for relationships yet are often intimidated by them and tend to have fractious and unsuccessful ones.

Aram regards this interlinked process of panic and shame as a response to deep-rooted fears to do with inclusion and exclusion and the consequent potential for being humiliated and shamed. Panic arouses feelings of shame and humiliation because it is taken as a sign of weakness and immaturity. This fragile sense of self stems from the fragility and insecurity of attachment and often reflects early attachment and separation difficulties. Anxiety generated by endlessly waiting and preparing to be abandoned and rejected, reflecting past experience, is replaced with panic, anger, rivalry and fear of closeness. All of these are ways of expressing difficulties of relating. The processes of panic are, thus, entangled with those of shame, humiliation, embarrassment and fragile senses of self. Shame arising from the public symptoms of panic contributes to the dynamics of inclusion–exclusion, feelings of being the 'odd one out,' which in turn give rise to further panic.

Shame is an affect that arises in relation to others and has to do with looking and being looked at, taking the form of a wish not to be seen. Shame is converted to feelings of inadequacy and fears of exclusion. These feelings may, in turn, provoke violence and aggression.

> In Elias' view, shame is closely linked to aggression and violence: it is in situations where violence is impossible that shame becomes expressed as the fear of others' gestures of superiority. During long-term civilizing processes, problems of lapsing into inferiority become more difficult to resolve by resorting to physical means or aggressive behavior. Shame feelings appear as conflict felt within the person when he or she transgresses conscience-controls; . . . Fears centre on the possible loss of love and respect of others. People become defenseless against the gestures of superiority of others when they cannot resort to violence. This is because they automatically adopt the attitude towards themselves that is generated by the superiors' attitude towards them.
>
> (Fletcher, 1997, p28)

Dalal (2001) argues that guilt is the individual equivalent of the social process of shame, suggesting that the difference is not one of type but one of location. The social reference of shame and embarrassment recedes from consciousness and becomes an unconscious self-restraint. Transgressions against these unconscious forms of self-restraint in the private role-play are experienced as guilt.

To summarize processes of shame, humiliation, repugnance and disgust are all simultaneously individual and social. The particular kind of society people in the West live in requires that they conduct themselves in particular ways and their compliance is assured by particular kinds of personality and mental process, that is, particular ways in which people experience themselves. In other words, particular forms of society require particular kinds of 'we' and 'I' identities. All of this relies on processes of shame to sustain the particular kinds of self-restraint required by Western society at this time. In other times and in other places, social patterns and the way people experience themselves, their 'we' and 'I' identities, are all different and processes of shame and humiliation are patterned in different ways.

In this section, I have been describing how the complex responsive processes of shame and guilt, patterned as social and individual experience, not only sustain patterns of society but simultaneously lead to all manner of emergent difficulties for individuals. I have been describing how shame is closely intertwined with processes of inclusion–exclusion and so attachment–separation. These processes are linked to anxiety and fear and also the fear of the fear, which is panic. And panic, which is a bodily experience of waiting for unconsciously feared shaming breaks in attachment, often further increasing the shame itself and the breaks in attachment. This whole constellation of social/individual processes easily triggers aggression and violence. This may take the form of envious attacks that destroy the attachment bonds of others, where some try to spoil what others have because they want it but cannot have it. Or the attacks may arise from threat to 'we' identities when it is felt that beliefs and actions in another group threaten the way of life of one's own group. Paradoxically, then, the very processes required to sustain Western society are also processes highly destructive of it.

What I have been pointing to here is a way of understanding individual distress and difficulties with relationships that is essentially social rather than intrapsychic.

Unconscious processes

On many occasions in this chapter, and in previous ones, I have been drawing attention to unconscious communicative interaction and power relating as it is understood in Elias' process theory. He talks about the automatic, self-compulsive nature of self-control instilled in individuals brought up in the kind of society that has evolved in the West, in which so much is banished behind the scenes. The impact of charisma on one group and stigmatization on another and how this is tied up with the evolution of 'we' and 'I' identities are all processes that are largely unconscious. This 'habitus,' which is both social and individual at the same time is unconscious and so is the role of ideology in sustaining power relations, as is the shifting dynamic of inclusion and exclusion that accompanies it. The same applies to the turn taking and turn making of ordinary conversation. It also applies to that constellation of processes to do with shame, anxiety, inclusion–exclusion, panic and aggression, all of which are destructive of social and individual mental life. Throughout, these unconscious processes are simultaneously individual and social as is conscious communicative interaction and power relating. In this section, I want to explore the nature of the unconscious aspects of communicative interaction by distinguishing between different ways in which one might understand what unconscious means.

First, the term unconscious has a physiological meaning, referring to a body that is alive but in a coma, anaesthetized, knocked out or fainting. I am not using the term unconscious in this sense. Physiological consciousness is a state of bodily activity, either awake or asleep, and physiologically conscious bodies can relate to each other in ways that one can characterize as unconscious in the following senses.

A physiologically conscious body could act in a purely instinctive, reflex manner. An example of this would be ants laying and following pheromone trials. They are interacting and communicating but in purely reflex ways. Another example would be the conditioning of laboratory animals to perform experiments. Human acts based purely on reflex actions could be described as unconscious. This mindless action is also not what I mean by the term unconscious.

A conscious body can communicate with another body in a direct way in the medium of what I called protosymbols in Chapter 4. Here the gesture of one body does not call forth in itself the same response as in the one gestured to. Instead, the body rhythms of one are thrown together with the body rhythms of another to form protosymbolic meaning. These bodies are communicating with each other, they are mindful of each other, they are resonating with each other, but they are not conscious of the communication's meaning. Their communication is unconscious. For example, the intricate conversation of gestures between infant and mother described in Chapter 5 is largely unconscious in this sense. Another example is when adults unconsciously communicate how they feel to each other. This is the basis of intuitive communication between people and it is one important sense in which I am using the term unconscious, namely, communication between bodies and between a body and itself, in the medium of protosymbols.

However, human bodies also communicate with each other in the medium of significant symbols (see Chapter 4). This means that the gesture of one calls forth in that one similar responses to those called forth in the other. This physiological capacity creates the potential for knowing what one is doing, that is, for being conscious in a mental and social sense. However, this is a potential, not an automatic guarantee. So, some processes of communication in the medium of significant symbols may be unconscious in the sense that the gesturer is not realizing the potential for knowing but is still communicating. For example, I might say something to another that provokes a hurt response, which I feel I did not intend, but then I immediately realize that I vaguely did, or could have known that this

would be the response. This is another aspect of what I mean by unconscious. It takes the form of communication between people where the
meaning of the communication is not formulated or articulated. I draw on
the work of the relational psychoanalyst, Donnel Stern (1983), who has
developed the notion of the unformulated unconscious and the intersubjective psychoanalysts, Robert Stolorow and colleagues (1994), who have
developed the notion of the unvalidated unconscious (see Chapter 12).
However, I recast these notions as communication rather than as features
of 'the unconscious.'

Briefly, unformulated communication consists of vague tendencies,
which are potentially articulable if allowed to develop. Here clarity and
differentiation of meaning is not yet known in terms of language. Such
communication is a beginning of insight not yet formulated and conscious
communication is constructed as progressive articulation of this unformulated and hence unconscious communication. Unformulated communication is communication not yet consciously grasped and Stern regards it as
creative disorder from which the new emerges. Unvalidated communication
is also communication that is not articulated but not because it is not yet
formulated. The communication is not articulated because a history of the
absence of validating responses has meant that it never could be articulated. This occurs because of a lack of attunement, or some traumatic
event, usually in childhood, makes it impossible, pointless, or highly
dangerous to articulate a particular communication. Neglect, futility and
the danger of traumatization prevent articulation. Unformulated and
unvalidated communication is the second sense in which I am using the
term unconscious.

The third sense in which I use the term unconscious is as follows.
Communication in the sense of gesture–response that takes place in
significant symbols, and which is formulated and articulated, can become
habitual and so easily repeated automatically. In this sense communicative
interaction becomes unconscious. This is communication that was once
formulated, validated and articulated but its meaning is now so taken for
granted that those communicating are unconscious of it. This is not the
same as the reflex behavioral conditioning described above because such
behavior never was conscious in the first place. Also, the meaning of
unconscious processes that I am referring to here is not necessarily that of
some active form of repression. It is simply a consequence of skilled behavior. This notion of unconscious process draws on Stolorow and colleagues
(1994) who propose the notion of a pre-reflective unconscious, which is
recurring patterns of communication that become invariant principles
unconsciously organizing subsequent experience (see Chapter 12). As an
example, they point to organizing principles that derive from a child's
perception of what is required of him/her to maintain ties that are vital to
his/her well-being. The idea I am putting forward here is similar to

Stolorow's notion but here it is a process of communicative interaction not a feature of an internal world. However, some communication may once have been formulated and recognized in the response, being in that sense validated, but the response might have been experienced as hostile or dangerous, and hence excluding. Such a pattern of communicative interaction is then repeatedly blocked from consciousness in a manner that might be described as repression. This is similar to Stolorow's formulation of the dynamic unconscious in which particular themes are prevented from crystallizing into consciousness because they are associated with danger, particularly the danger of threatening current configurations of interaction that allow people to cope. In this chapter there is a similar notion of what is unconscious but again without any notion of an internal world to be found in Stolorow's writing (see Chapter 12).

The forms of unconscious communication just described can also easily take place in the medium of reified symbols patterned in abstract-systematic form as theories. We frequently take for granted the assumptions upon which such communications are based and so are not conscious of these assumptions. We also experience the danger of contradicting dominant theoretical positions if we wish to remain members of a community.

To summarize, I am using the term unconscious in the sense of bodily communicative interaction and power relating that is unconscious in an individual mental and social sense at the same time. These processes constitute what Elias called 'habitus,' which can be thought of as:

- Communicative interaction in the medium of protosymbols, that is, as direct bodily communication of feelings.
- Communicative interaction in the medium of significant symbols with the potential for conscious meaning, which is either not yet formulated or never had the possibility of formulation in a powerful history of being unvalidated.
- Communicative interaction in the medium of significant and/or reified symbols, which was once formulated, validated and articulated but has become automatic and taken for granted. Alternatively, such communicative interaction may once have been formulated but met with so hostile and dangerous a response that it is never consciously experienced again.

I want to stress a number of points about the notion of unconscious communication described above. First, each of the patterns of unconscious communication distinguished are aspects of processes of communicative interaction and they cannot be separated from each other. They are simultaneously occurring aspects of processes not separate types that can be experienced separately in some pure form. Second, there is no boundary between conscious and unconscious communication because they are aspects of temporal processes of communication, not spatial concepts located anywhere. What I am describing as unconscious are aspects of processes of communication that cannot be separated from other aspects. I think of these aspects in fractal terms so that within any aspect that we might call conscious there are aspects that we might call unconscious and vice versa. Third, conscious and unconscious communications apply simultaneously to interaction between bodies, the social, and the interaction of each body with itself, mind. In dialectal terms the contradictions of conscious and unconscious, individual and social are transformed into the dynamic of human knowing. It is impossible to know, to find meaning, which is either simply conscious or simply unconscious, simply individual or simply social. Meaning is at the same time conscious and unconscious, individual and social.

I am suggesting, then, a way of thinking about that which is unconscious in terms of communicative interacting and power relating between people and this is a completely different notion to any idea of intrapsychic mechanisms, or 'the unconscious.' Psychoanalytic theories of the mind are built on the assumption that the mind is an internal world of representations and 'the unconscious' is an agency in that internal world operating as an efficient cause of individual human actions. According to this view an individual does what he or she does because of:

- instinctual wishes and modes of repressing and defending against them understood as the dynamic unconscious (Freud);
- universal, inherited fantasies of aggression and persecution and mechanisms of splitting, introjection and projection, all of which are unconscious (Klein);
- thoughts originating in formless beta fragments, which are unconscious (Bion).

In these formulations that which is unconscious has a very particular meaning as 'the unconscious.' This is an individual-centered perspective in which it is defenses against unacceptable wishes to discharge drives that are unconscious. 'The unconscious' refers to the drives as representations of innate instincts seeking discharge (the id). It also refers to the repression of socially unacceptable wishes and the subsequent causal agency of these repressed wishes as they return unconsciously to cause behavior (ego defenses and superego). There are separate logics, or modes of thinking, for unconscious and conscious agencies of the mind and consciousness is understood as a property of language. Or, from an object relations perspective, 'the unconscious' consists of inherited fantasies elaborated by experience of relationship with others. Individuals are assumed to unconsciously put individual mental contents into each other. In group terms, it is assumed that individuals anonymously donate mental contents to group unconscious processes (Bion, 1961). Later psychoanalysts developed notions of a separate social unconscious (Fromm, 1980; also see Chapter 12).

Freud's notion of 'the unconscious,' then, is one of an agency that represses experience, which is unproblematic in terms of formulation and validation. The unconscious distorts and blocks but the Freudian unconscious can always be put into words if the defenses are lowered. Freud also drew a boundary between the conscious and the unconscious. Although they are interrelated they always retain separate meanings. The unconscious is defined in terms of primary processes where there are no contradictions and no time. Consciousness is defined in terms of secondary process where there is differentiation and time. Later psychoanalysts have almost always continued with this notion. For example Matte Blanco (see Chapter 15) draws a distinction between symmetrical logic, very similar to primary process, and asymmetrical logic, very similar to secondary process.

From a complex responsive processes perspective, these separate spatial notions, based on the idea of internal worlds, have no place. Although I have drawn on important insights about unconscious processes by relational and intersubjective psychoanalysts, I will argue in Chapter 12 that their formulations continue to rely on the distinction between inside and outside, which the theory of complex responsive processes avoids. From a complex responsive processes perspective, unconscious refers to aspects of communicative interaction and power relating that cannot be separated from conscious aspects. We are talking about communication not intrapsychic mechanisms or supra systems. The complex responsive processes theory of mind/social drops the assumptions to do with drives and moves away from the individual making it necessary to abandon any notion of 'the unconscious' and any distinction between the individual and the social unconscious. Rejecting the notion of the internal world also means rejecting the assumption of internal object relations, including self objects, and the notions of innate fantasies and universal positions such as the schizoid-paranoid and depressive.

In the theory of complex responsive processes, interaction between people is understood to pattern itself. Interaction does not produce anything other than further interaction. There is no whole, system or supra individual outside of this interaction. From a complex responsive processes perspective, the notion of unconscious process also excludes any idea of a collective unconscious, a separate social unconscious, or any other kind of system above the direct experience of interaction. The proposition that interaction has intrinsic patterning properties also makes it unnecessary to posit any cause of form or pattern outside of interaction. In other words, there is nothing above, below, in front of, or behind interaction causing it or being produced by it. The theory of complex responsive processes does not rely on any intrapsychic agencies or on the notion of 'the unconscious' as a causal agency, a source of motivation for action that has been repressed and lies outside that action. According to Freud, psychological life, and social relationships for that matter, arise in the vicissitudes of the drives whereas in the complex responsive processes perspective individual mind and social arise simultaneously in the vicissitudes of attachment and separation, that is, in the dynamics of inclusion–exclusion, power relating and communicative interaction and clearly related dynamics of shame, panic and aggression. From this perspective, 'the unconscious' of psychoanalysis is a social construct rather than a psychic reality and there is no hidden reality located in the individual.

> We owe to Freud a great advance in the understanding of group processes during which men's self-controlling agencies grow into shape. Freud himself, however, conceptualized his findings largely in a manner which made it appear that every human being is a *homo clausus*. He recognized the specifically human capacity for learning to control and, up to a point, to pattern their malleable libidinal drives according to their experiences within a norm-setting group. But he conceptualized . . . controlling and orientating functions at the personality level of a human organism, which are patterned through learning, as if they were organs at one of its lower levels, which are little affected by learning. . . . As a result he advanced the concept of human beings' self-controlling functions – an ego, a superego or an ego ideal, as he called them – to the point where they have the character of functioning in what appears to be total autonomy within the single individual. But the layers of personality structure that remain most directly linked to the group processes in which a person participates, above all the person's we-image and we-ideal, lay beyond his horizon. . . . in the case of such personality functions as ego-image and ego-ideal, the emotive fantasies represent purely personal experiences of a group process. In the case of we-image and we-ideal, they are personal versions of collective fantasies.
>
> (Elias & Scotson, [1965] 1994, ppxlii–xliii)

So, Freud focuses on intrapsychic agencies and fantasies, while Elias argues for an understanding of the intertwining of individual and collective identities and fantasies. Freud takes the superego as a universal and describes its formation in terms of paternal domination, fear and fantasies around parents, the Oedipus complex, the primal image, the incest taboo, the primal horde and the murder of the father (see Chapter 9). Elias, on the other hand, describes the formation of conscience in terms of participation in the reality of social groups of individuals engaging in communicative interaction and power relations.

However, as I have argued above, the move from intrapsychic notions relying on the spatial metaphor of an internal world does not exclude unconscious processes. Instead, unconscious processes are understood as aspects of communicative interaction and power relating. Nor does abandoning the meta psychological construct of 'the unconscious' mean abandoning the rich insights into human emotions and fantasy lives, as well as the ubiquitous distortions in human communicative interaction, that psychoanalytic writers and practitioners have been developing for a century now. Indeed the relational and intersubjectivity schools of psychoanalytic thought have themselves been making moves, for decades now, from Freudian meta psychology of 'the unconscious' and developing different notions of unconscious process (see Chapter 12). Instead of abandoning these insights, the perspective of complex responsive processes points to the need for understanding them afresh from a perspective that is simultaneously individual and social.

In the theory of complex responsive processes, consciousness and unconsciousness are aspects of the narrative and propositional themes, elaborated in fantasy, patterning the experience of being together. As far as individuals are concerned, unconscious processes are forms of communication of the body with itself that take the same form as social processes, rather than primitive processes, present at birth, arising originally in individuals. Both individual mental and social change is change in the themes organizing communicative action and power relating and that change emerges in the interaction of organizing themes. Looked at like this, there is no notion of individuals moving mental contents from on to another. Since the mental and the social are the same process, nothing is internalized and interaction is not simply mimicry but continuous iteration or reproduction with the potential for transformation. I may or may not be conscious of the patterns of narrative themes reproduced and transformed in the private role-play of mind. At the same time, we may or may not be conscious of the pattern of narrative themes reproduced and transformed in our public relating. We are talking about the same process.

The nature of unconscious processes in the theory of complex responsive processes can be illuminated in terms of Mead's description of communicative interaction between organisms. Communication in the medium of significant symbols means that when A gestures to B, this gesture potentially calls forth similar responses in A as in B. When the potential is realized then we may say that the communication is conscious. In what ways might this potential not be realized, that is, in what ways may the communication be unconscious?

One central concept in psychoanalysis is transference. What happens in transference is that A's gesture to B calls forth in A responses that have often been experienced in A's previous experience of interaction with C. In the strict meaning of transference, C is one of A's parents. One might say that A mistakes B for C and is not conscious of doing so. In psychoanalysis, B's response to A's gesture is countertransference. However, B's response becomes a gesture to A and this may well call forth in B a response that B has often experienced in previous relations with D. As a result, the communication in the present between A and B involves the repetition in the present of past patterns that have become automatic for both of them. This is normally understood in psychoanalytic terms as a distortion in current communication, which could lead to a great deal of misunderstanding. However, from a complex responsive processes perspective, A and B will always be communicating in a way that is simultaneously selected by the past experience of each and called forth in the present by each other's responses. We are always iterating and constructing reality in this way and the potential for the transformation of repetitive patterns lies in the spontaneous amplification of small differences from one present to the next. Transference and countertransference then lose their special meanings and come to be particularly repetitive themes having very little scope for amplification into some new pattern of relating. I am suggesting then that the notions of transference and countertransference remain useful in thinking about the patterning of complex responsive processes. We will always be iterating themes from our past but when we do so in very rigid ways, communication becomes stuck in repetitive patterns that are not understood because they are automatic and unconscious. The resulting distortion of communication can be very distressing and the concepts of transference and countertransference are drawing attention to this possibility.

The psychoanalytic concepts of projection and introjection are much more problematic in terms of the complex responsive processes perspective. Both are terms appropriate to a spatial metaphor of inside and outside, and a sender–receiver model of communication. Projection is understood to be the evacuation of unwanted mental contents from inside the internal world of one person into another person who is outside, mistaking that other for an unwanted aspect of oneself in the process. Introjection is understood as the incorporation of aspects of an outside other into one's internal world. These terms have no meaning from a complex responsive process perspective since it is not based on spatial metaphors and avoids sender–receiver notions of communication. One might talk of A's gesture to B calling forth a response in A that has to do with habitual/imagined themes in A's silent conversation rather than B's response but to call this projection or introjection would be to bring in spatial metaphors. The same point applies to projective identification, which is understood as a process in which one person puts unwanted feelings into another who then feels them as his or her own, while the first has the fantasy of controlling the other from within. From a complex responsive processes point of view, there is no putting of feelings into each other but the phenomenon that projective identification is getting at would be understood as direct communication in protosymbols, the resonance of one person's body rhythms with those of another. One might talk about A's gesture calling forth a response in A that is a fantasy of controlling B from within and B might well get caught up in this so that it becomes a powerful theme organizing their communication but the use of the term projective identification again brings in spatial metaphors and is avoided in the theory of complex responsive processes.

Chapter 8

Some clinical implications of a theory of complex responsive processes

The Conductor, on the other hand, is the instrument of the group, or should be. He can be said to be the first servant of the group. He should follow the group's lead in turn. His lead should really be a service to the group and be understood as such. He should never need or use the group for his own sake. . . . the Conductor is directing the process, but in order to direct it he must let it develop and not disturb it by his interference. . . . By submitting himself completely to the needs of the group he sets at the same time a most important example.

(Foulkes, 1948, pp139–140)

This chapter explores the consequences of thinking about the therapy group as complex responsive processes of relating between its members, including the therapist. The first consequence is that as a therapist I am thinking about the group in process terms, rather than in terms of some combination of systems thinking and psychoanalysis. By process I mean the direct interaction between human bodies in which meaning and further interaction emerges, perpetually creating the future as continuity and potential transformation in the living present. This is in contrast to a systemic/ psychoanalytic approach in which process is understood as the interaction between parts of a system in order to create a whole, which is inevitably outside the direct experience of interaction (see Part II). From the complex responsive processes perspective, participation means participating with each other in self-organizing processes of meaning in which our individual and collective identities emerge as continuity and potential transformation. Individual minds are understood as private, silent versions of public, vocal social relations between people. There is nothing above or below this interaction because it is interaction itself that has intrinsic patterning capacities. As interaction is iterated from moment to moment it has the potential for transformation because of its property of amplifying small differences in interaction. Both individual mind and social relating are patterned as narrative themes and change is change in these themes.

Healthy minds and healthy social relating are characterized by the para-dox of continuity and transformation at the same time, where health is a paradoxical dynamic of stability and instability at the same time and illness is the repetition of thematic patterning with very little potential for trans-formation. Illness is a stuck pattern of stability in the private role-play/ silent conversation of a body with itself, mind, and rigid, stable patterns of interaction between bodies, social. Health and illness are always reflected simultaneously in individual minds and in social relations. The move from illness to health is a move from stability to more complex, variable patterns of relating of a body to itself and of bodies to each other. In other words, therapeutic change can never be either individual or social but is always both individual and social at the same time.

The purpose of a theory is to focus attention on some aspects of a phenomenon and so inevitably ignore others. The process theory I have been exploring in previous chapters focuses attention on relationships, belonging and communication just as Foulkes did in his development of group-analytic practice. The medium of the therapy is the group, under-stood as processes of individuals relating to, and communicating with, each other. This relating and communicating is individual and social at the same time. All of this is very much in line with Foulkes' account of group-analytic therapy. However, Foulkes then often switches from a process account to one drawn from systems thinking and psychoanalysis (see Chapter 15). I intend to avoid doing that in this chapter and stay with a purely process perspective. Instead of adopting a dualistic, figure-ground way of thinking about the individual and the group, I want to stay with the paradox of the individual and the group emerging at the same time, moment by moment, in the interaction. Staying with a process perspective in this way immediately focuses attention on emerging narrative themes and power relations in the group and the inevitable dynamics of inclusion and exclusion that are an aspect of power relating. Another way of putting this is to say that instead of focusing attention on the vicissitudes of the drives, the process account I am suggesting focuses attention on the vicissitudes of attachment and separation. Instead of moving back into the past to focus strongly on childhood experience as internalized in the internal world of an individual, the process approach focuses attention on the living present of relating between people in which they are continually re-creating the past in anticipation of the future, all in the living present.

The concept of what I am calling the 'living present' is very different to the notion of the 'here-and-now' as it usually seems to be understood. The 'here-and-now' is usually distinguished from the 'there-and-then.' Focusing on the 'here-and-now' in a group then means focusing only on the emotional aspects of the communicative interaction taking place at a particular moment in the room in which the group is meeting. Any discussion about relationships outside the room, as well as any kind of intellectual discussion, is then regarded as a distraction or a defense. This is a linear view of time in which the present of the 'here-and-now' is a point separating the past from the future. The living present, on the other hand, is a circular notion of time in which expectations forming in the present about the future affect the iteration of the past that is forming the expectation of the future. In other words, the living present is simultaneously the reconstruction of past relating and the anticipation of future relating in the present moment of interaction. In each moment, people are reconstructing their pasts as the basis of their expectations for the future and their expectations for the future are affecting how they are reconstructing their pasts. Reconstructions of the past are not simple retrievals from the long term memory of what actually happened but rather newly told narratives that are always changing, if only in minute ways. There is then no distinction between the 'here-and-now' and the 'there-and-then' in the notion of the living present. Whatever people are talking about, whether intellectual or emotional, about the past or the future, it is all part of the communicative interaction in the living present in which power relations are re-configuring in terms of inclusion and exclusion, that is, attachment and separation.

To illustrate what I am talking about, I would like to present a group that ran for two-and-a-half years.

Inclusion and exclusion in the therapy group

Towards the end of the life of this group, we experienced a very familiar pattern of interaction, but this time much more intensely than ever before. One member exploded in anger, railing at the group for its inadequacy, while another member picked up on the first's complaints and used them to mount a cold and calculated attack on other members and on me. This left me feeling particularly helpless and despondent. I was disappointed at my inadequate understanding of what this repetitive pattern of dissatisfaction with the group, and angry explosions at it, was all about and I strongly disliked the feelings of incompetence this lack of understanding left me with. I could interpret what the pattern might mean in terms of the emotional lives of the individuals concerned and in terms of transference/countertransference.

However, I felt that I had an inadequate grasp of what this recurrent pattern of attacks on the group meant in terms of the social process of the group. I found the reasons for these attacks somewhat puzzling. The two angry members, one aggressively and the other contemptuously, consistently attacked the group for two reasons on which they both agreed. First, they complained that 'the group' did not deal with emotions but simply went around the same circle of behavior over and over again, frequently taking the form of what had come to be known as the 'tea party' and this, they said, made the group unsafe. Sometimes this complaint seemed quite justified. However, much more frequently, the complaints about lack of emotion followed soon after someone had cried or had clearly demonstrated their depression and distress. People in the group definitely were expressing and talking about emotion quite often so the 'tea party' accusation mostly seemed to be about something else. One way of thinking about what was going on would be in the psychoanalytic terms of projections and transference but exploration along these lines did not seem to make much sense to the members and I too felt dissatisfied with them.

The second complaint made by these two members was that 'the group' was variable, inconsistent and unreliable and this left them feeling unsafe: some members had left and new ones had joined; people were absent; and they tended to come late, bursting in and disturbing what was going on. However, on face value this was an odd complaint because the group was unusually stable. During its two-and-a-half years of meeting, only two of the eight members left and were soon replaced. For eighty per cent of the sessions there were six or more members present, the smallest attendance being three and this occurred only twice. The practice of informing the group about absences was consistently followed and although people sometimes came late this rarely exceeded five minutes. Breaks were not excessive and although I sometimes changed the pattern of breaks, these changes were announced many weeks in advance.

There were six sessions, spread across the group's years of meeting, in which there were significant eruptions of anger and attacks on the group, followed by a number of sessions in which these rather traumatic events were discussed and worked with by group members. These sessions and those immediately preceding and following them displayed particular patterns. Sessions in which the angry eruptions were discussed were followed by sessions in which members talked about their unsatisfactory relationships with their parents and particularly with their fathers. For example, take the following sessions.

Ben explodes

Two weeks before a break, Andy announced that he was going to do a degree in some esoteric subject. Jane showed excited interest in this and Ann soon joined the conversation between them. Andy did describe how apprehensive he felt about going to the admission interview and how this brought up some of the distressing feelings around his breakdown, but mostly it was a very abstract discussion. With fifteen minutes to go before the end of the session, a very angry, white-faced and trembling Ben exploded. Shouting, he said that the last few sessions had been like tea parties in which working with feelings was banned. He seemed not to recognize that Andy and others had been talking about rather painful experiences in between abstract discussions during the past few sessions. As

far as I was concerned the sessions Ben was referring to had been productive. Jane suggested that Ben might be seeing elements of Leo, his
stepson, in Andy and might be furious at the attention that she and Ann
had been paying to Andy, rather like the attention his wife had lavished on
Leo. Ben, however, ignored the comment.

I now understand what was going on as an example the dynamics of
inclusion and exclusion in the living present of the group. Two members
were paying a great deal of attention to one member, in effect excluding
others. I was not paying much attention to anyone in particular during the
session in which Ben exploded and, having just returned from one break,
we would shortly be off on another that I had unexpectedly introduced.
Also, this session followed a fairly long run of sessions in which I had been
idealized by the older women in the group, namely, Jane and Ann. There
seemed to be an 'in' group consisting of Andy and me and an 'out' group
consisting of Ben and others who received little attention. This may well
have aroused feelings of having needs that are not met while those of other
people are. Perhaps the feeling was one of separation while witnessing the
attachment of others. This, in turn, could stir feelings of rivalry and competitiveness, jealousy and rage. These themes, in turn, might trigger a range
of defensive responses: withdrawal into a seminar, debating society or tea
party for some, and the expression by Ben of rage.

Attendance at the following session was the smallest up to that time: only
the four main protagonists in the previous week's session were present.
After repeated attempts to avoid dealing with what had happened in the
previous session, they finally began to explore the similarity between Andy
receiving a great deal of indulgent attention from the two older women in
the group and Leo receiving his mother's attention while Ben was ignored.
Ben connected with this. He had been thinking during the week about the
last session and realized that it was connected with his wife and his deep
bitterness at being left out. Ben, it seems, was talking about a rather
repetitive pattern of relating that he had experienced many times before.

In the session after this, a number of members expressed some curiosity
as to what I was making of events in the group and quite explicit expression
of fears that I might not like people or might be angry with them. Then
there was a break and after that the main theme running through the
conversation in the group was that of fathers who did not understand the
emotional needs of mothers and left children feeling rejected. The group
continued working for some weeks, with the anger rumbling around but
not surfacing at all powerfully.

From a psychoanalytic perspective, one might understand what had been
happening in the group in terms of transference in which I came to occupy
the role of the father. However, this focuses attention on intrapsychic
mechanisms, which I argue in Part II provide a highly problematic way of
making sense of human interaction. An alternative way of trying to

understand what was happening in the group runs in terms of the unconscious processes of inclusion and exclusion as I have already mentioned. This could be understood as the iterating of past patterns of interaction in the living present of the group's meeting.

Ben is angry again and Andy takes a sabbatical

Andy started his new course and discovered that he had an important seminar, the timing of which would make it difficult for him to get to the group on time. He dealt with this difficulty over a number of sessions by arriving at the group an hour late, completely disrupting the session when he entered. There were also other changes in the pattern of group meetings. In order to cope with other work pressures, I cancelled the summer break and announced additional one week breaks at the end of October and the middle of November. Also the membership of Nancy, who had missed many sessions and never replied to any of my letters, was terminated and the group then faced the prospect of a new member. Once again, it was Ben who was angry.

Ben told us that he felt completely unsafe in a group in which no one talked about their emotions while he was sitting choking on his – he was trembling. I tried to make a connection between his anger and the changes in the group. Ann responded to this, saying that the removal of Nancy's place and the prospect of a new member left her feeling replaceable and disposable. Ben reported that he was annoyed at the lack of consistency in the group, a matter that I seemed to do nothing about. I had let the situation with Nancy run on for a very long time and I was doing nothing about Andy's late arrivals. Soon after Ben disclosed his irritation with what was going on, Andy arrived late, complaining that to do even this he had to leave his seminar early and rush through the traffic. He asked if we could meet later, or on another day, since he wanted both his seminar and the group. However, he made it clear to us that if he had to choose he would choose his seminar – it was part of the core of the course. Changing the group time was out of the question but we did agree that Andy would take a sabbatical from the group. He would stop coming to the group until his seminars ended when he would return and in the meantime I would see him every six weeks or so to maintain his link with the group. For the rest of the year the group met without Andy, although he was often referred to, and at the end of the year a new member arrived, Terry, replacing Nancy.

The return of the 'prodigal son'

Terry's first session was not an easy one. The group ignored him while he sat blank-faced and hunched-up. After twenty minutes he gave an aggressive interpretation of another group member's behavior. Andy was still on sabbatical, but he was mentioned and this led Terry to wonder whether he had replaced Andy. Someone told him that it was Nancy whom he had replaced. For the next session, Terry arrived out of breath, having lost his way to the group room, to find a completely unexpected Andy basking in the group's indulgent attention. Andy was telling us that he had found it too difficult to cope with being a member of an academic institution and was probably going to give his course up. Andy and Terry introduced themselves to each other and a long silence followed which I broke by observing that it might be difficult to deal with the return of the prodigal son and the integration of a new member. Andy did not like being referred to as the prodigal son and somewhat contemptuously told the group that he had not missed them and he was not sure whether he would come next time: in fact, he might go to Spain. This provoked an angry response from the group during which I felt very concerned about the manic feel to Andy's behavior and the growing antagonism he was provoking. During this session I was also very aware of Terry who was being totally ignored while the group paid all its attention to Andy. Again there were the dynamics of inclusion and exclusion.

In the session after that, Andy was very quiet, apart from resisting my attempts to get him to take account of the importance of continuing his therapy, while Terry told us about his relationship with his father. He had hoped that the shared experience of his mother's death might draw him and his father together for the first time in his life, but his father had simply withdrawn further into a bitter resentment in which he blamed Terry for her death.

In the next session, Andy was still prevaricating about continuing his membership of the group, while Ann and Jane took up most of the time talking quite emotionally about relationship problems. Suddenly, towards the end of the session, Terry quietly said that he was wondering what 'they' were all doing there. Without any sign of emotion he said he felt very angry with Jane and Ann for chattering away without disclosing their feelings. They responded angrily, particularly when Ben backed Terry. I felt that I had encountered very deep hatred, the hatred aroused by exclusion and separation. The lack of attunement to Terry's needs, in which I too was participating, may have provoked feelings of rage and jealousy that he could not acknowledge, perhaps because he feared retaliation or complete rejection. The position of Andy in the group and Terry's attacks on Ann, and also Jane, continued to feature as central themes organizing the experience of being together for the next eight consecutive sessions.

After an absence of two sessions, during which members speculated about his whereabouts, Andy sent me a letter, which he invited me to read to the group. He informed us that he was going away to Spain and did not know when he would be back: he invited us to think of him as the absent member of the group. The group responded with indulgent amusement, just as I had done on first reading it. The image of the prodigal son was present once again: we would forgive him anything just to have him back. Terry, however, distanced himself from what was going on. He had noticed how 'they' were talking about Andy now that he was not there but had not talked to him when he was there. He somewhat bitterly observed that Andy had clearly had an impact on 'them.' Terry then said, 'perhaps *we* did something that has caused him to go.' He talked about competitiveness in the group and felt that he might have driven Andy out and taken his place in some way.

Reflection

I have argued in previous chapters that the dynamics of inclusion–exclusion, reflecting physiologically-based processes of attachment–separation, are directly linked to social/individual processes of shame/guilt. In a society in which dependency is often judged as weakness, where competition for attention provokes similar condemnation as being childish, it is shaming to be seen to be needy and trying to receive attention. The social prohibition on displaying these feelings leads to their expression in disguised forms, such as rage and envy. The dynamics of inclusion–exclusion arouse competitive feelings and consequent rage that cannot be directly expressed for fear of losing or destroying what is depended upon, the source of attachment. Instead of direct expression, therefore, there are covert attacks on the therapist and other members, alternating with the idealization of the therapist and the denigration of the group. This provides a way of understanding what is going on as simultaneous processes of individual/social communicative interaction and power relating, rather than in terms of innate fantasies or intrapsychic mechanisms. It is a way of thinking about the group that focuses on the iteration of patterns of interaction in the living present of the group's meeting. In this living present members are reproducing patterns of behavior from their past and those patterns are being called forth by interaction in the present. The therapy lies in the potential for amplifying and transforming differences in the reconstruction of past patterns.

Group processes and the role of the therapist

As a group therapist, I am *participating* in the simultaneously social and individual processes of exploring together our 'habitus' as members of that particular therapy group and all the other groups each of us belongs to. As I have said earlier on, I understand these paradoxically social and individual processes in terms of communicative interaction and power relating in which we are iterating, together and separately, the narrative themes patterning our experience of being together. Those themes are reconstructing the past and perpetually constructing the future in the present, all at the same time. As therapist, I am participating in these processes along with all the other members of the group but I am doing so in a manner that is somewhat different to the others. I have convened the group and I decide when and where it will meet, when it will commence and when it will end. There is then an immediate figuration of power relations in which the power is tilted towards me. Furthermore, I do not contribute the narrative of my own experiences outside the therapy group in the way that other members do and this too has consequences for the power figuration in the group.

This power difference is a very important part of our relationships with each other in the group. There is an immediate process of inclusion and exclusion that continues to have an impact throughout the life of the group. I am included in the healthy and they are excluded from this notional group, experiencing themselves in the group of the ill. I am included in the group of mental health professionals and they are excluded from this group, experiencing themselves in the group of laypersons. In terms of the inclusion–exclusion dynamics discussed in the last chapter, I am ascribed charisma and they are stigmatized as the mentally ill and the less skilled in the kind of exploration we are together undertaking. As we meet together in the group we inevitably iterate these themes to do with health and illness, expert and novice, that are so prevalent in wider social processes around mental health. These are all aspects of our 'habitus,' which we take so much for granted, and as such they are largely unconscious. It is part of my role as therapist to pay particular attention to the unconscious aspects of our communicative interaction with each other and to avoid taking for granted or even exacerbating the power differential between us. This is matter I will return to below.

One could think of therapists as the established (the professionals) and the other members of the group as outsiders (the sick). For example, members of one group often refer to my co-therapist and me as the 'professionals' and some say that we do not really get involved or feel emotions as the others in the group do. One member frequently said that we could not really understand him because we had never experienced panic attacks. Our non-disclosure helps to sustain this view. This stance, as well as our insistence on members not socializing outside the group, can be understood as an ideology that sustains the power difference between us. New members also face the established and the outsider dynamic on entering a group.

The importance of the 'we' identity

The therapy group, then, displays the same dynamics as those of Elias and Scotson, pointed to in the last chapter. Elias' emphasis on the interaction between 'I' and 'we' identities is helpful in understanding the nature of this

dynamic. As a therapist my 'we' identity, which I am not normally conscious of, is a powerful factor tilting the power ratio in the group towards
me. For example, I am a member of the Institute of Group Analysis and a
registered therapist with the UK Council of Therapists. I am also a member
of the teaching staff of the University of Hertfordshire and a member of
editorial boards of professional journals. As Elias insisted, these powerful
'we' identities are integral aspects of my own 'I' identity and these inextricably interwoven aspects of identity unconsciously pattern the way I interact
in the group. Contrast this with the 'we' and 'I' identities of most of those
who join therapy groups as patients. They are almost always experiencing
relational difficulties for one reason or another. With great frequency they
are isolated and cut off from others, and that often means that they are not
in regular employment. With great frequency, they are experiencing frag-
mented, persecutory and other difficult family dynamics. In other words,
their 'we' identities are markedly weak and problematic. It follows that
their 'I' identities will reflect this in a lack of self-esteem, depression, and so
on. This difference between therapist and patients in the iteration of
identity patterns in interaction is importantly reflected in the power relations between them.

Of course, all of the members of the group have some kind of 'we'
identity no matter how weak or problematic and the further weakening or
loss of these identities can itself be a trauma. For example, one group
member repeatedly held that his panic attacks and depression had started
some years before when a major reorganization in the company he had
worked for all his life had led to his redundancy. Afterwards he could not
bear to pass the offices of the company or see its logo on passing vans.
Thinking in psychoanalytic terms, I saw this as simply the reactivation of
some deeper and earlier traumas. He insisted for a very long time, however,
that his life before this had been very happy and that there were no major
problems in his childhood. Of course I thought this was a defensive reaction
and therefore kept probing for earlier traumas. Indeed, it did eventually
emerge that his previous life had not been nearly as trouble free as he had at
first indicated.

However, I now realize that I was not taking seriously enough the
trauma of the organizational change and the loss of his 'we' identity.
Another member of this group kept returning to the trauma of her first
marriage, which she had ended. Again, taking a psychoanalytic perspective,
I took this to be a secondary manifestation of a much earlier trauma. She
too resisted this notion and I have now come to think that again I was not
taking her experience of the first marriage seriously enough in its own right.
She often explained her repeated thinking about this first marriage as a lost
opportunity. This man had been of a higher class than she and had been a
'good catch.' Now, years later, she still seemed to be deeply regretting what
she had let go of, even though she knew she could not have been happy

with him. One can take her view more seriously and make more sense of her experience if one thinks in terms of lost 'we' identity. Her 'we' identity could have provided her with a greater feeling of self esteem, or so she now seemed to be thinking. Another member often talked about how much his responses to life had been formed in his years in the police force, where he never felt he fitted. Now he was trying to establish a 'we' identity by joining a club of fiction writers.

From a complex responsive processes perspective, therefore, the therapist pays a great delay more attention to the importance of the various groups people belong to, or have lost, in terms of understanding their 'we' identities.

Thinking in this way about the therapy group as social processes of inclusion and exclusion, reflecting wider 'we' and 'I' identities, immediately points to an important aspect of the healing potential of the group experience. In joining the group and becoming a regular member of it, patients acquire a 'we' identity, perhaps one of the very few such identities available to them at that point in their lives. Members of groups talk about how important the group is to them. They ask for group breaks to be shorter and comment on how lucky they feel to have the group. From a psychoanalytic perspective, these statements might be understood in terms of the 'group-as-a-whole' as collective unconscious fantasies, such as experiencing the group as the 'good mother' or the 'mother's womb.' Or, these statements might be interpreted as regressive dependency, or idealization of the group, or transferential attempts by members to persuade the therapist not to abandon them. From a complex responsive processes perspective, however, one would not think in this way because all of these formulations are in terms of something outside of the direct experience of interaction in the group in the living present and they are regressive rather than prospective. They are formulations basically relying on the notion of mind as internal world.

Instead, from a complex responsive processes perspective, I understand people in the group to be talking about the importance of their 'we' identity of which they are not all that conscious. When I ask members what it is about the group that is so important to them, why they feel lucky to be a member, they talk about the importance of the other members to them and the good fortune of having understanding others to whom they can talk. In my role as therapist, I realize that my attitude towards other members can either foster or hinder the development of a powerful 'we' identity. I think that this is more than the therapeutic factor of cohesion, which Foulkes emphasized. Although such cohesion is important, the formation of 'we' identity is much more than cohesion because 'we' identity is so closely part of individual 'I' identities. The purpose of the therapy is, of course, to enable the transformation of 'I' identities, which are causing the problems that bring people to the therapy group, and the transformation of 'we' identities simply through belonging to the group is a direct and powerful therapeutic factor. Foulkes certainly stressed this in regarding the experience of belonging as fundamental to group analytic therapy.

Power figurations in the group

Continuing with the theme of power differentials in the group, I now want to consider how my attitude as a therapist enhances or diminishes power differentials.

While other members engage freely in conversations about their lives outside the room in which the group meets and their feelings while they are interacting in the group, I do not talk about my life outside the group at all and I only sparingly articulate my feelings during the group meeting. However, direct bodily communication means that people, nevertheless, intuit a great deal about what I am feeling, as I intuit what they are feeling. In taking a much less disclosing stance, I am creating yet another difference between me and other members and in doing so, I am undoubtedly widening the power differential between us even further. Foulkes insisted, and I agree, that the evolution of the group should be towards a diminution in the power differential, so, why do I adopt the non-disclosing stance?

I think there are advantages in non-disclosure that outweigh any impact on power differentials. A great many of the people who join therapy groups have had very little experience in childhood, and often later on, of being listened to, understood and validated. Many have had experiences of parents and others whose needs came first, with long-lasting consequences for how they iterate their past in the present. What they are iterating is experience in which the more powerful are the ones who are to receive the most attention for it is their experience that has the most validity. One might understand this as particular patterns of 'we' and 'I' identities that the group experience offers the potential for transforming. That potential for transformation, I think, is greater if the unconscious connection between being more powerful and receiving more attention and validation is broken. This potential is enhanced, I think, when I do not take up group time with my needs but make it clear that I am there to attend to the needs of other members.

This reason for the stance I take is quite different to those reasons based on the belief that the therapist is a screen for, or container of, projections and transferences, available to be emotionally and unconsciously used by members of the group. That kind of reasoning is based on the assumption of internal worlds and sender–receiver models of communication, which the perspective of complex responsive processes avoids. A similar point applies to the psychoanalytic notion of therapist abstinence or neutrality, according to which the therapist should not disclose his or her own opinion or feelings. Such feelings are thought of as countertransference and are to be used by the therapist as the basis of understanding the unconscious experience of the patient. The abstinence or neutrality relates to that aspect of the therapist's countertransference that relates to his or her own experience rather than to the response aroused by the transference of the patient. The former must not be disclosed because it does not belong to the therapeutic relationship – Bion talked about the therapist leaving behind memory and desire. The latter part of the countertransference is the basis of interpretations of the patient's unconscious life. From the perspective of complex responsive processes, the therapist is inevitably a participant and cannot leave behind memory or desire and nor should he or she try to do so because that would mean severing genuine participation. Instead, the therapist participates and recognizes his or her participation as inevitably involving both memory and desire. Indeed, how the therapist feels is an important part of the genuine interaction with patients and it may well be both appropriate and very helpful for the therapist to disclose the feelings evoked by what the patients are talking about. So, while I feel that I should not take up the group's time talking about my life, I do not feel at all restricted from expressing opinions or reporting on how I feel if it seems appropriate and in this I am no different from the way I am in any other group.

The particular power figuration of therapist and patient has another aspect that I would like to comment upon. Members of the group perceive the therapist to be in control and to some extent this is true but group members tend to greatly exaggerate such control. For example at a recent group session, a very heated exchange occurred between two members who became very angry and aggressive toward each other. A new member commented that it was a good thing that my co-therapist and I were in control because otherwise real violence could break out. There was some reality to this because we did intervene and suggest that we all pause and try to make sense of what was going on. The exaggerated nature of this collective fantasy of the therapist being in control is reflected in the belief some patients firmly hold that as therapist I do know what they should do in order to feel better but I am waiting for them to discover it themselves. From a psychoanalytic viewpoint, I might be tempted to think about patterns such as this in terms of dependency. One might think in terms of transference in which the therapist is being treated as a parent and the patient has regressed to early states. From a complex responsive processes perspective, I am dubious about such formulations, based as they are on notions of representations of object relations in the patient's internal world. Instead, I think about the exaggerated belief in my ability to control and heal as understandable aspects of real adult relationships in the living present that are evoked by the power relations set up between us and the differing 'we' identities this reflects and generates. In this way I avoid infantilizing patients and I avoid thinking about them as regressing to primitive states because such thoughts inevitably exacerbate the already large power differential between us.

I find the notion of 'we' and 'I' identities useful in thinking about the meaning of the agreement I form with members of the group to do with their not socializing outside the group and the agreement that they will leave messages when they are not able to attend sessions. Clearly this is another way in which I emphasize the unequal power ratio in the group. In one group, a member would periodically become angry about this rule. He wanted to be able to assist others when they were having a bad time and call on others when he was having a bad time. One way of understanding this may be that the 'we' identity was important to sustain even when the group was not meeting. His anger may have had something to do with the shame triggered by being seen to have broken the rules and finding that he had to openly discuss this.

There are, of course many other aspects that have to do with the relative power differential between therapist and other group members. The therapist's technique in relation to waiting in silence versus actively participating has power implications. The therapist's silence can easily be felt to be persecutory or as a demonstration of superior power, which has the effect of widening the power ratio in the group. From a psychoanalytic perspective, this might be justified as not blocking the free floating conversation of the group and the associations of its members. The silence might also be interpreted as a defense against doing the work of therapy on the part of members. From the complex responsive processes perspective, however, such intrapsychic notions have no place and silence is understood in terms of its power implications. On this basis, as therapist, I rarely sit in silence in a group. On the contrary, the understanding of myself as a full participant in the group's conversational life means that I am prepared not only to say a lot but to compete with group members, on some occasions, for turns.

The notion of participating fully also makes it feel natural, I think, to adopt an educative, didactic role from time to time. For example, when the challenge comes around the no-socializing rule, it seems important to explain, even in a rather didactic but not patronizing way, just why it feels important to me to sustain that arrangement. The same point applies to other challenges to the direction a group discussion might be taking. For example, in one session, my co-therapist and I were encouraging the group to explore, in some detail, why a particular member had intentionally not left messages about his absence. Another member felt that we were wasting the group's time and ought to be attending to the needs of other members who had been having a difficult time. Instead of interpreting this as a challenge to the group or to our authority, I adopted a didactic approach and tried to explain why we were exploring the matter of not leaving messages and how this might actually have some connection with the distress of the member we were supposedly ignoring. In one way, taking this didactic role enhances the power ratio in my direction, but in another way it does the reverse because I am not treating members as if they were children or very fragile.

Unconscious processes

The immediate focus of my attention as therapist is on the narrative patterning of our interaction in the group, in which we are reconstructing past experiences in this and other groups at the same time as perpetually constructing our future together in this group and outside it. I have given an example of what I mean by this in the group discussed above. What I am doing is continuing to explore this narrative patterning, rather than simply taking it at its face value. I am encouraging the exploration of the unconscious aspects of the communicative interacting and power relating between us.

In this I am being group-analytic in the sense that I am attending to differences and trying to tease out the detail of interactions for further and even more detailed exploration and discussion, all as a way of understanding the more widespread patterns of communicative interaction. This is the opposite of holism. I am not trying to understand some whole – the group-as-a-whole, the matrix, and so on. I am also not trying to synthesize the experience of the group. I am participating in a group-analytic manner, therefore, because my thinking takes the form of analyzing, of teasing out difference, instead of thinking holistically or in terms of synthesizing. Instead of wholes, there is widespread patterning, which is itself a form of synthesizing or integrating, but this is what is emerging in the interactions in the group. It is not anything I am doing. I am paying attention to the emergent themes across the group and to how each person is resonating to them, in the way described in the group sessions reported earlier in this chapter. I am avoiding thinking of the group in terms of wholes or of myself as synthesizing because they are notions that presuppose something, a system or an individual, outside the direct experience of interaction.

This attitude of focusing on differences enhances the possibilities of the amplification of difference and so the potential for the transformation of identity, which is the essential purpose of the therapy. I understand change to be change in 'I' identities and 'we' identities at the same time and this amounts to shifts in the narrative patterning of silent conversation and private role-play and shifts in the narrative-like patterning of interaction in the group. My role is to follow and contribute to the emerging pattern, pointing to what I am making of our 'habitus,' that is, the unconscious aspects of our being together. I am not trying to interpret intrapsychic fantasies, such as Oedipal complexes, which, as contents of internal worlds, have no place in the complex responsive processes way of thinking.

My attention is also directed in another way that is different to that which the psychoanalytic perspective encourages. In psychoanalysis the patterning of the individual world is understood to have been formed in early childhood and the therapist's attention is focused on the past. The effect of the past on the unconscious mental patterning of the patient must be uncovered to remove distorted thinking and relating. However, from a complex responsive processes point of view, my attention is focused prospectively on the future that is now emerging in the group as interaction between people iterates their pasts in expectation of their futures, all in the living present. The focus is then on how narrative themes are being iterated as continuity and potential transformation.

As described in Chapter 7, I understand unconscious processes of communicative interaction and power relating, in three ways:

- as direct bodily communication in the medium of feelings. Here as therapist I am noticing how I feel and wondering what these feelings reflect in terms of themes organizing our experience of being together. Such speculations will be influencing what I am saying and sometimes I will directly disclose what I am feeling;
- as themes patterning communicative action and power relating that are unarticulated because they are unformulated or unvalidated in the past experience of individual members of the group. Through asking questions about why members were doing what they were doing in their narratives and about why they are doing what they are doing now in the group, I and other members of the group are participating in the emergence of many articulations of patterns of relating that have not been articulated before. We are validating what has previously been unvalidated;
- as themes patterning our experience that seem to be automatic or habitual, either because they have been repeated so many times before that they have become skilful performances, or because they are repeated as ways of avoiding dangerous or traumatic articulations. Here again my responses and questions, along with those of other members, are a form of participation in the emergence of many articulations.

Taking the first of these unconscious forms of communication, Damasio (1999) provides a striking example. David is a patient who has brain damage to the hippocampus and the amygdala. As a consequence, he cannot learn any new facts, including recognizing any new person, and he cannot remember anything about a new person. However, he is conscious and he may know briefly what emotion he is experiencing, for example, happiness when watching a pleasant scene. Despite his inability to learn in any conscious, knowing sense, he showed consistent preferences for some people while avoiding others. In an experiment, he was exposed repeatedly, in varying circumstances, to 'a good guy,' 'a neutral guy' and a 'bad guy' (who was also a very attractive woman). After this he was shown four photographs and asked to select a friend. When the good guy was shown he selected this photograph 80 per cent of the time, while the neutral guy was selected 25 per cent of the time (making this a purely chance choice). The bad guy, however, was almost never chosen. David could not remember any of them and could not explain why he did or did not choose them. He manifested an unconscious preference for the good guy. Damasio suggests that he did so because the photos induced in him repetitions of emotions of previously experienced emotions. David's body/brain could generate actions/make choices on the basis of emotions of which he was not conscious. The link between emotions and reasonable ordinary, everyday choices in conditions of ambiguity and uncertainty is, therefore, of great importance. The explanation suggests that emotions that are unconscious may play a role in reasonable or appropriate behavior. This is probably what we mean by intuition.

This is a particularly persuasive example, I think, and even though it relates to someone with brain damage, it does point to an unconscious mode of communication that is always present in human interaction, including therapy groups. When a therapist 'works with unconscious process,' one could understand this to mean that the therapist is sensitized to, and pays particular attention to, unconscious emotional communication of this kind, by paying particular attention to his or her own bodily feelings. For example, during one group session, one woman was in the middle of a tearful disclosure of some painful aspect of her experience when we were interrupted by someone entering the room to look for something. The incident was over very quickly but I immediately felt that I was going to vomit. I was on the verge of leaving the room but managed to stay and think about why I would suddenly feel like this. I connected this to the woman who had been interrupted and asked how she was feeling. She talked about having to push the emotion down into her stomach. I suggest that this may be an example of the kind of unconscious process involved in direct bodily communication.

When it comes to themes that either have not been articulated for some reason, or have been but have since become automatic for some reason, the therapist's role is to pay attention to a number of closely interlinked aspects of the processes of communication between members of the group. These aspects have to do with the vicissitudes of attachment and separation reflected in processes of inclusion–exclusion, 'we' and 'I' identities shame/ guilt, anxiety/panic, as well as various forms of aggression and reparation. These are all aspects of processes of relating and as such they are simultaneously social and individual processes. From a complex responsive processes perspective, the therapist thinks about what is going on in the group in terms of these social processes and not in terms if intrapsychic mechanisms or sender–receiver models of communication. One is trying to understand what is going on not in terms of internal fantasies but in terms of relational, communicative processes. I illustrate this in the following clinical experience.

Example

Some four years after this group's first meeting, one member, Paul, who has been in the group for some two years announces, at the start of a session, that while he does not want to leave the group he has decided that he needs a period of absence. He has recently ended his marriage and moved to another town, which means that he has to make a rather long journey each week to attend the group. This is expensive and he is finding it disruptive. He has decided that he needs a period of time when he can just stay in his new home, settle down and begin to build a new life. Tom immediately supports this decision and Greg thinks it is perfectly understandable. The other three members of the group, all women, say nothing.

My co-therapist and I then question Paul, inviting him and other members to explore his reasons for this decision, and how he and the others feel about it. He insists that there is nothing at all complicated about his decision – he simply needs time on his own to settle down. However, we therapists persist in exploring his thinking about this decision to absent himself from the group and point to how he has just presented the group with a fait accompli, making any kind of negotiation impossible and, indeed, suggesting that there is no point in any further discussion about the matter. I understand what we are trying to do as follows. Through our questioning we are participating in, and inviting other group members to participate in, attempts to articulate themes that are unconsciously patterning our present interaction, namely his announcement, the immediate, unreflective support of the other two men in the group, and the silence of the three women members. What we are trying to explore is 'habitus' in the group – themes that may never have been formulated, themes that have never been validated, themes that have become automatic and taken for granted, perhaps because articulating them may repeat some kind of trauma such as rejection, a form of separation. In other words, we are seeking to tease apart, to analyze, differences in articulating unconscious processes patterning our experience of being together. These may cast some light on automatic patterning in the experience of individual members of the group at the same time as those processes are patterning our collective experience. This is a way of thinking that does not rely on intrapsychic mechanisms or fantasies – we are focusing on thematic patterning in the group that is simultaneously individual and social, conscious and unconscious.

As the exploration continues, two of the women disclose that they are rather disappointed that Paul will not be coming because they will miss him, but nevertheless it is acceptable for him to take a holiday from the group. My co-therapist asks Paul if he had thought that he might be missed in this way and he expresses his surprise – it had not occurred to him that others would be affected. By this time Tom and Greg are becoming visibly irritated and ask why all this fuss is being made. It is all perfectly clear and logical and Paul has a right to a break from the group if he wants to, especially since he has provided very sensible reasons for doing so. I then ask why they are becoming annoyed and why they think that other members' feelings about Paul's absence are not important. Greg replies that we are wasting time when we should be listening to how people have been getting on in the past week. Here again, I am asking questions as an invitation to explore the unconscious themes patterning our discussion of the importance of Paul's announcement and our desire to move on to another topic.

At this point, Lisa says that she is finding Paul's behavior arrogant. She has accused him of arrogance on one occasion before, after he had talked about how painful he finds it, and always has found it, when his mother accuses him of being arrogant. She, then, is saying something that she presumably knows is hurtful to Paul. The exploration now turns to her action and it becomes clear that she is very angry about Paul's decision and the matter of fact, closed way in which he has announced it. What begins to be articulated as themes unconsciously organizing our experience together is something to do with presenting a fait acompli in order to avoid facing the fact that others may feel affection for one and that therefore one's actions might hurt others. Lisa begins to articulate a theme around feeling angry with Paul because she has become fond of him, respects him and relies upon him to support her in the group – and now he is leaving for a while, which she understands as preliminary to his leaving the group altogether. By this time Tom and Greg are even more annoyed at what they regard as a waste of time, when we should be attending to Kate who is very depressed.

As co-therapists, we were as active as any other group member during this session. We were persistently questioning everyone about their responses and their feelings about those responses. As I have already said, we were doing this in order to assist in the articulation of emergent themes unconsciously organizing our experience of being together. We were not understanding the group in terms of individual intrapsychic fantasies, intrapsychic defensive mechanisms or individual contributions to the group-as-a-whole. We were not thinking in terms of a matrix that exists outside our direct experience of interacting with each other.

At the next session, Paul is absent because he is on a four-week leave of absence. Tom is also absent without leaving any message. Lisa starts the session by telling us how upset she was after the last session, so much so that she had not been able to return to work. She had been upset all weekend and did not attend work on Monday either because of this. What had been going on? She spent the entire time feeling angry and upset with Paul because she felt he was about to leave the group but these feelings alternated with fantasies of a romance with him, despite the fact that he was considerably older than her. She had been greatly tempted to go to his new town over the weekend and see if she could bump into him. Then she felt stupid about the whole thing, but also felt it was also important to tell the group about it. Group members find this story very exciting and began to question her about her motives and feelings and my co-therapist and I join in this questioning. I was mindful of her childhood experience. Her parents' marriage had ended when she was twelve and her father had moved away. Her mother had blocked the attempts of the father to see her and a key theme in her life had become the anger and distress at feeling abandoned by her father. She seemed to keep reproducing this anger in her relationships with men, whom she always tested to see if they would leave her. Her life could be understood very much in terms of the vicissitudes of attachment and separation. She is surprised by my drawing attention to the link between her experience of her father and the way she now feels about Paul. Here I am trying to understand Lisa in terms of her interaction in the local situation of the group in the living present as simultaneously social and individual themes are unconsciously iterated. I am not trying to understand her in terms of Oedipal complexes for reasons which should become clear in Part II.

Tom misses the following session as well and then appears again at the next one. He begins the session by stating that he had not attended the two previous ones and he had intentionally not left a message because he wanted to explore how well he was. He wanted to test whether he could now get along without the group as a kind of experiment to see whether he was ready to leave it. He had discovered that he was now much stronger and could stand on his own two feet because even though he had not come to the group or left a message he had not experienced any recurrence of his panic attacks. Some other group members say they are pleased that he is getting so much stronger and after a few comments of this kind it looks as if the group is about to move to another topic. I ask Tom why it had been necessary not to leave a message in order to find out if he was strong enough. He simply repeats what he said before and someone else starts talking about something else.

After a short period I raise the question of Tom not leaving a message again. This time one of the women says she had been worried about him and Greg discloses that he too had worried and had tried to phone Tom but to no avail. It then emerged that Tom usually gave Greg a lift to the group. Tom may feel a little guilty at this and then he says that actually he had been a bit annoyed during the session in which we endlessly discussed Paul's decision to have a break from the group. What then begins to be articulated is Tom's anger at what he felt had been the therapists giving Paul a hard time and wasting the precious time people had to talk about their problems. I ask if he had been angry. No, he had not been angry. But then he says that perhaps he had been angry. Kate suggests that his not leaving a message was a retaliatory attack on the group therapists for wasting precious time. At first Tom denies this and then says that it might perhaps have been the case.

Tom keeps suggesting that we are wasting time and should go on to someone else but the topic keeps returning to his absence, mainly due to my co-therapist and me. He keeps saying that he is now much stronger and feels that he could challenge the therapists and the group. For example, he says how much he disagrees with the rule about no socialization outside the group, which the therapists insist upon. Furthermore, we therapists are being inconsistent or hypocritical because although members are not supposed to socialize, we said nothing when Lisa met a former member of the group. Lisa then brought this former member into the group by reporting how she was getting on, including having a minor relapse. This was not something Tom wanted to hear. He did not want hear how this other group member was deteriorating. He wanted to hold on to the memory of the healthy happy person who had left the group 'cured.'

An argument then ensues about the rules and at this point I take up a rather didactic role to try to explain, yet again, why we have the agreement not to socialize while people are in the group and that the matter of socializing once they have left had nothing to do with the agreement.

At this point, Lisa becomes very angry. She feels that Tom is telling her that she is doing the wrong thing and this is because he is jealous that the former member has not chosen to contact him. At this point, I intervene to suggest that we pause for a bit and think about what is going in. Eventually we begin to understand something of why Tom has become so angry. It seems to have become part of his automatic pattern to rely on fantasies of everything being happy. The former member in the group had left in a healthy state and it was important for Tom to believe that this had continued, after having had a close relationship with her. He seemed to be dealing with losing her by sustaining a fantasy that she was perfectly well. I linked this to the persistent fantasy he expressed about having had a perfectly happy childhood and a perfectly happy marriage until his breakdown some ten years earlier. Again his way of dealing with loss and separation seems to have been attachment to a fantasy of perfection. The fantasies of this kind are so important to him that he ends up being hurtful to others even while he is constantly trying to help them. This is an explanation of how the group works to articulate unconscious themes patterning the experience of being together. These themes are reconstructions of the past in articulation of the future, all in the present. I am not thinking of them in terms of intrapsychic mechanisms but in terms of simultaneously individual and social processes.

What I am describing in this example is a therapist's stance that is highly participative. We were participating in processes of emergent articulation of narrative themes patterning our experience of being together. I am not trying to analyze individual psyches, understood as internal worlds of representation, but I am taking an analytical attitude to the simultaneously social and individual themes patterning experience as reconstructions of the past and anticipations of the future in the present. From the complex responsive processes perspective this activity is therapeutic because it is processes of enriching conversation. The social interaction of conversation becomes more complex than many have experienced before and in the process the silent conversations of people with themselves is also enriched and made more complex. Mental distress is understood as rigid, repetitive, impoverished patterns of relating to oneself, unconsciously blocking richer articulations. The group process is obviously a social process and in enriching communicative interaction between people, it has the potential to enrich and complexify the interaction of an individual with him or herself. The therapist's technique is essentially one of trying to amplify small differences without knowing where they will lead because it is in such amplification that novel relational patterns potentially emerge.

The link to group-analytic practice

The perspective of complex responsive processes I have been illustrating above focuses attention on individual/social processes of relating. This is central to Foulkes' practice of group analysis. He emphasized the importance of socialization, mirroring and resonance, which are all relational processes rather than intrapsychic ones (see Chapter 15). As soon as one understands the process of change in a group to be one of self-organizing shifts in the themes patterning individual/social experience in which small differences may be amplified, then the wisdom of Foulkes' approach becomes apparent. He saw the therapy group functioning therapeutically when the discussion was free floating. This means that the therapist must avoid setting any agenda but rather follow the themes that emerge spontaneously in the group. However, Foulkes stressed the participative nature of the therapist's activity, meaning that the therapist is also a member of the group. In avoiding setting an agenda and following the emergent themes, therefore, the therapist is not simply passively following. As I have described above, in picking up an emerging theme the therapist is greatly elaborating it and so the emerging process produces patterns that are different to what they would have been if the therapist had been less active. The therapist is actively co-creating with others what emerges. The therapist's role is to be attentive and appropriately supportive, but Foulkes also stressed how the therapist's own personality influenced the group process.

Foulkes downplayed the activity of interpreting. This fits well with the complex responsive processes perspective in which the action of the group is not thought of as regressive but prospective. In other words, the therapist avoids thinking in archaeological terms about recovering lost memories, digging back into what actually happened in the past and striving to make the unconscious material conscious. From the perspective I am suggesting, narratives about early childhood are reconstructions in the present that are always slightly different. They may help to make sense of current patterns of interaction. Also later experiences may be just as important in accounting for how people may have become stuck in unrewarding patterns of behavior. The departure from Foulkes comes in avoiding thinking of the group-as-a-whole, that is in terms of some system or whole that is outside the direct experience of interaction. Also there is an avoidance of thinking in terms of primitive, infantile sexuality, Oedipus complex and so on, which Foulkes saw no need to abandon. One is not concerned with innate fantasies but how people are currently elaborating what is going on in a fantasy manner in the present and so distorting communication. Furthermore, fantasy is recognized as being close to imagination and, therefore, that there is a positive aspect to fantasy. As therapist, I am not trying to uncover the past or interpret intrapsychic defenses. I do not think in terms of regression or the primitive but, rather, I am concerned with patterns of relating in the living present and how this may change reconstructions of the past.

As therapist, I also do not think about myself as containing anxiety because this is a spatial notion and a reification of the relational process of anxiety. Moving away from spatial notions of containing also means moving away from the notion of boundaries. I think the idea of a boundary is not at all helpful when thinking about human interactions and human minds. It immediately imports spatial notions of inside and outside. Instead, I am trying to understand what is happening in the group in terms of enabling constraints that arise in our interactions in the group in the living present. In other words, instead of thinking about systems and their boundaries I am thinking about processes of power relations. Relationships between us and others in the group give rise to constraints on what it is appropriate for any of us to do. Those constraints may refer to rules but they are always in negotiation. It is also these constraints that enable us to continue relating. Constraints inevitably configure power relations and those power relations are unconsciously sustained by ideology. The ideology has the purpose of sustaining or shifting power relations.

Part II

Internal worlds and social systems
Defining the difference between the perspective of complex responsive processes and psychoanalysis

Part I of this book presented a complex responsive processes perspective on human activity with particular reference to the therapy group. That perspective is one which focuses on human communicative interaction and power relating understood as processes of interweaving human motives, intentions, plans and actions. The distinctive feature of this complex responsive processes perspective is that individual mind and group/social are understood as the same process, the former being the private and silent action of a body directed toward itself, while the latter is the public and vocal actions directed by bodies to each other. Since this is an action theory, it makes no use of the spatial metaphors of mind inside a person and social outside. Instead, persons are understood as social selves and group/society as the interaction of such individuals. Healthy human interaction is characterized by spontaneity, or complexity, that is, what Foulkes called 'free floating communication.' Disturbed human interaction is that which has largely lost this spontaneity, or complexity, and has collapsed into the simplicity of either repetitive stability (continuity with little or no transformation) or random instability.

A key source upon which the complex responsive process perspective draws is the thought of Elias. In an interview towards the end of his life, reported in *Group Analysis*, Elias had this to say of Freud:

> I think his theory of society is quite wrong.
>
> (Brown, 1997, p523)

In his *Reflections on a Life* (1994), Elias also made the following comments:

> Many scholars, not least Freud himself, seem inclined to see in opposites of this kind [individual and society] an unalterable fact of human existence, one of the tragic fundamentals of life with which one has to come to terms . . .
>
> (Elias, 1994, p143)

Apparently, Elias was working on an explanation of remarks of this kind but he died before completing it. The chapters in the following part of this book present my own explanation of why I agree with Elias' remarks.

The chapters in Part II, therefore, explore the differences between the perspective of social selves developed in Part I and psychoanalytic theorizing about the individual and the group/social. I will be arguing that a central concept running through psychoanalytic thinking from Freud to present times is the primacy it accords to the individual psyche understood as an internal world. However, as soon as one posits the individual mind as 'inside,' it follows that group, or social, reality must be 'outside.' This spatial distinction between inner and outer is, with very few exceptions, a defining characteristic of psychoanalytic thinking, a matter to be discussed in Chapters 9, 11 and 12. This distinction makes it easy to develop psychoanalytic theory in terms of systems where there is an internal psychic system and external social systems. This whole question of systems thinking will be discussed in Chapter 13. Another conceptual consequence flows immediately from this conception of an internal world and an external social system. Communication between people, between separate internal worlds, takes the form of sending contents from one to be received by the other. In this sender–receiver model, people send each other signals conveying information/meaning and in some psychoanalytic theories they are actually thought to put parts of their mental contents into each other. Through these processes of communication, individuals create the social system, which then imposes on, structures or shapes, the internal worlds of individuals. Psychoanalytic thought is also built on a particular view of evolution, which is easily extended into evolutionary psychology. Chapter 14 will explore this and will point to the difference from the view of evolution in the complex responsive processes perspective in Chapter 2.

Although psychoanalysis has always accorded primacy to the individual, it does not set up a dichotomy between the individual and the social. Instead, I will argue that it understands them as a dualism or a duality that eliminates the paradox of contradictions existing at the same time. This is completely different to the complex responsive processes perspective outlined in Part I where the relationship between individual and social is understood in terms of Hegelian dialectic or paradox. In other words, my argument is that the theories of psychoanalysis and complex responsive processes are substantially different and are derived from very different philosophical traditions. Chapter 10 will review these traditions and provide my reasons for this assertion. Chapter 9 will review Freud's thought on the relationship between the individual and the social and how it has been developed by later thinkers.

Before turning to Chapter 9, however, I think it is important to clarify the differences between a number of concepts that have to do with opposites because concepts of opposites will be used throughout Part II to make distinctions between different ways of thinking. Opposition can be expressed in a number of ways:

- Dichotomy. This is a sharply defined division into two, a binary classification.
- Dilemma. This is closely related to dichotomy in that it is an argument forcing a choice between two alternatives, both of which are unfavorable.

Here opposition or contradiction is dealt with as 'either . . . or' thinking; one must make a choice and so eliminate the opposition. This accords with Aristotelian logic where any contradiction is a sign of faulty thinking.

Now consider some rather different concepts to do with difference and opposition:

- Antimony. This is a contradiction in law or between two laws, where one statement denies the other.
- Paradox. This is two or more self-contradictory statements, or statements that conflict with pre-conceived notions of what is reasonable or possible.

One might distinguish between two distinct ways of thinking about antimonies and paradoxes:

- First there is the 'both . . . and' thinking of a dualism, which is the way that Kant dealt with paradox (Griffin, 2001). In a dualism, one holds first one pole of the contradiction and then the other in a sequence, or one allocates one pole to one space and the other to another space. In this way the dualism resolves or eliminates any contradiction or paradox. In a dualism, the two poles are kept apart or if they are brought together their essentially contradictory meanings remain the same. When one thinks in terms of a duality one proceeds as in a dualism but then makes a conceptual connection between the two poles so that each affects the other while they remain separate. An example of dualism/duality is the Kantian dialectic in which a thesis is opposed by an antithesis and this is followed by a synthesis that contains both thesis and antithesis. The principles of Aristotelian logic are preserved in that any contradiction is eliminated by locating the opposites in different time periods or spaces and then alternating between them or simply placing them together without changing their meaning.
- Second, however, there is thinking in terms of 'both . . . and at the same time,' which retains paradox. This is the essence of Hegelian dialectical thinking, which represents a logic completely different to that of Aristotle and should not be confused with the Kantian dialectic.

Hegel's dialectic must also be distinguished from another use of the word where it refers to rhetoric, or a didactic method of questioning, or simply a dialogic engagement between different ideas. Hegelian dialectic is different to this in that it is not a rhetorical method, or even simply a method of logic. It is, rather, a process of social knowing, a process of forming social selves, and a process of the movement of thought.

The distinctions outlined above will all be explored more fully in Chapter 10 but they will also be useful in Chapter 9, which looks at the difference between Freud (and later psychoanalytic thinking on the group/social) and the complex responsive processes approach suggested in Part I.

Freud on the individual and the group

This chapter reviews Freud's thinking about the individual and the group for which purpose I will draw on those of his papers that deal explicitly with the group/social in some way. These are *'Civilized' Sexual Morality and Modern Nervous Illness* (1908), *Totem and Taboo* (1913), *Group Psychology and the Analysis of the Ego* (1921), *The Future of an Illusion* (1927), and *Civilization and its Discontents* (1930). For Freud, the individual mind or psyche is an 'internal world' consisting of innate drives, developmentally shaped through interaction with an external world of reality. He, therefore, draws a distinction between individual psychology, the inside, and group psychology, the outside, stating that the oldest is group psychology:

> The contrast between individual psychology and social or group psychology, which at first glance may seem to be full of significance, loses a great deal of its sharpness when it is examined more closely. It is true that individual psychology is concerned with the individual man and explores the paths by which he seeks to find satisfaction of his instinctual impulses; but only rarely and under exceptional circumstances is individual psychology in a position to disregard the relations of this individual to others. In the individual's mental life someone else is invariably involved, as a model, as an object, as a helper, as an opponent; and so from the very first individual psychology, in this extended but entirely justifiable sense of the words, is at the same time social psychology as well.
>
> (Freud, 1921, p95)

This quote is often taken as evidence that Freud united the individual and the group, or the social. He, in common with most great thinkers, certainly did not think of the individual and the social as a dichotomy. It was never a matter of choosing one and ignoring the other. However, he did bring the individual and the social together in a particular way that is completely different to that of Mead and Elias, upon whose thinking the perspective of complex responsive processes is built. It is also true that the main focus of Freud's attention was on the intrapsychic and in this sense he accorded primacy, if not priority, to the individual. In the above quote, Freud says that individual and social psychologies are the same in the sense that the individual's internal world consists of objects, that is, internal representations of external others. The external social world is thus represented in the individual internal world. He also thinks of the external social world, the relationships between people, as being created by individual psychic processes. The inside affects the outside and the outside affects the inside but at the centre there is *both* the individual psychic processes consisting of internal representations of the social *and* the social which is created by those psychic processes. The psyche is forming the internal representations of the social and then the psyche is forming the social, which of course acts back on the psyche so that there is nothing paradoxical in the sense of 'at the same time.' Rather, Freud's formulation is that of a dualism or a duality in which there is no sense of a paradoxical relationship between the individual and the social because the individual, in the end, is creating both of them. The social affects the individual but only through the representations that the individual psyche forms.

This is very different to Elias' notion of long-term social processes which form individual minds *at the same time* as those minds form the social processes. It is also very different from Mead's social act consisting of gesture and response in which individual mind and the social are the same process so that there is no distinction between inside and outside. The formulations of both Elias and Mead are the paradox of 'forming while being formed at the same time.' These are temporal action theories, rather than spatial ones, and do not depend on any notion of innate universals, internal worlds and representations. In contrast, Freud defines individual psychology in terms of the satisfaction of innate impulses and treats the group as if it were a supra individual created by individuals. The group is understood analogously with the individual and treated 'as if' it were an individual writ large. His theory explains 'the psychology of groups on the basis of changes in the psychology of the individual mind' (Freud, 1921, px). In this way, Freud presents a dualism or a duality of 'both . . . and' with dual agency and dual causality and thereby eliminates the paradox of 'at the same time' (Griffin, 2001).

The following sections set out the reasons for reaching the above conclusions about Freud's thinking on the relationship between the individual and the social. His thinking about the nature of human groups is based upon the myth of the primal horde and this is what he means when he says that group psychology is older than individual psychology.

The primal horde

Darwin speculated that the primitive form of human society might have been a horde, by which he meant a small group, probably ruled over by a powerful male. Freud developed this idea in *Totem and Taboo* (1913), arguing that the primal horde had left indestructible traces in human history and in the human psyche. He admitted that the primal horde was a hypothesis but argued that it brought more understanding. The primal horde 'corresponds to a state of regression to a primitive mental activity' (Freud, 1921, p155). As such it forms the basis of any subsequent human group:

> This group appears to us as a revival of the primal horde. Just as primitive man survives potentially in every individual also the primal horde may arise once more out of any random collection; in so far as men are habitually under the sway of group formation we recognize in it the survival of the primitive horde.
>
> (Freud, 1921, p155)

Here we immediately see the basis of Freud's thinking in which the group is fundamentally a regressive phenomenon likely to have adverse effects on individuals, except in special circumstances, namely, when groups are organized. People who spontaneously come together to form a group are pulled down by regressive forces. The immediate implication is that social spontaneity is very dangerous and must be curtailed by, for example, hierarchy. From the complex responsive processes perspective, however, there can be no individual without a group. Both mind and social emerge at the same time in continual interaction between human bodies. Humans cannot survive as individuals but only as social beings. It is in groups that humans accomplish the sophisticated cooperation upon which their ways of life, their very beings, depend. It is the 'regressive' that is exceptional. This is not to say that human interactions, groups, produce only the good, for while they are doing this they also produce the destructive and the bad. Spontaneous group formation is of the essence of human life and inter-action itself creates its own coherence and continuity, not necessarily reliant on external organization.

Freud clearly saw group psychology as coming first and the individual as later, a progressive development with subsequent involvement of indi-viduals in groups as a form of regression to the primitive. For him, progress produces individuals and any steps they take to form groups immediately encounter regressive forces.

> We have said that it would be possible to specify the point in the mental development of mankind at which the advance from group psychology to individual psychology was achieved by the individual members of the group.
>
> (Freud, 1921, p168)

Freud located this point in what he calls the 'scientific myth' of the father of the primal horde. This father produced all the sons who formed the first group and to them he was the creator of the world, the ideal of each of them. Although they honored the father, they also feared him and were enraged by his power to deny them access to the females. So, they banded together, killed him and cut him to pieces. None of the sons were powerful enough to succeed the father and their ensuing rivalry only ended when they formed the 'totemic community of brothers' in which they were all equal. They were united by 'totem prohibitions' that preserved the memory of the murder and atoned for it. However, this united group of brothers eventually moved to the point where one became the chief and this ended the period of female rule that had followed the murder of the father. But the old times were not quite restored because now there were many fathers limiting each other's power.

> It was then, perhaps, that some individual, in the exigency of his longing, may have moved to free himself from the group and take over the father's part. He who did this was the first epic poet; and the advance was achieved in his imagination. The poet disguised the truth with lies according to his longing. He invented the heroic myth. The hero was a man who by himself had slain the father – the father who still appeared in the myth as a totemic monster. Just as the father had been the boy's first ideal, so in the hero who aspires to the father's place, the poet now created the first ego ideal. . . . The myth, then, is the step by which the individual emerges from group psychology.
>
> (Freud, 1921, pp169–170)

In other places, however, Freud says that individual psychology is just as old as group psychology because 'from the first time there were two kinds of psychologies, that of the individual members and that of the father, chief, or leader. The members of the group were subject to ties just as we see them today, but the father of the primal horde was free' (Freud, 1921 p155). The father loved only himself and was independent and isolated. The dualistic form of thinking is again in evidence here. The father is a free autonomous individual and the members are subject to ties and so not free, just as people are today, according to Freud. From this it is an easy step to think of the group as a system, as later psychoanalysts were to do, upon which the autonomous leader imposes ties. In the next chapter I will be arguing that this represents a particular use of Kantian dualism, quite the opposite of any form of Hegelian dialectic.

Freud describes how the original father prevented his sons from satisfying their direct sexual impulses, forcing them into abstinence and into emotional ties with him and one another. He forced them into group psychology through his sexual jealousy and intolerance, which was the cause of group psychology. The sons were driven out and separated from the father, and identified with one another in homosexual object-love, which freed them to kill him. Freud says that the possibility of sexual satisfaction offered the way out of group psychology, transforming group into individual psychology. The hero emerged to take the role of the slain father and he is the one who is free, under the sway of individual psychology. Here we see a theme that mostly still characterizes psychoanalytic thinking, namely, that healthy development is a move from dependency to autonomy, in which an individual autonomously takes his or her own authority for what he or she does. This autonomy represents the rational individual, significantly freed from the body which requires others for the discharge of drives. In the next chapter I will point to the similarity between this and Kantian thought.

> Even today the members of a group stand in need of the illusion that they are equally and justly loved by their leader; but the leader himself need love no one else, he may be of a masterful nature, absolutely narcissistic, self confident and independent. We know that love puts a check on narcissism, and it would be possible to show how, by operating in this way, it became a factor of civilization.
>
> (Freud, 1921, p155)

The family is important because it is the only group in which the illusion of being equally loved by the father can have some reality and the role of love is to check the narcissism of the most powerful.

Freud, then, sets up an antagonism between group and individual psychology and regards the latter as a more civilized phenomenon, restricted it seems to heroes. What he ends up with is an explanation of groups in terms of a myth plus individual intrapsychic processes that this myth foreshadows and from which the individual frees himself as hero. The group experiences a collective version of the Oedipus complex that is then recapitulated in the development of individual mind: individual psychology, ontogeny, recapitulates group psychology, phylogeny. The notion is one of the group as an external object distinct from the individuals, taken into each of their minds. The group is treated as if it were a child, an illusion that is fundamentally regressive, as well as basically inimical to the individual. There is both the group and the individual without any sense of paradox and the explanation is based on universal, ahistorical principles that apply to all of humankind in which thousands of years of the history of social evolution play no part. This is clearly what Elias was disagreeing with in the quotes given in the introduction to Part II. The internal world that is the individual psyche consists fundamentally of representations of instincts – drives seeking discharge – and these are innate forms, the most important being the Oedipus complex which recapitulates the primal horde. Clearly this is a completely different explanation to that provided by Elias where the way that an individual experiences him or her self is constructed in social evolution, which is at the same time constructed by how people experience themselves. Freud's theory has no notion of this kind of socially constructed 'habitus.'

In some places, Freud argues against the notion of a group mind but in others he talks about a group mind, indicating how he sees the group as a distinct entity, a kind of supra individual with a mind, quite outside the individual:

> Each individual is a component part of numerous groups, he is bound by ties of identification in many directions, and he has built up his ego ideal upon the most various models. Each individual therefore has a share in numerous group minds – those of his race, of his class, of his creed, of his nationality, etc. – and he can also raise himself above them to the extent of having a scrap of independence and originality.
>
> (Freud, 1921, p161)

This notion of a whole, a system, a group mind outside individual minds has continued to characterize psychoanalytic thinking as will be explored in Chapters 12 and 15.

The clash of individual and social

Freud repeatedly emphasizes how the social arises in the individual's renunciation of his or her instincts:

> Generally speaking, our civilization is built upon the suppression of instincts. Each individual has surrendered part of his assets – some part of the sense of omnipotence or of aggression or vindictive inclinations of his personality . . . Besides the exigencies of life, no doubt it has been family feelings, derived from eroticism, that have induced the separate individuals to make this renunciation. The renunciation has been a progressive one in the course of the evolution of civilization. The single steps in it were sanctioned by religion: the piece of instinctual satisfaction which each person had renounced was offered to the deity as a sacrifice, and the communal property thus acquired was declared 'holy.'
>
> (Freud, 1908, pp38–39)

Here we immediately see how renunciation of erotic feelings is accomplished in the family. This is highly characteristic of Freudian thinking in that it moves from some prehistoric, innate universal principle established by biological evolution to repetitions in each individual's experience in his or her family. We jump from pre-historic times to an individual's family relationships as if there has been no intervening thousands of years of social evolution. Contrast this with Elias who talks about a long-term social process in which higher degrees of self-control emerged in a manner strongly linked to shame. Elias' theory of self-control is far wider than the family and it is not focused upon sexuality. There is no hint of universalism and little reliance on the innate as he talks about a gradual social process in which individuals learn to exercise self-control reinforced by the social process of shame.

Freud also repeatedly stresses that the group is a threat to individuality:

> Civilized society, which demands good conduct and does not trouble itself about the instinctual basis of this conduct, has thus won over to obedience a great many people who are not following their own nature. Encouraged by this success, society has allowed itself to be misled into tightening the moral stand to the greatest possible degree, and it has thus forced its members into a yet greater estrangement from their instinctual disposition.
>
> (Freud, 1908, p71)

Here he postulates a true nature for the individual, while reifying society and ascribing intention and agency to it. He also reifies and ascribes agency to the individual unconscious:

> What, we ask, is the attitude of our unconscious towards the problem of death? The answer must be: almost exactly the same as that of primeval man. In this respect, as in many others, the man of prehistoric times survives unchanged in our unconscious. Our unconscious, then, does not believe in its own death; it behaves as if it were immortal.
>
> (Freud, 1908, p85)

In his 1921 *Group Psychology and the Analysis of the Ego*, Freud reviews the accounts of Le Bon (1895), McDougall (1920) and Trotter (1916) on collective mental life. In summarizing Le Bon, he extracts, with approval, the following points. According to Le Bon, the 'psychological group' forces mental change in the individual who becomes possessed by a collective mind in which his particular distinctiveness vanishes. The group spreads a kind of contagion, a form of hypnosis and suggestibility leading the individual to a feeling of invincible power in which he is no longer conscious of his acts but acts as an automaton. Here, Freud does not go along with a kind of collective mind so he recasts the group process thus:

> For us it would be enough to say that in a group the individual is brought under conditions which allow him to throw off the repressions

of his unconscious instinctual impulses. The apparently new characteristics which he then displays are in fact the manifestations of his
unconscious, in which all that is evil in the human mind is contained as
a predisposition.

(Freud, 1921, p101)

Here, Freud seems to be saying that joining a group universally provokes
regression. He says that simply being a member of a group causes one to
descend several rungs in civilization and that this process can be explained
not by contagion or suggestibility but by the psychoanalytic notion of the
unconscious, which produces group phenomena similar to the mental life of
primitive people and children. Note here how the individual unconscious is
primary in the sense that it forms the group, which is talked about as if it
were a child or a primitive individual.

A group is extraordinarily credulous and open to influence, it has no
critical faculty, and the improbable does not exist for it. . . . the feelings
of a group are always very simple and very exaggerated, so that a group
knows neither doubt nor uncertainty.

(Freud, 1921, p104)

Both Le Bon and Freud admitted that the morals of a group could be
higher than those of an individual in certain circumstances and recognized
the stimulation provided by a group and its achievement of language.
However, they both also held that great achievements are only possible for
an individual working in isolation. In the 1921 paper, Freud then explains
the contradiction between regression and creative tendencies with reference
to the work of McDougall.

In *The Group Mind*, McDougall (1920) suggests that regression can be
avoided and creative processes activated through organization. He con-
trasts a crowd, which has only the rudiments of organization, with a *simple
psychological group* consisting of members who have something in common
(interest, object, emotional bias) and consequently some degree of reciprocal influence. The higher the degree of this mental homogeneity, the more
readily do individuals form psychological groups and the more striking the
manifestation of group mind. The most striking result is the intensification
of emotion in the form of the pleasurable experience of surrendering
unreservedly to merged passions. In this state, the individual loses his
power of criticism and increases the excitement of others under the compulsion to do the same and remain in harmony. Freud says:

A group impresses the individual as being an unlimited power and an
insurmountable peril. For the moment the group replaces the whole
of human society which is the wielder of authority, whose punishment

the individual fears, and for whose sake he has submitted to so many inhibitions.

(Freud, 1921, p113)

In such a group the minds of lower intelligence bring down those of higher ones. McDougall then provides five principles for the organized as distinct from the simple group: continuity of existence; a definite idea of the nature, composition, functions and capacities of the group so that individuals can develop an emotional relation to the group; interaction with other groups, perhaps taking the form of rivalry; traditions, customs, habits; specialization and differentiation of membership. These conditions, to do with the clarity of organization, remove the psychological disadvantages of groups. This distinction between an organized group and one under the sway of regression was later greatly developed by Bion. Freud proposes another description of 'organization':

The problem consists of how to procure for the group precisely the features which were characteristic of the individual and which are extinguished in him by the formation of the group. For the individual, outside the primitive group, possessed his own continuity, his self consciousness, his traditions and customs, his own particular functions and position, and he kept apart from his rivals. Owing to his entry into an 'unorganized' group he had lost his distinctiveness for a time. If we thus recognize that the aim is to equip the group with the attributes of the individual, we shall be reminded of a valuable remark of Trotter (1916), to the effect that the tendency towards the formation of groups is biologically a continuation of the multicellular character of all higher organisms.

(Freud, 1921, p115)

Here Freud makes it clear that he thinks of a group 'as if' it were an individual. It can only function in a creative way if it has the attributes of the individual because only the individual is free and effective.

Freud then goes on to explore the mental change which is experienced by the individual in a group. Instead of suggestion, he turns to the notion of libido as:

the energy, regarded as a quantitative magnitude (although not at present actually measurable), of those instincts which have to do with all that may be comprised under the word 'love.'

(Freud, 1921, p119)

The nucleus of libido consists of sexual love with sexual union as its aim. He proposes that love, emotional ties, is what constitutes the essence of the group mind. In developing his argument he draws a distinction between leaderless groups and those groups with leaders and between natural groups (the family) and artificial groups (the Church and the army). He starts with artificial, highly organized groups that have a leader. Taking the Church and the army, despite their differences, there is in both the illusion that there is a leader who loves all its members equally. Everything depends on this illusion. The leader is a kind of elder brother, a substitute father and the libidinal ties that unite members of the group with the leader, or with a leading idea, unite them with each other. The alteration in the individual joining the group is due to these two libidinal ties and if these mutual ties cease to exist, then the individuals panic and there is contagion. An increase in common danger or a reduction in libidinal ties leads to neurotic anxiety and the loss of the leader, or the birth of misgivings about him, engenders panic. The tie with the leader is the ruling factor.

Freud then turns to how different kinds of group, more or less stable, arise spontaneously. He argues that it is groups with leaders that are more primitive because they contain a sediment of aversion and hostility, a readiness for aggression and hatred that only escapes perception through repression. Group formation causes this repression to vanish because individuals behave as though they are uniform, a feeling that is produced by libidinal ties with others. In addition to this, there is the process of identification. In the early stages of the Oedipus complex, a boy identifies with his father, taking him as his ideal. A little later he develops a true object-cathexis with his mother. He now has 'a straightforward sexual object-cathexis towards his mother and an identification with his father' (Freud, 1921, p134). They coexist for a while but because of the 'inexorable advance toward the unification of mental life' they come together in the 'normal Oedipus complex.' The boy's identification takes on a hostile coloring because the father stands in his way but then the Oedipus complex is resolved by introjecting the father as ego ideal and identifying with it. The ego ideal, later called the superego, is a critical agency, or conscience, as a self-observing censor and chief influence on repression. It gradually gathers up the influences of environmental demands. Thus identification is the original form of emotional tie and it may arise again in relation to another person with similar qualities to the father. The emotional ties in a group are essentially of this identification kind. Primary groups are

> . . . those that have a leader and have not been able by means of too much 'organization' to acquire secondarily the characteristics of the individual. . . . *A primary group of this kind is a number of individuals who have put one and the same object in the place of their ego ideal and have consequently identified themselves with one another in their ego.*
>
> (Freud, 1921, p147)

Freud therefore describes the process of primary group formation as a primitive process, defined in terms of intrapsychic action, which is distinguished from a secondary group that has organization in the sense of having the characteristics of a mature independent individual. The implication seems to be that an organized group is a collection of mature independent individuals who do not rely on their leader in a primitive manner but take their own authority, compared to the primary group, understood as a primitive or a child, in which people have surrendered their authority.

The civilizing process

For Freud, the social is seen as a kind of individual in that

> . . . the development of civilization is a special process, comparable to the normal maturation of the individual.
>
> (Freud, 1930, p287)

Civilization is built on the renunciation of instinct and the resulting frustration that dominates the field of social relationships. However, in addition to identification as an intrapsychic process of forming primary groups, Freud points to another important intrapsychic process that generates the social, namely, sublimation.

> Sublimation of instinct is an especially conscious feature of cultural development; it is what makes it possible for higher psychical activities, scientific, artistic or ideological, to play such an important part in social life.
>
> (Freud, 1930, p286)

Immediately one can see, that the sublimation and renunciation of instinct, intrapsychic processes, occupy in Freud's scheme the place of communication and negotiation, social processes, in that of Elias and Mead. For Freud, then, groups pull people down while individuals freed from group pressures by the achievement of maturity and autonomy repress their sexual drives, sublimating them into the greatest achievements of civilized society. On the other hand, for Elias and Mead, the achievements of humankind and its destructive and degrading manifestations are all social processes. For Elias and Mead, the social is the necessity of relating and the need to work in common, together with power relations that inevitably accompany relating. Loving and hating, creating and destroying, are all natural aspects of this process.

When Freud talks about civilization resulting from the repression of sexual and aggressive instincts through the prohibition exercised by the family on the growing child, it sounds like the same starting point as that of Elias. However, the explanation rapidly diverges. Elias sees the innate as a very generalized capacity and learning or cultural evolution as the major process in how people come to experience themselves. Freud, however, ties the civilizing process to innate individual sexuality and aggression, the restriction of this by society, and the possibility of sublimating this individual sexual energy. Elias takes the long-term cultural evolution in a specific place, Western Europe, and traces how people have come to experience themselves as self-controlled individuals due to increasing chains of interdependence and the monopolization of violence, where shame plays a very important molding role. This process is then reflected in specific families as a socialization process. Freud on the other hand jumps from genetically determined biology formed over 100,000 years ago to current family life and universalizes this, placing sexual pleasure at the centre as the motivating force and society as reflected in the family as the repressing constraint. In this way he universalizes patterns in Western European culture of the late 19th/early 20th centuries. Following Freud, one focuses attention on the process of repression of the sexual drive in early family life but following Elias one focuses on culture specific patterns in which shame plays a very important role.

Elias describes how growing interdependence and the monopolization of violence, as social processes, lead to self-control. For Freud this is the feat of the individual in the clash with society reflecting primal history and he does not look for any subsequent account in social evolution. For him it is just individuals controlling their instincts. Because civilization requires the restriction of sex and aggression man is never content with civilization.

> ... I adopt the standpoint, therefore, that the inclination to aggression is an original, self-subsisting instinctual disposition in man, . . . it constitutes the greatest impediment to civilization. . . . Civilization is a process in the service of Eros . . . collections of men are to be libidinally bound to one another . . . But man's natural aggressive instinct, . . . opposes this program of civilization . . . the evolution of civilization . . . must present the struggle between Eros and Death.
>
> (Freud, 1930, p314)

Comments on Freud's view of the individual and the group

Freud's thought represents a major revolution in explaining how we experience ourselves. In one sense, he radically decentered the subject understood as the rational autonomous individual who is free to choose goals and actions. He did this by arguing that our actions are frequently driven by unconscious motivation so that we are not as free as we think. In this he moved away from the philosophy of Kant, to be discussed in the next chapter. However, the rational autonomy of the individual remained as a more or less achievable goal so that the move away from Kant was not as great as at first appears. Freud's was a psychology that was closely linked to the experience of the body and in this he moved away from the philosophy of Descartes. However, the mind was squarely located inside a person as an internal world of representations of bodily instincts and bodily functions. In this sense, the mind and the body were not one so that the move away from Descartes is also less clear than at first appears.

Freud's thinking was revolutionary in other respects too. He established the central importance of anxiety and human responses to it, bringing into view more clearly than before the importance of fantasy and emotion, particularly as this was linked to anxiety and the defensive and repressing mechanisms used to deal with it. He developed a detailed understanding of the major impact of childhood experiences in the repetitive patterns of adult behavior, firmly linking repetition, defenses, fantasy, and anxiety to psychopathology.

Throughout his writing on the individual, the group and the relationship between them, between 1908 and 1930, Freud consistently made a number of fundamental assumptions:

- There is a natural continuity between the dynamics of the individual and of the group so that the psychology of the group can be explained in terms of the psychology of the individual. Individuals form groups through identification with the leader so that aspects of their ego ideals are projected onto the leader, attributed to him and reintrojected. In addition to this identification with the leader, individuals in a group libidinally attach themselves to each other. Group behavior then recapitulates the individual Oedipal situation, just as that individual Oedipal situation recapitulates a mythical overthrow of the primal leader and the incorporation of his ideals. Groups are therefore understood in terms of the Oedipal family model and the formation of groups is basically regressive to infantile and primitive states.
- The individual is threatened or incapacitated by the group except in so far as it can contain anxiety through forms of organization and except in so far as individuals can free themselves from its regressive pull and move to autonomy, independence and rationality.
- Understanding the group and ensuring individual capacity to function requires the resurfacing of the past, the primitive and the infantile. This frees the individual because the present is usually simply recapitulating the past. This is fundamentally different to the notion that individuals in interaction as groups are perpetually constructing their future.
- The group is external to the individual and the individual mind/psyche is an 'internal world'. That internal world is composed of ideas or

drives representing innate instincts, which are the basic motivations of behavior with the libido (sex) and aggression (death instinct) as primary. These motivations are thought of in terms of psychic energy seeking satisfaction at any cost and so encountering the prohibition of the group/society. Communal life is basically a constraint on individual satisfaction.

- The internal world is structured by this clash and so is basically conflictual. The conflict is dealt with intrapsychically in a dynamic in which 'the unconscious' is central.
- A key feature of the individual's relationship with others is that pattern of relating called the Oedipus complex. It is a universal and innate experience of infantile sexuality and its resolution is expressed in both the individual psyche and in the group.
- Groups can be understood in terms of individual psychological processes.
- Group and individual are thus thought of as a dualism or duality. Any dialectic is of the Kantian 'both . . . and' kind in which the Hegelian paradox of 'at the same time' is eliminated. This point will be explained in Chapter 10.

Freud's theory is thus essentially based on innate, universal features of primitive humans recapitulated by all their descendents to this day. This theory is substantially different to the perspective of complex responsive processes in the following ways:

- Instead of directly linking behavior to instinct, the complex responsive processes perspective understands evolution as having produced the kinds of bodies we have, which enable and constrain in particular ways. For example, an individual body cannot regulate itself but requires connection with other bodies as explained in Chapter 6. What are inherited, then, are not innate, universal patterns of behavior but physiological capacities that create the possibilities of human action. That action is then specific and unique to particular local situations and particular time periods in long-term historical processes.
- Instead of focusing on the individual and then using 'both . . . and' thinking to take account of the group, the complex responsive processes perspective thinks of individuals and groups as simultaneously forming and being formed by each other.
- There is no such thing as psychic energy in the action perspective of complex responsive processes.
- There is also no need for the notion of a mind representing and storing anything because a mind is the action of a body. This is more consistent with the views on the brain described in Chapter 6.

- The dubious notion of an 'inner world', with its inside, outside and boundaries is not required in the complex responsive process perspective.
- Innate or universal ideas of infantile sexuality and the Oedipus complex do not feature in the complex responsive processes perspective.
- Unconscious processes are not thought of in terms of an individual dynamic unconscious from the complex responsive process perspective. There is no distinction between individual and group unconscious processes as explained in Chapter 7.

Freud regards the individual and social as different ontological levels and treats civilization/culture/society as if it were an individual, claiming that the whole of humanity had an Oedipus complex in which the primal horde killed the primal father to get at the females. The individual and the social are both due to the same universal, the Oedipus complex, and the method of studying the social is through studying the universal mental processes of individuals (Freud, 1991, p237). There is no dialectic of individual and social as there is in Mead and Elias and no long-term history of civilizing processes forming a 'habitus' as there is in Elias.

Freud also talks about the social as constraint that is internalized as superego as the individual Oedipus complex is resolved. Elias talks about individuals acquiring higher degrees of self-control in the course of social evolution but he does not talk about the Oedipus complex and a mythical murder. His concern is with the detail of growing interdependencies and the monopolization of violence leading to self-restraint as a cultural phenomenon. For Elias and Mead, individual and society emerge simultaneously. Society enables and constrains individuals and the focus is not on energy or instinct but on communicative interaction and power relations as sophisticated cooperation. Civilization is sophisticated cooperation in the medium of language not sublimated sex drive. Social evolution is not a universal – it differs from place to place and time to time. The causality is not determinism nor is the thinking 'both . . . and'. Instead, the causality is transformative and the thinking paradoxical/dialectical: forming and being formed by. The group is not thought of as an individual writ large, rather, group processes and individual mental processes are the same.

Klein and Bion on the group and the individual

Klein's (1988) object relations theory greatly developed Freud's notion of the individual internal world, positing innate fantasies of an anxiety laden, aggressive and conflictual kind. Intrapsychic conflict is thus innate and so occurs from birth, not just arising in the conflict with society. Such intrapsychic conflict is dealt with by mechanisms of splitting, projection, introjection and projective identification. Klein, therefore, retained Freud's central assumptions of internal worlds communicating with each other using mechanisms of transmitting and she greatly elaborated them.

Bion (1961) developed these intrapsychic notions into a theory of group functioning. Individuals coming together in a group anonymously and unconsciously contribute mental contents to the group. The group itself is an illusion formed in the internal minds of the individuals constituting it through their anonymous contribution. Like Freud, Bion also thought of the group as a regressive phenomenon in which it is very difficult for individuals to function rationally and autonomously. For Bion, individuals are at war with their groupishness and are continually in danger of being overwhelmed by primitive group processes. Individuals inevitably experience great anxiety in groups and find themselves sucked into roles required by the group, primarily to defend against the anxiety of group life. Bion also recognized the reality of group life in which the performance of some task was required and like Freud he ascribed this capacity to organization taking the form of a work group. However, he reasoned that this performance of a real task was continually undermined by the primitive operation and regressive pull of the group on individuals. The implication is that the task can only be accomplished by a grouping of mature autonomous individuals freed from the regressive pull of the group and its defensive processes of fantasizing, scapegoating, and so on, and this in turn requires clear organization.

Bion drew attention to particular universal defenses employed in group life to defend against its innate anxieties. These take the form of the well-know basic assumptions. Group members find themselves unconsciously taking up roles in relation to dependency, fight–flight and pairing fantasies, all of which are inimical to thought and the performance of the group's task. Bion argued that all human groups consist of two kinds of group simultaneously present. The first is the basic assumption group to which members unconsciously contribute contents and take up defensive roles in relation to dependency, fight–flight and pairing. The second kind of group is the sophisticated work group. Only when the former is held at bay can the latter function and it functions essentially through individuals taking their own authority, in a sense freed from the pull of regressive forces in the group. The group, then, recapitulates the infantile primitive defenses of splitting, projection and projective identification of the internal world of the infant just as in Freud's thought.

Bion, then, extended Freud's thinking about the group by drawing on Klein to argue that the group expresses not only Oedipal but also pre-Oedipal concerns to do with the mother. The group came to be understood as a maternal environment. Bion considered that the ultimate sources of all group behavior lay in primitive anxieties of the part object kind, recapitulating those of early infancy in the Kleinian scheme. For Bion, the group is the container that absorbs and directs the primitive anxieties aroused in individuals by group membership. The group must contain the primitive if work is to take place. This idea of group as container was based on the relationship of the infant to the mother's breast so that it was thought of as a maternal entity.

Later examples of psychoanalytic thinking about groups

Object relations theory elaborated Freud's basic view of the group and its relationship with the individual. This elaboration has continued to exert an enormous influence on other psychoanalytic thinking about the individual and the group. For example, Ezriel (1952) worked very much in the tradition of Bion. He talked about three kinds of object relations that are evident in the manifest material of group communications. These were the required, the avoided and the calamitous relationships. He said that the group analytic task was to identify these relationships and also to find the common tension in the group by focusing on the group as opposed to the individuals.

> That is to say, the total material produced by *all* the members of the group is treated as if it had been produced by *one* patient in an individual session, and the object relationships that correspond to the common group tension are abstracted as the common denominators of this material.
>
> (Ezriel, 1952, p121)

One can see here the continuation of Freudian thinking about the group, which treats the group as if it were an individual. He talks about individuals in a group driven by forces beyond their control and about the group needing a leader as if the group had needs and exercised an agency quite apart from the individuals composing it.

Another example is Anzieu (1984) who regards groups as the consequence of individual projections, without which there would be a mere aggregation of individuals, not a group. In their projective activity, individuals are said to create an overarching group psychical apparatus.

> The only way a group can protect itself and make use of external stimulation, and the wishes and drives with which it is cathected by its members, is to fabricate an overarching group psychical apparatus on top of those of the individuals composing it. . . . thus the group is organized around the same agencies as the individuals composing it.
>
> (Anzieu, 1984, pp100–101)

Anzieu thinks of this group psychical apparatus in terms of the same kind of fantasies that Klein believed to characterize the individual internal world.

I shall deal with examples of phantasies of the group as breast–mouth or womb toilet, phantasies of breaking-apart, phantasies of the group as machine, phantasies of paradoxical resistance. These phantasies are expressions of libidinal, aggressive or self-destructive wishes, and are more or less regressive. In fact, group phantasies are produced by a circulation of individual phantasies among group members; for the group is the result of the economic and topographical organizations, which it represents and disguises. But in turn it produces particular effects on the thoughts, affects and behavior of group members.

(Anzieu, 1984, p101)

Like Freud and Bion, Anzieu sees the group as a primary threat to the individual. For him the Oedipal complex accounts for the anti-group attitudes and wishes that have always existed everywhere. The group favors the pleasure principle over the reality principle and people become like children in groups. He talks about individuals being drowned and lost in the group but also sheltered, enveloped and warmed as by the mother's body:

Does all this not point to the central, unconscious presence of the maternal imago in human groups, reduced to an infant's mouth, to devouring teeth, to the warmth of breasts and to a gigantic stomach in which swarm hundreds of digested substances and beings waiting to be born.

(Anzieu, 1984, p139)

Anzieu talks about group versions of id, ego and superego, and about the group as a dream or an illusion.

Whitaker (1985) also sees the group as a phenomenon existing at a different level to the individuals composing it. This phenomenon has special characteristics such as group moods, emotional contagion, shared themes, norms, beliefs and collusive defenses. She focuses attention on nuclear conflicts experienced by group members in their childhoods and how these are recreated as focal conflicts in the group.

Another prominent psychoanalyst who has addressed the matter of the group is Kernberg (1998). He talks about groups exerting an immediate regressive pull on individuals, which activates defenses and primitive object relations. He too sees the group as a pre-Oedipal mother posing a basic threat to individual identity. In exploring the functioning of organizations he attaches great importance to the pathology of individual leaders, as do many other psychoanalytic writers on organizations. Bureaucracy and ideology are regarded as defenses against the activation of primitive sexuality and aggression.

Ganzarain (1989) combines object relations theory with general systems theory, placing great emphasis on boundaries. His method involves the interpretation of projections and transference and he also uses the mother metaphor for the group, in particular the fantasy of the group as bad mother. The group is said to use an individual as a spokesperson.

Helen Durkin ([1983] 2000) draws attention to the impact of cybernetics and general systems theories on group psychotherapy. She says that Bateson was the first to apply cybernetics to therapeutic communication, followed by Watzlawick et al (1967) and then systemic family therapists, particularly the Palo Alto group, for whom family is *the system*. Durkin holds that cybernetics is based on a machine model and that the Palo Alto group became so obsessed with the family as system that they lost sight of the influence of individual family members. General systems theory, on the other hand, is based on the organism model. General systems are open and homeostatic, having many levels of operation with emergent properties at each level. They are autonomous because they have the inherent ability to control the permeability of boundaries. Living systems stabilize or transform themselves by monitoring the permeability of their boundaries to sustain equilibrium. Durkin drew on general systems theory for a different way of looking at clinical events and talked about individuals in energy exchange with parental systems, having varying abilities to close and open boundaries with them. Relationship problems are really boundary problems and the goal of therapy is to re-mobilize the full original system experienced in infancy. The therapist is the organizing subsystem and takes responsibility for boundary functions in terms of openness and closure. Cognitive processes sustain boundaries and emotional ones open them up.

In systems perspectives, then, the structure of a family is defined by the nature of the boundaries separating individuals, generations, parental and sibling subsystems. Rigid boundaries lead to blocked communication while those that are too open lead to lack of identity. In Agazarian's (1994) systems-centered approach to group therapy:

> The systems of the group-as-a-whole develop from simple to complex by splitting into differentiating subgroups which have the potential to remain in communication with one another across their boundaries . . . In a system-centered group, the basic unit is not the individual member, but the subgroup . . . In the systems-centered approach to the phases of development in group psychotherapy, the group is not left to develop 'naturally' while the therapist 'contains' the process and judiciously interprets it to make it conscious to the group, as is the case when the approach is primarily psychodynamic. Rather, group forces are deliberately exploited; certain group behaviors deliberately encouraged, others discouraged; and all dynamics are legitimized so that they can be exploited and understood . . .
>
> (Agazarian, 1994, p37)

Ansbach and Schermer (1994) continue in much the same way to combine a basically Freudian view of the individual and a systemic view of the group.

> Thus, the paradigm linking psychoanalysis and group dynamics calls for the observation of the relationship among three or more systems or processes: the internal or intrapsychic system of the person in the group; the system of communications and 'acts' among two or more persons; and the group *qua* group. These are not discrete units, but rather processes which translate from one to the other. To a great extent, the intrapsychic representations are internalized group systems, as for example dreams are often about significant others. Groups are projections of inner objects. Communications include empathically conveyed inner states and projective identifications of part objects into a container and may also represent 'monitoring' and 'transport' activities across organizational borders . . .
>
> (Ansbach & Schermer, 1994, pp14–15)

Both the individual and the group are said to emerge from a primal unity as a boundary is created differentiating one from the other.

In this brief and selective review of the continued impact of Freudian thinking about the individual and the group, I have made no reference to Foulkes because his thought and its further development by group analysts will be examined in more detail in Chapter 15.

This chapter has looked in some detail at Freud's thinking about individual and group and then pointed to how this thinking has continued to condition psychoanalytic theorizing on the individual and the group to the present time. His thinking has been incorporated into a systems way of thinking about the relationship between the individual and the group. I have pointed to how different this thinking is to the complex responsive processes perspective developed in Part I. The key differences have to do with the way psychoanalytic thought proceeds in terms of representations of external reality, stored as memory, in an internal world. None of these assumptions are made in the complex responsive processes perspective. Furthermore, psychoanalytic thought proceeds in systems terms, a notion not used at all by the purely process, activity theory of complex responsive processes. Also, psychoanalytic thought continued to develop the sender–receiver model of communication, which also does not feature in the complex responsive process perspective.

The next two chapters seek to further identify what this difference in thinking consists of. Chapter 10 will prepare the ground by exploring some key developments in the history of Western thought and Chapter 11 will look at how these developments influenced Freud's thinking. It will be argued that a very different strand in the development of Western thought influenced Mead and Elias, key foundations upon which the perspective of complex responsive processes is built. Chapter 12 will review recent thinking in psychoanalysis and the extent to which this has moved from its Freudian foundations. Again it will be noted that when psychoanalysis moves toward real relationships it does so within systems thinking. Chapter 13 will explore the problems raised by thinking about humans as systems.

Chapter 10

The movement of Western thought: pointing to the antecedents of complex responsive processes and psychoanalytic perspectives

In the last chapter, I described Freud's thinking about the relationship between the individual and the social. In essence, the individual is understood as an internal world. The social, or the group, is constituted by the projective and introjective movement of mental contents between individual worlds. And the social so constituted acts as a constraint, in fact, clashes with, the natural, innate inclinations of the individual internal worlds and it is in this clash that internal worlds are shaped. This is a very different way of thinking to that set out in the first part of this book, where individuals are thought of as social selves, forming and being formed by the cooperative and competitive interactions that are the social. In this way of thinking there are no internal worlds, only private and public role-plays, that is, actions of bodies. Such social selves are not fundamentally at odds with the social since they can only come into being in the social, although as individuals in society they may, of course, find themselves at odds with each other. In this chapter, I will explore the different origins of these two ways of thinking and in the next two chapters I will explore how these different origins continue to affect the further development of those ways of thinking. Exploring the historical development of different strands of thought greatly illuminates the nature of their differences.

Consider again the way in which people in the West have, over the last three to four hundred years, come to think and so experience themselves. In the Middle Ages, people thought that nature moved according to universal, unchanging laws that revealed the glory of God's creation. Humans were unquestionably a part of nature; indeed, humanity was the pinnacle of God's creation. Humans were a part of nature but they differed from other creatures in having souls, making them free to choose whether or not to act according to the universal ethical principles (laws) that were revealed as dogmas. Humans were rewarded when they acted according to these principles and punished when they did not. People also thought that humans could come to know something about the eternal laws of nature through authoritative revelation. People not only thought like this; they experienced themselves far more in terms of their role in the community than they later came to do.

The scientific method represented a major departure from this way of thinking. Instead of through authoritative revelation, it came to be thought that the universal, timeless laws governing nature could be discovered by the scientist who objectively observed nature, formulated hypotheses about the laws and then tested them, so progressively moving toward a fuller and more accurate understanding of the laws. These laws were understood to take the form of linear 'if–then' causal links and humans began to experience themselves as reasoning individuals. In other words, the empirical approach began to question the dogmatic one and it came to be thought that nature had laws of its own, no longer necessarily a reflection of God's order. Furthermore, it seemed that humans were also subject to these laws, creating a problem for the notion of human freedom. In addition to this, another key question arose. How it is that reasoning individuals are able to formulate hypotheses? In other words, how are humans able to categorize phenomena in nature and identify relationships between them?

This scientific revolution extended over more than a century. In the early 16th century there was the work of Copernicus and by the early 17th century that of Galileo and the writings of Bacon and Descartes. Descartes powerfully articulated the way in which people were coming to experience themselves in this period as individual 'thinking things.' By the early 17th century, then, these writers were presenting a very clear picture of what Elias called *homo clausus* (see Chapter 2). People in the West had come to experience themselves as individuals with a mind inside them but separate from their bodies, taking the form of an internal world, which they could access through introspection. In the late 17th century, the work of Newton, Leibniz and Locke typified the maturing scientific revolution. The shape of this revolution and the nature of the scientific method was by then clear and the notion of individuals with minds inside them was firmly established. This view of how people experienced themselves was concisely formulated in the philosophy of Leibniz. He saw individuals as windowless monads who internally represented external worlds, perceived both consciously and unconsciously, and related to each other across an existential gulf. Again, this is a clear depiction of what Elias was later to call *homo clausus*, a way of people experiencing themselves that was part and parcel of the evolution of modern society. Modern societies were producing modern selves and modern selves were simultaneously producing modern societies.

By the late 18th century, however, the scientific method came under intellectual threat. This threat came from Hume's skeptical position but Kant countered it with his dualistic philosophy that eliminated paradox and thereby continued to provide a philosophical basis for science in the form of critical or transcendental idealism. Central to Kant's thinking was the autonomous individual and the innate universal categories of the individual mind. There was no challenge to *homo clausus* here. Then in the early 19th century there was the reaction to Kant and the further development of

German idealism by Fichte, Schelling and Hegel as romantic or absolute idealism. What is striking about the development of thought in absolute idealism was the importance attached to the historical evolution of social processes in experiencing oneself and knowing. For the purpose of this book, this was a development of major importance. For the first time in Western thought, social processes were understood to play the major part in the construction of knowledge and self experience, as well as of society itself.

The rest of this chapter looks in more detail at the evolution of thought that I have just outlined and the next chapter looks at the origins of Freudian thought in this evolution.

The scientific revolution and the philosophy of Leibniz

A common assumption that united prominent figures in the movement of thought known as the scientific revolution was that the basis of knowledge lay in the human mind and its encounter with the real world. This was philosophically a realist, materialist position taking for granted the existence of an independent reality outside the mind. This real world could be observed, couched in the language of mathematics, and explained through reductionism and experimentation. Science could generate certain knowledge and truth. Descartes' philosophy expressed all of this. He exposed everything to radical doubt and concluded that the ultimate reality was the ability to think and this ability was located in the mind as distinct from the body. Knowledge was acquired by reduction and by testing doubts. Descartes resolved his doubts about the reality of the external world by appealing to the existence of God. His work appeared in the middle of the 17th century and the work of another key philosopher of the scientific revolution, Leibniz, was published early in the 18th century. Since it has been suggested that Freud was influenced by Leibniz's philosophy, this will be reviewed in the next section.

Leibniz

Leibniz (Leibniz, 1992; Rescher, 1991) sought to understand both nature and human beings in much the same way. He looked for the fundamental irreducible elements of all phenomena, a kind of atomism, and found them in what he called monads. Monads constitute the world and are the basic units of reality in that they have no spatial parts and so cannot be divided. However, they have qualities and they are distinguished from each other by intrinsic features, namely, their modes of action. All natural processes are a matter of reassembly or transformation of pre-existing monads, which cannot be created or destroyed other than by God.

Leibniz distinguished between different kinds of monads:

- Entelechies are created monads in general amongst which there are simple, or basic, entelechies which have unconscious perception and lack memory and awareness;
- Souls are ruling monads in animals and souls have consciousness as perception and memory;
- Spirits are ruling monads in rational creatures. These are humans with minds capable of self consciousness and reason.

For Leibniz, perception was not a capacity of a specific kind but pervaded nature. He strongly opposed the idea that all mental life was conscious and held that unconscious perception lying beneath the threshold of conscious awareness was crucial. He held that humans function not only at the highest level but also at the lower levels, including the lowest unconscious level. Perception does not have to be noticed and there are many minute perceptions that are too small to be noticed. These minute perceptions constitute something distinct through which the perception of the monad reaches out to embrace the universe. The entire history of the monad is programmed internally in its natural make up. Leibniz held that it was only on the basis of unconscious perception that the continuity of our mental life could be assured. For him, self consciousness and reason were the same and humans were free to choose on the basis of reason.

Leibniz's conception of a self is thus that of a human individual capable of self consciousness (apperception), both conscious and unconscious perception, and reason and choice. He had more than this to say about all monads, including human individuals. For example, nothing can affect monads from outside of them – they are windowless. However, although windowless, each monad expresses and represents the rest. They mirror each other. There is a harmony in which everything is adjusted to everything and this ensures consonance without any actual interaction. All monads perceive the same thing but from a different point of view within a pre-established harmony. All monads are interconnected and whatever happens at one point affects all at other points. Leibniz viewed nature as a nested hierarchy of functional complexity and this required knowledge to be developed as a co-coordinated system.

The inner nature of a monad, that is, its defining notion or complete individual concept, fixes everything about it. However, monads do change but only as a result of inner programming and not by external causal impetus. While monads cannot act upon one another by way of causality, their inner states can be aligned to each other by way of coordination or synchronization, effecting a mutual adjustment that is not causal but ideal. Because of such reciprocal coordination through alignment, monads are not totally independent although in causal terms they are. Each monad provides a representation of the entire universe, although in different ways, from different points of view, and the universe as a whole is an integrally connected system of coordinated monads.

Change is the most fundamental feature of monads and it proceeds under the operation of natural laws that are mathematically continuous so that there are no gaps, leaps or discontinuities. Change is defined in terms of each monad's characteristic mode of operation and the pre-specified internal principle regulating a monad's changes is called appetition, a word that connotes appetite or desire. The inner active force of appetition is a program specifying the manner in which the monad's entire history unfolds in a predetermined fashion. The complex internal state of a monad at any given temporal juncture consists in the perceptions by which it represents its whole environing world. Appetition, or self-development, is the internally programmed drive from one family of perceptions toward another. The appetitive drive is to a fuller realization, a self-aggrandizement. Appetition is a drive or force responsible for all change and the monad unfolds from within, from its own inherent nature. Because monads change from within, they are agents and each has a complex inner structure establishing its identity, which cannot be separated into parts. It is this complex structure that differentiates one monad type from another. Monads relate to each other by internalization through mutual attunement and the basis of their agency is this ongoing readjustment always naturally produced from internally pre-programmed changes and never caused from without.

Unlike Descartes, Leibniz did not have a dualism of mind and body since both are monads and unlike Kant, to be discussed in the next section, he did not have a dualism of organism and human action. For Leibniz, the mind and the body are completely interdependent and human beings are very much part of nature. All are different degrees of development of the same living force, which he identified with God. It was this kind of metaphysics that Kant was to reject and it was something like this idea of living force that Fichte, Schelling and Hegel were later to resurrect in reaction against Kant's dualisms.

The sharp difference between Leibniz and the thought of Mead and Elias discussed in Part I is clear, as is the connection between Leibniz's philosophy and many Freudian ideas. In both Leibniz and Freud there is the focus on the self-contained individual, the mind as an internal world, the formation of representations, connections between individuals through processes like internalization and the distinction between conscious and unconscious perception. There is a similar kind of determinism and emphsis on the innate. There is also a similar notion of the nature of interaction.

The notion of an individual forming representations of reality and thus knowing was to generate a considerable debate later in the 18th century and the philosopher Locke, in some ways, laid the foundations for that debate.

Locke

The empiricist Locke, was a contemporary of Newton and Leibniz. He argued that there was nothing in the intellect that was not first in the senses so that all knowledge of the world rested in sensory experience and reason required sensory experience. Intrinsic rational thought could be mere speculation or even spurious, making it impossible to proceed by pure deduction since this could only reveal tautologies. Reason had to be concerned with appearances in a procedure to uncover probable rather than absolute truths. Locke, therefore, did not accept the belief in innate ideas found in the philosophies of both Descartes and Leibniz. As rationalists, the latter held that the mind alone achieved knowledge through its recognition of clear distinct truths. For Locke, the mind has innate powers but instead of having innate ideas, it is, in the beginning, a blank tablet waiting for experience to write upon it. In other words, the mind receives sensory impressions that represent external, material objects. Locke saw the problem that the idea of representation created, namely that there is no guarantee that the idea/representation corresponds to reality. Such a view threatened to undermine scientific knowledge making it unreliable and relative. Locke proposed to get around this by distinguishing, as Galileo and Descartes had done, between quantities inhering in objects and qualities inhering in human senses. By focusing on the former, science could gain reliable knowledge, while the latter had to be left to more speculative ventures.

I want to draw particular attention to this notion of representation and its implication of an internal world because it came to be so central to psychoanalytic ways of thinking. The underlying idea is that of the mind as an internal space, tablet or world that constructs internal representations of external objects through sensory perception.

The notion of representations and internal worlds

By the end of the 17th century, the camera obscura had become the common metaphor for the structure of the human eye – both were devices that caught pictures (Leader, 2000). Vision no longer had its base in the object but in the eye. Do we see an external object or do we see the retinal image of the object? If it is the latter, how do we know that it conforms to the former? Then the terms that had been used to describe the act of seeing, or the propagation of light rays, came to designate the act of understanding, a shift from the eye to the mind, thinking and knowing. The camera obscura became a metaphor for the mind as 'inside.' It became a way of knowing how the mind worked, rather like how the metaphor of the computer came to be the basis for understanding the brain in the late 20th century. Locke wrote of the mind as a dark room with small windows that let in resemblances of 'ideas' of things outside, where they would stay as understanding. These 'ideas' were precursors of 'internal objects.' Locke was countering the notion of innate ideas to form an empirical philosophy where contact with the world established the content of thinking. In this way an optical view of the mind was established in tension with innate ideas.

However, if retinal objects, not actual objects, are the immediate objects of sight, then the immediate objects of thought are not external objects but internal objects. How do we know that the two coincide?

The Scottish philosopher, Reid, was concerned with how we perceived 'outness' and argued against the notion that a 'veil of ideas' separates us from external objects. According to this notion, ideas have their own ontological status, they are 'things' that separate us from the external world. Reid, however, argued that ideas are not things but acts of cognition. By talking about ideas as things in the mind, we introduce a misleading topology of internal and external. It is the *act* of thinking that matters. Reid used the term 'internal object' to damn the view that ideas are third terms between a thinker–perceiver and an external object. He was against Plato's cavern and Locke's dark room. Knowing something was different to containing something in one's mind. Reid and other critics of the camera obscura and the 'veil of ideas' showed that the spatial model of mind was based on confusion between being spatially and cognitively present. They were critical of the idea that the mind had contents. Despite their critique however, the notion of an internal world populated by internal objects came to be common and very much taken for granted.

Berkeley pointed to the weakness of the distinction Locke had made between quantities and qualities, one in the object and the other in the senses. He concluded that all aspects of reality were in the mind and there was no conclusive inference of a world even existing. Since one cannot get outside the mind, the whole notion of representations was groundless. However, for Berkeley, objectivity still existed because God, the universal mind, produced regularities.

Writing around the middle of the 18th century, Hume followed Locke in positing that sensory impressions were the basis of all knowledge. The mind imposes an order of its own on the chaotic volley of sensations. It draws from its experience an explanation, an association of ideas, a habit of human imagination through which it assumes causal connections. Cause is the accident of repeated connection in the mind. Ideas result from connections in experience, not from an independent reality, and intelligibility reflects habits of mind, not the nature of reality. Hume claimed that there was no necessary order to our ideas other than the ways they were combined in our minds according to habit and the laws of association. With this argument, he threw into doubt the Enlightenment idea that reason could unaided discover the order of the world. Berkeley and Hume's idealism doubted everything except one's own self. The philosophy of Descartes,

Leibniz and Locke no longer seemed to provide a firm foundation for science. This skepticism, with its conclusion about the relativity and unreliability of knowledge, threatened the very basis of science and it was this that awoke Kant from what he called his 'dogmatic slumbers.'

Kant: autonomous individuals and natural systems

Kant had been educated in the philosophy of Leibniz and had accepted its metaphysics in which the concepts of the individual and an external reality were in a pre-established harmony because they were both part of God's creation. However, the arguments of Berkeley and Hume brought Kant to the conclusion that we cannot say that simply because we have a concept it exists in reality. This conclusion led Kant to the dualism of the noumena, reality itself, and phenomena, the appearance of reality to the senses. Kant argued that it was impossible for humans to know anything about the noumenal, that is, about reality itself. All we could know is appearances as we sense them, that is, representations. However, this does not mean that all reasoning is relative because Kant also posited that the human mind contains innate categories, such as time, space and cause–effect, which enable us to order appearances in a non-relative way. Kant argued that the metaphysics of Descartes and Leibniz, based on the concept of the absolute as a supernatural entity outside of nature, was impossible because the supernatural, the noumenal, was unknowable. A supernatural entity tran-scends human understanding, which has to rely on dogma, because making an explanation, a metaphysics, of the supernatural was impossible. Kant, therefore, rejected a metaphysics involving direct knowledge of the absolute.

However, he retained a kind of metaphysics of universals in the form of innate categories according to which our minds give laws to nature. In doing this, Kant was proposing a transcendental logic where transcendental means knowing in advance the form that something will take. In other words, the forms of reason are given beforehand and knowing is then outside of the present experience itself. It is in this sense one might say that there is something metaphysical about transcendental logic. However, transcendental, that is, prior to experience, does not mean the same as transcendent, or outside of experience altogether and thus unknowable.

> But forms do not determine what the content will be. They determine how we shall experience that content when we do experience objects, but we cannot tell in advance what particular experience we shall have. We do know in advance what form it must take, because the forms of experience are given to the world by the mind itself. In that sense Kant could legitimately speak of the mind giving laws to nature as well as to society.
>
> (Mead, 1936, p42)

So, the form that reason takes is already determined outside of experience and what experience does is simply provide a particular content. This does not leave much room for spontaneity and Kant was aware of this. He located any spontaneity in nature and in human action in the noumena, in effect saying that we cannot directly know anything about spontaneity.

At this point I would like to make a connection between Kant's transcendental logic and Freud's thinking. Freud's structural theory of the psyche posits the id consisting of drives, which are 'representations' of innate instincts. He also posits innate stages in the development of the drives through bodily stages of the oral, the anal and the genital. Freud, like Kant, therefore, is saying that the forms are given outside the present experience and what experience provides is simply specific variants of these forms. I will be returning to this point in the next chapter.

Countering Hume, Kant argued that any object we perceive has a certain unity that is more than the association of one experience after another in a habit. The unity is an organization holding together experiences within a certain form and grasping that unity is an act of judgment. Our perception is a process of organizing different elements into a whole and Kant called this transcendental (a priori) apperception (i.e. more than a perception), which relies upon an 'I' or 'ego' that judges.

> The Kantian self, . . . had two aspects. One aspect is purely formal as it appeared in the transcendental unity of apperception, that unifying power which holds together, constructs our percepts, makes them different from bare sensations, and gives unity to them. But this unity was a pure function from Kant's standpoint, it was not an entity, was not a spiritual being; it was just a function of unity. The other aspect of this self, . . . appears in the *Critique of Practical Reason*. . . . We find ourselves accepting responsibility for our own actions. We could not lay any such responsibility upon ourselves unless we were free, unless actions were our own. . . . but in the world of experience . . . everything is subject to the laws of mind, . . . – the categories. What takes place there takes place in accordance with the laws of cause and effect. . . . thus freedom cannot be found in the world of experience as we know it. Kant's assumption is that we must postulate a self which, so to speak, lies in a different realm from that of the phenomenal, namely, in the noumenal world of 'things-in-themselves.'
>
> (Mead, 1936, p667)

As I understand it, Kant proposes a formal, functional self that is noumenal and cannot be known. We could say that this aspect of self is unconscious. The other aspect of self is found in experience, that is, conscious, rational human agency that takes responsibility for action. Spontaneity and freedom, however, belong to the noumenal unconscious aspect.

This seems to be a significant move from the Leibniz notion of unconscious, which seems to relate to many small perceptions below the level of awareness. It seems to me that the kind of self that Kant proposes foreshadows Freud's postulates. The Freudian id (unconscious) is the source of spontaneity. Freud proposes a universal Oedipus complex as that which realizes the structure of the psyche. So there is a kind of noumenal self, which is realized in the actual empirical experience of an Oedipal situation in the form of conscious aspects of the ego and the superego, that is, practical agency.

Kant reversed the conception of truth in which truth consists of the correspondence of our representations with things that exist independently of them. This is because it is impossible to get outside our representations to see if they conform to reality. So Kant says we see truth as the conformity of our representations with certain universal and necessary concepts already in our minds that determine the form of our experience. The standard of truth is then within consciousness itself when we ask whether our representations conform to the universal and necessary forms of consciousness itself.

Furthermore transcendental idealism applies only in the sphere of appearances so ensuring the autonomy of reason, its freedom from the determination of experience and history because the standards of reason do not operate in nature at all. Kant's transcendental idealism rejects both traditional realism and traditional idealism. There is reality but we cannot know it and idealism is not simply perception because of the transcendental categories. He limits knowledge to experience alone and says traditional realism and idealism are metaphysical propositions, which he rejects. Kant argued that there were rationally necessary rules for the combination of ideas and these could be derived from the condition of the agent's coming to be conscious of himself.

Kant said that as embodied beings we are part of nature, the objective world, but as subjective beings we do not appear in nature. Instead this subjectivity is a transcendental condition of conscious experience, that is, of a subjective point of view that unifies our being in the world and our point of view on the world.

One of Kant's categories was the innate capacity to formulate regulative ideas. By this he meant that we can observe nature and formulate hypotheses about the purposive movement of nature where those hypotheses take the form of 'as if' intention. We are able to understand nature 'as if' it were moving toward some end and he suggested that this end would be a mature state of itself. However, this purpose is not in nature itself but, rather, it is we, as objectively observing scientists, who can understand nature 'as if' it were moving towards the end that we have postulated. Kant incorporated this notion of 'regulative ideas' into a systemic approach in which organisms in nature are understood as wholes consisting of parts and in the interaction of the parts, both those parts and the whole emerge. So, we can understand nature in terms of hypotheses we formulate in which organisms are thought of as systemically self organizing wholes to which we ascribe a purposive movement toward end states which are mature forms of themselves, all as a way of more deeply understanding nature. The hypotheses we formulate could well be wrong and then we have to formulate others, so gradually improving our knowledge.

Turning to humans, Kant argued that although they are part of nature they are different and cannot be understood as parts of a whole, or system. They cannot be understood in this way because then they would be subject to the whole and as such not free. Instead, he argued that we have to think of ourselves as autonomous individuals. This means that each individual, having a soul, is free to choose how to act, unless he allows his actions to be directed by the passions of the body, in which case he is subject to the laws of nature and so not free. Kant was bringing a teleological perspective to human action and arguing that individuals could set their own goals and strategies using their powers of reason. The question then became how an autonomous individual could know which acts to choose so that autonomous individuals could live together. In other words, the question was how autonomous individuals could know what ethical choices were. For mediaeval thinkers the answer was to follow the revealed dogma. In Kant's time dogmatic rationalists presented a new alternative to revealed dogma, arguing that the dogma, the ethical principles, could also be identified by human reason on its own. Kant argued that the notion of the 'regulative idea' could be applied to human conduct just as it could to nature.

In the case of human conduct, the regulative idea was Kant's categorical imperative, that is, his notion of ethics. This meant that in matters of ethics, just as in relation to nature, autonomous individuals as scientists could objectively observe their own conduct. Ethical actions could be understood 'as if' they were actions that could be performed by everyone because then the principle behind the action would reflect a universal law. This is the categorical imperative. So an individual could formulate hypotheses about an ethical action, testing them against the regulative idea or categorical imperative 'as if they could be performed by everyone.' As people proceed in this way, different formulations of the categorical imperative emerge, for example, 'treat others as you want them to treat you' and 'do not treat other people as means to an end since all people are ends in themselves.' These imperatives have the character of universals but they do not dictate what to do in any specific situation. In specific situations people have to choose what to do, testing their actions against the categorical imperatives and using them to justify what they have done. In this way, just as we can progressively build up a body of knowledge about the timeless universal natural laws governing nature, so we can progressively build up a body of knowledge on timeless, ethical imperatives for human conduct. Ethics is firmly based on the reasoning capacity of the autonomous individual who can discover the universal principles of good conduct through what amounts to the scientific method.

Kant developed a 'both . . . and' way of thinking that resolves paradox in that there are both natural laws and autonomous individuals without any sense of this presenting a paradox. Essentially the same way of thinking applies to both nature and human action in that both are to be rationally understood through the scientific method of testing hypotheses as regulative ideas. These regulative ideas are applied to systemic wholes, in the case of nature, and they are to be understood as ethical imperatives reflecting a metaphysics of a not-to-be-defined whole in the case of human action.

By way of summary consider some key points about Kant's way of thinking:

1. He uses a dualistic mode of thinking ('both . . . and') to resolve or eliminate some key paradoxes.

    i.   First, there is the paradox of inside and outside and the question here is how an internal representation of external reality can be taken to accord with that reality. One approach is to say that inner representation and outer reality accord with each other because they are parts of the same whole, as in Leibniz's *holistic* thinking. Another approach is *either* to say that one cannot take an internal representation to accord with reality at all, as in the radical idealism/skepticism of Berkeley and Hume, *or* to say that there is only an objective reality, as in the realism of science. This is a way of thinking in *dichotomies*: 'either . . . or.' Yet another way of thinking is that of *dualism*. Instead of excluding one or the other entirely, Locke suggests a dualism in which quantities inhere in objects and so are real, while qualities inhere in humans and so are ideal. Kant developed the dualistic way of thinking into a complete philosophical system. So in his thinking there is *both* reality as noumena which we cannot know *and* appearances or phenomena which we can know through the senses upon which the categories of the mind impose order. What is inside the mind is what we know and what is outside is what we cannot know. This has an echo of consciousness and unconsciousness. In making a clear distinction of internal consciousness and external unconsciousness, Kant eliminates any paradox.

    ii. Next there is the paradox of nature and human autonomy. This is eliminated when one causality is assigned to nature and another to rational human action. Nature can be understood as mechanism operating according to efficient 'if–then' cause or as organism thought of as a system. Such a system is a self-organizing whole in which its form is caused by a process of development from embryo to mature adult. Causality here is not of the efficient kind but of the formative kind. The system is understood as operating according to a regulative idea, an 'as if' posited by the observing scientist. Such an idea is regulative, that is, hypothetical – one cannot posit a constitutive idea because this would mean claiming to know how nature actually was. When it comes to human action yet another causality is posited. Human action is not bound by the laws of nature but by a causality of freedom enabling people to set their own goals using reason and to act accordingly – rationalist causality. However, the human body is part of nature and so subject to its laws and when a person acts in accordance with the passions of the body his or her actions are subject to the laws of nature so removing freedom. Kant, then, ends up with a causal dualism. Formative cause applies in one sphere and rationalist cause applies in another sphere. It is worth noting that Freud too has an aspect of the psyche that is governed by the laws of nature (the id) and an aspect of rational autonomy and agency (the ego).

2. In dealing with paradox in a dualistic way, Kant adopts a kind of dialectical thought. He refers to the thesis of humans being part of nature, and so not free, and the antithesis of humans being free, and his transcendental logic is the synthesis he proposes. Later in this chapter I will draw attention to how Hegel's dialectical logic differs profoundly from this. Kant's dialectic is about removing paradox just as in Aristotle's logic any paradox is regarded as a failure to think properly. Hegel's dialectic is essentially about the movement rather than the resolution of paradox.

3. A key to Kant's way of thinking is the notion of universals. All humans have minds with innate categories. All humans know appearances (conscious) and none know reality (unconscious). All humans are autonomous individuals whose behavior is determined by rational goals and all humans are bodies with passion that when acted upon render them unfree.

4. Kant reinforces the Western notion of the rational, autonomous individual who objectively observes the world, positing regulative ideas about it, and himself, positing hypothetical imperatives about the categorical imperatives that should guide his behavior.

5. Kant rejects a metaphysics of the absolute or the supranatural relying instead entirely on human reason.

In the next chapter I will be exploring the similarities and differences between Freud's thought and that of Kant.

The response to Kant: Hegel and social processes

Kant distinguished between *understanding* (concepts, categories) as an active, a priori, intellectual faculty outside space and time giving universal form to experience, and *sensibility* (intuition) as a passive, a posteriori sensing faculty in space and time that is particular and contingent and supplies the matter of experience. However, empirical knowledge requires the interchange between understanding and sensibility and the problem is how we can know that the a priori concepts of understanding apply to the a posteriori intuitions of sensibility. Fichte and others argued that since one was outside time and space and the other inside, they could not interact other than through some mysterious pre-established harmony. The task became how to overcome the dualism of the subject and the object, the ideal and the real. But in our experience there is a distinction between subject and object, idea and reality. The problem is how to have the identity of subject and object so that they interact and also difference (non-identity) between subject and object that we experience, all at the same time.

The philosophies of romantic idealism responded in the late 18th and early 19th centuries to the problem by identifying the object of knowledge with the process of knowing to be found in the self. They were particularly concerned with self consciousness where the subject is an object to itself. It is the self that is real and all experience is carried back to this immediate experience of the self. The reflexive position becomes central. Kant held that the mind encountered antimonies in the attempt to go beyond the phenomenal world to the noumenal. They were warnings of a mind going beyond its limits. For the romantics (Fichte, Schelling and Hegel) experience also takes place in the contradiction of opposites but they dealt with this in a different way. For them the contradictions were inherent in the movement of thought. Fichte deals with this in terms of moral experience, Schelling in terms of aesthetic experience and Hegel in terms of the experience of thought. Their common problem is how the world, which seems to be independent of the self is brought into the experience of the self. They looked at the self as process and saw each self as an expression of the absolute self, so reversing Kant's dismissal of metaphysics.

In reviewing the movement of thought known as romantic idealism, Mead has this to say:

> . . . the self itself and the relation of things to the self are the important factors in experience. I again want to refer to a peculiar aspect of this self, namely, that it is both subject and object. . . . The Romantic attitude is the ability to project one's self upon the world, so that the world is identified in some fashion with the self.
>
> (Mead, 1936, p75)

This quote emphasizes the move the romantic idealists were making away from transcendental logic with its already given forms of thought outside of experience to a dialectical logic in which human consciousness and self consciousness in experience is central to knowing. Furthermore, a particular notion of consciousness and self consciousness was being developed in terms of the unity of the relationship between subject and object as the source of meaning. Even more striking is the interconnection that was seen between individual selves and social relations. This thinking is the basis for the development of the idea of social selves by Mead and Elias as outlined in Part I of this book.

> But the Romantic philosophy pointed out that the self, while it arises in the social experience, also carried with it the very unity that makes society possible, which makes the world possible. . . . It is our thinking, our perception of the world, that gives it its unity. . . . It is the self which organizes the world; but when it has organized it, it has really organized that which is identical with itself, it has organized its own experiences. It has, in one phase of its nature, discovered what it is in another.
>
> (Mead, 1936, p125)

Romantic idealism moves to focusing on experience itself as historical processes of social consciousness and self consciousness. In doing this it represents a powerful break with the notion of the autonomous individual.

Although Fichte and Schelling were important romantic idealists, for the sake of brevity, the next section will focus on Hegel whose thought represents the culmination of romantic idealism.

Hegel

Hegel's is a philosophy of evolution, that is, of living processes that take on successively different forms. These are subject–object processes that exhibit the differences we experience in the world and contradiction, or paradox, is the process by means of which the object arises in the subject–object relationship. The development of thought, therefore, takes place through conflict and the world of our experience is the world we are creating in our thought. Hegel drew on Leibniz's notion of matter as living force that surmounted the dualisms to argue that mind and matter are not separate substances but different degrees of organization of the same substance.

Kant had proposed that we could think about nature as an organism, that is, as a self-generating and self-organizing whole having the cause of its motion within itself. That cause, however, was regulative in the sense that it was an 'as if' hypothesized by the scientist. Hegel, however, insisted that nature *is* a self-organizing whole with the cause of its motion within it and that this is not simply regulative but constitutive. There is a single universal substance in nature, the absolute, consisting of living force and it is neither subject nor object but the unity of both. Nature conforms to a purpose, plan or design that is inherent in matter itself rather than being created by God. The ideal, therefore, is the underlying purposiveness and rationality of nature itself, which is manifested in the mental and the physical, the subjective and the objective (Beiser, 2000). Hegel argued that the mental and physical are only degrees of organization and development, with mind as the most organized development of matter, and matter as the least developed form of mind. *For Hegel, Geist (spirit/mind) is the highest degree of organization and development of the organic powers within nature.*

Hegel's metaphysics is, therefore, not a form of speculation about supernatural entities such as God or the soul. The absolute is not a kind of thing, an entity, but the whole of which all things are reflections. Hegel banishes all occult forces and explains everything in terms of natural laws, rejecting Leibniz's metaphysics not because the supernatural is unknowable but because it does not exist. We can know the absolute by knowing nature as given in our experience. The purposes of nature are internal to itself and not imposed by some external designer.

Hegel said that the absolute has to be given constitutive status, that is, it actually exists and he also said that it exists within the subject–object dualism of our experience. Only if the subject–object identity exists within the subject–object dualism (non-identity) of our experience is it possible to explain the conditions of empirical knowledge. In other words, the absolute is simultaneously subject–object identity and the identity of subject–object identity and subject–object non-identity. For Hegel the absolute is a single infinite substance, living force, with attributes of the subjective and the objective. All nature is organism and the knowing subject is only part of it making possible the interaction of subject and object. They are all reflections of the absolute and the highest reflection of all is society.

Hegel and the social formation of meaning

Hegel held that one cannot begin, as Kant had done and as Freud was later to do, with an isolated individual subject experiencing the world and then ask how a world of objective experience gets built up out of the inner world of purely subjective experience. Rather, one must begin with an already shared world of subjects making judgments in the light of possible judgments by others. Hegel also emphasized the idea of mutual recognition to argue that there is an intersubjective unity of mutually recognizing agents in the natural world, which he called the absolute ethical life. Pinkard in his biography of Hegel says:

> Hegel argued that the 'ethical life' . . . of any particular 'people' must be construed entirely in terms of the patterns of entitlements and commitments that those individuals confer and sustain by acts of mutual recognition: it must not be construed by any kind of separate realm requiring its own special causal powers, nor as simply the result of natural process.
>
> (Pinkard, 2000a, p171)

Notice how Hegel argues against any separate realm outside of experience. In this, he moves decisively away from Kantian ethics (Griffin, 2001) or any notion of a system lying outside experience and causing it. He accords central importance to recognition, linking it to desire, particularly the desire for desire of the other. Here he is emphasizing the cooperative aspects of society, although power and competition were also central to his view.

Hegel argued that there were always elements of inequality in relationships so that some have more power than others. Without the right kind of social mediation, therefore, there will not be complete mutuality of recognition but rather relations of domination, which he explored as follows. In their encounter with each other, each self conscious agent makes his own judgment about his right to have his desires fulfilled in accordance with his life project. He seeks to confirm these norms of his behavior and so requires the other to recognize this. The demand for recognition becomes a struggle to death when one party decides that his own self-conception is more important than life itself. One party then submits to the authority of the other and both enter into a relationship of master and slave. Taking as an example the relationship between master and slave, Hegel says that the master imposes his norms on the slave and the slave allows this. The master's project for his own life determines the project of the slave. However the claim to superiority of the master's viewpoint is compulsion and the slave comes to understand that his submission is contingent on passions, luck and uses of personal power. This realization undermines his allegiance to the principles set by the master. Also, the master comes to realize that the slave does not really recognize him but is simply submitting. This undermines his own allegiance to the principles of the relationship. The relationship cannot provide the free recognition he requires and the internal contradictions of the relationship lead to its transformation.

The term for the process of transformation is *Aufhebung* meaning transforming through a process of negation and preserving. Our commitments to certain basic kinds of judgments carry with them other kind of judgments that at least at first seem to be incompatible with each other – so negating – but which when viewed from another standpoint are understood to have their own legitimate place – so raising – and whose tensions are never fully abolished – so preserving. Hegel is pointing to the process of social evolution as dialectical in a distinctive sense. In the unity of the relationship, the strength of one's demand for recognition generates the very lack of the required recognition. The submission of the other generates the objection to submitting. Dominating and submitting are not separate but a unity where dominating and submitting are changed. In the next chapter I will discuss Ogden's view that it is possible to interpret in this way the kind of relationship Freud posits between ego and id.

Hegel emphasized the historical specificity of human self-conceptions upon which society is founded. However, for Hegel, the concepts of 'person' and 'subject' were only abstractions insufficient to provide a content for human rights and moral duties. These abstractions foster what he called a 'spirit of atomicity' separating individuals from each other and their common social life. The abstractions of person and subject are given content only by the social institutions in which each individual achieves social identity through interdependence and mutual recognition. In the civil society, individuals are drawn into connections with others and this brings about changes in the individuals and their ends.

These social institutions are reflections of absolute spirit, or *Geist*. However, by spirit, Hegel does not mean something distinct from human activity in the objective world but conscious activity that makes or actualizes itself by doing something outside itself and coming to understand itself in the light of an interpretation of what it has done. History is the history of the objective social forms that spirit gives itself. The activity of spirit is the:

> . . . dialectical interplay between self-knowledge, self-actualization, and practical striving, in which the striving for a given set of goals, founded on a given knowledge of oneself, leads in time to a new self-knowledge, new goals, and so to an altered striving. Spirit is this kind of self-transformative activity considered socially or collectively.
>
> (Wood, 1993, p428)

> Hegel['s] . . . theory implies that it is spirit's nature continually to transform its nature in fundamental ways by deepening its self-knowledge, and it locates this self-transformation mainly in social structures. That means that his theory does imply that radical social change will occur, and that the nature of this change will decisively depend on the growth of human knowledge. More specifically, it implies that rational knowledge of the ethical principles of a social order is available only after the order has reached maturity. This means that Hegel's theory does imply that those who take the first steps in creating a new social order cannot have a rational comprehension of the nature of what they are creating. They cannot predict what future society will be like, because they lack the knowledge of spirit necessary to understand how the new society will actualize spirit's nature.
>
> (Wood, 1993, p439)

Mind or consciousness is manifested in social institutions, that is, ways of life, which give identities, self-concepts, to individuals. As social beings, our experience is of a subject–object duality (non-identity), that is, the position of the objective observer, and at the same time, subject–object identity, that is, participation. The dialectic is the interplay between opposites of observation and participation as an identity. This also applies to oneself in that one observes and participates in self consciousness. This is a self-organizing process. Kant's dialectic, on the other hand, is subject–object antimony, resolved in thought by a dualism (synthesis) that eliminates paradox as 'both . . . and' thinking.

Each person is self consciously, purposively directing himself but each is also dependent on the other. Self-determination by a free subject can only occur through another person who is also a self-determining subject and is doing the same. Another self conscious subject offers resistance to the realization of my desires by testing or challenging me and my self-world conception. It is inevitable that two self-determining, self conscious subjects will conflict and struggle in a world of finite resources. In their struggle each negates the other as a subject. They become an object to each other. Paradoxically, however, each also confirms the subjectivity of the other in genuine mutual recognition. This is the dialectical process of the social in which we come to know. Each possible resolution represents a self-determined relation to objects and others, and there is no reason why they should determine or affirm each other's moves. We develop a commitment to rationality – it is not already there. Self consciousness achieves its satisfaction or realization only in another self consciousness.

> . . . Hegel is suggesting that how we come to understand or to make judgments *about anything* must be a function of some sort of mutually sanctioning process *among* such subjects, and that this process can be understood only by considering such subjects as practical, purposive, or living beings.
>
> (Pippin, 1993, p71)

Hegel argued that individual autonomy could only be achieved in a social context:

> Briefly, Hegel held that individuals are fundamentally social practitioners. Everything one does, says, or thinks is formed in the context of social practices that provide material and conceptual resources, objects of desire, skills, procedures, and the like. No one acts on the general, merely biological needs for food, safety, companionship or sex; and no one seeks food, safety, companionship or sex in general. Rather one acts on much more specific needs for much more specific kinds of objects that fulfill those needs, and one acts to achieve one's aims in

quite specific ways; one's society deeply conditions one's ends because it provides specific objects that meet those ends, and it specifies procedures for obtaining them. Even so, Hegel realized that this fact does not render individuals subservient to society. First, what individuals do depends on their own responses to their social context. In addition, Hegel argued that there are no individuals, no social practitioners, without social practices, and vice versa, there are no social practices without social practitioners – without individuals who learn, participate in, perpetuate, *and who modify* those social practices as needed to meet their changing needs, aims, and circumstances.

(Westphal, 1993, p236)

In contrast to Kantian thinking, where there is a duality of the individual and the social, Hegel presents a perspective in which they cannot be separated. Indeed, individuals arise in the social, which they are simultaneously constructing. This is clearly a paradoxical or dialectical perspective in which individuals are simultaneously forming and being formed by the social.

A brief note on the dialectical method

In the next chapter, I will explore suggestions that Freudian thought can be interpreted in terms of Hegel's dialectic. To prepare the ground for this exploration, this section provides a summary of Hegel's dialectical method. Central to this method is the idea of contradiction.

> The antimony in knowledge, instead of being the indication that we are trying to know something that we cannot know, is the very process by means of which knowledge itself arises. The antimony is a stage in the process of knowledge. This process is called after the term which was used in the old Greek speculation – 'the dialectic.' Of course, what 'the dialectic' means is a process of discussion, conversation in which the ancient Sophist sought to entrap his opponent in contradiction. . . . but for Socrates the process was not simply a game; it was a means of getting back to certain fundamental realities (p120–121). . . . What I want to point out is that here we have the dialectic as a means of advancing from contradictions to a truth.
>
> (Mead, 1936, p122)

Hegel's dialectical method of thought is reflected throughout his discussion of the social evolution of consciousness, self consciousness and knowledge. Dialectic refers to the social processes of power difference and mutual recognition in which self consciousness arises. The dialectic is the experience of self consciousness consisting of self-examination, that is, the subject–

object identity, in which one is an object to oneself. This is not a dualism in which the subject simply observes itself as an object but a paradox of participant observation in which the subject and object are moments in one action. Hegel's notion of dialectic needs to be distinguished from that of Kant's thesis–antithesis–synthesis posited by an objective observer in relation to a natural system as regulative ideas or in relation to a human action also as regulative ideas. For Kant the dialectic is the hypothesizing of the autonomous individual about an object. In Hegel, the dialectic of consciousness is constitutive as participant observation, as subject–object identity and essentially as social process.

Hegel's dialectic, in purely technical terms, is a way of thinking, a particular kind of logic to do with the paradoxical movement of thought. It is a logic in which there is the unity of opposites in their dissolution and transition, that is, *Aufhebung*. Aufhebung means negating opposites and preserving them, so raising or transforming them, all at the same time. In this paradoxical movement a unity of thought emerges. The new unity of thought not only preserves the opposites but also abolishes them because while they are preserved, their original meanings are modified and the distinctions between them are negated.

The concept of mathematical chaos provides a technical example of this logic. In thinking about the weather, one notices its stability, for example, in terms of the seasons predictably following each other. However, one also notices the instability as storms unpredictably alternate with sunshine. One could think about the weather in Kantian dualistic terms as both stability and instability, locating stability in one place or time and instability in another place or time. In other words, one could think of the weather moving from the dynamic of stability to the dynamic of instability and back again. The thesis of stability and the antithesis of instability are then combined in the synthesis of the weather system. This is a Kantian dialectic in which the two opposites or antinomies are preserved with their meanings unchanged in a synthesis that does not yield anything substantially new and in a way that paradox is resolved or eliminated.

However, from the perspective of chaos theory, one thinks of the weather as mathematically chaotic. This is a distinctive dynamic, which is a combination of stability and instability at the same time. In this sense the opposition of stability and instability is preserved but at the same time it is destroyed because these opposites can no longer be separated and so do not mean the same as they did. Instead the opposition is transformed, is raised, to a new unity, a new dynamic, in which stability is always found in instability and vice versa. New meaning emerges in the tension of opposites and the paradox remains. Indeed the paradox is the source of the new meaning. The concept of spatial and temporal fractals is close to that of mathematical chaos. No matter what the degree of detail in which one examines a fractal, it always displays self similar patterns, which are stability in instability and vice versa. The 'edge of chaos' is also a concept of a dynamic characterized by stability and instability at the same time. In all of these cases there is no notion of moving from stability to instability and back again – the opposition of stability and instability is always present at the same time.

However, Hegel's dialectic is not just a technical logic but the movement of thought as a social process expressing a human self consciousness encountering, desiring and recognizing the self consciousness of others where the unity is that of meaning and the social. Mead expresses the essence of Hegelian dialectic in his gesture–response between human bodies constituting the social act, which is meaning. This was discussed in some detail in Chapter 4. That chapter makes the following point. In terms of Hegel's dialectic, one thinks of the individual and the social in much the same way. The distinction between, the opposition of, the individual ('I,' or subject) and the other (another 'I' or object) is both retained and dissolved in the unity of social selves/society. The unity is society in which there are still distinct individuals but the meaning of individual 'I' (subject) and individual 'other' (object) is changed in the unity of social selves/society. Each individual is social, is thoroughly social to the core, in that the social self is the bodily interaction of an 'I' or subject with a 'me' or object that is the attitude of society. And society consists of individuals in that it is in the communicative interaction of individual bodies that society arises. The individual is always found in the social and the social is always found in the individual in fractal processes.

Dialectic, as a form of logic, is a movement of thought in which a statement and its opposite (negation) are taken as phases of one inseparable act. The unity of meaning arises so that the statement (for example, stability or the individual) and the negation (for example, instability or the other) are retained but in a way that transforms, lifts them up, to a new meaning (for example, chaotic weather or social selves/society). If one holds that all thought is the action of a body having the gesture–response structure of the social act, then one would also say that dialectic logic is articulated in public role-play/vocal conversation (I–you) and in private role-play/silent conversation (I–me). But this kind of dialectic conversation (reflecting dialectic logic) must be distinguished from the dialectics of the Socratic rhetoric, which is a form of teaching. The latter is a didactic process rather than a distinctive kind of logic.

Hegel criticized Schelling's reduction of 'thesis–antithesis–synthesis' to a 'lifeless schemata' externally applied to a subject matter instead of being allowed to emerge and he himself never used this formulation, although he did not reject the formulation either (Forster, 1993, p161). Hegel saw the history of thought as a process in which genuine self-contradictions arise and act as motives driving us to escape them by enriching our conceptual resources in ways that enable us to avoid them. This process cannot be thought of as pure thought (transcendental) applied by an independent free self. For Hegel the thinking subject is part of the world, interacting with other selves and nature.

Post Hegel

In the middle of the 19th century, Feuerbach argued that Hegel's metaphysical structure of absolute spirit was a transcendent mystification of human reflective processes. Self consciousness was an attribute of people not a universal subject manifested in nature and history. He and others were thus translating Hegelian metaphysics into a humanist terminology. This focused on actual historical process and the realization of self conscious human beings in an ethical community in which individuals achieved autonomy and fulfillment of their potentials through identity with others. The meaning of reality emerged in the actions and relations of individual human beings.

Marx recognized that Feuerbach had in effect translated rather than erased Hegel. He declared his independence of Hegel, grounding his thought in what he claimed had been invisible in Hegel. For Marx, reality was the sensuous reality of individuals who related to the natural world in order to produce their means of subsistence. For Marx, existence was practice as productive labor, a social practice that reshaped individuals within systems of production and their historical transformation. Marx and Engels rejected Hegel's philosophical system (absolute spirit), while expressing their allegiance to his dialectical method. However, the leading Marxist theorist of the time, Kautsky expressed the notion of dialectic in the now well-known 'thesis–antithesis–synthesis' formulation, which comes not from Hegel but from Kant.

Kierkegaard also declared his independence of Hegel but in a different way to Marx, arguing that the reality of human being was a passionate inwardness of personal ethical will. For Kierkegaard the passionate commitment to self-actualization brought individuals face to face with God.

Hegel's thought also exerted a powerful influence on James, and the school of American pragmatism (which includes James, Dewey and Mead) also rejected Hegel's metaphysics but Mead particularly took up his dialectic of social process and developed the symbolic interactionism that forms one of the foundations of the basis of the approach suggested in Part I of this book. Elias rejected all philosophers but is closer in thought to Hegel shorn of any metaphysics than to any of the others reviewed in this chapter. The approach presented in Part I of this book therefore very much has its origins in Hegelian thinking about the social process.

Elias broke with his supervisor Hönigswald because of his views about Kant:

I could no longer ignore the fact that all that Kant regarded as timeless and as given prior to all experience, whether it be the idea of causal connections or of time or of natural and moral laws, together with the words that went with them, had to learned from other people in order to be present in the consciousness of the individual human being.

(Elias & Scotson, [1965] 1994, p91)

Elias mentions Hegel:

But at that early stage in my learning process I envisaged the succession of stages in a social development as a sequence of mental structures. . . . My earlier view was probably an outcrop of the process model most familiar to a philosophy student at that time: that of Hegel. I did not yet distinguish clearly between 'process' and 'system,' but I already understood that a historical fact is a function of its position within this process . . . In the experience of those who come later even what comes afterwards, the 'consequences,' in part determine the way in which something which happened earlier, the 'reason,' is experienced and understood.

(Elias & Scotson, [1965] 1994, p12)

However it was Kantian thinking that exerted the most powerful effect in the further evolution of Western thought with its notions of system and the autonomous individual, rather than Hegel's notions of historical process and the social. The next chapter will explore the strands of thinking that most affected Freud. I will be arguing that his thinking reflects the frameworks of both Leibniz shorn of metaphysics and Kant. Although it is possible to interpret Freud in accordance with a technical definition of Hegel's dialectic (see Chapter 12), Freud's thought cannot be located in the kind of dialectic social process that Hegel was expounding.

Chapter 11

Locating Freud's thought and its later developments in the tradition of Western thinking

The previous chapter provided a brief review of some of the major movements of Western thought that are relevant when it comes to putting into context the thinking about the individual, the group and psychotherapy. That chapter paid particular attention to Leibniz, Kant and Hegel and concluded by pointing to the link from Hegel to Mead and Elias, both of whom rejected Hegel's notion of absolute spirit but took up, in different ways, his dialectical logic in understanding the development of selves and society. Others, however, largely rejected Hegelian thinking and continued to develop the Kantian tradition and also the tradition of Leibniz. An example of a thinker in these traditions is Herbart and although he is not a well-known figure, his work is relevant here because of the influence it exerted on Freud. Quite consistent with the philosophical traditions of both Leibniz and Kant was the enormous development in mainstream science reflecting a realist, materialist and positivist way of thinking. And one example of this was the medical work of Helmholtz and Brücke, relevant again because of the influence exerted on Freud's thinking. During this period, Lamarck and Darwin were also developing their theories of biological evolution and they too had an impact on thinking about selves and society, being taken up in rather different ways by those developing the Hegelian strand of thought compared to those in the traditions of Kant and Leibniz.

I am, then, drawing a distinction between two substantially different lines of development in Western thought about individuals and groups over the last few hundred years. First, there is a tradition reflecting a view of humans to be found in Leibniz's monad and in Kant's autonomous individual. These were approaches based on the objectivity of the observer and positivist science. It was in this tradition, augmented by the evolutionary thinking of Darwin, that Freud built his distinctive theory and practice in the first part of the 20th century. It seems to me that Freud followed in the tradition from Descartes and Leibniz, through Kant to the psychologists of the late 19th century in placing the individual mind at the centre of his attention. The internal world of the individual and its representing function is central to his thought. This leads to the particular view of society and the particular view of how the individual and society are connected, which was reviewed in Chapter 9. I argued there that psychoanalytic interpretations of the individual and the group have continued to be characterized by a view in which there is *both* the individual *and* the group, where the latter is understood as if it were either an individual or a system.

Second, over the same period, there was another tradition flowing from Hegel through the psychology of James and other American pragmatists, who built on a secularized, but not materialist, development of Hegel's thought in relation to the importance of the social and the understanding of the self as social. It was in this tradition that Mead developed his original view of self and society in the first part of the 20th century. In this view, individual and social are paradoxically the same process, forming and being formed by each other at the same time. The work of Elias, a little later in the 20th century, reflects an explicit rejection of Kantian thinking and takes a perspective quite compatible with Hegel's emphasis on long-term historical processes of social development. Mead and Elias take a completely different route, in terms of the history of thought, from that taken by psychoanalysis and so present a radically different picture of individual minds and the relationship with the social. I will argue in the next chapter that this history of origins continues to affect psychoanalytic theorizing as it moves from focusing on the individual to focusing on the relational and the intersubjective. In this chapter, however, I will explore the evidence for locating Freud and subsequent psychoanalytic thought in the tradition of Leibniz and Kant rather than Hegel.

I should start, however, by admitting that this distinction is not quite as neat as I make it sound in the above paragraphs. Ricoeur points to both the similarities and the difference between the thought of Freud and Hegel. Also, Ogden provides an interpretation of Freudian theories in terms of Hegel's dialectic. I will take up the views of Ricoeur and Ogden later on in this chapter and argue that attempts to interpret Freud in Hegelian terms do not, in the end, address the dialectic of individual and social in a Hegelian manner. I argue that this is because Freud and most psychoanalytic writers are located in an intellectual tradition which regards the relationship between individual and social in a 'both . . . and' manner that eliminates paradox as in the tradition of Kantian thinking. This is not compatible with Hegel's view of self in society, at least as understood from the perspectives of Mead and Elias, in which selves form society while being formed by it at the same time. Here paradox is not resolved or eliminated but is of the essence of the explanation.

The origins of Freud's thought

In his introduction to Volume 12 of Freud's collected works, Strachey says:

Behind all of Freud's work, however, we should posit his belief in the universal law of determinism. Freud extended the belief uncompromisingly to the field of mental phenomena.

(Freud, 1991, p17)

Strachey traces this influence, through Freud's medical training, from what became know as the 'School of Helmholtz' and also, indirectly, through Herbart's philosophy relating to mental phenomena. Freud's was, of course, not a straightforward determinism because he emphasized the way in which mental phenomena are over-determined in the sense of having many causes. However, it is deterministic in the sense that all mental phenomena are causally determined. The unconscious operates as a causal agency, providing causal continuity where there are discontinuities in conscious causal agency. The concept of psychic energy and the process of cathexis are direct imports from classical physics. The reflection of Descartes, Newton and Leibniz is unmistakable here.

In reviewing the scientific origins of Freud's thought, Leader (2000) cites the many authorities, in addition to Strachey, who claim that the 'School of Helmholtz' was of central influence. This school was said to have originated in the 1840s and to have consisted, amongst others, of Helmholtz and Brücke, the latter being Freud's teacher. Helmholtz was a physician and he and members of his 'School of Medicine' rejected any teleology in nature. They believed in the materialism and tangibility of matter, and in observation and experimentation as the way to understand the forces determining an organism. Their philosophy was explicitly that of scientific materialism and positivism, freed from speculative and metaphysical concerns. Helmholtz was said to take a materialist perspective in viewing the mind as a machine fuelled by electrical and chemical forces that could be traced and measured. Many writers have said that his 'physicalist psychology' impressed the young Freud, leading him initially to aim for a quantitative, physiological understanding of mental functioning and the establishment of psychology as a natural science. Freud's innovation was said to be his later move away from the materialist view that the mental could be reduced to neurology to his project of providing a science of mental phenomena. It is also argued that Freud abandoned a psychophysical and psychochemical program to take up an evolutionary one. The view that has been propagated, then, is that Freud started in the Helmholtz School and then moved on to develop a completely novel psychoanalytic theory arising from his practice rather than academic psychology or philosophy.

However, Leader contests this standard view, ascribing it to an attempt to create a myth of Freud as a lone intellectual and scientific genius, relatively little affected by other thinkers. Leader points to Freud's debt to the neo-Kantian, Brentano, who also, at much the same time, influenced Husserl and his development of phenomenology. As an example of this influence Leader takes Freud's paper 'The Negation', seeing it as a direct development of Brentano's work on the function of judgment. Here it can be seen that the kind of issues dealt with by both Brentano and Freud were common in philosophy and psychology at the time. For example, the problem of relating judging to concepts goes back at least to Kant.

Furthermore, Leader produces evidence to back his view that a 'School of Helmholtz' never actually existed and that Helmholtz and his colleagues were not the extreme materialists that they have been portrayed to be. Helmholtz wanted to explain the functioning of an organism in terms of material components interacting according to the same natural laws that those components followed outside of an organism, but this left room for many non-materialist perspectives. In thinking in this way, Helmholtz seems to be reflecting Kant's notion of organism as system. So the location of the origins of Freud's thought in the mechanism and materialism of Helmholtz is dubious, according to Leader, as is the major innovation Freud was said to have made all on his own. Leader argues that the importance Freud attached to quantity in his theory of mind could be linked not so much to Helmholtz but to the philosopher Herbart who introduced the idea that the structure of the mind, which produces the quality of experience, is amenable to the language of mathematics. Herbart continued Leibniz's program of research into the dynamics of ideas and Leader argues that Freud continued that work. Freud's use of many terms, for example, 'resistance' and 'repression,' is linked to Herbart's use of these terms. However, despite these obvious connections and despite information available about them since the 1930s, historians of psychoanalysis have paid little attention to Herbart's influence on Freud. Leader suggests that this is because it contradicts the myth of the scientist and sole founder of psychoanalysis. In other words, the standard view locates the origins of psychoanalysis largely in the individual Freud rather than in the social process reflected in the wider development of Western thought.

What, then, was the influence of Herbart on Freud? Herbart was born in 1776 and died in 1841. He was thus a young man of 28 when Kant died and a contemporary of Hegel. He studied philosophy under Fichte at Jena and developed work on the ego, drawing on Kant and Leibniz, and succeeding to Kant's chair at the university in Konigsburg. Herbart's mathematical theory of psychic structure was concerned with the dynamics of a chain of psychic *representations*.

> This introduction of mathematics enabled Herbart to take up the challenge bequeathed by Kant, who had claimed that psychology could not become a science due to its inamenability to mathematical treatment. Herbart assigned numerical values to different degrees of physical intensities at play in chains and rows of ideas. An increase in one idea's intensity results in a decrease in another's, to give a dynamic

model of the psyche that could be formalized with equations. As representations exclude each other from consciousness, their mutual resistance turns them into forces, which then oppose or consolidate each other. And since consciousness is dependent on the antagonism of representations, all consciousness will in principle involve pain. Representations inhibit and repress each other like colliding forces, and without a mutual resistance would merge. Pushed out of consciousness, they will strive to be represented again.

(Leader, 2000, pp26–27)

It is striking how resonant the above passage is with Freud's notions of psychic energy, object cathexis, repression and repetition compulsion. I also provide the above quote to point to the link between Herbart and Kant. Hegel too may have had some influence on Herbart's thinking in terms of the emphasis on contradiction expressed as antagonism and the need for the transformation, or Aufhebung, of conflict:

The theory of the ego in Herbart is based on the notion that the antagonism between representations needs to produce an *Aufhebung* of a representation as a prerequisite to the functioning of the ego. This is developed into the distinction between mediated and unmediated reproduction of representations, and Herbart's idea of mediated reproduction seems to bear exactly on the notion introduced by Freud in the *Project* under the heading of reproductive thinking.

(Leader, 2000, p42)

Herbart was also concerned with the relation of representations to desire.

However, here he was not thinking in terms of the tradition of Hegel in the sense that he focused on individual psychic functioning as a system or an internal world separate from the social.

Leader refers to other influences on the thinking of Freud. He takes the central concept of representations and internal worlds, in turn closely linked to the concept of introjection, which is usually ascribed to Ferenczi in psychoanalytic literature. Leader shows how the concepts of internal worlds and introjection were actually developed by Avenarius (1843–96) in a context critical of spatial concepts of the mind. For Avenarius, the inner–outer distinction was unfounded and grounded in the erroneous notion of a mind enclosed in a body. The fallacy of introjection, he said, was to assume that when one sees a tree one is seeing an internally reproduced picture containing an idea inside oneself. Introjection, then, is the notion of a mechanism through which an internal representation of an external event is formed. Avenarius held that the premise of 'inside' and 'outside' and the mechanism of introjection were false ones. For him, it was the task of science to overcome the illusion of introjection. Ferenczi, however, picked up on the idea of introjection and used it not to deride transactions across an inner–outer divide but to designate a process involved in cognition.

It was just this inside–outside split that Freud built his thinking upon and that still largely characterizes psychoanalytic thinking, with the notable exception of Schafer (1976; [1983] 1993), who says that mental processes do not occur in space at all and so calls for an action language in which to talk about psychoanalysis. As explained in Part I of this book, Mead's scheme is based on action, the action of a body, and so does not require a notion of an internal world and therefore of processes of introjection and projection. Mead, like Avenarius, talked about an act, a change in the state of the organism, as the basis of mind. Foulkes (see Chapter 15) and Elias were both critical of the inside–outside distinction. Freudian thinking, with its 19th century concept of an internal world, requires the send–receiver, transmission processes of introjection and projection, while the frameworks suggested by Mead and Elias do not.

In this section, then, I have been arguing that Freud's thought is located in the tradition from Descartes, Leibniz and Kant in that he focuses on the autonomous individual with an internal world of representations. In this sense it is radically different to that of Mead and Elias, the foundational thinkers for Part I of this book. I have also indicated how this difference in origin and further development has major implications for how one thinks about the practice of psychotherapy in terms of processes such as introjection and projection. As I have already said, however, there remains the question of the extent to which Freudian thinking might also reflect the Hegelian tradition. In relation to this question, the work of Ricoeur is informative.

Ricoeur on Freud

First, I want to point to the comparisons Ricoeur makes between Freud and the thought of Descartes, Leibniz and Kant. In locating desire, motivation, and much of agency and meaning in the unconscious, Freud's theories dissolve Descartes' 'I think.' Freud showed how the 'I' of 'I think' has no clear meaning.

Of Leibniz, Ricoeur says:

> But perhaps the one who most clearly prefigures Freud is Leibniz . . . It is well known that the monad expresses the universe and in this sense perceives it.
>
> (Ricoeur, 1970, p455)

He is here linking Freud's notion of representations with that of Leibniz. Freud said that an instinct was unknowable and could only enter the psychic field by means of its ideational representative:

... the psychical cannot be defined by the fact of being conscious, by apperception; on this point the affinity with Leibnizian concepts of appetition and perception . . . is very instructive and renders the Freudian concept of a physical representative of an instinct highly plausible.

(Ricoeur, 1970, p430)

Ricoeur mentions how Leibniz took account of unconscious perception and how Freud added the notion of the barrier between the conscious and the unconscious provided by repression.

Referring to the Freudian notion of behavior depending upon the drives, Ricoeur says:

This dynamic point of view has long prevailed over the preconception of the old empirical psychology and its *tabula rasa*; psychology has opted for Kant and against Hume.

(Ricoeur, 1970, p351)

Kant held that the mind contained universal categories while Hume argued that perceived connections were simply the result of habitual association, about which there was nothing necessary. Freud, then, continued in the Kantian tradition of ascribing innate structure to the mind that determined perception and behavior. It seems to me that Freud's theories dissolved the taken-for-granted agency of Kant's autonomous individual in much the same way as it dissolved Descartes' 'I think' because the action of any individual is thought to be determined by 'the unconscious' not simply by rational decisions. However, Freud's practice was built upon the assumption that analysis could develop the agency of the conscious ego and the successful outcome of an analysis was the increased autonomy of the individual. A person was not thought to be born autonomous but could become so through thinking and reflecting. Kant's autonomous individual and Descartes' 'I think', it seems to me, have not in practice been dissolved.

Ricoeur also draws attention to the Kantian 'both . . . and' structure of Freudian thinking:

. . . Freud says . . . 'Internal objects are less unknowable than the external world.' It should be noted that [this] . . . is couched in Kantian language . . .

(Ricoeur, 1970, p435)

This is Kantian language because Kant said that humans knew anything through the structure of the mind, the internal objects, because reality was unknowable. We then get both a knowable internal world and an unknowable external one. Freud thinks in this way about both the individual and the social.

> The same emotional core, that of the Oedipus complex, lies at the
> origin of neurosis and culture; each man, and the whole of mankind
> viewed as a single man, bears the scar of prehistory carefully obliter-
> ated by amnesia, a very ancient history of incest and parricide.
>
> (Ricoeur, 1970, p448)

Note how Ricoeur also sees the point I made in Chapter 9, namely, that in Freudian thought, the social, the whole of mankind, is viewed as a simple man. Having pointed to the unmistakable reflection of Leibniz and Kant in Freudian thought, Ricoeur then makes a connection to Hegel. Ricoeur says that the need to be in close contact with other beings is fundamental to the human mode of being. In other words, intersubjectivity is fundamental to human beings, which is one of Hegel's central notions. For Hegel, human desire is the desire of the other's desire, that is, a demand for recognition. Desire itself is an unanswered demand. Ricoeur argues that Freud's topographical model is solipsistic in that the unconscious does not rely on any intersubjective relationship; its desire is entirely internal. However, the structural model (referred to as the second topography) does rely on intersubjectivity, according to Ricoeur, superegos are set up in the intersubjective field.

> . . . if desire were not located within an interhuman situation, there
> would be no such thing as repression, censorship, or wish-fulfillment
> through fantasies; that the other and others are primarily bearers of
> prohibitions is simply another way of saying that desire encounters
> another desire – an opposed desire. The whole dialectic of roles within
> the second topography expresses the internalization of a relation of
> opposition, constitutive of human desire; the fundamental meaning of
> the Oedipus complex is that desire is a history, that this history involves
> refusal and hurt, that desire becomes educated to reality through the
> specific unpleasure inflicted upon it by an opposing desire.
>
> (Ricoeur, 1970, p387)

Ricoeur then compares this with Hegel's notions of the movement to self consciousness of desire in desire; the education of desire in the struggle for recognition; and the inauguration of the struggle in a nonegalitarian situation, namely, the master–slave relationship. Ogden follows a very similar route and I will, therefore, comment on this in the next section, which reviews Ogden's thinking.

However, having pointed to some similarities, Ricoeur identifies a very important difference between Freud and Hegel.

> Freud expressly stated that the discipline he founded is not a synthesis but an analysis – i.e. a process of breaking down into elements and of tracing back to origins – and that psychoanalysis is not to be completed by a psychosynthesis.
>
> (Ricoeur, 1970, p460)

Hegel's dialectic, on the other hand, moves in the opposite direction:

> This dialectic constitutes a progressive synthetic movement, which contrasts with the analytic character of psychoanalysis and the 'regressive' (in the technical sense of the word) character of its economic interpretation. In the Hegelian phenomenology, each form or figure receives its meaning from the subsequent one. . . . the truth of a given moment lies in the subsequent moment; meaning always proceeds retrogressively. . . . In such a phenomenology it is a question of the production of the self (Selbst), the self of self consciousness. . . . the positing or emergence of the self is inseparable from its production through a progressive synthesis; hence the self does not and cannot figure in a topography; it cannot appear among the vicissitudes of instincts which constitute the theme of the economics.
>
> (Ricoeur, 1970, p464)

What he is referring to here is the fundamentally synthesizing and progressive direction of Hegel's thought and the basically analytic and regressive, or archaeological, nature of Freud's thought. Mead expresses the future directed synthesizing movement that Hegel refers to in his process of gesture and response in which the meaning of the gesture emerges in the response. It is the whole social act of gesture–response that constitutes meanings and this social act has the time structure of the living present. That time structure is a circular one in which the future, the response, changes the past, the gesture, all in the present. It is in the living present that the individual and the social continually emerge in forward movement into the future, a movement in which the past is continuously reconstructed. In Freud, however, meaning, as well as the behavior and the nature of the person, are to be found by uncovering the past. In Hegel, the self is continually constructed in a synthesizing progression into the future.

The object of desire according to Hegel cannot be generated by mere evolution from the earlier to the later as in Freud. Ricoeur argues that Hegel's view of desire has affinities with Freud's but it is the opposite of a genesis of the higher (ego) from the lower (id) or from the past to the present. Instead Hegel is talking about the meaning and conditions of desire appearing in later moments. This is because my desire now, being a desire for the desire of another, can only have meaning later in the other's desire or lack of it. This is very different to Freud's archaeology, but very close to

Mead's notion of the gesture only finding its meaning in the response. Each present includes in it the element of the not known – how the other will respond. Because of this, Hegel sees recognition as a struggle to tear from the other an avowal that one is self conscious. For Freud, however, man is constantly dragged back to his childhood.

Ricoeur mentions how Freud thought in terms of opposed pairs and how this could be interpreted in dialectical terms. This is just what Ogden does and it is to his interpretation of psychoanalysis as dialectical that the next section turns.

Ogden's interpretation of Freud and object relations theory

Ogden (1994) reviews the thought of Freud and its developments in the form of object relations theories, arguing that all of them can be interpreted in terms of Hegel's dialectic. I will argue that Ogden's interpretation of Freud and object relations theorists is not consistent with the full concept of Hegelian dialectic. Ogden, I suggest, presents a technical interpretation of interaction between abstract mental agencies in the context of a concept of mind as an internal world. Communication then has to take the form of the sender–receiver mode in which contents are sent from one internal world to another. There is a fundamental assumption of minds inside people and reality outside them, which is clearly Kantian thinking. Hegel's dialectic, particularly as presented by Mead, does not involve inside or outside; it does not involve internal worlds and sender–receiver modes of communication. Instead it involves human knowing through the encounter between real persons who desire recognition from each other. Although he uses the terminology of Hegelian dialectic, I argue that Ogden really presents a Kantian dialectic of thesis–antithesis–synthesis that eliminates the paradox of the individual and the social. The Hegelian dialectic, on the other hand, sustains the paradox of individuals simultaneously forming and being formed by the social. Mead clearly reflects this paradox in that individual mind and social interaction are the same process of gesture and response. Elias' process theory represents much the same way of thinking.

Freud and dialectic

Ogden puts aside what he calls Freud's more mechanistic formulations and selects a number of passages from Freud's writings, which he claims support a dialectical interpretation. Ogden argues that the process by which the Freudian subject is constituted is dialectical in Hegel's sense because the subject is created, sustained and decentered through the dialectical interplay of consciousness and unconsciousness. He says that Hegel's dialectic is a process in a movement tending towards integration that is never achieved.

Ogden defines subjectivity as an *individual's* capacity to generate a sense of experiencing 'I-ness' (subjectivity), however rudimentary and non-verbally it is symbolized. He argues that in Freud's thought, subjectivity is not equated with the ego, or consciousness, but is the experience of 'I-ness' as the outcome of the dialectic between consciousness and unconsciousness. Consciousness is Freud's *system*, pre-conscious/conscious (Pcs/Cs), and unconsciousness is his *system*, unconscious (Ucs) by which he means the dynamic unconscious consisting of repressed wishes of a sexual and aggressive nature. Ucs is meanings felt to be incompatible, unacceptable, and threatening to Pcs/Cs. Ucs is devoid of self awareness and it operates according to different principles of mental functioning, that is, different forms of psychic representation, different rules of transformation, and different types of temporality. The system Pcs/Cs is concerned with perception, speech, motility and self consciousness. Ucs and Pcs/Cs are mutually dependent, each defining, negating and preserving the other with the existence of one depending upon the existence of the other. The systems Pcs/Cs and Ucs co-exist and subjectivity is the relationship between the two. The qualities of experience are created in a discourse between them and this discourse generates the *illusion* of a unity of experience.

Notice how Ogden takes two systems comprising the internal worlds of the individual and argues that they create, preserve and negate each other in a discourse that produces an illusion of the unity of experience. Ogden also says that Freud's structural model can be interpreted in terms of Hegel's dialectic:

> Freud's (1923) structural model represents a system of dialectics built upon (and by no mean replacing) the topographic model. In the structural model, the mind is conceived of in terms of mutually defining dialectics constituted by the ego (the I), the id (it that is not me and yet within me), and the superego (that part of me that lords it over me threateningly and protectively). . . . The subject of the structural model is located in the dialectically constituted stereoscopic illusion of unity of experience constituted by the negating and preserving discourse of the id, ego, and superego.
>
> (Ogden, 1994, p20)

Notice again how Ogden takes abstract systems or agencies in an individual mind and argues that they define, negate and preserve each other to produce an illusion of the unity of experience.

Evaluation

I want to argue now that Ogden's interpretation of Freud is not the Hegelian dialectic of subject–object, 'I-not I,' and 'I-me.' The opposites that Ogden identifies in Freud's thought are all to do with the individual, that is, aspects of the subject or 'I.' Hegel's dialectic is a movement of thought, a process between self conscious persons seeking recognition from each other, while the dialectic Ogden ascribes to Freud is intrapsychic, involving a movement between abstract psychic systems.

First, take what Ogden calls the dialectic of the conscious–unconscious. The system unconscious is the opposite of the system conscious. To be conscious in a Freudian sense is to symbolize or verbalize one's wishes, motives and intentions as causes of one's actions. Consciousness here means self consciousness. It means knowing what I am doing and why I am doing it. The Freudian unconscious, on the other hand, involves repressed wishes, motives and intentions as causes of one's actions. There is no verbalization here and while I may know what I am doing I certainly do not know why I am doing it. Subjectivity is the dialectical interplay between consciousness and unconsciousness. From the perspective of complex responsive processes, built on Mead's interpretation of Hegelian dialectic, the notions of conscious, self conscious and unconscious have very different meanings.

For Mead, consciousness is the capacity to gesture to another in significant symbols and this means that the gesture calls forth in oneself a similar response to that called forth in the other. Furthermore, the response being called forth in oneself may simply be a feeling of awareness, a felt intuition of potential response not expressed in verbal terms at all; significant symbols need not be verbal ones. Unlike Freud, therefore, being conscious in Mead's terms does not require verbalizing. Also, consciousness is not equated with self consciousness because the latter is an additional reflexive process in which one is taking oneself as object to oneself, that is, taking the attitude of one's society to oneself. For Mead, self consciousness is the 'I-me' dialectic. This is only possible because the 'me' is the gesture of the community to the 'I,' which is a response to that gesture. Self consciousness is also not purely a matter of language. Consciousness and self consciousness, then, are simultaneously individual and social processes in which interacting people are taking the attitudes of others towards their actions and each is taking the attitude of the community to himself or herself. By implication, what 'unconscious' means is interaction with others in which the attitude of others, the attitude of society towards oneself, is *not* taken. If one gestures in a way that does *not* call forth a similar response in oneself as in the other, then one cannot be conscious of what one is doing. Unconsciousness, just like consciousness and self consciousness, is a process of interaction that is both individual and social at the same time because it is individuals interacting *without* calling forth the attitude of others in themselves.

In defining subjectivity as the dialectic of consciousness and unconsciousness, Ogden is locating the emergence of subjectivity in intrapsychic processes and thereby focusing entirely on the subject pole. The object pole of the other, the community, is absent. He does not make an essential link to the other but talks about the dialectic between one individual's conscious and unconscious. He does this, of course, because this is the essence of Freud's thinking. In Mead's interpretation of Hegel's dialectic, subject and object are moments of one act, a unity in which they are preserved as new meaning, that is, consciousness/self consciousness, and what is negated is the split between subject and object. In Ogden's interpretation of Freud, consciousness and unconsciousness may negate each other but the split between them is not negated and the unity created is simply an illusion. They do not take on a new meaning because each continues to have its own separate functioning principles. Consciousness is characterized by asymmetric logic (secondary process) and the unconscious by symmetric logic (primary process) (Matte Blanco, 1975). Asymmetric logic is the Aristotelian logic of the conscious mind where paradox is a sign of faulty thinking. This is much the same as Kant's autonomous reasoning individual or Leibniz's monad. The symmetric logic of the unconscious does not even sense logical contradiction or paradox and is timeless. This is the opposite of logic and Kant would see it as man ruled by the passions. The opposites, conscious and the unconscious are said to operate simultaneously. But what is the unity that is created by this tension? When Freud talks about translating the unconscious into consciousness, bringing to the surface unconscious meaning and unconscious cause, he is talking about moving from one space to another. This is not opposites constituting something new in which they continue to be simultaneously present but with different meanings. Instead, this is oscillation from one pole to another. This is Kantian, not Hegelian, dialectic. The conscious and the unconscious are simply synthesized or added together in a resolution of paradox and the meaning of the opposition does not change. Ogden is using Hegel's terms but in a different way – there is no *Aufhebung*, that is, raising to a new meaning in which the opposites cannot be separated because they are one act.

For Mead, consciousness, self consciousness and by implication unconsciousness are all impossible outside of social processes. The conclusion I reach is that Freud's topographical model cannot claim to be Hegelian dialectic simply because it focuses on the individual internal world, just as Ricoeur pointed out earlier in this chapter.

Now consider Ogden's dialectical interpretation of Freud's structural model. In the structural model, the ego and superego arise in the clash between the id and society represented by parents and they function as psychic agencies, mediating between internal and external worlds and prohibiting free discharge of drives. The superego is a representation of the society's (the father's) prohibition. There is no reflexive notion here of an 'I' taking the attitude of the society to itself as 'me'; there is no subject taking itself as an object to itself. Instead there is an innate agency having nothing to do with society, the 'id,' conflicting with another agency, the 'superego' which represents society and imposes its wishes on the id. In Mead, the 'me' is not a representation or an imposition but the reflexive action of taking the attitude of society to oneself. Self consciousness is bodily interaction, social processes. Right at the start it is processes of communication between bodies, of action, of social processes of enabling–constraining interactions, not an imposition from outside on an internal world. It is noteworthy that in Ogden's discussion of Freud, there is no mention of the key concept of innate drives. As soon as one takes account of the drives it becomes evident that Freud's model is not dialectical in the Hegelian sense. This is because the 'id' is already given as inherited drives and so cannot be said to be created in dialectic interplay between id and ego. Again, I think Ogden uses Hegelian terms to describe an individual, intrapsychic process that does not involve the social in Hegel's or Mead's reflexive sense.

Notice also Ogden's interpretation in terms of universals and systems. The mind is understood as a system consisting of interacting subsystems that follow universal principles of functioning and make representations. This leads to the outside/inside distinction, which is not Hegelian paradox but the elimination of paradox in Kantian 'both . . . and' thinking.

Another point to notice about Ogden's argument is this. The unity of experience is said to be an illusion. This seems to mean that the individual mind is creating an illusion of unity in its experience of the world, which is actually divided in the discourse of id, ego and superego. However, the way in which Mead takes up the Hegelian dialectic is one in which a unity of experience is actually constituted. Group and society are real experience, not illusions created by individual minds.

Ogden does recognize that Freud focused on the intrapsychic and that one has to put aside what he called his more mechanistic formulations if one is to establish Freud as a thinker in the tradition of Hegelian dialectic. He suggests, however, that object relations theorists provide a more inter-subjective dialectic.

Ogden's interpretation of Klein and Bion

Ogden holds that the dialectic of intersubjectivity is implicit in Klein's concept of the paranoid-schizoid and depressive positions, as well as the notion of projective identification.

Taking the concept of the positions first, Ogden says that they are psychological organizations that determine the ways in which meaning is attributed to experience. This implies that the positions are transcendental wholes, that is, something before, something outside of experience, which is giving meaning to experience. Note immediately the difference from the formulations of Mead and Elias (see Chapter 4). For them, meaning is experience rather than something attributed to experience. Associated with each Kleinian position, there is a particular quality of anxiety, particular forms of defense and object relatedness, particular types of symbolization and particular qualities of subjectivity. Ogden says that each position is a fiction, a non-existent ideal never encountered in pure form and together they constitute a state of being. Again the difference from Mead and Elias is striking. They talk about real interactions between real persons and a real unity of experience rather than illusions of unity and fictitious positions never encountered in their purity.

The paranoid-schizoid position is, according to Ogden, a psychological organization generating a state of being that is ahistorical, devoid of experience of an interpreting subject, part object related, heavily reliant on splitting, idealization, denial, projective identification, and omnipotent thinking. It constitutes the immediacy and intensity of experience. The depressive position is a psychological organization generating a state of being (experience) characterized by an interpreting 'I-ness,' historically rooted sense of self, relatedness to others, concern, guilt and forms of defense like repression and mature identification. It generates experience endowed with symbolic meaning. When Ogden talks about a historically rooted sense of self, he means an individual's history rather than the kind of social history of ways of experiencing ourselves as psychic structures talked about by Elias. Also, for Mead and Elias, symbols are actions and meaning emerges in the social act. In Ogden's formulation, however, symbols are something behind experience that endow it with meaning, a very Kantian concept.

Ogden then introduces a third position, which he calls the autistic-contiguous position. This is a mode of psychological organization dominated by protosymbolic impressions of sensory experience. Rhythmic and sensory contiguity contributes to an elemental sense of continuity. This is generated within the invisible matrix of environmental mother and provides a sensory floor of experience. He understands the three positions to be simultaneously present, with none of them being the locus of the subject. It is important to note here the combined assumption of an internal world, now described in terms of positions, and therefore quite inevitably, the notion of something outside, namely, the invisible matrix of environmental mother.

The three positions are described in terms of the developmental process. After a hypothetical moment of unity with the mother at birth, the Kleinian psyche enters into an ongoing process of splitting of ego and corresponding division of internal objects, that is, representations. Note here how this means that the process of splitting and the object representations are implicitly already there at birth, that is, they are innate and not socially constructed.

Ogden describes the dialectic as one of splitting, that is, the paranoid-schizoid position, and integration, that is, the depressive position. The

Kleinian subject exists in the dialectic tension between these paradoxes. Each creates/negates/preserves the other. His justification for saying that they create each other is simply that they are necessary for each other's definition.

Ogden admits that his interpretation of Klein so far is one of an entirely intrapsychic dialectic, as it was for Freud. He then moves from the intrapsychic to the interpersonal, claiming that projective identification powerfully addresses this dimension. Projective identification is the psychic process by which aspects of the self are projected into psychic representation of external objects in a way that is felt to control the object from within the object and leads to the projector experiencing the object as part of himself. This is psychically depleting because it requires high psychic energy to try to control the other. The other then feels that he is being manipulated to play a part in someone else's fantasy. Projection as an intrapsychic process becomes interpersonal because it exerts pressure on the other to behave and feel in a particular way through actual interaction. Klein talked about an infant projecting split-off parts of the ego into the mother and in so far as she contained them she was not felt as separate but to be the bad self. In the Kleinian concept, the projector feels that he is in control of the object from within, experiencing the object as part of himself. Note here the sender–receiver model of communication.

Bion's formulation of container and contained, according to Ogden, makes a significant move from Klein's notion of projective identification as an intrapsychic process to a notion of projective identification as an interpersonal process. In this process, the infant projects unwanted contents (the contained) into the mother (the container), eliciting thought in her in such a way that the unwanted contents are detoxified:

> From the point of view of the container/contained dialectic, projective identification becomes a conceptualization of the creation of subjectivity through the dialectic of interpenetration of subjectivities. In this dialectical relationship, projector and 'recipient' enter into a relationship of simultaneous at-one-ment and separateness in which the infant's experience is given shape by the mother, and yet (in the normative case) the shape that the mother gives the infant has already been determined by the infant. The other allows herself to be inhabited by the infant in her 'counter-identification' . . . with the infant and in this sense is created by the infant at the same time as she is creating (giving shape to) him.
>
> (Ogden, 1994, pp45–46)

Ogden holds that Bion was here beginning to articulate a notion of *interpersonal space* in which subjectivity and the capacity for thinking was created and sometimes attacked. Ogden says that in Bion's exposition, projective identification was not just intrapsychic but an interpersonal event in which the projector exerted pressure on the other to behave in congruence with the projector's omnipotent fantasy. Projective identification is a process where the infant's thoughts/feelings that cannot be thought/felt are elicited in the mother and if she is available for use in this way then he can investigate his own feelings in a personality powerful enough to contain them. When she refuses to be a repository of her infant's feelings it damages the impulse to be curious upon which thinking and learning depend.

The subject is no longer located in the individual, according to Ogden, but arises in the space between them, in the 'interpretive space between':

> . . . the subject is conceived of as arising in a dialectic (a dialogue) of self and other. Paradoxically, the subjectivity of the individual presupposes the existence of two subjects who together create an intersubjectivity through which the infant is created as an individual subject.
>
> (Ogden, 1994, p47)

Note here how the assumption of an internal world, an inside, is inevitably followed by the positing of an outside called 'intersubjectivity' or 'space,' which the interacting individuals create. In the complex responsive processes perspective, interaction is an ongoing process in relation to which inside and outside have no meaning. Intersubjectivity is interaction and there is no space; interaction simply creates more interaction. For Ogden, however, the interacting couple are creating this third called intersubjectivity, which is another whole existing between them. This is not what Hegel and Mead are saying. They are talking about the forming of selves who are simultaneously forming the pattern of interaction. They are not creating some whole that will then affect them.

To summarize, Ogden is suggesting that subjectivity arises intrapsychically through the dialectic of the three positions: schizoid-paranoid, depressive and autistic-contiguous. Then he says that subjectivity arises as a third in a space between two individuals in the dialectic of projective identification. He formulates his position by saying that subjectivity does not arise exclusively within an individual but also in a dialectic (a dialogue) of self and other. This immediately imports Kantian 'both . . . and' thinking. At some times we can think about a dialectic of innate positions and splitting processes entirely in the individual, an internal world. At other times we can think about an intersubjective dialectic in terms of projective identification understood as container-contained and the creation of an 'outside whole' called intersubjectivity. Although he focuses attention on one process after another as paradox, his thinking eliminates the paradox of the individual and the group in which they simultaneously form each other and in which there is no inside and outside. Instead, the social/group/intersubjective becomes a space between, a tension between, a single personality system, a third. This is understood 'as if' it was another individual and the concepts of intrapsychic process are simply applied to the new third individual, namely, projective identification. This is a Kantian way of thinking rather than Hegel's dialectic.

Ogden then argues that Winnicott's thought is dialectical in the Hegelian sense.

Winnicott

According to Ogden, the implicit dialectics of Freud and Klein became the foundation of Winnicott's efforts. For Winnicott, the living, experiencing subject existed neither in reality nor in fantasy but in a potential space between the two. The subject, subjectivity, does not coincide with the psyche of the individual because it is between the two.

> Winnicott's conception of the creation of the subject in the space between the infant and mother involves several types of dialectic tension of unity and separateness, of internality and externality, through which the subject is simultaneously constituted and decentered from itself.
>
> (Ogden, 1994, p49)

Winnicott held that for the infant the mother is initially an invisible felt presence, which the infant experience as at-one-ment with mother and at the same time as being distant. The infant sees himself in the mother's face – the mother looks and what she looks like is related to what she sees. In recognizing and identifying with the infant's internal state (mirroring), the mother enables the infant to see himself as other, that is, to be an object to his observing experiencing self. This is a difference between I and me (self-as-subject and self-as-object) and is rudimentary of experiencing self consciousness, self-reflection, observable me-ness. The mother in role as mirror provides *thirdness* that allows for the division of the infant into an observing subject and a subject-as-object with a reflective space between the two. In the course of development the infant experiences transitional object relatedness in which the object is experienced simultaneously as created (fantasy) and found/discovered (reality). The question as to which it is never arises. At first the infant treats the mother ruthlessly as a 'subjective object,' an externalization of an omnipotent internal object mother. Later, however, the infant recognizes the 'I-ness' of the mother. The subjects are creating each other in their recognition of each other in an 'I-Thou' dialectic. Subjectivity becomes aware of itself. This is the development of the infant's capacity to 'use' the mother as an external object and to feel concern for her as subject. Both involve forms of recognition of alterity that are different but related to transitional object relatedness. The subjectivity of the infant, therefore, takes place in the potential space between the

234 Complexity and group processes

mother and the infant. This space is defined by a series of paradoxes generating a third area of experiencing as the place where we live.

Evaluation

I want to try to understand what Winnicott is saying and how Ogden is interpreting it by means of a comparison with Mead.

Mead explains the process of communicative interaction between adults in terms of gesture–response. One gestures to another, simultaneously calling forth in himself a similar response to that called forth in the other and that response by the other is simultaneously a gesture calling forth in herself a similar response to that called forth in him. This is consciousness in the sense that both parties can know what they are doing and are signaling to each other how the social act of gesture–response might unfold and thereby, of course, creating its evolution. Simultaneously with this, however, there is self consciousness since each of the parties is not only conscious of what they are doing but conscious of themselves as selves. This means that in gesturing, the one person is not just gesturing to the other but also simultaneously to the 'generalized other.' In other words, in gesturing, that person is not only calling forth a similar response to that of the other but also simultaneously taking the attitude of the group towards the gesture in his or her own private role-play. When one person says something to another, they are not simply experiencing how the other might react but also at the same time how the group would view the gesture. Would other people think one is being reasonable or justified in making this gesture?

Furthermore, in gesturing, the first person is also simultaneously responding as an 'I' to a 'me,' where the 'me' is the attitude of the society to that person. In other words when one person says something to another, they are not simply experiencing the possible response of that specific other and the attitude of the group to what they are saying but also the attitude of the group/society towards him or her as a person or self saying what he or she says. This is simply another way of saying that what he or she says reflects on him or her and what others will think of him or her and therefore who he or she is – we are back to the fundamental need for recognition. We do not have to account for what we say or do to another just to that other but to the group or society in general. When two people are gesturing and responding to each other, when they are interacting, it is not simply a matter of a dyad but necessarily involves the group/social. And at the same time as the first person is simultaneously gesturing to another, to the group and responding to the group, that other is simultaneously doing the same. And all of this, you will recall, is the living present, that is, the iteration of the past in anticipation of the future, always with the potential for transformation.

Mead, therefore, does not take an isolated dyad in which each is simply gesturing and responding to the other because interaction between the two is always simultaneously the gesture–response of each to group/society. Wider social relations are always intrinsically implicated in the interaction between any two people, indeed in the interaction of any one person with him or her self. For human beings anything else is an impossibility. And in this highly complex interaction in the living present, notice the multiple operations of desire and recognition. When he gestures he expresses a desire not just for her as an object but for her responding desire, that is, recognition of his desire, and this is true of her too. Furthermore, both are desiring the desire, the approval or recognition of the group and society.

Recall that Mead talks about symbolic interaction. The communicative interaction takes place in the medium of symbols and, for Mead, symbols are actions. The significant symbol is the bodily action of gesturing calling forth the bodily action of responding, together constituting social acting, which is meaning. The symbol is meaning and that is a social act, a unity in which gesture and response are simply moments. Mead's whole approach, then, is about the actions, the communicative interactions, of bodies. There can be no inside or outside in relation to an action. Self and society are not separate but the same process of ongoing communicative interaction between bodies in sophisticated cooperation in the present iterating of the past and expecting of the future.

Now compare Winnicott's formulation with that of Mead. Winnicott takes the mother–infant dyad as prototypical of interaction between people. He and those many psychoanalysts who have taken up his thinking, move straight from this dyad to the analytic dyad of analyst–analysand. This is the first difference from Mead who does not locate his explanation in infancy alone. Winnicott also describes interaction entirely in terms of the mother–infant dyad. There is no simultaneity with, no inescapable implication of, the group/society. Others, such as father, siblings, mother-in-law may sometimes feature as context introduced after the dyadic interaction is understood. As far as the mother and infant are concerned there is no notion of calling forth in the way that there is in Mead. The mother, when adequate, is attuned in a good enough way to the feeling state of the infant. Instead of 'calling forth' in each other, Winnicott talks about the mother's mirroring role. In this role she is recognizing and identifying with the infant's internal state and by doing so she is enabling him to see himself as other, that is, as object to his observing subject. Ogden then equates this with the 'I-me' dialectic. In this formulation Winnicott made a very important move from the Freudian emphasis on interaction with others as constraint, for here interaction is enabling a sense of self. However, this is certainly not the 'I-me' dialectic of Mead, nor is it the kind of social dialectic of Hegel. Consider why.

In her mirror role the mother recognizes and identifies with the infant's internal state. This is the key move for it means that the mother is reflecting back to the infant his true self, a pre-existing innate self. What the infant sees in the course of normal development is his true self or essence. Here, the 'me' is not the attitude of the society towards him, his self, as expressed in the mother's recognition, but the attitude of him to himself. This is an intrapsychic dialect of his 'I' relating to his 'me' and the good enough other is simply instrumental in helping him to have this experience. The 'social' interaction of mother and infant, when it works normally, mirrors what is already there. What the social interaction is enabling and also shaping to some extent is the expression of the true self. This is still a Freudian way of understanding the social and it is very limited compared to that of Mead and Elias. There is no idea here of the infant's self being in the process of perpetual construction in the social interaction where there is no true self at all. In Hegel, and very much in Mead, the self is forming and being formed by the social at the same time. Here there is no true self, once one abandons Hegel's metaphysics of absolute spirit. Furthermore, the Winnicott model of interaction is one that involves one party, the infant, who cannot initially be said to be self conscious. As a prototype interaction it is thus very limited.

Next compare Mead's notion of symbol with that of Winnicott. Winnicott's theory of symbol is very much an intrapsychic one. The first symbol for an infant is the transitional object. This is a real object that represents, stands for, another in fantasy. In the infant's mind a representation of an external real object stands for the mother object in fantasy and this is a symbol. The connection between the fantasy and the real, the symbol, is an illusion. Winnicott takes this as the foundation of thought and culture, society, because they all involve symbols. The very foundations of culture and society are thus intrapsychic processes representing, through individual fantasy and illusions, early actual interactions between mother and infant. This is the same kind of thinking as that of Freud. The separation between self and society, inside and outside is retained and the social is an illusion of individual minds.

For Winnicott, the first symbol is the transitional object and the implication is that the infant's communication with the mother before this does not take place in the medium of symbols. I argued in Chapter 5 that right from the start the communication between infant and mother is in the medium of protosymbols, that is psychological/physiological attunement, of attachment and separation in the form of the hyperstructure, a socio-physical temporal process (see Chapter 6). When does this medium become symbol proper? It does so when the infant calls forth in himself a similar response as in the mother. This is likely to occur long before the 'transitional object.' For example, the hungry infant's crying, as gesture, seems to call forth in himself similar distress, frustration and fear as that called forth in his mother. In Mead's terms, this is significant symbol and this social act means hunger–feeding. What then is the significance of the transitional object in these terms? It seems that this is one of the first observable signs of the infant developing the ability to engage in private role-play, which constitutes mind. This is the same as developing imagination or fantasy. In the place of direct communication with the mother, the child communicates with an object. The gesture is directed to the object and this gesture calls forth in the child the same responses as he is imagining to be called forth in the object. The object and the object–response is now part of the child's private role-play, the precursor to silent conversation. The infant can only engage in this because he has already engaged in the public 'play' with the mother and others. The communication has already been in the medium of symbols so this transitional object cannot be the first symbol. The infant's mind only becomes possible because he is living in a human society. The capacity to engage in private role-play depends upon ongoing social play of public communication in the medium of significant symbols. For Winnicott, however, the social and the cultural depend upon prior existence of symbols and he presents an intrapsychic view of how they are formed.

Winnicott is using a spatial metaphor and coming up with the idea of a space between, a third, and so on. Why does he do this? This is an important question because so many, including Ogden, have taken this idea up.

Winnicott assumes that initially, for the infant, there is no separation between inner and outer reality because the infant experiences the mother as part of himself due to her nearly perfect attunement to him. The transition is from this undifferentiated subjective omnipotence, or oneness, to object relating and a sense of two-ness. For the transition to occur, the near perfect attunement has to be ruptured and the infant has to experience frustration and thus separation. Transition is the moment at which this happens and it creates a gap between the two. The transitional object plays an important part in this moment. This transitional object is something the baby uses that is not part of his own body but a bit of the external world, for example, a blanket. The transitional object is not wholly part of the self, nor is it completely separate from the self. Through its use the actual space between the infant and the mother does not open up, only the potential space between them   the transitional space between complete attachment and complete separation. The baby experiences a 'me' and a 'not me' and its creative solution to the gap is the fusion of 'me' (image of mother) with 'not me' (blanket) so that 'a new subjective object has been formed that seems to perpetuate the unity with the mother that is being lost' (Wright, 1991, p72). In commenting on Winnicott's notion, Wright says:

> We can speak . . . of outer reality, a world of shared experience and meanings in which we all live . . . we can also speak of a world of inner reality, of thinking, of fantasizing, and dreaming. But Winnicott wants to point us to a third area of 'experiencing,' which lies in some sense

between the other two. In the outer world meanings are fixed and cannot change. In the inner world, they are fluid, subjective, and idiosyncratic. But in the transitional area, which can be thought of as being at the interface between the other two, there can be dynamic interchange.

(Wright, 1991, pp74–75)

Winnicott holds that this third area is immensely variable in that one baby creates a transitional object and plays while another might not. Whether the baby does or does not depends upon the mother and whether she provides good enough holding. However, the third is very much the creation, the creative solution of the individual infant, only being assisted by the mother. This creation of transitional objects, transitional and potential space is taken as prototypical of the artistic, the cultural and the social, all regarded as areas in which the sustaining of illusion is important.

Why does Winnicott find that he has to posit a third and why do some many other psychoanalytic theorists do the same in positing some kind of third, something between, transitional space, field, background or matrix? The answer, I suggest, has to do with the spatial metaphor and its central notion of an internal world separated from other internal worlds by a gulf. If it is then held, in the absence of any evidence at all it seems to me, that the infant starts in a fused omnipotent state then one must explain how this infant comes to experience being separate. Even if one did not start with this assumption but held, as Stern does, that the infant already has a sense of a separate self, then given the assumption of an internal world, one must still explain how internal worlds can communicate across the gulf. There has to be some notion of transmission of something from one internal world to another. In other words, something must happen in the 'space between.' As soon as one poses two internal worlds, one has to pose a third, a 'between.' One then conceives of this as transitional space, or a third, or a matrix. In other words, one has to think of a system, a womb, a matrix or field, in which the two participate. This third then is an abstraction from the direct *interaction* of two bodies.

However, if you think in temporal terms of direct interaction between bodies having pattern or form then there is no in-between; there is only interaction. The question then becomes how the interaction comes to have form, comes to be patterned. This normally would lead one to look for the system or field causing it and one is then back to some kind of third. However, insights from the complexity sciences (see Chapter 3) provide an analogy donating a different possibility. This is that interaction itself has intrinsic pattern forming properties. From this perspective one does not assume that an infant has no sense of separateness. The hyperstructure (see Chapter 6) strongly suggests that this would not be possible. From birth the baby's bodily regulation in terms of opioids and arousal hormones requires alternating attachment and separation provided by the presence of another. Attunement then has to do with this hyperstructure, which is fundamentally physiological and social at the same time and is present at least from birth if not before. The question of a tabula rasa does not arise because the baby is born with a body and the action of a body is the basis of mind. It makes no sense to ask whether action is a tabula rasa. This question only even arises when you have a spatial notion of the mind as an internal world.

Ogden's interpretation of Freud is not Hegelian because there is no recognition of the other. However, in Bion and particularly in Winnicott there is much stress on recognition. So here there is something of the social. However it is incorporated in a very particular way that is quite different to Mead's interpretation of Hegelian dialectic. Essentially the recognition is the recognition of one's true self rather than taking the attitude of the other. Ogden is talking about a direct apprehension of one's own subjectivity as reflected in the other. Mead, however, talks about a gesture calling forth in oneself the attitude of the other to oneself and this is social processes in which self is perpetually constructed. Even when social relations are taken into account by Bion and Winnicott, this is not done in a way that is consistent with Hegel.

I am arguing then that Freud and the object relations theorists who followed him all continued within the Kantian tradition of thought. To the extent that their thinking is dialectic it is so in the Kantian sense. It does not work to try to force psychoanalytic thinking into the framework of Hegel's dialectic because in Hegel's thought paradoxical social processes are central in a way that is completely different to Freud and object relations theorists.

Chapter 12

The development of relational and intersubjective psychoanalysis

In this chapter I will review three significant developments in psychoanalytic thinking that have taken place over the last few decades. The first is by a group of psychoanalysts who have developed a relational perspective, the most notable names here being Mitchell, Greenberg, Stern, Benjamin and also Ogden, whose thinking has already been reviewed in the previous chapter. The second closely related development has come to be known as intersubjectivity theory and the most prominent names here are Stolorow, Atwood, Brandchaft and Orange. Finally I will briefly refer to the thinking of Schafer. Taken together these developments represent a significant shift from Freud's theory and practice of psychoanalysis.

Mitchell and Aron (1999) provide a brief review of the history of relational psychoanalysis, claiming that it represents a distinctly new tradition in America. In the 1930s and 1940s Harry Stack Sullivan, Eric Fromm and Clara Thompson contributed to the development of interpersonal psychoanalysis, which emphasized interpersonal phenomena and tended to downplay intrapsychic ones. This theory pointed toward a departure from Freudian drive theory and this, perhaps, accounts for its relatively small impact at the time. Bowlby's work on attachment after the Second World War also had little impact at first but, together with interpersonal theory, has recently gained more attention. More recently, Kohut's work broke away from American ego psychology and established a powerful presence. In the late 1970s and early 1980s an American brand of psychoanalytic feminism developed and this pointed to the importance of social relationships. All of these developments emphasized actual relationships with significant others in contrast to earlier psychoanalytic thinking, which tended to emphasize fantasized relationships. It was out of this mix of influences that relational psychoanalysis developed, with Greenberg and Mitchell (1983) using the term to bridge the traditions of interpersonal relations and object relations. The term relational began to encompass developments in self-psychology, intersubjectivity theory and social constructivism. Relational here means that the analytic process is thought of as the transformation of the relational configuration between therapist and patient and constructivist means that this configuration is co-created in the interaction between the two participants. This accords with Sullivan's concept of the interpersonal field where mind is not inside us but emerges in relations with other minds – it is transpersonal and contextual.

Before reviewing the development of relational psychoanalysis, I want to make some comments on one of its foundational thinkers, namely, Bowlby.

Attachment theory

John Bowlby (1969; 1973), the developer of attachment theory, was a child psychiatrist and somewhat maverick psychoanalyst who adopted a position that was not at all fashionable in psychoanalytic circles in the post Second World War period. He held that it was real interpersonal experiences, rather than intrapsychic processes and fantasies, which accounted for the psychological development of the individual. In his work with children he discovered that parents had a tendency to use their children to satisfy needs not met by their own parents, as well as to displace hostility felt towards their parents onto their own children. Here he was pointing to psychic development as an intergenerational phenomenon. It was this experience that led to the formulation of attachment theory, which holds that the individual always lives in an interpersonal and intersubjective context. From the moment of birth, a child becomes attached to his or her parents and a few others. In the course of this attachment experience, the child develops mental representations of these attachment bonds and those representations then organize the individual's internal world, so affecting personality development. Representations are developed into internal working models of self and other. Anxiety is a response to the threat of losing the attachment object. Psychopathology originates in faulty real life attachment bonds rather than innate fantasies. Bowlby was, therefore, proposing a theory in direct opposition to Freud's emphasis on fantasy and on Melanie Klein's object relations theory. However, he was not moving away from the notion of mind as an internal world, which was fundamental to the thought of Freud and Klein. For Bowlby, the object of psycho-analytic study was not the individual in isolation but the individual in the social context.

Bowlby and his colleagues conducted research demonstrating that the psychological reactions of the small child to separation from his or her mother could have long-lasting effects on later developments. This research showed that children who experienced consistent, reliable and empathic parental care developed patterns of secure attachment with their parents and this became the basis for reasonably stable relationships in later life. On the other hand, children who experienced parental neglect, rejection, abandon-ment or abuse tended to develop insecure attachment patterns, which persisted through later life. The research also indicated that the defense mechanisms against separation anxiety were not internally generated but were responses to interpersonal events. Defenses were not originally shaping experience; rather it was experiences that were shaping defenses. In constructing developmental theories along these lines, Bowlby challenged traditional psychoanalytic thinking, questioning the notion of unconscious fantasy and downplaying notions such as the Oedipus complex.

However, Bowlby did not move away from the Freudian reliance on instinct. Instead of basing psychic development on sexual and aggressive instincts he postulated a basic attachment instinct and he understood psychic development in systemic terms in which the psyche was likened to a cybernetic system (Marone, 1998; see also Chapter 13). By instinctive, Bowlby meant persistent, predictable patterns of behavior common to a species that occur without learning. In adopting a cybernetic model of the psyche, Bowlby was thinking in terms of goal directed behaviors in which any gap between the goal and the actual outcome is fed back as a further determinant of behavior such that the gap between goal and actual is reduced. This is a view of behavior tending towards a pre-given equilibrium.

The major similarities and differences between attachment theory and the theory of complex responsive processes developed in Part I can be seen from this very brief review of attachment theory. Attachment theory is based upon the spatial metaphor of the mind as an internal world consisting of representations and models, which are understood as cybernetic systems. The theory of complex responsive processes adopts a completely different view of individual mind. It is understood in process terms as the action of a body directed toward itself in private role-play and silent conversation, essentially the same process of acting that constitute social relations. There is no internal world and no system, only the temporal process of action. Furthermore, attachment theory continues to rely on instinctually determined behavioral patterns, while the complex responsive processes theory posits no link between instinct and human action. The theory of evolution it is based on is one in which evolution produces the physiology of the human body such that it requires attachment–separation behavior for physiological regulation but the patterns of such behavior are entirely learned.

The relational and intersubjectivity developments in psychoanalysis, to be reviewed in the following sections, continue attachment theory's reliance on the notion of internal worlds and systems.

Relational psychoanalysis and the field

I will first review how real relationships are taken into account in relational psychoanalysis and then return to the notion of a field as it is used by relational psychoanalysts. After that, I will review concepts of the unconscious before looking at shifts in the practice of psychoanalysis.

Real relationships

Mitchell (2000) argues that when Freud abandoned the seduction theory for instinct theory, significant others became largely fantasized others as extrapolations from inborn drives. Drive theory was a kind of object relations theory in which fantasies about others rather than their actions were crucial. This opened the way for a rich exploration of human fantasy and imagination, the intrapsychic, but it sidelined relationality. Other people faded into the background as the mind came to be thought of in terms of body-based, constitutionally wired primal fantasies such as Oedipal triumphs, fratricidal murders and primal scenes of parental intercourse. Given this starting point, it was necessary to explain why people would relate to each other at all and these reasons were found in individual urges for pleasure, needs for dependency and desires for recognition. The result was a monadic, individualist theory in line with Western thought as expressed by Descartes. Mitchell calls for a move from this individual centered notion of subjectivity to one that regards subjectivity as arising alongside intersubjectivity in that one mind presumes other minds. For him, we become human through our attachments to, and internalizations of, caregivers.

Greenberg (1986) suggests that Freud's drive/structure model is an individual psychology while the relational/structure model is a field theory. The drive model understands psychic structure as the transformation of original drive energies, while the relational one sees structure as the consequences of early interpersonal exchanges. For Greenberg, Freud's model of the analyst is based on the position of the observing scientist as understood in the 19th century, derived from Cartesian philosophy. There is a direct line from the Cartesian stress on the observer's externality to the drive model. Relational models are not based on Cartesian philosophy but more on theories of relatively and uncertainty. Greenberg refers to Sullivan's notion of participant observer and Fairbairn's interventionist stance as the basis of a relational attitude in psychoanalysis.

Greenberg also says that *every relational model postulates some idea of an internal object world, a representational world, as the means of the transformation of relationships with others.* These representations have motivational and structural properties. He sees the analyst as fitting into the patient's representational world, either assimilated into an old relational pattern or experienced as new. Repression always has interpersonal components and takes place in a context that makes an impulse feel dangerous.

It is noteworthy that while the relational model moves to real interpersonal relationships it does so in a particular way. The notion of mind/psyche as an internal world of representations remains firmly in place. There is *both* an inside, what goes on in the psyche, *and* there is an outside, what goes on in the social field. I will come back to the notion of a field but here I want to draw attention to the 'both . . . and' structure of relational psychoanalytic thinking. These writers are suggesting that early actual relations form an internal world, which is then the basis of later relating to others and is also the means of transformation. First we have the intra-psychic and then we have the interpersonal. The paradox of forming and being formed by, which was stressed in Part I of this book, is eliminated by this 'both . . . and' way of sequencing the intrapsychic and the inter-personal. In the psychoanalytic relational model, one does not find the radical questioning of inside and outside as in the thought of Elias and Foulkes (see Chapters 2 and 15). The key assumption about internalization and internal world in the relational model points to a major difference between this way of thinking and that set out in Part I, based on the action theory of mind to be found in Mead and Elias.

Furthermore, the two-person model is clearly at the centre of relational thinking, while the wider group is central to thinking in terms of complex responsive processes. This group approach is social in a way that one and two person models are not. The relational theorists hold on to the dyadic situation, retaining the notion of innate psychic processes that are now structured by real relationships rather than the drives. The shift to thinking and practicing in terms of the group is profoundly different, I suggest, because it is a shift to a wider, interactive view of relationships. Instead of object relations as representations in an internal world, the complex respon-sive processes perspective focuses on the actions of bodies and the patterning of their communicative interaction as themes simultaneously forming and being formed by the actual experience of interaction between real people.

The notion of a field or a third

Ogden's thought was reviewed in some detail in the previous chapter, which referred to his understanding of interaction between two people as con-stituting a field or a third. He develops this notion more fully in relation to his view of psychoanalytic practice.

Ogden defines the analytic third as the intersubjective space between analyst and analysand. He sees this as a dialectic construction in that there is a tension between subject and object that immediately reveals itself to be a new source of dialectical tension. Analyst and analysand are subjects creating and created by, destroying and destroyed by one another, and in the process generating an analytic third. This is the middle term sustaining and sustained by the analyst and analysand as two separate subjects who come into being in the process of the creation of the analytic subject. This analytic third is a subjective (intersubjective) phenomenon that differ-entiates psychoanalytic experience. The analytic third is constituted in a process of mutual negation/recognition but it does not reflect each of the subjects in the same way – transference and countertransference reflect each other but are not mirror images. Although they jointly create and are created by the analytic third each of the parties experiences it differently because they are separate subjects in dialectic tension.

What is immediately striking about this formulation is the creation of a third. By this Ogden seems to mean a whole in which the analyst and analysand participate. Two separate subjects, two internal worlds, interact and in doing so they create a new subjectivity (intersubjectivity) that then creates them. It is outside of them and is experienced differently by each of them. Although he is using Hegelian terminology, Ogden is using it to describe a movement that seems to me to be quite different from Hegel's description. As I understand it, Hegel was talking about a process in which each party desires to be desired, that is, they seek mutual recognition. It is in this process of seeking mutual recognition that they experience negation. For example, the master seeks to dominate but his domination is negated by the fact that such domination requires the acceptance of the slave, which means that the slave is not being dominated in a simple way. Hegel is pointing out how the self consciousness of each party is emerging in the tension of their interaction. This is different to positing that another whole is emerging in the interaction. In the Hegel formulation the parties are not participating in anything other than the interaction between them. They are not creating anything other than their own self consciousness. It is certainly in this sense that Mead understands the Hegelian dialectic and it is fundamentally different to the Ogden version.

With respect to Klein's theories, Ogden says that projective identification was only implicitly a psychological–interpersonal concept. He then says that Bion extended the notion of projective identification to the psychological–interpersonal with his container–contained framework. Ogden develops this further, arguing that projective identification creates a 'subjugating third', which subsumes within it the separate individual subjectivities of the participants. He seems to me to be saying that an essentially individual process subjugates/subsumes individual psychic processes to become a social process, the subjugating third as a kind of interpersonal system of which the individuals become parts.

> Projective identification can be thought of as involving a central paradox: the individuals engaged in this form of relatedness unconsciously subjugate themselves to a mutually generated intersubjective third (the subject of projective identification) for the purposes of freeing themselves from the limits of who they had been to this point. . . . the new intersubjective entity that is created, the subjugating analytic third, becomes a vehicle through which thoughts might be thought, feelings might be felt, sensations might be experienced, which to that point had only existed as potential experiences for each of the individuals participating in this psychological–interpersonal process.
>
> (Ogden, 1994, p101)

The notion of interaction as the creation of a third, a field, or a system is also central to the work of all the other relational psychoanalysts. For example, Greenberg (1986) holds that relational models are field theories and Benjamin (1990) takes a similar position. For her, relational approaches encompass *both* intrapsychic *and* intersubjective phenomena and she sees subjectivity as established by *both* processes of recognition or affirmation *and* destruction/negation *at the same time*. Drawing on Hegel's master–slave analogy she points to the paradox that in the very moment of recognizing our own independence we are dependent on the other to recognize it. However, having provided a paradoxical formulation, she then picks up on Ogden's notion of the third and says that this implies something outside each of us to which we orient ourselves. She says that it is only from this standpoint that we can be separate yet connected and she speaks of a primary dialogic form of mutual recognition, a form of play, which creates thirdness as an intersubjective space, that is, as an essential aspect of relationships of recognition. The third is the music, or the dance, which the partners follow. They do not necessarily match each other's moves but align themselves to a third, making it up as they go and feeling as though they are oriented to something outside themselves. The co-constructed history of this dialogue is ultimately the container.

Relational theorists retain the emphasis on the intrapsychic as innate and conflictual and they replace the drives as the structuring force with the relational. In doing so, however, they stay with two person relationships and do not move to the group. They all use spatial metaphors of space, field or third. Despite protestations to the contrary, it seems to me that relational psychoanalysts continue to see the relational in terms of transactions between monads rather than as social co-construction. Despite sometimes using Hegelian terms, they in fact think in terms of Kantian dualisms of the 'both . . . and' form that eliminates paradox.

The unconscious

In their introduction to Stern's (1983) paper, Mitchell and Aron (1999) suggest that some of Freud's notions cannot be separated (for example, infantile sexuality and the Oedipus complex) but others are not necessarily conceptually joined. For example, classical psychoanalysis joins the concepts of unconscious, repression and instinctual drive as if they were different facets of the same phenomenon. Drives emerge from the body and exert pressure on the mind for discharge. The drives are asocial and dangerous and so many are repressed to become unconscious. Relational theories reject the notion of the drives and are then accused of rejecting unconscious repression. Stern's paper, however, theorizes about a distinctly psychoanalytic unconscious in non-drive terms. He picks up on Sullivan's suggestion that much of what is normally thought of as unconscious is merely unformulated. Sullivan never developed this suggestion and Stern sets out to do so with the notion of unformulated experience as composed of vast domains of sensation, perception and thought rather than specific repressed contents. The unformulated unconscious becomes a source of creativity. This is similar to Stolorow's notion of the unvalidated unconscious to be discussed later in this chapter. In making this move, Stern lays the ground for a shift from:

- repression as the prototypic defense to dissociation;
- drives to the importance of language in the construction of experience; and
- a view of memory as the tapping of static unchanged images to a view of memory as perpetually transformed and reconstructed in the present.

For Stern, drawing on Dewey, unformulated experience consists of vague tendencies, which if allowed to develop to the point where they can be articulated would become lucid experience. Unformulated experience lacks clarity and differentiation and is not yet knowable in the definable terms of language, perhaps a beginning of insight not yet formulated. Freud's thought is built on the assumption that perception is a sensory given so that any lack of clarity in a psychic element always had to be the consequence of later events, a distortion of drive and defense. The contents of the Freudian unconscious are not unformulated in that unconscious elements are carriers of meaning that could be put into words if the defenses could be lowered. Thing presentations, primary thinking, await only cathexis by secondary process to become word presentations and so conscious. This transformation does not represent growth, evolution or transformation because in entering consciousness the repressed wish is tamed and so becomes less itself.

However, in entering consciousness the unformulated becomes more itself. Here, experience is not a given but is constructed and its construction proceeds in levels of progressive articulation. Unformulated experience is not indicative of pathology or conflict; it is just that consciousness cannot yet grasp it. However some unformulated experience may be defensively motivated in that its lack of clarity protects against noxious articulation. This is unformulated experience that has never been formulated clearly enough for traditional repression to operate. Terms like memory and distortion cannot be applied to unformulated experience. In contrast, Freud claimed that the unconscious contained veridical historical truth that needed to be uncovered. Stern regards the unformulated as creative disorder from which the new emerges:

> In this view, then, psychoanalysis is not a search for hidden truth about the patient and the patient's life. It is instead the emergence, through

curiosity and the acceptance of uncertainty, of constructions which may never have been thought before. Furthermore, these constructions are not merely sensible stabs at history and description: As Sullivan was the first to see, they are part and parcel of the new world patient and analyst are creating between them. . . . In the same vein, Loewald (1960) proposes that change in psychoanalysis is the result of the reorganization of experience, not of the uncovering of fully formed truth.

(Stern, 1983, p100)

This notion of what is unconscious in human interaction, together with the similar notion of Stolorow's unvalidated unconscious, is quite consistent with the complex responsive processes perspective and it was taken up in Chapter 7.

Practice

Mitchell (2000) talks about the implications of a relational perspective for practice. Instead of thinking about the analytic relationship as the sterile operating theatre Freud believed it could be, Mitchell argues that it is not different from other human relationships, as Freud wanted it to be. The intersubjective engagement between analyst and patient is the very vehicle of deep change. Mitchell talks about the passionate feelings that the analyst has for the patient whereas classical practice was largely prohibitive and characterized by pervasive restraint. Mitchell holds that the neutrality, anonymity and abstinence of classical practice were largely negative principles and that silence and emotional flatness simply made it safer for the analyst. From a relational perspective there is a sense of liberation for the analyst because it is now possible to use appropriate self-disclosure, breaks in the frame and deep emotional engagement with the patient. Mitchell is not arguing for an abandonment of restraint but for disciplined self-reflection and the bringing of love and hate back into the analytic relationship. The patient's love and hate are not simply transference but also relate to the real analyst and surrender of the analyst to deep emotional engagement is the precondition of effective treatment. The analyst needs to form judgments in specific circumstances about concealing or disclosing his love or hate. This is not simple, however, because love and hate are shaped and cultivated within contexts that are slowly constructed over time. There is nevertheless an asymmetry in the roles of analyst and patient.

From a relational perspective, the analyst's interpretation is no longer regarded as the ultimate authority – the conversation between analyst and patient, the disciplined and thoughtful process itself, becomes more important than the truths arrived at (Spezzano, 1999). Sometimes it is useful for the analyst to accept the need to act under personal motivations of which he or she is unaware before those motivations can be thoroughly investigated (Renik, 1999). Sometimes one needs to react spontaneously on the basis of intuition. Appropriate gratification for the analyst is an essential feature of the successful treatment. The best way to facilitate a patient's self-exploration may be for the analyst to present his own different view and even argue persuasively for it. The most effective way of avoiding the danger of imposing a subjective construction on the patient is not to try to abandon it but to acknowledge it and make every effort to identify and question the ways in which the analyst is idealized as his or her own constructions are given undeserved authority.

Aron (1991) says that a communication process is established between analyst and patient in which influence flows both ways – they affect and are affected by each other in a relationship established and continually re-established through ongoing mutual influence. He says fantasies and memories are not just carriers of infantile wishes and defenses but are plausible interpretations of the patient's experiences with significant others. He also says that care must be taken with metaphors of the good enough mother, or of the analyst, as holder or container of the patient's pathological contents because this infantilizes the patient and deprives the analyst of subjective content.

The relational turn, therefore, signaled a significant shift in psychoanalytic practice. Central technical concerns to do with neutrality and abstinence have been called into question and there is a move from the view that the analyst is trying to make the unconscious conscious through interpretation to the view of the analyst as engaging in a relationship. This shift in technique directs attention to real relations with others in the present and the links with the past have more to do with enriching the narrative.

I turn now to a similar development, that of intersubjectivity theory. One feature distinguishing this development from relational theory is the much more critical attitude taken to object relations theory.

Intersubjectivity and systems thinking

Stolorow and Atwood provide a succinct description of the intersubjectivity theory they have developed:

> Intersubjectivity theory is a field theory or systems theory in that it seeks to comprehend psychological phenomena not as products of isolated intrapsychic mechanisms, but as forming at the interface of reciprocally interacting subjectivities.
>
> (Stolorow & Atwood, 1992, p1)

Stolorow and his colleagues argue that psychological phenomena cannot be understood apart from the intersubjective contexts in which they form and so they propose to focus not on the individual mind but on the larger system created by the interplay of subjective internal worlds. Individual mind/psyche is a psychological product crystallizing from within the nexus of intersubjective relatedness and that individual mind serves psychological functions. The larger field or system constitutes the proper domain of psychoanalytic inquiry and the larger system they talk about is always the dyad of parent–child or analyst–patient. They specifically exclude from their view of intersubjectivity the interpersonal (what people are actually doing in their interaction) and the social (defined as outside causes of behavior). They also do not regard intersubjectivity as a developmental achievement since it is always present.

Consider first the view of Stolorow and colleagues that their theory of intersubjectivity is a systems theory and then how they understand subjective internal worlds, which they identify as subsystems in an intersubjective supra system.

Intersubjectivity as a systems theory

When Stolorow and colleagues talk about systems theory, they have in mind the general systems theory of von Bertalanffy (1968):

> Within a general system philosophy, any living system is part of a hierarchy. Each system contains subsystems, or elements, that constitute the whole. Two or more systems interacting cooperatively form a supra system. From this perspective the mental activity of the individual child or patient is a subsystem of the larger child–caregiver or patient–analyst supra system. One- and two-person psychologies have tended to be reductive because they proposed comprehensive explanatory theories grounded in one level only of a living system hierarchy.
>
> (Orange, Atwood & Stolorow, 1997, p75)

However, they clearly see one of the fundamental problems of systems thinking, namely, the objective observing stance that the first order systems thinker takes in relation to the system of interest. While this stance may be reasonable in relation to non human systems, systems thinkers have for a long time seen that such a stance is not appropriate in relation to human 'systems' because the supposedly objective observer is a part of the system. This is the problem that second order cybernetics has tried to deal with but, as I will argue in the next chapter, it has not succeeded in doing so. Stolorow and colleagues also argue that one can only ever work within the intersubjective field, or supra system, and can never step outside of it to objectively observe it.

. . . intersubjectivity theory differs from systems theory, as defined, for example, in the family-systems theory of Bowen and his collaborators. Intersubjectivity requires subjectivity, or rather two or more subjectivities, and retains its focus on the interplay between differently organized subjectivities. We cannot work within the intersubjective field and simultaneously step outside it, as family-systems theorists attempt to do, from a God's-eye view.

(Orange, Atwood & Stolorow, 1997, p4)

However, they do say that analyst and patient can together reflect upon their intersubjective interplay. I do not think that they really develop the implications of this point. What does it mean to reflect upon interactive experience within that experience? I think they would find it difficult to explain this without implying a move outside the direct experience of interaction itself because the intersubjective field is a higher-level system consisting of the intersection of internal subjective worlds. In Mead's explanation, which is not a systems theory, each party calls forth in him or herself responses similar to those called forth in the other. This is how each can know what he or she is doing, can signal to the other how the act might unfold and in fact can know something of how the other feels. All there is here is the paradoxical process (forming while being formed) of bodily interaction and you clearly cannot step outside of that – you can only continue to interact. The basis is the actions of bodies with particular kinds of nervous systems and there is no field or higher and lower level systems so that the question of stepping outside one or the other does not even arise.

What does it mean to reflect upon interaction from this process perspective? Clearly we can and do reflect upon our interaction, that is, take our current interaction including reconstructions of our past interactions as objects to our subject (social consciousness) just as each of us can take ourselves as an object to ourselves (self consciousness). Note that in Mead's dialectical theory there is a subject and an object, a gesture and a response, and the unity of the two, where the unity is in no way outside or supra. The unity just is the two taken together as meaning and nothing else. To put it another way, we can reflect upon the themes of being together that we are forming and that are simultaneously forming our experience of being together. Of course, when we do this we are not stepping outside of our bodily interaction, we are simply engaging in further interaction, that is, forming themes that are forming us at the same time. We are not constructing a field or a system; we are forming while being formed by the themes of being together. We begin to see more clearly why the conceptual difficulty about getting outside of the field arises. It is because conceptually it is outside the internal world and outside direct interaction between people. Retaining the notion of an internal world as system and a system outside of this immediately brings in the individual–social, the inner–outer problem.

Consider further how Stolorow and colleagues use the systems idea.

> . . . the intersubjective viewpoint does *not* eliminate psychoanalysis's traditional focus on the intrapsychic. Rather it *contextualizes* the intrapsychic. The problem with classical theory was not its focus on the intrapsychic, but its inability to recognize that the intrapsychic world, as it forms and evolves within a nexus of living systems, is profoundly context-dependent. . . . the concept of an intersubjective system brings to focus *both* the individual's world of inner experience *and* its embeddedness with other such worlds in a continual flow of reciprocal mutual influence. In this vision, the gap between the intrapsychic and interpersonal realms is closed, and, indeed, the old dichotomy between them is rendered obsolete. . . . The very distinction between one-person and two-person psychologies . . . is rendered obsolete, because the individual and his or her intrapsychic world are included as a subsystem within the more encompassing relational or intersubjective supra system . . . The very idea of a two-person psychology continues to embody an atomistic, isolated-mind philosophy in that two separated minds (the 'windowless monads' of the philosopher Leibniz) are seen to bump into each other. Such a conception fails to recognize the constitutive role of relatedness in the making of all experience. We ought to speak of a contextual psychology.
>
> (Orange, Atwood & Stolorow, 1997, pp67–68)

Here they distance themselves from Leibniz's (and Freud's) monads and posit instead a supra-relational/intersubjective system of which the internal subjective worlds (consisting of organizing principles) of two individuals are parts. The supra system provides the context within which the internal subject worlds form and evolve and in which they are embedded. The supra system is also described as a continual flow of reciprocal mutual influence constituted by the intersection or interplay of the subjective worlds. Stolorow and colleagues then talk about their theory as bringing to focus *both* the subjective worlds (intrapsychic realm) *and* the intersubjective context (interpersonal realm). This is the Kantian way of thinking that eliminates paradox and they do not notice the paradox of subjective worlds forming the intersubjective context while the intersubjective context forms the subjective worlds at the same time. Because they locate them at separate levels in a hierarchy of systems, they have dissolved a dichotomy and replaced it with a duality. Interaction is understood as a system/field/context, implying that the participation of the individuals is participation in a system/field/context, that is, a whole outside of direct experience of interaction. This is a different view of participation to one in which participation is simply the direct interaction between bodies.

Subjective worlds

Stolorow and his colleagues argue that the subsystems forming the inter-subjective supra system, or field, are the subjective internal worlds of a dyad: infant–caregiver and patient–analyst. The particular thematic structure or organizing principles of a child's subjective world evolve organically from critical formative experiences that mark his/her unique early history and the individualized array of personal motives that develop as their result. Development is motivated by the child's need to organize experience and the basic process that mediates the functional relationship between experience and action is concretization, that is, the encapsulation of structures of experience in concrete sensorimotor symbols. Note how action and experience are separated and how they are mediated by symbols – in Mead, actions are symbols, which are experience. Once the child has established a relatively stable psychological organization, it serves as a prereflective frame of reference into which structure he/she will unconsciously assimilate subsequent experience. The developmental process is an intersubjective one shaped at every point by the unique interplay between the child's evolving psychological world and the worlds of caregivers. In other words, the field/system produces the subjective worlds of minds and the interpenetration of the subjective worlds produces the field so that they influence each other sequentially.

The 'subjective world' refers to the contents of experience and the 'structure of subjectivity' designates the invariant principles unconsciously and recurrently organizing those contents according to distinctive meanings and themes. So the theory posits invariant principles (distinctive meanings and themes) constituting 'structure,' which is recurrently organizing the 'contents' of experience. In other words, there is an intrapsychic system that is attributing meaning to experience, where experience seems to be understood as the sense of self (cognitive and affective) in interaction with others. For example, the patient is said to organize his or her experience of the analyst according to archaic organizing principles – the transference. So here there is an individual mind as a system of invariant principles that gives meaning to a particular interaction and this applies to the other individual in the interaction too. It seems to me that this theory has not really moved away from two monads interacting across a boundary.

The unconscious

In intersubjectivity theory, there are three different senses in which subjective internal worlds are unconsciously organized: prereflective, dynamic and the unvalidated.

Prereflective unconscious. Recurring patterns within the developmental system (infant–caregiver) result in the establishment of invariant principles that unconsciously organize the child's subsequent experience. The unconscious ordering principles, crystallized within the matrix of the child/caregiver system, form the building blocks of personality development. This is a realm of unconsciousness called the prereflective unconscious. People enter any situation with a set of such principles but which is activated depends upon the context. For example there are self-object and repetitive dimensions in patient–analyst relationship. In the former the patient yearns for the analyst to provide self-object experiences, in the latter the patient expects and fears a repetition of the early experience of developmental failure. These oscillate in a figure-ground way and which appears at any moment depends not just on the patient's transference (invariant principles) but also on aspects of the analyst's stance. The treatment provides new relational experiences and together with greater self-awareness this facilitates the establishment of alternative organizing principles thereby enlarging the experiential repertoire. Prime examples of prereflective unconscious organizing principles are those that derive from the child's perception of what is required of him to maintain ties that are vital to his well-being (normally covered by the term superego).

Dynamic unconscious. This is formulated in terms stripped of meta psychological encumbrances. Repression is understood as a process whereby particular configurations of self and object are prevented from crystallizing into awareness. The dynamic unconscious is configurations that consciousness is not allowed to assume because of their association with conflict and subjective danger. Particular memories, fantasies, feelings and other experiential contents are repressed because they threaten to actualize these configurations. These derive from the realm of intersubjective transaction, namely, the mutual regulation of affective experience within the developmental system. This happens when central affect states cannot be integrated because they fail to evoke the requisite attuned responsiveness from the care-giving surround. The result is life long inner conflict in which affect-dissociating operations are called into play, defensively walling off central affect states rooted in early derailment of affect integration. The dynamic unconscious here is not repressed instinctual drive derivatives but rather the dynamic of affect states defensively walled off to protect against re-traumatization. This is not just a name change because now the boundary between conscious and unconscious always forms within the system as a product of specific intersubjective contexts. Conscious experience becomes progressively articulated through the validating responsiveness of the early surround. When a child's experiences are consistently not responded to he perceives that aspects of his own experience are unwelcome or damaging to the caregiver and this experience must then be sacrificed to preserve the tie. Repression is understood as a negative organizing principle operating alongside a positive one that does materialize in conscious experience.

The unvalidated unconscious. Other features of experience may remain unconscious, not because they are repressed, but because in the absence of validating response they could never be articulated. This is the unvalidated unconscious. This is a similar notion to Stern's concept of the unformulated unconscious. The boundary between consciousness and unconsciousness is thus fluid and shifting, a product of changing responsiveness. In the realm of experience in which consciousness increasingly becomes articulated in symbols, unconscious becomes coextensive with unsymbolized.

Psychoanalytic technique

Stolorow and his colleagues define psychoanalysis as the study/interpretation of organizing principles that are unconscious:

> Only the consistent working through in the analysis of the developmentally determined, invariant organizing principles can achieve the structural change so hopefully envisioned by the pioneers of our calling.
>
> (Stolorow & Atwood, 1992, p97)

They see themselves as psychoanalysts, despite the significant departures from Freud, because they work with unconscious mental processes, transference and countertransference, and the fantasies of the patient. However, instead of regarding the dissolving of the transference as a sign of ending, they think a remaining tie with the analyst could continue as a source of emotional sustenance. They attach great importance to the analyst's subjectivity, regarding resistance as something to do with the analyst's stance. For example, the analyst may be re-enacting the patient's early trauma.

How intersubjectivity has moved from Freud and object relations theory

Intersubjectivity theory makes a decisive move away from viewing motivation in Freudian terms as the working of a mental apparatus processing instinctual drive energies. Instead it views motivation as arising in lived experience as the unfolding of affect-laden exchanges with the other. This is a shift from drive to affect as the central motivational construct and affectivity is not the product of an isolated intrapsychic mechanism but the property of the dyad system. They dismiss notions of ego, id and superego as mechanistic reifications.

Classical psychoanalysis assigned ontological priority to the body and its drives with the organization of experience as a secondary expression of bodily events. Intersubjectivists regard this is a materialist doctrine in which concepts from the natural sciences are reified. Instead, they hold that the boundaries between subjectively experienced mind and body are products of specific, formative intersubjective contexts. Empathically attuned verbal responses foster the gradual integration of bodily affects into symbolically encoded meanings as body sensations become verbally articulated as conscious subjective states. The extent to which one comes to experience affects as mind (feelings) rather than solely as body depends on the presence of a facilitative intersubjective context. This evolution can fail. Subjective experience can become concretized, that is, encapsulated by concrete, sensorimotor symbols. This is dramatized and reified as action or enactment so as to maintain the organization of the subjective world. For example, early erotic experiences may be concretized and retained as a way of maintaining the cohesion and stability of a sense of self and a bodily substitute may be created for some conflictual experience. They express in anatomical symbols what must not be expressed or cannot be heard. Here they move away from the universals of Freud, regarding even the Oedipus complex as a metaphor that becomes salient for some people as the result of failure of attunement. Early erotic experiences are not universal but a form of bodily action that substitutes for failed attunement.

In terms of practice, intersubjectivity does not regard psychoanalysis as the uncovering of actual memories of past fantasies, so abandoning Freud's archaeological model. A different perspective on the transference is taken in that it is not seen as regression to infantile states, but rather, takes the form of archaic organizing principles. While Freud saw transference as repetitive reliving of the past in the present, intersubjectivity theorists argue that nothing is removed from the past and attached to the present. Instead they talk about invariant organizing principles that have remained salient through the patient's life and the patient's experience of the analysis is not simply determined by his/her past but also by the current relationship with the analyst. They do not see transference as distortion because this implies that the analyst knows reality. They reformulate transference as organizing activity, an expression of the continuing influence of organizing principles that crystallized in the patient's early formative years. They do not see transference as a biological compulsion to repeat the past but as the continuing influence of themes connected to early derailment.

From the classical perspective, the success of the analysis is gauged in terms of the extent to which the patient sees the events of the analysis according to the basic concepts informing the analyst's observations. The unchallenged assumption is that the analyst can know the objective reality that the patient is distorting. Stolorow and colleagues, on the other hand, argue that through empathy and introspection the only reality to be known is subjective reality – that of the patient, analyst and the field created by the interplay between the two. They claim that traditional methods are cures by compliance and that analysts adopting traditional techniques often recreate the primary trauma of the patient. For them the therapeutic alliance is sustained empathic inquiry as reflection on the organizing principles. They explore intersubjective conjunction and disjunction as reflecting early trauma and derailment.

Analysts drawing on Klein think of the transference as a manifestation of projection. For example, Racker (1968) thought of transference as the projection of rejecting internal objects on to the analyst and Kernberg (1976) attributed certain transference reactions to projective identification. Stolorow and colleagues argue that this locates everything in the patient. The alternative they propose is to think in terms of developmental arrests. They object to the idea of the patient putting something into the analyst, arguing that what happens between them is co-created. Projective identification, however, is the notion that the patient translocates parts of his psyche by unconscious intent into the analyst, as if the analyst is playing no part in it. Simply because the analyst *feels* taken over by this supposed unconscious intent of the patient does not mean that this is what is actually happening. There may be a correlation but the linear cause and effect that the notion of projective identification suggests is untenable. As an explanation of infant development, projective identification implies a hidden intent on the part of the infant to communicate unwanted feelings but Stolorow and colleagues argue that there can be no *intent* to communicate an experience that has not yet been symbolized. We can say that there is unconscious communication in non-verbal forms but this does not require us to posit processes such as unconscious intentionality and the projection of objects. Kleinian theory builds on the assumption of monads with deep aggressive drives, encapsulated in isolation, struggling to find a means of communication. Stolorow and colleagues dismiss as untenable this Kleinian picture of an infant with complex fantasy activity in the pre-symbolic stage – they reject the notion of projective identification altogether (Stolorow, Orange & Atwood, 1998).

However, despite the significant move from Freud and object relations, the theory of intersubjectivity remains individual centered. The theory originated in studies of the subjective origins of the theories of Freud and others. These studies argued that theories derive to a significant extent from the subjective concerns of their originators and a theory of subjectivity itself was therefore needed, meaning a unifying framework to account for the phenomena the theories address and also for these theories themselves. The studies were not concerned with the wider cultural mix in which the theories were developed. In its origins therefore intersubjectivity theory takes a reflexive turn purely in relation to an individual and never looks at the wider culture/society. Despite strictures against focusing on the individual mind, the origins of the theory displays just this focus and its development never moves past the dyad. Also, developmental derailment occurs when the individual is deprived of a developmental progression in which he could come to rely on his own spontaneous, authentic and noncompliant experience (Stolorow, Atwood & Brandchaft, 1994, p72). This occurs when the child is hostage to the response of another for determination and definition of who he is. He is imprisoned in responsibility for the state of mind of another. This implies a true self, whereas Mead's 'I-me' dialectic requires the view of the other to become oneself. This shows how Stolorow and colleagues stay within the Freudian tradition.

Furthermore, the internal worlds and the supra system they form, in which they then crystallize, are strongly reminiscent of Kant's self-organizing systems and of his 'both . . . and' elimination of paradox. Intersubjectivity theorists sometimes use the figure–ground allusion and they do not seem to notice the paradox of subjective worlds creating the system that creates them. They eliminate the paradox by looking at these phenomena sequentially. In some important respects the basics of Freudian thought are retained. There is still the notion of the individual mind as an internal world even though the contents are now not drives or objects but organizing principles. The focus of the analytic experience is still upon a dyad and in particular on the history of the patient in terms of another dyad – the infant–caregiver system.

If one moves to thinking about the individual and the group in dialectical terms as paradox of forming while being formed at the same time, as in Part I, then organizing principles emerge in the interaction between people and at the same time in the interaction of each with him/herself. There is no internal world or external field or system, only the bodily actions, the process of interaction patterning interaction. Agency is not simply located in a subjective world nor is it simply located outside people. Agency and interaction coincide.

The question of agency is central to Schafer's development of psycho-analysis.

Schafer and psychoanalytic action language

Perhaps the biggest move that Schafer (1976; [1983] 1993) makes away from Freud is his rejection of spatial metaphors in meta psychology, including the notion of an internal world or any kind of internalization process. He rejects Freud's language of force, energy, cathexis, mechanisms, sublima-tion, function, structure, drive and adaptation. He also describes Kleinian object relations theory as carrying reification to grotesque extremes (Schafer, 1976). What he proposes in place of the internal world is action, by which he means that the person as the agent of actions is to be distinguished from bodily or environmental happenings. In doing this he moves from the notion of an internal world to that of the autonomous individual as agent of action. This is a move back to the unambiguously autonomous individual. While Freud limited individual agency in the form of the id and the drives, and the complex responsive processes perspective limits individual agency in the need for others, Schafer does not seem to limit individual agency at all. Instead, he posits individual agency as a given.

> These action locutions (presented here only to clarify a narrative alternative and not as a standard to be imposed on the analysand) establish the analysand as single or unitary and fully responsible, even if conflicted and puzzled, agent. Now the analysand is someone who is acting as a person in a world made up of other people who are also agents. Gone is the populous, animistic 'inner world' and gone is the posture of either commander or a detached, passive, helpless witness of dramatized psychological events. . . . Now the analysand is not so much harnessed by mental life as engaged in clarifying, extending, and communicating the complex, uncertain, distressed, or pleasurable aspects of his of her activity. In one way, not having fragmented and distributed himself or herself in an 'inner world' narrative, the person as agent is more alone; in another way, having maintained personal agency, he or she is at least potentially involved in intersubjective or social relationships and communication.
>
> (Schafer, [1983] 1993, p247–248)

> . . . interpretation brings home to the analysand the extent to which, and the terms in which, the analysand has been the author of his own life . . . [and] . . . has been disclaiming this activity.
>
> (Schafer, 1976, p8)

> In my recent publications (1976, 1983), I have identified many of the locutions analysands use to disclaim their own actions. Examples are: 'The impulse overwhelmed me' . . . What is being defensively disclaimed is the personal agency that would be plain if the analysand were to say instead: 'I did the very thing that I consciously and urgently did not want to do' . . . By attributing agency to impulses and thoughts rather than to oneself, the analysand disavows responsibility.
>
> (Schafer, [1983] 1993, p248)

From these quotes it is clear that in abandoning the notion of an internal world, Schafer has not made the move to social selves. Instead, he has recast, in action language, the psychoanalytic aim of increased individual autonomy and the taking of personal responsibility.

> Refined and stabilized personal agency is one way – the action language way – of referring to what is more familiarly known as increased autonomy of adaptive, self-reflective, and synthesizing ego functions; a moderation of superego functions and defensive ego functions; as mature narcissism and increased cohesiveness of the nuclear self; as

genitality or postambivalent object love; as the further development of the separation–individuation and object constancy; or as development though and beyond the infantile depressive position. Personal agency is refined and stabilized by the analyst's insightful retelling of both disclaiming and excessive claiming agency . . .

(Schafer, [1983] 1993, p190)

Schafer does not talk about individual minds/selves emerging in the social process as the paradox of forming and being formed at the same time. Although he abandons the notion of mind as 'inner world' he strongly retains the notion of individual agency without relating it to the social process. He does, however, regard the analyst and patient as co-creating the analytic situation and he talks of both analysand and analyst presenting what he calls their second selves in the analytic situation, a presentation evoked by the situation. The two are creating something that then affects them.

If as I have proposed, the analytic relationships amounts to a meeting and a development of two-second selves, defined to a large extent by the nature of the analytic project, then it follows that this relationship may be called *fictive*. Fictive, not in the sense of artificial, inauthentic or illusory, but in the sense of a relationship constructed by both people under highly specialized dialogic circumstances. . . . All relationships have a fictive aspect in that they are constructed by both parties involved; they are constructed out of what is conversationally realistic and expectable and what is fantasized unconsciously.

(Schafer, [1983] 1993, p52)

. . . the second self – and the first self too, for that matter – are for systematic purposes better conceptualized as actions and modes of action. The analytic second self is a way of conducting an analysis. It does not refer to an essence that lies behind the actions and expresses itself through them. And it does not refer exclusively or without amendment to the analyst's self-description. Indeed the designation second self is best thought of as a narrative device, a form of description of interpretation of the analyst insofar as he or she is working effectively as an analyst . . .

(Schafer, [1983] 1993, pp52–53)

Schafer (1976) regards analysis as an encounter between two agents each narrating to the other. He talks about emotions being actions, which define, as they are defined by, the agent's situation; the agent defines as he is defined by these situations, actions or modes. Schafer proposes an action language focusing on the person as agent who pursues narrative strategies.

Each account of the past is a reconstruction that is controlled by a narrative strategy. The narrative strategy dictates how one is to select, from a plenitude of possible details, those that may be reorganized into another narrative which is both followable and expresses the desired point of view about the past. Accordingly, this reconstruction, like its narrative predecessor, is always subject to change. For whenever new explanatory aims are set and new questions raised, new slants on the past will be developed and new evidence concerning the events of the past will become available.

(Schafer, [1983] 1993, p193)

Schafer's view of time is very similar to that of Mead discussed in Part I of this book in that he too stresses the narrative thematization of experience and how it changes in the retelling. This is not Freud's view of excavating the past.

To summarize, Schafer's thinking abandons the notion of the mind as an internal, world and leaves behind the problematic distinction between what is inside the mind and what is external to it as reality, relationship and the social. Like Mead he sees mind as silent private action. He thinks of experience in narrative terms and has the same notion of the living present as that discussed in Part I of this book. He understands interaction in terms of narrative performance co-created by those participating in it. However, he retains a straightforward view of the agency of the individual and in the relationship of concern to him, the analytic relationship, he does see the pair creating something called the analytic situation or the fictive account which then affects them. This is close to Ogden's analytic third and the field or system of the relational and intersubjective psychoanalysts. Schafer has moved from the idea of the individual possessing an internal world to the notion of the individual as an active agent narrating histories of experience. He does not focus on the construction of experience in interaction nor does he deal with the group or society but focuses on the dyad. The analyst as actor retells the analysand's story according to particular rules of psychoanalysis and focuses on the 'second' story, that is, the unconscious one. He occasionally refers to the story as a joint product emerging in interaction but this does not seem to me to be central to what he is saying.

The last chapter and this one have traced out a significant move away from Freud's meta psychology and his focus on intrapsychic phenomena. These chapters have also indicated major developments in terms of practice. However, the notion of the internal world and the distinction between inside and outside, with its Kantian dualism of 'both . . . and' thinking, remains a central feature of both theory and practice, with the notable exception of Schafer. Even for him, however, the focus of practice is on the dyad and the theory is developed in terms of a dyad. While he leaves behind the notion of inside and outside, he does so by focusing almost entirely on the individual. Furthermore, psychoanalysts have retained a particular view of the social inherited from Freud but now clothed much more clearly in the language of systems thinking. In the next chapter, I will explore the drawbacks of systems thinking. These two assumptions, that to do with internal worlds and that do with interaction as system, are the central features distinguishing psychoanalysts from the theory of complex responsive processes outlined in Part I of the book.

Chapter 13

The incorporation of systems thinking into psychoanalysis

Chapter 9 traced the development of Freudian thinking about the relationship between the individual and the group in the work of Bion and later psychoanalysts and those influenced by them. Throughout this development, the basic view was retained of the group as a phenomenon promoting regression in individuals unless clear group organization and high levels of rational autonomy in individuals prevented this. Some formulations drew on general systems theory, for example, Durkin. Yet others, for example, Agazarian, presented an understanding of the group in terms of cybernetic systems. The analyst, or therapist, was the objective observer of the systems. Foulkes and subsequent group analytic writers also incorporated systems thinking into their approach to group therapy, but in a somewhat different way to be explored in Chapter 15.

Freud had thought of the group as an individual writ large where both individual and group followed the same universal developmental process, particularly the Oedipus complex/primal horde. The introduction of systems thinking into psychoanalysis recast the individual and the group in terms of universal systems constituting wholes that interacted with each other according to universal developmental processes, for example, basic assumptions, splitting, and so on.

A similar movement of thought was described in Chapter 12 in relation to the development of thinking about the psychoanalytic dyad. Freud's original focus on intrapsychic phenomena was steadily transformed into a focus on relationships between people, first through object relations theory and interpersonal perspectives on psychoanalysis and then through the relational and intersubjective theories of more recent years. There has been a shift from the analyst as objective observer of the patient's psyche to the notion of analyst and patient co-constructing the analytic situation. These relational and intersubjectivity theories have also been cast in terms of systems. Individuals interacting with each other as subjects are said to constitute a third, a field or a supra system, which then becomes the focus of psychoanalytic attention.

Systems thinking, therefore, has become an important component of modern psychoanalysis and it is the purpose of this chapter to explore the nature of systems thinking. I will be arguing that it is inappropriate to think about human interaction in terms of systems and I will point to how systemic perspectives differ from the process perspective presented in Part I of this book.

The origins and development of systems thinking

Chapter 10 described how Kant synthesized a central intellectual challenge of the Age of Enlightenment, namely, the antimony of human freedom and the determinism of the natural scientific method. In three 'Critiques' of the scope of human reason, action and judgment, Kant created a new dualistic paradigm of nature and human action that resolved these contradictions. This is the 'both . . . and' thinking that eliminates the paradox by positing two causalities and locating them in different spheres. One causality, determinist natural laws, applies to nature, and another, rational choices made by autonomous individuals, applies to human action.

Kant and systems thinking

In eliminating the paradox of determinism and freedom, Kant also suggested an additional way of thinking about nature when he made a distinction between mechanisms and organisms. A mechanism may be defined as a functional unity in which the parts receive their function as parts from the functioning of the whole. For example, a clock consists of a number of parts, such as cogs, dials and hands, and these are assembled into a clock, which has the function of recording the passing of time. The parts are only parts of the clock insofar as they are required for the functioning of the whole, the clock. Therefore, a finished notion of the whole is required before the parts can have any function and the parts must be designed and assembled to play their particular role, without which there cannot be the whole clock. Before the clock functions, the parts must be designed and before they can be designed, the notion of the clock must be formulated.

However, the parts of a living organism are not first designed and then assembled into the unity of the organism. Rather, they arise as the result of interactions within the developing organism. For example, a plant has roots, stems, leaves and flowers that interact with each other to form the plant. The parts emerge as parts, not by prior design but as a result of internal interactions within the plant itself in a self-generating, self-organizing dynamic in a particular environmental context. The parts do not come before the whole but emerge in the interaction of spontaneously generated differences that give rise to the parts within a unity (Goodwin, 1994; Webster & Goodwin, 1996). The parts, however, have to be necessary for the production of the whole, otherwise they have no relevance as parts. The parts have to serve the whole, it is just that the whole is not designed first but emerges in the interaction of the parts. Organisms develop from simple initial forms, such as a fertilized egg, into a mature adult form, all as part of an inner coherence expressed in the dynamic unity of the parts. An organism is thus thought of as expressing a nature with no purpose other than the unfolding of its own form. The organism's development is thought of as unfolding what was already enfolded in it from the beginning. Kant described this as 'purposive' (see Chapter 10), for although an organism is not goal-oriented in the sense of having a movement towards an external result, it does move to a mature form of itself. The development to the mature form and the mature form itself will have some unique features due to the particular context in which it develops but it can only ever unfold the general form already enfolded in it. In talking about development being purposive, Kant introduced his notion of organism developing according to a 'regulative idea.' Since he held that we could not know reality, it followed that we could not say that an organism actually was following a particular regulative idea. In other words, we cannot make the claim of a constitutive idea in relation to the organism. Instead, as observing scientists, we can claim that it is helpful to understand an organism 'as if' it were moving according to a particular purpose, namely, the regulative idea of realizing a mature form of itself, that is, its true nature or true self.

For Kant, the parts of an organism exist because of, and in order to sustain, the whole as an emergent property (Kauffman, 1995). Organisms are self-producing and therefore self-organizing wholes, where the whole is maintained by the parts and the whole orders the parts such that it is maintained. The link with modern complexity theory and its notions of self-organization and emergence is clear (see Chapter 3). It should be noted that in suggesting that we think in terms of systems Kant was introducing a causality that was teleological and formative rather than the simple, linear, efficient (if–then) causality assumed in the traditional scientific way of understanding nature as mechanism. In systems terms, causality is formative in that it is in the self-organizing interaction of the parts that those parts and the whole emerge. It is 'as if' the system, the whole, has a purpose (teleology), namely, to move towards a final state (teleology) that is already given, namely, a mature form of itself. In other words, nature is unfolding already enfolded forms and causality might be referred to as formative teleology (Stacey, Griffin & Shaw, 2000) in which the dominant form of causality is the formative process of development.

However, Kant argued that this explanation of how nature functioned could never be applied to humans because humans have a soul. For Kant, then, human action had to be understood in a different way, and this was in terms of autonomously chosen goals and autonomously chosen actions to realize them. The predominant form of causality here is teleological, namely, that of autonomously chosen ends made possible because of the human capacity for reason. The principal concern then becomes how autonomously chosen goals and actions mesh together in a coherent way that makes it possible for humans to live together. This is a question of ethics and Kant understood ethical choice in terms of universals, namely, choices that could be followed by all people. We may call this rationalist teleology (Stacey et al, 2000).

So, Kant developed a systems theory with a theory of causality we may call formative teleology, to explain how nature developed, arguing that this could not be applied to humans, and another kind of explanation for human action, which we may call rationalist teleology, that did apply to human action. The human body can be thought of as a system because it is an organism. As such, it is subject to the laws of nature and when human action is driven by the passions of the body then it too is subject to the laws of nature and so not free. However, when acting rationally, humans could not be thought of as parts of a system because then they would exist because of, and in order to maintain, the whole. A part of a system is only a part because it is interacting with other parts to realize themselves in the purposive movement of the emergent whole and the emergence of that whole is the unfolding of what is already enfolded, so excluding any fundamental spontaneity or novelty. If a part is not doing this then it is irrelevant to the system and so not a part. However, a part in this sense cannot be free, that is, it cannot follow its own autonomously chosen goals because then it would be acting for itself and not as a part. Furthermore, as parts of a whole that is unfolding an already enfolded final state, neither whole nor parts can display spontaneity or novelty. There can be nothing creative or transformative about such a system.

It is particularly important to note these points because when systems thinking was developed during the 20th century, it was directly applied to human action and individuals came to be thought of as parts in a system called a group, organization or society. It immediately follows that any such explanation cannot encompass individual human free choice. Nor can a systemic explanation encompass the origins of spontaneity or novelty. To explain these phenomena within systems thinking, we have to rely on the autonomous individual standing outside the system. In other words change of a transformative kind cannot be explained in systemic terms, that is, in terms of interactions between parts of the system, with one important exception that I will come to later. Any transformative change can then only be explained in terms of the intrapsychic functioning of the individual. This is a particularly serious drawback for relational, intersubjective or group theories of psychotherapy where it is the interaction between people, not simply the attributes of individuals, that is posited to bring about change of a transformative kind.

Note also how the understanding of nature as system is quite consistent with the natural scientific method in that it is the human objective observer (understood from the perspective of rationalist teleology) who identifies and isolates causality in natural systems (understood as formative teleology) and then tests hypotheses ('as if' or regulative ideas) about those systems. The classical psychoanalytic view of the therapist very much accords with the notion of the objective observer who formulates hypotheses as interpretations and manages the boundary around the analytic situation. Although the view of the therapist's role from a relational or intersubjective perspective is substantially different, the analyst still retains a version of the objective observer role, but now in relation to the system, field or analytic third that is being co-created with the patient. The therapist is still in the role of objectively observing and forming hypotheses about something outside him or herself that he or she has co-created with the patient. From the complex responsive processes perspective, the therapist thinks of himself or herself always within the paradox of participant observer in interaction with patients as participant observers, in which they are together producing nothing other than further interaction. The focus of the therapist's attention is on the thematic patterning of that interaction.

The rest of this chapter is a further exploration of the points just made in the light of the development of systems thinking in the 20th century.

First order systems thinking

In the late 18th century Kant, then, introduced a systems theory and it reached a position in subsequent philosophy that was to serve as the foundation of systems thinking, the main developments of which occurred around the middle of the 20th century. During 1930s and 1940s, a number of scholars worked in related areas, very much in conversation with each other, and their work culminated in the publication of some important papers around 1950. The related areas covered systems of control, the development of computer language and the development of a new science of mind in reaction to behaviorism, namely, cognitivism (McCulloch & Pitts, 1943; Gardner, 1985).

The new systems theories developed along three pathways: general systems theory (von Bertalanffy 1968, Boulding, 1956); cybernetics (Ashby, 1945, 1952, 1956; Beer, 1979, 1981; Wiener, 1948); and systems dynamics (Forrester, 1958, 1961, 1969; Goodwin, 1951; Philips, 1950; Tustin, 1953). All three of these strands began to attract a great deal of attention in many disciplines from around 1950, as did the new cognitivist psychology, and of course, computers. Engineers, bringing with them their notion of control, took the lead in developing the theories of cybernetic systems and systems dynamics, while biologists, concerned with biological control mechanisms, developed general systems theory. This systems movement, particularly in the form of cybernetics, has had a major impact on sociology and psychology and previous chapters have shown how it has come to be part of psychoanalytic thought. It is particularly important to bear in mind the underlying ideology of control that has been imported along with systems thinking. Some brief remarks are made on each of these strands of development in systems thinking before returning to the problems that systems thinking brings with it.

The central concept in general systems theory (von Bertalanffy, 1968) is that of homeostasis, which means that systems are thought to have a strong tendency to move towards a state of order and stability, or equilibrium, in which the system is adapted to its environment. Systems can only do this if they have permeable boundaries that are open to interactions with other systems. Such systems display the property of equifinality, which means that they can reach homeostasis from a number of different starting points along a number of different paths. It follows that history and context are unimportant. All that matters is a system's current state in terms of boundaries and how systems are relating to each other across these boundaries. Disorder is corrected at all levels by boundary and role definitions and change take place through change in boundaries.

Cybernetic systems are self-regulating, goal directed systems adapting to their environment, a simple example being the central heating system in a building. Here, the resident of a room sets a target temperature and a regulator at the boundary of the heating system detects a gap between that target and the actual temperature. This gap triggers the heating system to switch on or off, so maintaining the chosen target through a process of negative feedback operation. Clearly, this is a highly mechanistic way of thinking and this makes its application to human behavior problematic.

The third strand of systems theory was also developed largely by engineers who turned their attention to economics (Goodwin, 1951; Philips; 1950; Tustin, 1953) and industrial management problems (Forrester, 1958). In systems dynamics, mathematical models of a system are constructed, consisting of recursive, nonlinear equations that specify how the system changes states over time. One important difference from the other two systems theories is the recognition of amplifying as well as damping feedback. Another is the introduction of nonlinear responses into a chain of circular causality that could lead to unexpected and unintended outcomes, which means that it can no longer be assumed that the system will move to equilibrium. The system is then no longer self-regulating but it is self-influencing: it may be self-sustaining or self-destructive. Instead of thinking of a system moving toward an equilibrium state, it is thought of as following a small number of typical patterns or archetypes.

Second order systems thinking

When this kind of systems thinking is applied to human interaction, that interaction is thought to be a self-regulating or a self-influencing system and it is the formative process of self-regulation or self-influence (formative cause) that is organizing the pattern of behavior that can be observed. In all of these systems theories, the final form of the system's behavior (teleology), that towards which it tends, is a state already enfolded, as it were, in the rules governing the way the parts interact or in pre-given archetypes, or in the goals and visions that systems designers or leaders have put into it. However, as soon as one thinks of human interaction as a system that can be identified or designed, one immediately encounters the problem that the identifier or the designer, a human subject to rationalist teleology presuming free choice, is also part of the system subject to formative teleology in which there is no freedom. Furthermore, the system itself is in fact other humans who supposedly have free choice. If they have free choice how can their action be governed by the formative cause of the system? Systems thinkers have, of course, recognized this problem, which Kant warned of, and they have sought to remedy it in what has been called second-order cybernetics (Bateson, 1973; Bateson & Bateson, 1987; von Foerster, 1984; von Glaserveld, 1991).

Second order systems thinking is based on the view that human beings determine the world that they experience. A 'biology of observing systems' was developed by von Foerster who said that he was part of the universe and whenever he acted he changed himself and the universe. Second order systems thinking involves reflection upon how we operate as perceiving and knowing 'observers' who bring forth our experiential worlds through the actual functioning of our nervous systems and the cognitive operation of making distinctions. Second order cybernetics is a theory of the observer rather than what is being observed (first order thinking) and is the continual attempt of researchers to be aware of their tradition of understanding. Some argue that second order thinking does not replace first order thinking but is, rather, the latter's context. They are a duality of a process of science (first order) and the processes leading up to science (second order). While the basis of first order systems thinking is straightforward cognitivist psychology in which the individual mind forms representations of a pre-given reality and processes information rather like a computer, the second order tradition is based on a constructivist psychology in which the individual brain–mind selects or enacts reality.

Basically, second order systems thinking widens the boundary of the system to include the objective observer, the one who is identifying or designing it. In other words, the system is widened to include the observer observing him/herself. But then the question is: what means has he/she of observing him/herself as he or she is enacting, observing or designing the system of which he/she and others are parts? Something like a mental model, or an internal world, inside the individual has to be assumed. It is this internal world, or mental model, which is included when the system boundary is widened to 'sweep in' what was outside in first order thinking. Now, however, the internal worlds or mental models of all the individuals are parts of the systems and so subject to the formative cause of the system. There is then no scope for any spontaneity or novel change in individual internal worlds. The process by which the mental model/internal world changes in novel ways, therefore, has to be specified and this is usually expressed as something to do with satisfaction and dissatisfaction, or preference, and this is now outside the system definition. So, the system boundary has to be widened once more to include the observer observing him/herself changing his/her preferences, so changing his/her mental model/ inner world. However, there is now the problem of defining the process by which he/she becomes aware of the need to change preferences. Bateson (1973), for one, found he could not identify what this would be and concluded that such complex learning processes were beyond most humans and rarely happened other than in deep therapy or some kind of mystical experience, which he could not explain.

The problem with the move to second order systems thinking, then, is that it rapidly runs into an infinite regress and has to be abandoned to some kind of mysticism. The source of the problem, it seems to me, lies at the very roots of systems thinking in the split theory of causality it is built upon and the problem cannot be addressed simply by widening the boundaries of the system to include the observer. The system is always driven by formative teleology, moving to some optimal or archetypal state that is already embedded in it. This means that any human thinking about the system is confined to an observer outside the system. It is rationalist teleology that applies to the observer, that is, the observer has the freedom to choose goals for the system, even the freedom to design it. Systems thinking, therefore, right at its roots, proceeds by making a Kantian split, but unlike Kant, applies formative teleology to human beings. Free choice is thereby confined to the observer outside the system.

For me, a key problem with this whole conceptual framework is the split it makes between two levels of reality, namely, the individual level and the social/group level. Each of these levels is thought of as a system and attention is then directed to how each system functions and how each interacts with the other. This leads to causal dualism in that formative teleology applies to each as a system but choices to change the system are understood within some other causal framework. In systems thinking, mind is firmly located in the individual. The social level has to do with the enduring features of collective life, described as structure, culture, shared beliefs and values expressed in routines, traditions, procedures and habits. The two levels have an impact on each other. Individual minds, as systems, interact to form groups/social as systems. These collective levels feature in individual minds as shared mental models, or introjects, so affecting how individuals act.

The main point I have been indicating in the very brief review of systems thinking in this chapter is that in its development from first order to second order thinking, the systems movement has not been able to deal adequately with Kant's stricture against applying system thinking to human action. It cannot escape the dual causality of formative cause applying to humans as parts of a system and rational teleology applying to autonomous humans necessarily outside the system. In doing this spontaneity and transformative change can only be explained in terms of the individual. This conclusion is highly relevant to the movement of psychoanalytic thought away from the central focus on the individual towards relational, intersubjective and group explanations of transformative change. This movement has involved the incorporation of systems thinking and I am arguing that this incorporation is basically flawed because systems thinking cannot in itself explain transformative change and so always falls back on the individual. The move to systems thinking in psychoanalysis, therefore, does not provide a move from the individual to the interaction between individuals as the source of transformative change.

Complex adaptive systems

Earlier on in this chapter, I mentioned that there was one exception to the claim that systems thinking cannot, in its own terms, explain spontaneity or novelty. In other words, there is one kind of system model that does exhibit transformative change and this is a particular type of complex adaptive system (see Chapter 3). Complex adaptive systems consist of large numbers of components or entities interacting with each other in iterative nonlinear ways. In this they are similar to the models of the systems dynamics strand of systems thinking mentioned above in that they do not move to equilibrium as the models of general systems do. Instead they exhibit patterns of movement far from equilibrium, often involving unpredictability. However, systems dynamics models, and many complex adaptive system models too, are not capable of evolving in novel ways. They can only unfold what is enfolded in them. The exception I referred to is when the entities comprising a complex adaptive system are different enough to each other (Allen, 1998a & b). Then, given the characteristics of micro diversity, the model evolves, that is, it takes on a life of its own. Novelty, spontancity and by implication freedom are possible only because the nonlinear iteration of the model amplifies difference.

However, a system with a life of its own, where the entities comprising it are perpetually creating the system's future in interaction with each other, renders problematic the notion of a whole. The whole certainly cannot be given in any way because a system with a life of its own is evolving unpredictably into the future. The only way one can then talk about a whole is in terms of an 'incomplete' or 'absent' whole (Bortoft, 1985). This kind of whole is then never a whole and to my mind talking about a whole provides no explanation, only a mystification. The notion of entities being a part of a system also becomes highly problematic. If the whole is absent, then how can one determine whether a part is really a part or not? Bortoft talks about holographic systems in which the parts are in the whole and the whole is on the parts. However, in human terms, appealing to the metaphor of the hologram in this way comes very close to the notion that the individual is social because of representations of the social in the individual mind, with all the conceptual problems that internal worlds and representations bring. Furthermore, even though a system with a life of its own can produce novelty, the individual entities comprising it still cannot be free to choose because to be parts they must be fulfilling the purpose of the system, even though that purpose is evolving.

Systems thinking and psychoanalysis

When psychoanalysts and others, for example, Durkin and Agazarian (see Chapter 9), employ the explanatory constructs of first order open systems, their theories are subject to the same explanatory problems as those outlined above in relation to first order systems in general. The essence of the move to relational and intersubjectivity perspectives in psychoanalysis lies in the recognition of the co-construction of the therapeutic relationship by both the patient and the therapist. It is not just the unfolding of the patient's past patterns of relating in the form of transference but also the unfolding of the therapist's past in the countertransference. Together they create and are affected by the analytic third, or the field, or the intersubjective system. These perspectives, therefore, clearly fall within second order systems thinking. There is also an emphasis on the many different ways in which the patient's material can be understood and this is similar to the multiple perspectives stressed by modern critical systems thinkers (Jackson, 2000; Midgley, 2000). However, the difficulties identified for first order systems thinking remain. There is still a formative causality in which the already enfolded basic fault or primary trauma is unfolded in the analytic situation. There is also the split causality of the autonomous individual in the form of the therapist who interprets what the analytic pair are creating and this capacity is ultimately acquired by the patient as his or her unconscious is made conscious.

If one takes a systemic perspective, whether it is first or second order, then interaction, participation and process have a very particular meaning. As parts of a system, individuals are interacting with each other to produce a system. Participation means that they participate as parts of the system that their interaction creates. The meaning of process within the system is that of interaction to produce a system. In all of these cases, interaction creates something that is abstracted from the direct experience of interaction itself. Interaction creates a system above the interacting individuals who continue to be thought of as the individual systems of internal worlds, including the unconscious as a system underlying experience. Systems thinking focuses attention on the creation of a whole but this whole is an abstraction from our direct experience. In fact, it is a mystification of our experience. From the complex responsive processes perspective, interaction, participation and process all mean something completely different. The process is that of direct interaction between individual bodies, which produces further direct interaction between bodies. The process is direct interaction and participation means participation in this direct interaction. There is no creation of any third, system, field or anything else above, below, behind or in front of interaction.

Further implications of systems thinking in psychoanalysis

The paradigm shift brought about by systems thinking was to focus attention on interactions between entities, rather than purely on the nature of the entities. In doing this, systems thinking has questioned the notion of the observer. However, in focusing attention on interaction, the phenomenon of interest is thought of as a system with the following distinctive features:

1. A self-regulating, self-influencing or self-organizing *whole* consisting of interacting parts and following some kind of purposive path. Furthermore, systems thinking involves *hierarchical levels* in that any system consists of subsystems interacting with each other to produce the system and that system is interacting with other systems constituting a supra system called the environment, field, matrix, and so on. In other words, different levels of behavior are distinguished, usually with different governing principles, or laws, at each level.
2. *Boundaries* that separate the system from an environment consisting of other systems.
3. Some kind of *interaction* across these boundaries with other systems in the environment. Mostly, systems are thought to be open to the action of other systems in the environment. Open systems are said to import energy or information from the environment, process it in some way to produce something, and then export that something, or some form of waste, back into the environment. Some system theories assume closed boundaries as in the theory of autopoiesis (Maturana & Varela, 1992) in which case structural change in the system is triggered by perturbations in the environment but the nature of the change is determined by the system itself.
4. A *dynamic of internal change* in which the system adapts to changes in the environment in such a way as to preserve stability, equilibrium, homeostasis or identity, usually employing processes of feedback. Or the dynamic of internal change might produce disequilibria, which nevertheless display archetypal patterns.

In the process thinking developed in Part I there is no notion of wholes, hierarchical levels of explanation, boundaries or adaptations to environments. Process is not thought of as interaction between parts to produce a whole but as producing further interaction. The following sections explore the above key features of systems thinking in relation to psychoanalytic thinking.

The notion of the whole and hierarchical levels

Elias expressed his disagreement with systems thinking primarily in the form of criticisms of the sociology of Parsons, which was expressed in systems terms. In *The Civilizing Process* ([1939] 2000), Elias argued that Parsons conceived of individual and society as two separate phenomena that interpenetrate each other, while Elias (ibid., p482) claimed that his concept of figuration was neither an abstraction of an individual without a society nor an abstraction of a society as a system above individuals. Elias argued in *What is Sociology?* ([1970] 1978), that sociology could not be reduced to the psychology of individuals because the figurations of human interdependence cannot be reduced to the actions of individual people. On the contrary, the actions of individuals can only be understood in terms of their patterns of interdependence, that is, in terms of the figurations they form with each other.

> Some people tend to shrink from this insight. They confuse it with a metaphysical assumption of long standing which is often summed up in the saying 'the whole is more than the sum of its part.' Using the term 'whole' or 'wholeness' creates a mystery in order to solve a mystery.
>
> (Elias, [1970] 1978, p72)

In incorporating systems thinking to deal with the group, relational and intersubjective psychoanalytic thought also conceives of separate phenomena that interpenetrate each other. For example, in Bion's formulations there are individuals who anonymously contribute psychic contents to the group and there is the group that sucks them into roles and penetrates their psyches so that they fall under the sway of basic assumptions. Also, in the relational notion of an analytic third, or field, there are two individuals who create this third or field, which then penetrates their psyches. In other words, they create a whole that is more than simply the sum of the individuals and this is often spoken of in a way that sounds quite mysterious. The complex responsive processes perspective does not require any notion of a whole. Indeed, the notion of a whole makes no sense in a purely process perspective.

Also in *The Society of Individuals* (1991), Elias has this to say:

Since they can only conceive of regularities as the regularities of substances or of substantial forces, they unconsciously attribute to the regularities of human relationships which they observe a substance of their own beyond individuals. On the basis of these specific social regularities, they can conceive of society only as something supra individual. They invent as the medium supporting these regularities either a 'collective mind' or a 'collective organism' or, as the case may be, supra individual mental and material 'forces' by analogy with natural forces and substances. Opposed to them on the other side are groups whose ideas focus above all on human individuals. They see quite clearly what is concealed to the others: that all that which we call 'social structures and laws' is nothing other than the structures and laws of the relations between individual people. But like the first group they are incapable of imagining that relationships can themselves have structures and regularities of their own; like them they involuntarily think of these structures and regularities not as a peculiarity of relations *between* tangible units but as a peculiarity of such body units. But they, in keeping with their different social experiences and interests, believe the tangible substances of social structures and regularities to be located within the individual seen in isolation. . . . they involuntarily imagine that the explanation of the structures and laws of relations between individuals are to be sought in the 'nature' or 'consciousness' of the individuals, as they are in 'themselves' prior to all relationships.

(Elias, 1991, pp17–18)

It seems to me that the move to the relational and the intersubjective in psychoanalysis is a move, to some extent, away from the second group in the above quote, that is, those who understand the social in terms of the individual as they are in themselves prior to all relationships. However, in making this move they join the first group Elias refers to, that is, those who ascribe relational patterns to supra individual forces such as a field. The complex responsive process perspective falls into neither of these two groups but understands individual and group, not as different hierarchical levels forming a whole, but as the same processes of communicative interaction.

Systems thinking and human action

If one tries to understand human interaction as a system in which human individuals are averaged or assumed to follow the same rules, as is done in macro modeling of human interaction, then one cannot understand the emergence of novelty because the very feature leading to novelty, namely, diversity, has been assumed away. Instead there is the unfolding of the unfolded understood as a 'regulative idea' such as an inherent archetype or some kind of vision ascribed to the system by an objective observer. There is also no human freedom in such interaction. This problem is resolved in the 'both . . . and' approach of systems thinking which understands human action as both systemic and also rationalist. In the latter, it is the observer identifying or designing the human system who is free to choose and who may choose to change the system design in novel ways. There is no paradox.

However, if the designer of a human system were to understand the system as having a life of its own, because it consists of diverse individuals interacting with each other, then this designer could no longer choose its goals or purpose. The system would be developing its own purpose quite independently. What role can the observer now have? What could the participation of individuals within the system mean? What freedom could individuals have in such a system? These questions reflect the recognized but irresolvable problem that is at the centre of second order cybernetics. Second order cybernetics seeks to model a system in which those steering it are participants in it rather than observers of it. The system cannot be steered if we do not have a model of it. In other words, those proposing to steer a system must have some kind of model they can use to compute the effect of steps they take to correct deviations in its movement. First order cybernetics encounters no difficulty in designing the model of the system to be steered because the one doing the steering steps outside it, reflecting upon it from an external vantage point. However, second order cybernetics seeks to avoid this hypothetical stepping outside the system and designing the model required for steering from within. But this leads steering to lose its meaning because every small act of participation within the system defines the path along which the small acts of participation themselves are made. In the end, there is no logical recourse other than specifying some wider system of which the system to be steered is a part, this wider system being some kind of transcendent whole in which all participate in what has to be a mystical kind of union. The steering from within then becomes an act of surrender to a whole in which all participate.

To deal with the question of participation from a systems perspective, therefore, one has to slip into thinking in terms of some kind of transcendent whole in which individuals can choose to participate. For example, one could think of a group mind, a collective unconscious, a common pool of meaning, or nature as a whole. Individuals could then choose to hold themselves open to participation in this collective mind or in nature as a whole as a mystical, spiritual experience in which purpose emerges. Individuals may form this collective mind which then forms them, which is 'both . . . and' thinking. Or one could think of a transcendent whole in terms of nature itself (for example Gaia), or some mystical spiritual phenomenon which individuals could hold themselves open to participation in. Individual action is then understood as *both* system *and* as openness to some transcendent phenomenon and again there is resolution of paradox. Thinking about wholes, including any notion of an actively absent whole then easily slips into this kind of transcendent thinking. The prescription has to do with ways of humans getting in touch with the whole, which is the purpose produced by the system having a life of its own. Here the transcendent whole forms the individuals who do not form it, but merge into it. They get in touch with the 'regulative idea,' which is now thought of as ultimate reality rather than an 'as if' hypothesis.

Although one may try not to think of nature in terms of teleology, regulative ideas and so on, this is not possible in relation to human action where the idea of purpose is essential. If, in order to incorporate the possibility of novelty, one thinks of human interaction as a system with a life of its own, then one inevitably moves to something transcendent, a mystical whole. Ordinary individual freedom is then lost in being absorbed, becoming one, with the transcendent whole. The insight about diversity and novelty is lost because difference, conflict and power are all incorporated or covered over by the fusion into the harmonious transcendent whole.

How might one think of iterative nonlinear interaction between diverse humans, with its potential for novelty, if one is not convinced by the move to thinking in terms of transcendent wholes? How might one think if one wants to avoid any appeal to holistic accounts? How might one think if one wants to retain individual human freedom? One suggestion is to think of human action in terms of complex responsive processes of relating.

Boundaries and containers

The systemic notion of a boundary around a system has come to occupy an important place in psychoanalytic thought and in the everyday discourse of psychotherapists of a psychodynamic persuasion. Closely connected to the notion of a boundary is that of a container, both of which fit well with the spatial metaphors upon which is built the fundamental psychoanalytic notion of the psyche as internal world. The therapist is thought of as the 'holder' of the boundary and as the 'container' of anxiety in both dyadic and group therapy settings. This boundary relates to the stance of the therapist, the spatial setting of the therapy session and the timing of that session.

The therapist is thought of as operating at the boundary of the dyad or group and this means that the therapist refrains from disclosing personal material or feelings, focusing entirely on the patient(s). This is the classical stance of neutrality and abstinence or in Bion's terms relating without memory or desire. Chapter 12 has described how the relational and intersubjective turns in psychoanalysis have eroded the purist notions of abstinence and neutrality. However, the view remains of the therapist as boundary holder and container of the anxiety of patients. It is thought that the empathic stance of the therapist who makes only limited disclosures is anxiety containing for patients. There is also still a widespread view amongst therapists that strict adherence to time boundaries of therapy sessions and careful attention to the integrity of the space in which the therapy session takes place is also anxiety containing. Other rules of therapy are also understood as containers, for example, the group therapy rule about members not socializing outside of sessions and of patients not missing sessions or at least leaving messages when they do.

The complex responsive processes perspective does not rely on spatial metaphors and notions of boundary and container have no meaning in process terms. Instead, anxiety is understood in terms of the vicissitudes of attachment–separation as particular kinds of thematic patterning of communicative interaction between patients and therapist. There is no notion of any individual 'holding' or 'containing' anxiety since anxiety is not a substance but a pattern of relating linked to brain processes. Some patterns of relating enable those interacting to continue productively with each other while living with anxiety, while others do not. For example, patterns of relating having the quality of trust enable people to go on together despite the anxiety they feel while patterns of suspicion and mistrust exacerbate feelings of anxiety to the point where the thematic patterns of, for example, aggression or apathy might be triggered. Instead, then, of thinking of the therapist, or anyone else, as 'holding' or 'containing' anything, it is the qualities of relational patterns that account for the capacity to live with anxiety, uncertainty or other potentially debilitating effects.

This does not mean that rules to do with the therapist exercising care about personal disclosure, or to do with attendance at sessions and so on, have no meaning. It is, rather, that such rules are thought about in terms of the power relations they set up.

Interaction

In *The Civilizing Process* ([1939] 2000, p269), Elias refers to the incompatibility of talking about a free individual and a free social system. Elias criticized Parsons for presenting society as a 'social system' and dismissed his teleological perspective, that is, his assumption that all institutions exist to keep the 'system' functioning well in a kind of harmony or equilibrium. Elias said that this approach was profoundly misleading because it broke society down into elementary components such as human acts and the values that guided such acts. From the systems perspective, humans are treated like atoms of society and they must play the cards society deals them. Instead of putting acts at the centre, Elias puts people at the centre. He could not see how we could regard people as atoms and then say that they were parts of a smoothly working whole. He said that this was abstract, or ideal. For Elias, Parsons' abstractions were in service of a particular ideal, namely, the unified equilibrium society. Parsons' theories were disguises for subject-centered ideals in which long-term social processes played no part.

Of course, psychoanalysis has never held that society is a smoothly working whole system. Instead it has strongly emphasized the conflictual and destructive processes at play in human psyches and in human interaction. However, when the group is regarded as a system of basic assumptions, or when the dyad is regarded as a field unfolding unconsciously driven past behaviors, humans are being treated like atoms that must play the cards dealt them by the group or field. The alternative is the autonomous individual who has managed to escape from the pull of the group or field. This elevation of the autonomous individual is also a subject-centered ideal.

Psychoanalysis has significantly decentered individual agency and questioned the nature of human freedom. It might, therefore, be argued that it is irrelevant to criticize its interpretation of systems thinking for its inability to account for human freedom. From Freud through the relational and intersubjective psychoanalysts it is a central tenet that the internal world of the psyche contains a subsystem called 'the unconscious.' In Freud this was the repressed wishes that returned to determine patterns of behavior and in the intersubjective theories it is themes that prohibit other themes. Or the unconscious may be unformulated or unvalidated experience. Whatever the formulation, the effect is to limit rational individual agency. However, this does not mean that there is no rational individual agency. Indeed the whole purpose of analysis or therapy is to enable rational agency through freeing individuals to some extent of the grip of the unconscious. This is effected either by making the unconscious conscious in some way or by some kind of reparative experience through empathic attunement or good enough holding. What is then not explored is the nature of this conscious, rational, individual agency. I argue that it becomes impossible to explain this if one posits individuals as parts of some third, field or system, for the reasons provided in this chapter. In other words, having been freed to some extent from the grip of the unconscious, the individual still cannot be free to choose if that individual is immediately thought of as part of yet another system called the third, the field or supra system.

The notion of system is based on a spatial metaphor of an 'inside' and an 'outside.' A system is a 'whole,' an 'inside,' separated from an environment, an 'outside,' by a 'boundary.' This immediately establishes hierarchical levels. At one level there is a system and at another level there is the environment, usually thought of as a supra system, or more encompassing whole. Interaction between subsystems produces the system and interaction between systems produces the global supra system or whole. The human individual is thought of as a system called an internal world and the group is then a supra system of interacting individuals. The individual and the group are at different hierarchical levels and need to be understood in different ways. In other words, systems thinking inevitably involves causal dualism. In moving to the temporal notion of process, one abandons thinking in terms of an 'inside' or an 'outside,' a 'whole' and a 'boundary.' One also abandons thinking about different hierarchical levels of existence or explanation, at least as far as human action is concerned. If one is concerned with the temporal processes of human interaction, one is concerned with the actions of human bodies such as walking, talking and thinking. The notion of anything inside or outside of an action makes no sense, nor does it make much sense to describe acting as a whole separated by a boundary from something else. Most importantly, process thinking moves away from dualism and the elimination of paradox. It is based on a unitary, paradoxical causality of emergent continuity and transformation at the same time.

This chapter has pointed to the assumptions about human behavior that psychoanalysis has imported in it use of systems thinking. In essence these assumptions amount to the view that human action is to be understood, not in terms of direct experience, but in terms of abstracted wholes lying above, or beneath direct experience. The reliance on systems thinking continues the spatial metaphor of internal worlds and proposes boundaries around, and containers for, aspects of experience such as anxiety. This is a radically different perspective to the temporal process one on which the theory of complex responsive processes is built.

Chapter 14

Evolutionary psychology

Previous chapters in Part II of this book have traced the movement of psychoanalytic thought about the relationship between the individual and the group from the early formulations of Freud to more and more relational, intersubjective, group and social perspectives. This movement has involved the incorporation of systems thinking into psychoanalytic theory where the relationship between the individual and the group/social is understood in terms of systemic interaction between people. In recent years, there has also been a movement of thought in the other direction, namely, toward the universal, innate nature of individual human beings. The resulting evolutionary psychotherapy is built on the foundations laid by theories of biological evolution as it was taken up in sociobiology and evolutionary psychology. Here the relationship between the individual and the social is explained in terms of genetically determined survival strategies produced by evolution. The social is then genetically determined attachment behavior and there is a frequent appeal to Bowlby's development of attachment theory in psychoanalysis. This move to genetically determined survival strategies is highly compatible with Freudian thought, extending it to include not only the libidinal and aggressive drives but also attachment and altruistic ones. Evolutionary psychotherapy reflects a substantially different notion of evolution (see Chapter 3) to that upon which the perspective of complex responsive processes is built and this chapter explores that difference.

The origins of evolutionary psychotherapy

The two most prominent early thinkers in the area of biological evolution were, of course, Lamarck and Darwin. Lamarck held that acquired characteristics could be inherited so that variations of biological type could occur through direct adaptations to the environment rather than random mutations operated on by natural selection. For Darwin, variations occurred first and then there was environmental selection through which adaptation occurred. Although Darwin himself did not reject Lamarckism, most later thinkers did for reasons given below. The Darwinian approach, therefore, came to occupy the dominant position in theories of biological evolution.

Darwin was influenced by his reading of Malthus who held that permanent change in any species was impossible because of the pressure of increasing population on limited space and food resources in a struggle for survival. Darwin, however, turned the Malthus argument on its head and argued that it was precisely this struggle for survival that provided the motive force for change. In the struggle to survive, organisms developed biological variations that were more or less adapted to their environment, which included other organisms. The more adapted organisms survived and their numbers increased, while the less adapted perished. In this manner, adapted changes were retained in the population and at some point the cumulative adaptations resulted in completely new species, new forms that had not existed before. For Darwin, it was the formative process of adaptation of whole organisms that accounted for change of a truly novel kind. However, he did not see this as a process in which just anything could happen or as a process in which chance or accident was central. The need to adapt exercised a constraint.

Some of the central themes in Darwin's *Origin of Species* (1859) and *Descent of Man* (1871) run along the following lines. The body parts of an organism have particular functions, namely, those of enabling the organism to win in a struggle for survival in a particular ecological niche, the environment, that the organism finds itself in. A species consists of a number of organisms with much the same body parts, that is, mode of survival. Species change through variations at the level of the individual organism, some of which enhance its chances of survival, and thus reproductive success, in a changed environment. Other variations do not and so disappear from the species. In other words, some of the small individual changes turn out to be more adapted to a changed environment than others do. The more adapted changes, arising by unknown cause, spread through the species so that it gradually changes toward more adapted forms. If groups of the species are separated from each other by, for example, geographic barriers, then those groups are likely to change in different ways. In other words, they diverge, with each becoming more and more adapted to their separate local environments through the competitive sifting of more from less adapted changes, that is, through the process of natural selection. Eventually, the difference becomes so great that one could say that the divergent groups constitute new species.

Novelty, therefore, arises through a gradual process of changes due to unknown causes, sifted by natural selection, the struggle for survival, so that the most adapted forms survive to constitute a new species. Darwin, however, could not explain how these individual changes were passed from one generation to the next so as to spread through the population. An answer to this question was provided by Mendel who explained the genetic basis of inheritance. The combination of Mendel and Darwin became the neo-Darwinian synthesis to be discussed later.

Darwin's theory of evolution, then, was a gradualist theory in which chance variation at the individual level was operated on by natural selection as the struggle for survival. However, even in Darwin's time, there were dissenting voices.

Alternatives to some of Darwin's views

Thomas Huxley (1863) argued that novelty emerged in a sudden discontinuous fashion. For him, novelty arose before natural selection exerted its influence. He suggested that natural selection operated to refine the newly emergent species. However, he could not explain how this occurred, just as Darwin could not explain how variations in an individual organism were passed on to the next generation. Around the beginning of the 20th century, when Mendel's explanation of the genetic basis of inheritance began to attract increasing attention, William Bateson argued that mutations typically arose as small changes in genes in their recessive state where they were shielded from natural selection until they spread through the population and suddenly became dominant. Natural selection and adaptation to an environment were thus seen to be far less important in the origin of new species than Darwin thought.

Fisher (1930), Haldane (1932) and Wright (1940) developed this idea in rather different ways and later views of this kind were expressed in the idea of genetic drift. It was argued that random variation might lead to less fit species surviving as more fit ones were eliminated. Some species might survive contrary to selection, or for reasons that had nothing to do with selection, such as a disaster that wiped out the more fit species. Later, in the 1970s and 1980s, Eldridge and Gould (1972) took up this kind of argument and suggested that new species arise in discontinuous jumps in a way not due to natural selection. They called this punctuated equilibrium.

Another line of disagreement has to do with whether natural selection operates at the level of the individual or the group. Gould and Eldridge emphasized group selection, as did Lewontin (1974). The former pointed to the particular role of regulating genes that control other genes in a move that gives more emphasis to interaction between genes rather than a simple focus on chance variation in individual genes.

So, the primacy of natural selection and gradual change has been disputed from Darwin's time to this day. These different views look for the reason for change in *some kind of micro interaction* not initially subjected to selection and in the abrupt appearance of new species not necessarily due to adaptation. However, these dissenting voices have never come to occupy the dominant position, as the neo-Darwinian synthesis did.

Darwin and the neo-Darwinian synthesis

According to the neo-Darwinian perspective, variations take place in the process of reproduction. One cause of variation is the errors arising as genetic material is copied (random mutation) and the other cause is the somewhat random mixing of genetic material in sexual reproduction. New varieties of organism, therefore, appear by chance and accident lies at the heart of the process. The explanation of variation, and thus of the whole evolutionary process, shifts from the level of the organism to the level of the gene. The explanation is reduced to the level of the individual gene and interaction between genes is regarded as unimportant. At the most important level of the explanation of evolution, *the notion that interaction plays an important part thus disappears.* Natural selection, that is, competition for survival, then sifts out for further reproduction those variations that adapt most effectively in the competitive environment constituted by other species of organisms. Less adaptive variations perish, for it is only the winners who survive. Even in relation to natural selection, interaction becomes less important in this explanation and the idea that forms are evolving to the unknown slips into the background.

From this perspective, then, chance, or accident is a major cause of the emergence of any new species. In principle, any variation could emerge, the only constraints being the laws of physics and chemistry. The internal dynamic of the organism as a whole plays no part in the evolutionary process. Instead, the new form is 'caused' by the sifting operation of competitive selection on chance variations at the level of the genes. This evolution produces emergent outcomes in the sense that there is no blueprint or program for the pattern of evolving species but it does so by blindly cobbling together chance changes, retaining only those that compete most successfully. Even what appears to be altruistic behavior is explained in terms of survival advantage: cooperation occurs between relatives because this enhances chances of reproduction and so the survival of the family genes; cooperation occurs between non-relatives because this is a winning strategy. What of teleological causality? Neo-Darwinists refer to selfish genes that program organisms to reproduce in order that they, the genes, might survive, so that the teleological cause of evolution becomes the blind urge to survive.

The neo-Darwinians argue that Lamarckism is not possible in biological evolution. Weismann (1883) said that there was a 'barrier' between the organism and its genes, which ruled out the inheritance of acquired characteristics. Waddington (1962) argued that the genetic code had to be protected against the acquisition of acquired characteristics to prevent degradation and this is why the Weismann barrier evolved. Dawkins (1976) argues that any form of Lamarckism depends upon prior Darwinism because Darwinism explains why organisms seek to adapt to the environment whereas Lamarckism just assumes that they do.

However, Waddington and others following him have argued that evolution favors species that evolve 'evolvability' so that evolution produces the capacity to acquire characteristics.

> Although an 'acquired character' developed by an individual is not inherited by its individual offspring, a character acquired by a population subject to selection will tend to be inherited by the offspring population, if it is useful . . .
>
> (Waddington, 1975, ppv–vi)

Moving from the biological to the social, the neo-Darwinians argue that Lamarckism is not possible and that the social should be understood in terms of memes (ideas, concepts, images) that function like genes. Hodgson (2001) suggests that the social unit is not the meme but the habit to which a limited form of Lamarckism applies. An example of this is the human ability to imitate and replicate habits as explained by the American pragmatists (for example, Dewey) and institutionalist economists (for example, Veblen and Commons). Hodgson suggests that habits are the social analogues of the genes. Some habits are instincts and others are ideas (tacit) forming propensities to engage in particular activities. Habits are then adaptations and the capacity to acquire habits is the parallel of learning, which can be passed on through imitation, a kind of Lamarckism. Habits are not themselves behavior but dispositions, propensities, or acquired instructions that are carried inside the organism as a vehicle. Hodgson sees social evolution as the dovetailing of Darwinism and Lamarckism.

It is clear, then, that although neo-Darwinism has come to occupy the mainstream of thinking about biological evolution, it cannot simply be accepted as fact. Right from the beginning of evolutionary thinking there have been debates and there are credible alternatives to neo-Darwinian theories of biological evolution. The credibility of neo-Darwinism becomes even more tenuous when it is applied to social and psychological evolution. However, there has been a growing school of writers who do apply neo-Darwinism to the social and the psychological. Dawkins (1976) has played a prominent role in popularizing the notions of neo-Darwinian evolutionary theory and also in its extension from biology to sociology and psychology. E. O. Wilson (1992) is well known for the controversial development of sociobiology, which holds that all human behavior, including social interaction, can be explained scientifically in terms of the genes. More recently these ideas have been incorporated into evolutionary psychology where the most prominent writers are Cosmides and Tooby (1992), Pinker (1994; 1997) and Ridley (1997). Gilbert and Bailey (2000) have edited a useful volume of papers that provides a good overall view of how this evolutionary psychology has been taken into thinking about psychotherapy.

Psychotherapy and neo-Darwinism

Evolutionary psychotherapy is concerned with the nature of human passions, emotions and motivations, all understood in terms of animal heritage, which is said to lie behind human suffering and irrational behavior. However, writers in this tradition depart in significant ways from Freud who also started from this position. For Freud, a basic, evolved animal nature lies hidden beneath a veneer of socialization in humans and words and deeds are manifestations of unconscious motivations, mainly conflicting instincts of a wild and brutish nature, derived from early evolution. These instincts are unable to find permissible outlets and so appear as passions, dreams and mental illness and the role of society is to contain human passions and self-centered, anti-social behavior. Evolutionary psychotherapists, however, take a different view and argue that humans evolved to live together because this enhanced survival chances. They see mental illness and distorted thinking as due to previously evolved adaptive defenses that are no longer appropriate. Suffering can be traced back to thwarted needs for care, love and status that humans have been evolved to expect and require, and to rejection, abuse and neglect. They argue against Freud's view of the id as wild and brutish beneath the surface veneer of civilization. For them, what lies behind our behavior is a set of developmentally sensitive strategies where belonging, emotional needs, compassion, care, friendship and joy in relationships are as much evolved as violence, exploitation, anxiety and depression.

Evolutionary psychotherapists take without question the neo-Darwinian perspective on evolution. For them, the building blocks of organic forms are the genes, which provide, singly and in combinations, the information to build complex organisms. Genes are thought to have been designed by natural selection and now determine internal biological functions and structures, giving rise to adaptive traits that enable organisms to survive and reproduce. In other words, selective pressures, mainly competitions for mates and resources, are held to give rise to various emotional and behavioral predispositions for attachment, group living and social hierarchies. Although varying in specifics, these general traits are said to be common to all humans. These general traits are also called strategies. For example one such strategy is the genetically programmed strategy of favoring one's kin when it comes to altruistic behavior because this enhances the chance of passing on one's genes.

An important concept drawn on by evolutionary psychotherapists is that of inclusive fitness, which refers to the relative success of groups of biological kin assisting each other and so enhancing the chances of their family genes surviving and reproducing. The concept of inclusive fitness thus extends the selection process from individual genes in isolation to groups of individuals who assist each other, providing an explanation of altruistic behavior.

This is a very different view of the impact of biological evolution on current human behavior to that described in Chapters 3 and 6. Those chapters present a view of evolution in which evolution has produced human bodies with a particular physiology requiring attachment and separation interactions between bodies and brains that are so highly plastic that humans have to learn almost every kind of action they undertake. Evolution has produced bodies dependent on others and on processes of interactive learning, rather than any kind of specific behavior.

Evolutionary psychologists, however, focus on a period in which the early human species lived in small intimate groups and the need to belong was a fundamental and powerful drive. The group was essential to the well being of the individual and the fundamental distinction for animals organized into systems of kinship was that of the in-group and the out-group. In-groups were intensively intimate compared to out-groups and together they acted out species scripts in an intricate social ecosystem. According to evolutionary psychology this still characterizes humans today as evidenced by the manner in which we automatically classify people. This classifying activity is linked to fitness for survival and here fitness is not understood simply in personal terms but in terms of inclusive fitness. Inclusive fitness theory suggests that the stability of kinship categories and kin-based altruism are direct functions of genetic relatedness – they activate mechanisms of pleasure. The fact that we have evolved strong kinship ties that lead to altruistic behavior may not improve the fitness of any single individual but it does improve collective fitness so enhancing the chances of passing family genes on to the next generation. Here inclusion–exclusion is seen as genetically determined rather than as the kind of social process outlined in Chapter 7.

It is recognized, however, that people do form strong bonds with non-family members and act altruistically towards these non-kin. Evolutionary psychologists account for this by arguing that a few non-kin may be integrated into the in-group in a form of psychological kinship. An example of this is friendship. Friendship, it is argued, does increase fitness. However, modern societies bring us into contact with large numbers of strangers creating a nature–culture mismatch between ancestrally evolved selves and the modern context. The central role of togetherness in enhancing fitness has led to the evolution of human brains that are more social than technological. Hard-wired into the brain there are various social mentalities, or categories, of role taking behavior, social signaling, evaluating self and other in a kind of cost-benefit analysis. Evolutionary psychologists talk about modular like internal brain structures like archetypes. This, it seems to me, is not consistent with research showing high degrees of human brain plasticity.

A key distinction is drawn between distal causes of behavior, that is, those that enhance reproductive success, and proximal causes, for example, the accumulation of resources and power that enable people to prosper and thus ultimately satisfy the distal cause of enhancing reproductive success. What is relevant for human motivation is the proximal cause because we are not aware of the distal. When we get the resource of power right, then the distal cause is met. Humans have been designed by natural selection to strive for the achievement of specific goals or experiences such as acquiring resources, making friends, having high status and reducing unpleasant emotions. These goals are held to be responsible for most human behavior.

However, the strategies for achieving goals were evolved a long time ago and they may not always result in reproductive success in today's environment. Evolutionary psychologists ascribe the automatic, compulsive urging of much human behavior to a carry-over of the reptilian brain from our ancestors. Although we evolved self conscious perception to provide survival advantage, this same mechanism can be disadvantageous as, for example, in feelings of low self worth. Adaptation often involves compromises, cost-benefit tradeoffs, and they need not be all that advantageous.

The process of learning is also brought in by arguing that survival chances are increased when genes build organisms that can internally modify their own physiological processes by learning from the environment. The genes are held to build brains disposed to follow evolved strategies and display evolved traits, which are recreated or limited by the social environment. Social signals and relationships are powerful biological regulators emanating from the environment and social strategies operate to pursue certain biosocial goals. We are depressed or pleasured by their failure or success. In explaining how these strategies change, evolutionary psychotherapists focus on childhood experience. Development, as a history of received signals, is central because it is via early experience that social strategies take the form they do. Early environments select which social and reproductive strategies, for example, affiliative, become incorporated as affect control and self-systems. Adverse rearing can significantly affect maturation and functioning, which is a downside of physiological malleability. Again, the points being made by evolutionary psychologists are similar to those I have been making in Part I but the notion of learning in the complex responsive processes perspective is a social one, not one that is genetically determined.

So, evolutionary psychologists shift from Freud's perspective of the mind structured by the clash between evolved drives and society, to a view of drives as mechanisms evolved in the need to live in a society, to cooperate and to relate. The successful navigation of social change, the ability to handle relationships, is essential to reproductive success and the evolution of many mental mechanisms was shaped by social challenges. Humans evolved over millions of years in primate social groups and many of our basic social emotions and behaviors serve the function of enabling individuals to engage each other in different kinds of relationships. Evolved social strategies operate as psychobiological regularities of behavior, underpinning universal forms of social behavior (Cosmides & Tooby, 1992), for example, mating strategies where men are inclined to mate with young females and females are motivated to seek high status males. Other strategies are attachment and preference for kin and in-group individuals.

Evolutionary psychologists talk about the evolution of information processing strategies and algorithms such as:

- Care eliciting/seeking, which is evident in children and throughout life.
- Care giving/providing. Such behaviors take account of the cost of providing care and are especially devoted to kin and those likely to reciprocate. Various forms of deception have arisen because there is always a conflict of interest due to the cost of care giving. The brain has evolved to need signals of care and when care is given it has physiological effects on the brain and the immune system.
- Mate selection. There are innate, conflicting strategies for males and females when it comes to the selection of mates. Males follow evolved strategies of looking for many young mates while females follow strategies of homebuilding and are attracted to older wealthy males.
- Cooperation and the formation of alliances involving aggression inhibition, sharing, affiliation, friendship, group living and reciprocal altruistic behavior. This involves tracking favors given and received and it also involves cheating.
- Social ranking behavior involving competition for resources, as well as gaining and maintaining rank and status. Examples of this are dominance and leading strategies, making social comparisons of inferiority and superiority, accommodating those of higher rank, submission and following. All of this implies internal mechanisms for making predictions, for example, on when to submit. The social ranking process depends upon social symbols given and received to encourage being selected and chosen by others. In-group/out-group biases have evolved around sex, race and religion leading people to elevate and identify with one group while denigrating and seeking to dominate other groups.

From an evolutionary perspective, the aim of psychotherapy is to help people pursue biosocial goals and adaptive role taking, that is, to alter the modules or algorithms that no longer produce adaptive behavior. The therapy relationship is kin-like, a form of psychological kinship. Mental disorders are conditions of failed functions. Symptoms are reactions to situations associated with negative cost-benefit outcomes. The environment has a causative role because it determines the efficiency of functional capacities and adverse environments compromise the efficiency of strategies. Therapy should refine the capacity to assess the cost-benefit of behavioral strategies and develop revised models of the environment; so improving the capacity to select strategies for goal achievement.

The argument against evolutionary psychology

This section now takes the central argument of evolutionary psychology outlined above and considers the counter argument. First consider the role ascribed to genes in evolutionary psychology.

The role of the genes

In evolutionary psychology, biological evolution is understood in neo-Darwinian terms as the natural selection (competition for resources and mates) of chance variations in the genes. This process is held to have produced or designed human bodies with human brains that enable and constrain humans so that they pursue particular survival strategies, that is, particular patterns of behavior. Each newborn infant is therefore said to inherit genetically programmed survival strategies. This is a view of genetic programming that is increasingly contested.

Sole and Goodwin (2000) argue that the genes themselves are participants in the developmental process and do not occupy a privileged position in making decisions about alternative pathways of differentiation. Genes only constrain the pathways open to cells and do not determine those pathways. The issue is how genes interact within the context of cells so as to bring about structure and function. Genes can only function in living cells and they are highly sensitive to context so it cannot be the genes alone that generate the structures. Sole and Goodwin argue that the form of an organism is to be explained in terms of the dynamics of interaction and emergent properties.

Sole and Goodwin also refer to the work of Kauffman, who shows that the emergence of coherent pattern in a network of model genes depends upon the connectivity across the network rather than the nature of any gene or node in it. The numbers of connection operate as conflicting constraints – they constrain the developments of the entire network. At low levels of connection the network displays surprising degrees of emergent order, despite the random nature of the genes. At higher levels it operates at the edge of chaos where small differences can amplify to constrained changes in global pattern. These studies show how local interactions are exercising constraints on what emerges globally and how local interaction may amplify small differences and so differentiate the development of a network.

In other words the functioning of genes is far more complicated than the simple notion that they are a blueprint for the body and a program for an organism to follow specific survival strategies.

Genes consist of DNA and the neo-Darwinian notion of genes as self-producing replicators selfishly seeking their own survival is also contested. For example, Lewontin (2000, p141) disparages this notion in the following terms. First, DNA is not self-producing; only cells are. DNA is a dead molecule, which is why it can be recovered from mummies and mastodons frozen tens of thousands of years ago. It is produced by complex cellular interactions between proteins and it makes nothing. The nucleotides of the DNA are used by the cell to determine what sequence of amino acids is to be built into a protein and to determine when and where the protein is to be made, but the proteins are made by other proteins. It is not simply the genes that are passed on to the next generation but a complex apparatus of production formed in the egg in the course of its cellular development. We inherit not only genes made of DNA but an intricate structure of cellular machinery made up of proteins. Second, organisms are not determined by DNA. Since the DNA of genes bears information that is read by the cell machinery in the production process it cannot be regarded as a blueprint, master plan or master molecule. Lewontin points to the ideological position that has led to DNA as information bearer being transformed into DNA as master plan, a linear cause of the form of an organism.

In an article published in the *Sunday Times* on 8 July 2001, Lewontin writes:

> When this so-called 'annotation' of the human genome was done, it was estimated that humans had about 32,00 genes. [This is compared to the 100,000 previously estimated.] This seems a rather small number when the comparison is made with the fruit fly (13,000), the nematode worm (18,000), and the mustard weed (26,000). Can human beings really only have 75% more genes than a tiny worm and a mere 25% more than a weed? If, as the eminent molecular biologist Walter Gilbert wrote, a knowledge of the human genome would cause 'a change in our philosophical understanding of ourselves,' that change has not been quite what was hoped for. It appears that we are not much different from vegetables if we can judge from our genome. The reaction to the discovery . . . has been to call for an even more grandiose project. It is now agreed . . . that we now need to study the proteome, the complete set of all the proteins manufactured by an organism.

Rose argues that the nature of the human brain does not support the exaggerated role ascribed to the genes by evolutionary psychologists:

> Being and becoming cannot be partitioned into that tired dichotomy of nature versus nurture. Rather they are defined by a different dichotomy, that of specificity and plasticity. Consider the problem of seeing and making sense of the world we observe, processes subserved by eye and brain. The retina of the eye is connected via a series of neural staging posts to the visual cortex at the back of the brain. A baby is born with most of these connections in place, but during the first years of life the eye and the brain both grow, at different rates. This means

292 Complexity and group processes

that the connections between eye and brain have continually to be broken and remade. If the developing child is to be able to retain a coherent visual perception of the world this breaking and remaking must be orderly and relatively resistant to modifications by the experience of development. This is specificity. However, as both laboratory animal experiments and our own human experience show, both the fine details of the 'wiring' of the visual cortex, and how and what we perceive of the world are directly and subtly shaped by our early experience. This is plasticity. All living organisms and perhaps especially humans with our large brains show both specificity and plasticity in development, and both properties are enabled by our genes and shaped by our experience and developmental contingency. Neither genes nor environment are in this sense determinant of normal development; they are the raw materials out of which we construct ourselves.

(Rose & Rose, 2000, pp256–257)

The basis upon which the entire argument for evolutionary psychology is built is the role of the genes in transmitting to every newborn infant the survival strategies produced by evolution for the environment of 100,000 years ago. That basis is not supported by what is now known about DNA and genes or by what is now known about the human brain. The alterative argument is one that ascribes a more limited role to the genes and regards the form of an organism as emerging in the interaction between genes and context. The form that emerges creates both the physiological potential and the constraint for human behavior which is shaped by the long term evolution of society. This view of biological evolution was presented in Chapter 3. It is one in which human bodies/brains emerged in biological self-organization. A secondary role is ascribed to natural selection and the process of evolution has produced a particular kind of human body/brain that makes a wide range of potential behaviors possible. The particular patterns have emerged in the long process of social evolution and are not genetically determined.

Inherited survival strategies

The second step of the evolutionary psychology argument is this. Each person is said to inherit particular survival strategies produced by biological evolution, which have changed little since the small communities of hominids who lived some 100,000 years ago. The strategies modern people have inherited were adapted to that earlier environment but the environment has changed a great deal since then, creating problems for the strategies people continue to use. The resonance with Freud's notion of the primal horde is immediately apparent. It is also clear how this view largely dismisses the impact of thousands of years of social and cultural evolution in human behavior. This of course means that evolutionary psychology and the complex responsive process perspective developed in Part I of this book are mutually excluding. Adopting one perspective logically requires the rejection of the other because it makes no sense to say that we are still following behavior patterns formed 100,000 years ago and we are also behaving in ways that have been transformed fundamentally by 100,000 years of social evolution. Evolutionary psychologists claim that social evolution has simply given a specific shape to universal, inherited human action. The evolutionary perspective that the theory of complex responsive processes is based upon argues, on the other hand, that biological evolution has produced human physiology as it is but not specific patterns of human action. The evolved body makes human action possible and constrains humans from acting in other ways but the actions themselves, the survival strategies if you will, emerge as patterns of social evolution. Survival strategies are these social patterns.

The complex responsive processes perspective is consistent with the notion that modern people inherit the particular form of the human body/brain that emerged in biological evolution and that this particular form of physiology compels people to seek attachment and to separate in order to regulate their bodies. This is an enabling constraint that is elaborated and evolves in cultural history. However, the patterns of attachment and separation are precisely what is meant by the social and since we know that the social evolves into the unknown it cannot be determined in any way by genes. What is striking about evolutionary psychology is the way in which it links every human behavior back to natural selection and how the originally selected emotions are then patterned in every person's childhood without taking account of the social formation of how we experience ourselves, as Elias does. Evolutionary psychologists do emphasize relationships but regard them as formed by genetic evolution, saying little about the social formation of such dispositions and the way in which the civilizing process alters patterns of self regulation. The emphasis is on the innate and how it is coded in brain structure. What is then missed is the change from the spontaneous and violent expression of emotion, even as recently as the Middle Ages, to the self-controlled way we experience ourselves now due to the effects of growing interdependencies and the monopolization of violence. In focusing so much on the biological formations, evolutionary psychologists fail to apply evolution to the social, to the way our experiences of ourselves evolve, to how our modes of thinking evolve. They also take no account of self-organization and the amplification of difference but stick to the first ordering principle of natural selection and the chance generation of difference. This ignores and covers over power relations by continually looking for innate causes formed in the distant past.

In summary, there are a number of ways in which we could explain the coherent patterning of human interaction.

- One possibility is taken up by evolutionary psychologists, namely, that human interaction is patterned as innate design. This means that biological evolution, understood as natural selection applied to chance variation/combination, has preserved individuals with particular social dispositions that are structured in lifetime experience. The ultimate cause of current patterns of interaction lies in a blind urge to enhance reproductive success. Individual experience can distort the natural patterns rendering them sub-optimal/dysfunctional. Current interactions are then dispositions fixed a long time ago as adaptations to the then environment. Because biological evolution is slow and environmental change fast, the old dispositions are no longer appropriate. The distal cause is way back in the past and the proximal causes are in current lifetime development. This imparts rigidity to sex, gender, race and other important differences between people.
- Or one could say that human interaction is patterned by learning. Here one would say that biological evolution has produced the bodies we have but we are born with minimal dispositions and then learn to act. One then has to explain how we learn and socialization might be taken as imitation, involving the sender–receiver model of communication. This explanation is consistent with theories of culture as systems and a focus on lifetime learning, where problems are due to defective learning. Here culture evolves but as for the first explanation, we are looking for the causes of interaction outside of the interaction itself.
- Or one could say that human interaction is patterning itself, that is, that interaction has inherent ordering properties. This brings in the second ordering principle of evolution, namely, emergence and spontaneous self-organization. Here one could argue that over very long periods of biological evolution understood as spontaneous self-organization/ emergent pattern, both biological organisms and their patterns of interaction emerged at the same time. Selection plays a secondary role, no longer the designer with chance as the variety producer. Instead, social interaction amplifies difference in an emergent process of transformation. It is impossible to find specific causes for particular evolved patterns and everything is not linked to reproductive success. Now it is not simply the biological that is evolving over very long time periods but also social relations are evolving in shorter time periods as self-organization/emergence. We can then start to perceive the process over long periods of social evolution, of history, and not just of a lifetime. We then come to see how gender/race are not fixed but are ways of expressing ourselves and our attachment dispositions. Power/ideology come to the fore as evolutionary processes. Ways of thinking are then also understood to evolve. We can still retain the notion of innate disposition, in the form of a particular physiology, to seek attachment but the patterns of attachment are understood as emerging in processes

over historical time as well as over biological evolutionary time. We come to see the inheritance of innate dispositions as much looser bodily constraints. The key point here is the insight about nonlinear iteration having its own patterning properties so that we move from a notion of design to a notion of emergence.

The trouble with the first two explanations, I think, is that they do not take seriously the constitutive, constructive operation of interaction itself. Instead, causality runs in one linear direction: chance variation at the genetic level to natural selection at the body level and biology to behavior. Freud and Klein do this when they start with the individual inheritance of id/fantasy, holding that individuals inherit mechanisms such as splitting and universals such as the Oedipus complex. I argue that biological evolution as self-organization, paradoxically amplifying variations while reproducing continuity, yields emergent enabling constraints. What enables some function restricts it from being anything else. So, biological evolution yields enabling constraints and as we move from lower organisms to higher ones, the enabling constraints become more generalized. The human body, for reasons that have to do with evolved brain chemistry (se Chapter 6) is enabled and constrained to attach–separate.

When it comes to therapy, evolutionary psychologists keep going back from current problems to the inherited strategies appropriate 100,000 years ago. They explain to their patients that they are beating their wives because of human nature but because this is no longer appropriate, they must devise another strategy. This immediately implies that nature can be altered. However, if this is so, it must have been altering for a long time as cultural evolution. So why do evolutionary psychologists keep going back 100,000 years when strategies must have been changing since then? Surely this process of change will be even more important than genetic inheritance and this is where we should look for our explanation.

Part III

Dealing with paradox in thought
From eliminating to living with paradox

The chapters of Part II reviewed the development of psychoanalytic thinking about the relationship between individual and social and the evolutionary psychologists' explanation that is quite consistent with it. Those chapters traced how Freudian thought continued largely within the tradition of Leibniz and Kant to regard the individual as in some sense autonomous. Freud equated mind with an 'internal world' inside an individual and focused his attention on the intrapsychic dynamics of that world. For him, group or society was formed by these intrapsychic processes and it acted as a constraint on the individual as the individual and the social replicated each other according to particular universal patterns. After Freud, psychoanalytic thought continued to focus upon the internal world of the individual in a dyadic practice but it became more and more concerned with relationships between internal worlds. This development of relational and intersubjective psychoanalysis incorporated systems thinking into an understanding of the internal world as a system and the social as another system. Systems thinking is also very much within the Kantian tradition. A key feature of the Kantian way of thinking is its 'both . . . and' structure, which creates dualisms that eliminate paradox.

This final part of the book first reviews, in Chapter 15, the thought of Foulkes, a psychoanalyst who retained the central assumptions of the internal world of the individual. He was also one of the first psychoanalysts to apply systems thinking to understanding the group. What is distinctive about Foulkes, however, is the major innovation he made in the practice of therapy by moving to the group setting. He also developed innovative ways of explaining this new practice in what one might think of as the second strand in his thought. Here, he abandoned the spatial metaphors of internal world and moved to the notion of the individual as a social self based on the work of Elias. In doing this, he questioned the foundations of psychoanalysis. However, it is quite contradictory to hold that there is no inside and outside the individual and the group, on the one hand, and retain the notion of an internal world and an external system on the other. Foulkes did just this by employing the Kantian device of 'both . . . and' thinking.

Group analysts have largely continued within Foulkes' 'both . . . and' thinking to hold together two contradictory theories about the relationship between the individual and the group. Finally, Chapter 16 links back to the theory of social selves presented in Part I, describing its fundamentally paradoxical logic.

Chapter 15

Foulkes' dualistic understanding of the relationship between the individual and the social

Foulkes was a psychiatrist and psychoanalyst. His thinking was built on the foundations laid by Freud and therefore reflected the historical tradition described in Chapters 9 to 11. However, Foulkes made a number of highly significant innovations. First, during the 1940s, he shifted his practice from the psychoanalytic dyad to therapy in a group. Second, he explained what he was doing in ways that developed and also contradicted Freud. From the 1940s to the 1960s, he incorporated systems thinking into his group analytic theory of therapy, so anticipating the development of relational and intersubjective psychoanalysis from the 1970s onwards. However, he also contradicted psychoanalytic theory in his use of sociological theories, particularly those of Elias, to understand the relationship between the individual and the group (Dalal, 1998). This chapter reviews Foulkes' turn to systems thinking and sociology and then explores the manner in which he continued throughout his life to use both the Freudian perspective as developed in systems thinking and the sociological theories of Elias in a manner that eliminated the contradiction between them. In essence he employed Kantian 'both . . . and' thinking to eliminate the contradiction between two incompatible theoretical traditions. Consider first his appeal to systems thinking.

Systems thinking in group-analytic theory

Early in his career, Foulkes worked as an assistant to the neurologist Kurt Goldstein and was considerably influenced by him. Goldstein developed his own version of Gestalt psychology based on his work on the effects of brain damage (Goldstein, 1939). He thought of the central nervous system as a *network* of neurons, each neuron being a *node* in that network. He insisted that the nodes did not function in isolation but rather as elements in a *communicating* network. The functioning of the central nervous system, therefore, could not be understood simply in terms of the *parts*, the neurons, but had to be understood first from the perspective of the *whole* organism. The parts could only be understood as *figures* against the *ground* of the whole. Goldstein took a very clear position in which understanding requires first the identification of the significant whole and only later the analysis of the parts, because the whole is more than, different from, the sum of the parts.

. The impact on Foulkes can be readily seen in his understanding of the relationship between the individual and the group. He thought of a group as a transpersonal network in which its members were equivalent to nodes and the whole, the group, was primary and prior to the parts, the individuals. Individuals could only be understood in terms of the groups to which they belonged.

> Its [the group matrix] lines of force may be conceived as passing right through the individual members and may therefore be called a *transpersonal* network, comparable to a magnetic field. The individual is thought of as a nodal point in this network, as suspended in it.
>
> (Foulkes, 1964, pp258–259)

> The group as it were avails itself now of one speaker, now of another, but it is always the transpersonal network which is sensitized and gives utterance or responds. In this sense we can postulate the existence of a group mind . . .
>
> (Foulkes, 1964, p11)

What did Foulkes mean by transpersonal? He used the term transpersonal, as distinct from interpersonal, to indicate interactions between people that cannot simply be located in one of them (Foulkes & Anthony, 1975, p16). By *trans* he seems to have meant looking at patterns between people and across generations rather than from the point of view of one individual.

> . . . we speak of a matrix, a communicational network. This network is not merely interpersonal but could rightly be described as transpersonal and suprapersonal. Like neurons in the network of the nervous system, so the individuals in such a network are merely nodal points inside the structural entity.
>
> (Foulkes, 1964, p70)

> While having an eye on each individual member and on the effects they and their utterances have on each other, the Conductor is always observing and treating the group as a whole. The 'Group as a Whole' is not a phrase, it is a living organism, as distinct from the individuals composing it. It has moods and reactions, a spirit, an atmosphere, a climate, . . . One can judge the prevailing climate by asking oneself:

What sort of thing could or could not possibly happen in this group? What could be voiced?

(Foulkes, 1948, p140)

What Foulkes was doing here was quite clearly describing a system that is greater than, and outside of, individuals. It is a supra system, a whole, indeed, a living whole with a spirit of its own. According to Foulkes, then, when people come together in a group they create a new phenomenon, a suprapersonal psychic system, which he describes in a number of different ways as: the context of the group, that is, the background in which the individual is figural (Foulkes, 1973, p230); a total unified field of mental happenings of which the individual is a part (Foulkes, 1971, p214); transpersonal processes that go right through individuals like X-rays, but which those individuals can modify, elaborate and contribute to in their own way (1973, p229); and interacting mental processes that transgress the individual (1973, p229). By mental processes, he seems to have meant communications such as 'acts, active messages, movements, expressions, silent transmissions of moods . . .' (1973, p213) both conscious and unconscious. In the latter category he included resonance, transference and projection.

In his last paper on the group matrix, Foulkes (1973) says of a group-analytic group:

What an enormous complexity of processes and actions and inter-actions play between even two or three of these people, or these people and myself, or between two in relation to another three, and so on. What enormous complexity, quite impossible to perceive and disen-tangle even theoretically all at the same time. How is it that they can nevertheless understand each other, that they can to some extent refer to a shared common sense of what is going on?

(Foulkes, 1973, p227)

His answer to this question is 'the existence of a suprapersonal matrix' (1973, p227) and he sees this as an alterative to the view that what is happening in a group is due to the interaction of individual minds. He makes it clear (1973, p226) that he is talking about a psychic system, one of interacting mental processes, not individuals interacting to form a super-imposed social system. But his use of systems thinking is made quite com-patible with Freud through 'both . . . and' thinking when Foulkes turns from the suprapersonal system to its individual parts.

Individual communications can be considered as unconscious associ-ations to a shared theme, reactions against a shared theme or inter-pretations of a theme of others. Unconscious communications present regressive levels of all kinds simultaneously. They occur, according to group theory, in the matrix of communication and communion of the group and rest on the basis of unconscious understanding and of resonance. By the latter is meant the specific reaction of each individual to a stimulus touching a particular note in him.

(Foulkes, 1990, p243)

Consistent with systems thinking, Foulkes identified hierarchical levels in the supra system that is the group when he distinguished between the primordial, foundation, projective and dynamic matrices (Foulkes, 1964, pp114–116). The primordial matrix refers to the shared biological and instinctive inheritance of individuals and in communicating at this level members of a group express primitive images common to the race, much as in Jung's collective unconscious. The foundation matrix refers to the shared linguistic and cultural inheritance that individuals have acquired in their original family and other groups. They bring this shared foundation matrix with them to any therapy group and it is this stable background that they share which makes it possible for them to communicate. The projective level refers to the transferential manner in which people re-create early family patterns of relating and the projective manner in which they locate unwanted aspects of themselves in each other. The dynamic matrix refers to the web of communications that take place in the here-and-now as a group meets – a fluid, unfolding pattern of communication that includes both here-and-now interactions and the recounting of everyday personal experiences outside the group.

> . . . I have accepted from the beginning that even this group of total strangers, being of the same species and more narrowly of the same culture, share a fundamental, mental matrix (*foundation matrix*). To this their closer acquaintance and their intimate exchanges add consistently, so that they also form a current, ever-moving, ever-developing *dynamic matrix*.
>
> (Foulkes, 1973, p228)

> This pre-existing and relatively static part we call the 'foundation matrix.' On top of this there are various levels of communication which are increasingly dynamic. They develop under our eyes. This is called the 'dynamic matrix.'
>
> (Foulkes, 1971, p213)

He made it clear that the various levels of matrix in the supra system operate at the same time in various admixtures but said that for reasons of clarity one can distinguish between the

. . . relatively static and unalterable genetic foundation matrix and the rest, which is, to a greater or lesser extent, subject to change within the group-analytic group.

(Foulkes, 1971, p213)

Of course, the foundation matrix changes through biological and cultural evolution but such evolution takes a long time. It seems clear to me from these quotes, that as far as a specific group-analytic group is concerned, the theory postulates a suprapersonal psychic system having stable, static aspects and dynamic ever-changing ones, to be thought of as intertwined with each other as interacting mental processes.

As the group matrix evolves, that is, as patterns of relationship and communication emerge, the individual members of the group change through processes of insight and adjustment, of which the latter is the more important. By adjustment, Foulkes meant the restructuring of the internal worlds of individual members of the group, which is reflected in changes in relational and communicative patterns. He held that the group would reflect healthy social norms and linked neurosis with deviations from such norms, suggesting that the group experience would erode them while still respecting the basis of human individuality. The foundation matrix thus establishes the healthy norm and the dynamic matrix performs the function of grinding away at those deviations that are neurotic to produce some kind of healthy fit with society at large, leaving untouched the healthy aspects of individuality. Although he made it clear that he was not talking about compliance with the therapist's authority or with the current attitude of the group, Foulkes nevertheless did equate the sound part of an individual's character with group norms, or at least group approval:

The deepest reason why these patients . . . can reinforce each other's normal reactions and wear down and correct each other's neurotic reactions is that collectively they constitute the very norm from which they deviate. This is because each individual is to a large extent a part of the group to which he belongs. This collective aspect permeates him all through to his core. To the extent he deviates from the abstract model, the standard of this norm, he is a variant of it. Just this deviation makes him into an individual, unique which he is again all through, even to his finger prints. . . . The sound part of individuality, of character, is firmly rooted in the group and wholly approved by it. The group therefore respects and supports the emergence of the free development of individuality. Neurotic peculiarities and symptoms are relieved as the process of communication develops and brings about shared experience.

(Foulkes, 1948, p29)

In this formulation, Foulkes reflects the notion of homeostasis or dynamic equilibrium to be found in open systems theory. The foundation matrix seems to be seen as something given and stable, not itself evolving or emerging. It is primarily the social norm that the group represents and in relation to which each individual deviates in a unique way. Part of this deviance is the individual's neurosis and part is his unique, healthy individuality. Foulkes claims that the group process, presumably the dynamic matrix, gradually transforms the neurotic deviance but respects and approves of the healthy uniqueness. Healthy uniqueness is not seen as being itself determined by social interaction. Foulkes is thinking in terms of a foundation matrix as an already existing whole against which the parts are measured to determine what is neurotic or not.

I find this notion problematic for the following reasons. Healthy uniqueness is not some absolute but will itself be determined by social norms. It follows that it is only that uniqueness that the majority conventionally accept that will be respected and approved. Any deviance from acceptable deviance will be attacked as if it were neurotic. In fact the labels of 'neurotic,' 'deviance,' and so on, are themselves social constructs that change over time and vary from place to place. A particular group will thus operate according to the specific norms on acceptable deviance prevailing in its particular time and place: homosexuality used to be labeled neurotic and now it is often not. So thinking in terms of a foundation matrix as an already existing whole against which the parts are measured to determine what is neurotic or not is highly problematic. Furthermore, by definition the novel, the innovative and the creative entail a questioning and a breaking of some social norm or other. History is full of examples of creative, innovative individuals and groups who were rejected, ridiculed and persecuted by their groups and communities.

Furthermore, through the notion of the foundation matrix, Foulkes has brought the individual back to the central position because now mental processes interact in a way *determined* by instincts, predispositions and inner constellations and *decisively shaped* by early family life. This determination and decisive shaping clearly refers to the individual mind. Instincts, predispositions, and so on, constitute causative factors operative before the individual comes to a group to create the new phenomenon of the dynamic level of the suprapersonal psychic system. In fact, if their minds are *determined* and *decisively shaped* in the way just described, what is the causative role of the newly created dynamic level of the supra system of transpersonal processes that pass through individuals? The argument has moved from a dynamic multiperson interactive process in the present that is potentially constructing the future to one in which the future is the unfolding of individually enfolded instincts, predispositions and unconscious inner constellations. How these two are to be understood as processes in one newly constructed supra system is far from clear.

For me, the notions of a dynamic level of the psychic supra system, on the one hand, and a foundation level of inherited instincts and early pre-dispositions, on the other, are two mutually inconsistent explanations in a number of ways. One privileges the group as a psychic system transgressing the individuals and the other privileges the genetically/culturally determined individuals as constructing the group. One implies transformative causality in which the future is being constructed in the living present while the other implies formative causality in which the future is unfolded from what is already there. One emphasizes the possibility of the unknown and the other the likelihood of the known.

In his insistence that the total psychic supra system must be understood as one intertwined system consisting of foundation and dynamic matrices, Foulkes ends up with a 'both . . . and' explanation. On the one hand, there is the dynamic matrix understood as a jointly created whole of a supra system, above or across individuals, penetrating or transgressing them as their minds. This is a multipersonal phenomenon and thus a notion very different to classical psychoanalytic theory. On the other hand, there is the foundation matrix, suggesting something below or before individuals, which is explained in terms of biological determinism and decisive shaping by early family experience, fully in accord with classical psychoanalytic theory of mind as a single person phenomenon. Foulkes does not choose between these explanations but quite explicitly states his 'both . . . and' position (Foulkes, 1973, pp227, pp230–231). He argues that, against the background of the total field, one can focus on the group as a whole or on the individual, in which latter case psychoanalytic formulations apply. It all depends upon what one wishes to observe. He sees both as abstractions in terms of figure (group, individual) and ground (total field or psychic supra system) and regards both as being true from the position from which the observation is made. However, he does express a preference for the multiperson view of mind (Foulkes, 1973, p227).

The influence of Elias' process sociology on group-analytic thinking

In presenting Foulkes' combination of psychoanalytic and systems thinking in the previous section, I have been selective in my use of quotes, drawing on those that make clear Foulkes' use of systems thinking and his adher-ence to Freud. However, it is easy to find other quotes that point in another direction. The other tradition that he tries to combine with psychoanalysis and systems thinking lies in the thought of Elias by whom Foulkes was initially much influenced. For example, in the following passage Foulkes presents the argument to be found in Elias' *The Civilizing Process* ([1939] 2000):

In recent times, in fact since the end of the Renaissance, and in a society that stresses individual property and competition, a configuration has arisen that has brought about the idea of the individual existing in isolation. The individual is then confronted with the community and the world as if they were outside of him. The philosophy of Descartes starts from this premise, and its strict subject/object juxtaposition is still responsible for many pseudo problems of our time. Yet one of the surest observations one can make is that the individual is pre-conditioned to the core by his community, even before he is born, and his personality and character are imprinted initially by the group in which he is raised. This concerns his psychology even more than his genetic inheritance inasmuch as the former is developed in the interaction between him, objects and persons.

(Foulkes, 1990, pp151–152)

Foulkes recognizes quite clearly that this argument represents a departure from Freud's thinking about the relationship between the individual and the group:

Freud's explicit contributions, e.g. 'Group Psychology and the Analysis of the Ego' are not really relevant. He uses the group model in order to illustrate the operation of processes as revealed in the analysis of the individual patient in isolation.

(Foulkes, 1964, p15)

It looks as if we must reverse our traditional assumption, shared also by psychoanalysis, that the individual is the ultimate unity, and that we have to explain the group from inside the individual. The opposite is the case. The group, the community, is the ultimate primary unit of consideration, and the so-called inner processes in the individual are internalizations of the forces operating in the group to which he belongs.

(Foulkes, 1990, p212)

In the above quotes Foulkes still refers to the notion of the inside and the outside. However, Foulkes also clearly stated his disagreement with the spatial notion of an inside and an outside when it came to human individuals and their social interaction. The following quote also interestingly reveals how Foulkes strove to stay within the Freudian tradition.

Explicitly, however, Psycho-Analysis has not yet allotted to this social side of man the same basic importance it has to his instinctual aspect.

For Freud, and for the majority of analysts at the present day still, the social nature of man is a derivative from sexual love, or a reaction formation against incompatible destructive impulses. The infant is thought to be solipsistic, knowing nothing but his own instinctual urges, learning of the 'outside' world only by a painful trial and error method. This is quite true from the infant's own point of view, and not only from the infant's, but from that of every individual. But it becomes wrong as soon as we want to build up the 'world' and 'society' or even the family from the sum total of such intricate complexities of 'individual' interactions. It is the same mistake as it was to consider the whole as the sum of its parts. From a mature scientific point of view, the opposite is true: each individual – itself an artificial, though plausible abstraction – is basically and centrally determined, inevitably, by the world in which he lives, by the community, the group, of which he forms a part. Progress in all the sciences during the last decades has led to the same independent conclusion; that the old juxtaposition of an inside and outside world, constitution and environment, individual and society, phantasy and reality, body and mind, and so on, are untenable. They can at no stage be separated from each other, except by artificial isolation. Freud's own concepts were, of course, in this respect determined by his own epoch, and if he had lived fifty years later he would have been one of the first to correct them. He has, as it is, given sufficient evidence for this assumption.

(Foulkes, 1948, pp10–11)

Foulkes' struggle with the notion of inside and outside is even clearer in the following quote:

What is mind? It will have become clear that I do not think that the mind is basically inside the person as an individual. I think our kind of group clearly shows that. The mind that is usually called intrapsychic is a property of the group, and the processes that take place are due to the dynamic interaction in this communicational matrix. Correspondingly, we cannot make a conventional sharp differentiation between inside and outside, or between phantasy and reality. What is inside is always outside, what is outside is inside as well. . . . I think that the real nature of mind lies in each individual's need for communication and reception.

(Foulkes, 1990, pp277–278)

He clearly feels that the inside–outside distinction is problematic but instead of entirely abandoning it he claims that what is inside is outside and vice versa.

The 'both . . . and' elimination of paradox

In the two previous sections, I have described how Foulkes presented a theory based on a combination of psychoanalysis and system thinking, on the one hand, and on some aspects of the process sociology of Elias, on the other hand. His use of psychoanalytic theory in combination with systems thinking relies on the assumption of a boundary separating a mind inside from the social outside. But then he switches, sometimes in the same paragraph, to the sociological perspective and has difficulties with the notion of inside or outside in the sense that what is inside is also outside and what is outside is also inside.

Dalal (1998) has analyzed these two strands in Foulkesian thought in some detail and pointed to their contradictory nature. In the first strand Foulkes draws on Freud and individualism (orthodox Foulkes), and in the second he tries to develop a theory that gives primacy to the social group (radical Foulkes). Orthodox Foulkes sees the individual as *penetrated* by the social, while radical Foulkes sees the individual as *constructed* by the social. Dalal holds that this mixture gives rise to a series of unsustainable contradictions.

I now want to consider how Foulkes dealt with this contradiction. He did so in 'both . . . and' formulations. To illustrate what I mean take the following passage. First, he makes it clear how we cannot think of internal psychic processes on their own or as inside a person. Instead he emphasizes the group as a whole and explains how this does not remove the individual because the group and the individual are two sides of the same coin, very much the position Elias took. However, he then moves immediately from this formulation to the following, which is the same position as Freud.

> Psychoanalysis has shown that neuroses are based on conflict, conflict that arose early in life with respect to parents or their equivalents. This conflict at bottom is one between the individual's instinctive impulses and his group's cultural taboos. This becomes internalized – unconscious in the dynamic and systematic sense; that is to say, subject to the operation of primary process: primitive pre-logical mentality. . . . There is no need or any wish to abandon these foundations. Concepts like the Oedipus complex, patriarchal and matriarchal, assume a conflict based on the primary family group. Infantile sexuality and incest barriers are all based on the species and its cultural development.
>
> (Foulkes, 1990, pp154–155)

What he does here is to move from a formulation consistent with Elias to one consistent with Freud without noticing any contradiction. He holds both the view that there is no internal world and the view that there is, by moving his focus between the group and the individual. Foulkes' explanation provides the relief of retaining two contradictory theories by looking at them sequentially, keeping one for one purpose and one for another purpose. In so doing, the theory loses the dialectic, the paradox of groups and individuals simultaneously forming and being formed by each other in communicative processes.

The therapeutic process and the role of the therapist

The previous section has indicated how Foulkes constructed a theoretical account of the basis of his group analytic practice using the Kantian device of 'both . . . and,' which enabled him to present two completely contradictory strands of thought. The first derives through Freud and systems thinking from the tradition of Leibniz and Kant utilizing dualities of thought, while the second derives through Elias from the tradition of Hegel who opposed dualities and proposed a social dialectic. When it came to the practice of group therapy itself, however, Foulkes' descriptions perhaps display greater reliance on the notion of social selves although some psychoanalytic aspects of practice are retained. Although he considered himself to be a psychoanalyst to the end of his life, he was also very aware of the highly innovative and distinctive approach to psychotherapy that he developed.

> The treatment of the patient in a group setting is so far removed from the psychoanalytic set-up – one could almost say it is its opposite – that in the writers' opinion it is misleading to call it psychoanalysis.
> (Foulkes & Anthony, 1975, p22)

He understood neurosis and mental disturbances in group terms and he regarded the group as the agent of therapeutic change in the individual.

> At the basis of group psychotherapy lies the conviction that neuroses and other mental disturbances are in truth multipersonal phenomena. This multipersonal network of communication and disturbance is in fact the object of treatment. In group psychotherapy the group of people who are assembled and participate form also the agency of treatment.
> (Foulkes, 1964, p66)

His understanding of the therapy group in practice emphasizes the idea that the individual is social through and through:

> In group-analytic theory we do not orient ourselves by discerning 'intrapsychic,' 'interpersonal' and 'group dynamic' processes. We believe and can show that they are the same processes which can and must be described from different standpoints according to the task

which we pursue. 'Society' is inside the individual, just as well as outside of him, and what is 'intrapsychic' is at the same time shared by the group, . . .

(Foulkes, 1990, p184)

He repeatedly emphasized that in his approach it was the individual who was being treated in the group but he regarded pathology as the location in an individual of relational disturbances in a group. Although he adhered to the belief in the therapeutic effect of making unconscious material conscious, he greatly downplayed the importance of interpretation. Instead he introduced what he regarded as more important therapeutic processes of mirroring, socialization and support.

It was particularly in his development of the role of the group therapist that he introduced far reaching innovations that foreshadowed the much later development in technique of the relational and intersubjective psychoanalysts. The group analyst creates the group-analytic situation – dynamic administration. He does so through his handling of the situation rather than through giving instructions. People come to the group expecting a cure but what they seek a cure from actually serves some purpose for them so it cannot be overcome rapidly. Lectures and exhortation are likely to help little. Instead people are more likely to benefit if they are brought into a situation which they are 'continuously helping to create, to shape.' This forces them to come out with their own reactions and contradictions.

The Group Analyst, for this reason, wants to give the patient a minimum of instructions, of program or of rules, and maximum of freedom in self expression, a maximum of active participation in what is going on. The less defined the situation, the more the patient must stretch and strain himself, become engaged, in order to cope with it, the more he has to invest of his own mind into it.

(Foulkes, 1948, p71)

The keynote in group-analytic sessions is informality and spontaneity of contributions which leads to what I have described as 'free-floating discussion.' The Conductor gives a minimum of instructions and there are no set topics, no planning. While he is in the position of a leader, he is sparing with leading the group actively. He weans the group from wanting to be led – a desire which is all too strong – from looking upon him as an authority for guidance, for instance, as a doctor who will cure him.

(Foulkes, 1964, p40)

Given this freedom, patients engage in free floating discussion, which Foulkes equates with conversation and sees as a group version of free association. This group-analytic situation promotes active participation that awakens interest and communication in a permissive atmosphere enabling people to search for meaning for themselves. The group-analytic situation enables observation in a social setting (including self observation) that allows for living history, diagnosis and prognosis, adjustment and adaptation and insight. The group provides support by sharing anxiety and relieving guilt by confession.

> *The Group Conductor's aim is to let this [interpretations etc.] come from the group itself. The group is the instrument he uses whenever possible.*
> (Foulkes, 1948, p136)

> He is a participant, he observes, has his eye on the group as a whole, as well as on the individual members whom he perceives against this background.
> (Foulkes, 1964, p42)

> He loves and respects the group and his aim is to make its members self-responsible individuals. He wants to replace submission by co-operation on equal terms between equals. In spite of his emotional sensitivity, he has self-confidence, which comes from modesty, and the courage to lead, which springs from his social responsibility.
> (Foulkes, 1964, p65)

Further developments in group-analytic thinking about the individual and the social

Previous sections have described the two contradictory strands in Foulkes' thought. On the one hand, he provides formulations of the relationship between the individual and the social that are derived from Freud augmented by systems thinking. The central concept here is the matrix understood as a suprapersonal system and the meta psychology of Freud is retained where the mind is understood as an internal world of conflicting agencies   the id, ego and superego. On the other hand, Foulkes draws on the sociology of Elias to argue against the notion of a mind located inside an individual and in favor of the notion of minds and the social emerging together. Here he moves from the spatial thinking of systems theory to the temporal thinking of process theory. The two theories are fundamentally contradictory because the first is built on the spatial notion of inside and outside while the latter denies such distinctions. If one is to argue for both then logic demands an explanation of how it is possible for there to be an inside/outside and for there to be no inside/outside for the same phenomenon. Foulkes never dealt with this contradiction but rather eliminated it in the Kantian 'both . . . and' way of thinking. He stated clearly that there was no inside or outside, no separate individual or separate social, but then he said that the notions of individual and social were plausible abstractions. For theoretical purposes, therefore, he retained both notions and dealt with them using the device of figure and ground. Sometimes he thought in terms of one and sometimes he thought in terms of the other. This temporal and spatial separation follows Kant in his way of eliminating paradox.

In this section, I want to explore how this pattern of 'both . . . and' thinking has continued to characterize the development of group-analytic theorizing. The development of group-analytic thought, however, has been strikingly one-sided. It is the combination of psychoanalytic and systems thinking that has dominated the further development of Foulkesian thought. The strand of thinking based on Elias, while frequently acknowledged, has received very little attention. To illustrate the point, the rest of this chapter reviews the extension of group-analytic thought from its Foulkesian base to incorporate object relations theory. I then review thinking on the notion of the social unconscious, and the role of destructive processes, taken as examples of how group-analytic thinking has come to greatly emphasize the internal world and the external supra system, while continuing the 'both . . . and' tradition of claiming that the individual is social to the core.

The incorporation of object relations theory

Although Foulkes himself was critical of Kleinian object relations theory, there have been numerous writings incorporating object relations theory into explanations of group analysis. For the purpose of illustrating this incorporation, I will concentrate here on a paper by Brown (1994). Brown builds on Foulkes' (1948, 1964, 1971, 1973) views on the relationship between the individual psyche and the social by drawing on intersubjective perspectives in psychoanalysis (Stolorow, Brandchaft & Atwood, 1987), Stern's (1985, 1995) detailed studies of infant development, Merleau Ponty's (1976) phenomenology and object relations theory.

Brown talks about a process of communication, of empathic relating, between people in a group in which there is the potential for personal transformation. He describes the process using Foulkesian notions of mirroring in which group members find themselves in each other, and resonance in which they emotionally attune to each other. This is a highly participative perspective, so well described by Merleau Ponty as 'consummate reciprocity.' It is clearly a social process but in drawing on intersubjectivity theory it is, at least implicitly, a systemic view of the social. What people are producing in their reciprocal action is a social system. Brown then draws on object relations theory to formulate a view of individual psyche, which emerges in the social process, as an 'internal world' of representations of relationships between objects and between them and self objects. In other words, the individual psyche is social to the core because it is an 'internal world' of representations of social interactions. People represent in their internal worlds the social system that they have constructed.

Notice here how there is no appeal to Elias' understanding of the social process through which people in the West have come to experience themselves as having an internal world. The notion is simply taken for granted as a human universal. Brown's understanding of how the individual is social to the core is completely different to that developed in Part I of this book. There, to have a mind means to be aware of the possible conse-quences of actions, as those actions evolve, by means of silently conducted conversations in gesturing and responding. *Mind is silent, private role-playing of gesture–response* conducted during the vocal, public interaction of gesture–response that is social cooperation. This is not a view of the autonomous individual first thinking and then choosing an action but of individuals in relationships continuously evoking and provoking responses in each other, responses that each paradoxically also selects and chooses in reconstructing past history in the present. The private, silent conversation of a body with itself is the same process as public, vocal conversation between bodies and in this sense mind is always a social phenomenon even though it is an individual conducting the private silent conversation. Both are the communicative actions of bodies. There is no need to postulate a separate social level, or any kind of transpersonal processes, or any notion of a group mind. Nor is there any need to postulate something separate called a 'mind' *in* which meaning is arising. Instead mind is meaning arising in the communicative interaction of a body with itself. This avoids thinking about mind as an abstraction, as a place located somewhere containing representations of object relations. Rather, mind is processes; the actions of a body experienced in a body and it is this embodied characteristic that makes it impossible to say that a group has a mind or that people have an 'internal world.'

Drawing on Stern's (1985, 1995) detailed descriptions of mother–infant interactions, Brown (1994) says that the infant self emerges from a barely differentiated unity with the mother as the infant comes to experience objects as part of the self. These objects influence perceptions of what is inside the infant and outside, so that inside and outside mutually recreate each other. Later, relationships with others are internalized as representa-tions of self in relation to others, forming an 'internal world.' This internal world consists of representations of objects and relationships between them, all interacting with each other and the self, so becoming organized together with the ego and the superego. The ego mediates and adapts the mind to the outside world. Brown says that it might be thought of as rules for relating to objects and it scans the field, differentiating and synthesizing experience.

What is being postulated here is a 'system' of stored representations, which lies behind interaction and exercises causal powers over it. In the course of this internalizing, the relationships internalized are said to be impregnated by values, customs, history, and so on. In other words they are impregnated by the social and this is how the social is transmitted from one generation to the next. What is being postulated here is a 'system' of shared values and customs, which exists outside interaction itself and exercises causal powers over it. Then when we talk about an 'internal world,' we are positing another system in which agency is also located in, say, the mediating ego. It is also 'as if' this has purpose, or a kind of intention. What we do is then determined by the action of *both* the social *and* the 'internal world.' This is the kind of 'both . . . and' approach to be found in Foulkes' figure–ground thinking.

The perspective taken in Part I is completely different. There, interactions are thought of as bodily communications between mother and infant through touch, sound, gaze, odor and taste; what Mead called a 'conversation of gestures.' Stern infers that within days after birth an infant's sense of a coherent self emerges in the conversation of gestures. From Mead's perspective, mother and infant are forming the social, that is their conversation of gestures, while at the same time they are being formed by that conversation, for it is not simply the infant self that is emerging because the mother too changes in the process. When Brown places the emphasis he does on a theory of mind as internal world and the theory of the social as system, he continues in the tradition of thinking that accords primacy to psychoanalysis and treats the individual and the social as a dualism in the manner of 'both . . . and' thinking.

The incorporation of object relations theory into group analytic thought thus perpetuates the contradiction between the two strands of Foulkesian thought and it deals with the contradiction in exactly the same way, namely, the 'both . . . and' elimination of paradox.

The unconscious

I now turn to another example of the development of Foulkes' thought, this time relating to his notion of the social unconscious. As an example, I take a recent paper by Hopper (2001). He thinks of groups as open systems dependent on imports from across their own boundaries. He says that group analysts usually focus on the psychological context but in his paper he is concerned with the social context and how a group and its members are affected by it. From this formulation, it is immediately evident that he is thinking of the social as a context outside of the therapy group and of the therapy group as dependent on imports from this social context. He draws a distinction between, on the one hand, the constraints that social systems place on individuals and their 'internal' worlds and, on the other hand, the effects that their unconscious fantasies, actions, thoughts and feelings have on social systems. Social systems exert constraints on individuals and at the same time individuals affect social systems. Although he uses the words *at the same time*, Hopper is not presenting a paradox in the sense that I do in Part I when I say that individuals form groups while being formed by them at the same time. This is because Hopper is not talking about the same process of temporal interaction as I am, but rather about two distinct entities affecting each other. One entity is the individual 'internal world' and the other is a social system and they interact with each other. Hopper uses the spatial metaphor of Freud and the Freudian/systems strand of Foulkesian thinking to locate individual and social in different spaces. In doing this he continues in the tradition of 'both . . . and' thinking that immediately eliminates paradox.

Having set up this dualism of individual and social, Hopper then explains what he means by the social unconscious:

> The effects of social facts and forces are as likely to be unconscious as conscious. The social unconscious is not merely a matter of the preconscious, and cannot be reduced to questions of awareness. The social unconscious is lawful in the same sense that the dynamic uncon- scious operates according to primary process. Structural dilemmas and contradictions abound, and some arrangements and cultural patterns preclude others. The concept of the social unconscious refers to the existence and constraints of social, cultural and communicational arrangements of which people are unaware. Unaware, in so far as these arrangements are not perceived (not 'known'), and if perceived not acknowledged ('denied'), and if acknowledged, not taken as prob- lematic ('given'), and if taken as problematic, not considered with an optimal degree of detachment and objectivity. Although social con- straints are sometimes understood in terms of myth, ritual and custom, such constraints are in the realm of the 'unknown' to the same extent as the constraints of instincts and fantasies, especially in societies with high status rigidity . . . However, 'constraint' is not meant to imply only 'restraint,' 'inhibition,' or 'limitation,' but also 'facilitation, 'develop- ment' and even the transformation of sensations into feelings.
>
> (Hopper, 2001, pp10–11)

Hopper goes on to say that the social unconscious refers to social and cultural elements and processes that people were formerly aware of but no longer are (for example, the Oedipus complex), that they were partially aware of formerly but no longer are (for example, fantasy life before language), and that they were never aware of. He says that social systems do not have unconscious minds or any other kind of mind. He traces the notion of the social unconscious to Foulkes:

... the group analytic situation, while dealing with the unconscious in the Freudian sense, brings into operation and perspective a totally different area of which the individual is equally unaware. Moreover, the individual is as much compelled by these colossal forces as by his own id and defends himself as strongly against their recognition without being aware of it, but in quite different ways and modes. One might speak of a social or interpersonal unconscious.

(Foulkes, 1964, p52)

Hopper then says:

In various kinds of social systems, people tend unconsciously to recreate situations (in terms of actions, fantasies, object relations and affects) that have occurred at another time and space, such that the new or later situation may be taken as 'equivalent' to the old or previous one . . . although 'equivalence' is based on the social unconscious, it is analogous to a person's creation of symptoms or dreams in terms of unconscious fantasies emanating from the biologically based unconscious mind or id . . . Equivalence occurs through forms of externalization and internalization, including projective and introjective identification, in the service of expulsion or attack, mastery and control, but, above all, as a result of attempts to communicate nonverbal and ineffable experience, all of which may be considered as elements of the repetition compulsion. In fact, equivalence can be seen as a kind of group-transference of an unconsciously perceived situation from its social context to its present situation. The concepts of the social unconscious and of equivalence emphasize the importance of the experience of personal and social helplessness and powerlessness.

(Hopper, 2001, p13)

Notice how there is both the social system and an internal world, the effects of which may be unconscious. Notice the assumptions of inside and outside in the postulation of externalization and internalization. There is no notion here of the social as process as in Elias' thinking. Hopper presents an explanation of social unconscious processes as a phenomenon distinct from the individual unconscious and eliminates the paradox of the social and the individual in Kantian 'both . . . and' thinking.

Dalal (1998) develops a different perspective on the social unconscious, one based on the thinking of Elias, which was summarized in Chapter 7. Dalal points to the use of ideology to make power relations feel natural as an unconscious social process, where the hatred between the groups emerges without people being aware of or intending it. Power differentials are thus preserved through the unconscious use of ideology, also an unconscious process.

Dalal further develops the notion of the social unconscious in relation to the structure of language. He argues that humans categorize or partition experience in order to deal with it and this act of naming is intrinsically binarizing: the deep structure of language is a binary logic in that things are categorized as 'A' or 'not-A.' Dalal suggests that there seems to be an inevitable tendency, as humans frame their experience, to binarize and polarize it. In making this move, Dalal presents an understanding of unconscious processes that differs from the theory of complex responsive processes and also, it seems to me, from Elias' ideas. Dalal is making a distinction between experience, thought of as a continuous flow, and acts of categorizing and framing that experience. These acts are thought of as partitioning, cutting up, binarizing and polarizing experience. Language is then thought of as separate from experience. However, for Elias and Mead, and from the complex responsive process perspective, experience is the actions and interactions of bodies. It follows that experience is language and language is experience. As soon as one suggests that language does something to experience, one introduces an observer who is using language to operate on experience, partitioning it, making distinctions in it, and so on. However, from a complex responsive processes perspective, there is no observer using language to operate on anything, only participants in language as experience and there is nothing, such as deep structure, underlying language/experience. The experience of language is the experience of categorizing, of including and excluding, and as I argued in Chapter 7, this is a largely unconscious aspect of experience.

Dalal's next point is that there seem to be two different forms of logic used by humans to frame their experience, forms that Matte Blanco (1975, 1988) called asymmetrical and symmetrical logic. Asymmetrical logic establishes difference in that it distinguishes things from each other and locates them in time and space, much as in Freud's secondary process thinking. Symmetrical logic, on the other hand, treats all objects as the same, rather as in Freud's primary process thinking. Symmetrical logic homogenizes everything and recognizes no contradictions, no negation and no degrees of certainty or uncertainty. There is no difference, no space, no time. Asymmetrical logic is the opposite in all of these respects. Matte Blanco argued that both forms of logic are applied in all forms of thought at the same time. However, despite using the phrase 'at the same time,' there is no real paradox because symmetrical and asymmetrical logic remain distinctly different forms of logic so that their meanings do not change when they are brought together. They constitute a duality, not Hegelian dialectic.

We can now make a general statement and say that all thinking consists of fracturing the continuum of experience, of breaking it up into different parts, and relating those parts to each other. Thus between the parts, difference is emphasized, and similarity is obliterated – asymmetric logic. Whilst within each part, similarity is emphasized and difference obliterated – symmetric logic.

(Dalal, 1998, p166)

Dalal argues that conscious thinking tends to be more asymmetrical than symmetrical and unconscious thought tends to be more symmetrical than asymmetrical. He argues that the very act of naming or categorizing inevitably binarizes and polarizes an experience and at the same time the process of thinking makes the experience both heterogeneous (asymmetrical and conscious) and homogeneous (symmetrical and unconscious). So, when some in a group are named 'British,' the others all become 'not-British' and symmetrical thinking is immediately applied to both 'British' and 'not-British' in that homogeneity is imposed on each group. Within each group the differences between members are obliterated and the fact that this is being done is unconscious. At the same time there is asymmetrical thinking in that a difference is being drawn between the two groups.

. . . every sentence contains globules of homogeneity, which are connected by heterogeneity. . . . *Thus all thought could be said to consist of a weaving together of islands of unconsciousness.*

(Dalal, 1998, pp190–191).

Dalal then suggests that at the centre of identity there is symmetry, an unconscious symmetry that cannot be tested without destroying that identity. He sees this as an aspect of the social unconscious and links it with discourse. Within each discourse there are certain categories taken to be natural, the equivalent of identities, and these are homogenized and so hidden from questioning. It is these categories that constitute the social unconscious and what is being made unconscious is the power differential. People cluster around their similarity – the symmetrical – to hide the difference of power.

In continuing with the notion of language/logic as separate from experience, as fracturing the continuous flow of experience and applying different logics to it, Dalal continues to introduce the implicit observer of experience. In taking up Matte Blanco's separate logics, he implicitly brings in Freudian individual intrapsychic concepts of primary and secondary processes in a way that is quite different to the complex processes perspective. It seems to me that this loses the earlier Eliasian formulation of unconscious *social* processes. Nevertheless he is pointing to important aspects of unconscious processes of inclusions and exclusion. These aspects have to do with unconscious processes of inclusion as sameness and homogeneity and exclusion as difference or heterogeneity at the same time.

In his formulation of the social unconscious, Dalal (1998) builds on the social strand of Foulkesian thinking but in a sense presents a distinction between individual and social by positing two different types of unconscious. In a later publication (2001), he moves further to abandon the distinction between individual and social unconscious, arguing that they are the same process. In doing this he argues in the tradition of Hegel as understood by Elias, seeing unconscious behavior in terms of social processes. However, in continuing to split language and experience, and in positing two separate kinds of logic, he implicitly continues with individual, intrapsychic processes. It proves very difficult to draw on psychoanalytic notions and avoid 'both . . . and' thinking to stay with social process thinking.

Destructive and creative processes

Nitsun (1996) argues that Foulkes had an overriding tendency to emphasize wholeness and idealized wholes, as for example, in the notion of the group matrix. However, while Foulkes idealized the healing power of groups, Bion emphasized their destructive potential. For Foulkes, the group was a sociobiological reality, while for Bion it was a psychic illusion. Nitsun criticizes both of these positions, the former for its idealization and ignoring of destructive group processes and the latter for not taking account of the creative potential of groups or of how individuals actively mould the group. Nitsun seeks to bring these two positions together by incorporating into group-analytic theory the notion of the anti-group, which he thinks of as a phase in the development of a group. He uses Bion's concept of container and contained to define the anti-group as a failure of the container–contained relationship resulting in projective identification. He also conceptualizes the group as mother.

Nitsun holds that the demands of group existence arouse considerable anxiety and potential for regression and he explains these processes in terms of object relations theory.

> My vantage point is largely that of object relations theory . . . The link between internal representations and external relationships – the bedrock of all object relations theory – together with the emphasis on projective and introjective processes, I consider to be essential for the understanding of the psychopathology of the anti-group.
>
> (Nitsun, 1996, p106)

Nitsun, therefore, continues within the strand of Foulkesian thinking based on Freud/systems thinking and its later extension by others to include object relations theory. The underlying assumption is that the social and the individual exist at different levels, with the individual psyche as an 'internal world' of representations interacting with other 'internal worlds' through intrapsychic processes of projection and introjection as the link between internal and external representations. The spatial metaphor of inside and outside is fundamental to this thinking. The group is then an object outside of the individual.

> As a guiding principle, I start from the conception of the *group as object*. This formulation is implicit or explicit in the views of numerous writers. In Bion's work (1961), for example, the notion of a *group entity*, established through the operation of the basic assumptions, in essence describes a group object. Anzieu (1984) more explicitly describes a group object created through the fantasies and projections of the group membership. . . . the group becomes an 'object in the cultural field.' . . . Once established, the group as object, an entity in its own right, invites its own form of object relationships with the group membership, in a way which powerfully influences further development. In the case of the anti-group, the group as object becomes a fragile, dangerous, or aversive container . . .
>
> (Nitsun, 1996, pp106–107)

In this way of thinking, the group is a separate psychical system operating like an individual psyche and the determinants of the anti-group are the intrapsychic processes of regression, projective identification, envy, jealousy and greed and the death instinct. The anti-group is also characterized by interpersonal processes such as aggression, hatred rivalry, shame, humiliation, interpersonal disturbances due to the destructive effects of loss or unavailability in early 'primary' relationships, and the primal scene as precursor to the Oedipus complex.

The origins of the anti-group therefore lie primarily in universal intrapsychic processes and the potentially disturbed interpersonal relationships they lead to. This is a very different understanding of destructive processes in groups to that of Elias explained in Chapter 7.

Nitsun then suggests that the anti-group is not only destructive but also a source of creativity.

> . . . the group has particular transformational properties given its depth and width: it reaches deeply into the intra-psychic and social origins of self, while enhancing the intersubjective relationships . . .
>
> (Nitsun, 1996, p197)

He takes what he calls three key perspectives on transformational change. First, there is the systemic operation of positive and negative feedback. He says that feedback explains why the system maintains itself (negative feedback) or transforms itself (positive feedback). He also says that an initial stimulus triggers change but is not the cause because the transformation is already contained in the logic of the system. I would argue, however, that if the transformation is already contained in the logic of the system, then it cannot be truly transformative or creative in the sense of being novel. Nitsun is here taking the Kantian notion of a system that unfolds what is already enfolded in it. Second, he takes autopoiesis and says that the anti-group challenges its self-reference. Again, however, I would point out that an autopoietic system is one that sustains its identity and when its identity is transformed it ceases to exist. This too is a theoretical perspective that cannot explain the transformation of identity. I am arguing that this appeal to systems thinking cannot serve Nitsun's intention of explaining the transformative potential of a group. Third, he takes a dialectical perspective on transformation.

Nitsun talks about the dialectic of creative and destructive forces in a group, arguing that

> . . . the anti-group forms an essential part of the dialectic of creative and destructive forces in group psychotherapy, that it is in the movement between the two poles that the group develops, and that it is in the opposition of thesis and antithesis that a new synthesis, a transformation, may take place. In the complex system that is the developing group, the antagonistic force of the anti-group helps to shape the identity of the group, to define it as an autonomous and self-regulating system, and to evolve its therapeutic value system. It helps to deepen the crucible of change that is the therapy group.
>
> (Nitsun, 1996, p197)

Here, Nitsun uses Kant's terminology of thesis–antithesis–synthesis to describe the dialectic (see Chapter 10). When he talks about two poles between which the group oscillates, one of destruction and the other of creation, he is positing a Kantian dualism. Furthermore the whole argument is based on the group as an autonomous self-regulating system on the one hand, and the individual as an internal world of representations on the other. This is another Kantian dualism. Given that there are separate internal worlds, people interact with each other in the sender–receiver mode of projection and introjection and their experience is patterned by innate universals such as the primal scene. This again is Kantian thinking. The destructive processes Nitsun talks about are primarily couched in terms of the intrapsychic processes of object relations theory and the synthesis is a combination of these destructive forces (all related to internal worlds) and the group as a self-regulating system. Furthermore, the meaning of destruction and of creation remain the same in this synthesis. All of this is quite consistent with the Kantian dialectic.

Hegel, however, argued against Kant's dualisms and never used the terminology of thesis, antithesis and synthesis. In Hegel's dialectic, the tension of oppositional forces creates a new dynamic in which the opposition remains but with its meaning altered (see Chapter 10). For Hegel, the dialectic was a social process in which self consciousness arises in the desire of one for the desire of another, in the mutual recognition of interacting self consciousnesses.

Nevertheless, Nitsun claims that his theory is a form of Hegelian dialectic. He talks about the anti-group as a collapse to one pole of a contradiction and cohesion as a collapse to the other pole and provides an extended clinical illustration of the dialectic in practice.

> . . . the group presented illustrates the dialectical movement between creative and destructive forces, the anti-group acting as an essential, recurring polarity in the interplay between opposing tendencies in the group. Within this dialectical matrix, the group gradually gains shape, strength, and identity. It becomes a self-created, 'autopoietic' activity, a transitional space which awakens the zone of play and provides the context for therapeutic transformation for group and conductor alike.
>
> (Nitsun, 1996, p216)

The notion of dialectic is here linked with that of an autopoietic system. However, the essence of an autopoietic system is that it sustains its identity. This is a theory of change in which identity is maintained rather than transformed and while this is consistent with Kantian dialectic it is not consistent with Hegelian dialectic, which is a theory of identity transformation. Nitsun analyses the group's development in terms of movement from primitive and archaic fantasy images (Foulkes' primordial, projective and transferential levels) to ones of transformation. Here there is a reliance on concepts assuming an 'internal world' of universal, pre-given fantasies (for example, the primal scene and fantasies of the mother's body). Again, this is consistent with Kantian dialectic but not the kind of Hegelian dialectic taken up by Mead and Elias. Nitsun then goes through a number of group sessions and identifies a period of some weeks during which the group is said to be an anti-group of a dead, frozen kind, buried in its archaic past. Here one gets the movement back into the past of Freudian theory rather than the movement into the future of Hegelian dialectic. This is followed by a number of sessions in which there is transformation in the sense of reparative themes, changes in the group's relationship with the conductor and improvements in members' lives. Then an approaching summer break re-ignites the anti-group. After the break the group experiences a difficult start with denial when the conductor tries to take up feelings about the break. The group is attacked as inadequate and at the same time some individual members improve. The group attacks the conductor and some members drop out. This is described as a crisis, further evidence of the anti-group. However, this is followed by a period of intense transformation during which the group develop the capacity to play.

What Nitsun describes, it seems to me, is an oscillation between a phase of destructive anti-group behavior followed by a phase of constructive work, sometimes followed by another phase of anti-group. He then indicates how the one triggers the other. However, this kind of oscillation is the Kantian 'both . . . and' in that there is the predominantly anti-group in one phase and the predominantly constructive group in the other. Nitsun identifies a transformation but then says that it is already contained in the system – this is pure Kant. Nitsun is, therefore, describing a dialectic that is completely different to the one developed by Mead and Elias from Hegel, which forms the basis of Part I of this book. Hegel's dialectic is a social process of people recognizing each other. It does not involve internal worlds and external systems.

I am essentially arguing that a theory built on the individual and the social as two levels and a theory of process as a movement between poles cannot be other than a Kantian dialectic no matter how many Hegelian terms are used. It seems to me that valuable as his insights about destructive processes in groups are, Nitsun remains within that Foulkesian tradition which combined psychoanalysis and systems thinking and the Kantian form of 'both . . . and' thinking.

To summarize, I have argued that Foulkes drew on two very different strands of Western thought. In one he combined psychoanalysis and systems thinking and in the other he gave formulations drawn from Eliasian process sociology. The two are contradictory theories but Foulkes eliminated the contradiction using the Kantian device of dualism. He moved from one formulation to another depending on what he wanted to focus attention on. Using a sample of recent group-analytic writing, I then argued that group-analytic thinking has mainly continued in the Foulkesian tradition, with a few exceptions, such as Dalal. It has greatly emphasized the combination of psychoanalysis and systems thinking and greatly downplayed Eliasian process sociology without abandoning it altogether. The contradiction is normally not noticed in the continued reliance on 'both . . . and' thinking, in the shift between figure and ground, which eliminates paradox.

Chapter 16

Complex responsive processes: the movement of paradox and the transformation of identity

The premise of this book is that humans are fundamentally social animals, where social means processes of relating between human bodies. The argument is that over very long periods of time the processes of biological evolution have produced human bodies with distinctive characteristics. Human physiology is such that an individual body cannot regulate itself on its own because the biochemical mechanisms of calming and arousal are inextricably linked to actions of attachment to, and separation from, other bodies. Attachment actions of the body trigger releases of opioids in the brain, which calm the body, and separation actions trigger arousal hormones in the brain, which excite the body, so that humans are inevitably social at a fundamental physiological level. In the most basic way, humans have to belong together in groups and this physiological need is central to the cooperative and competitive joint action that is the basis of the survival of the human species.

The capacity for joint action has also evolved in two further distinctive features of the human body. The first is the capacity of the human body, due to the form of its central nervous system, to call forth in itself similar responses to its gesture as those gestures call forth in other human bodies. It is this physiological capacity that constitutes the basis of mind, that is, consciousness and self consciousness, and also the basis of communicative interaction between bodies, particularly in that form of vocal gesturing and responding called language. This physiological capacity makes possible increasingly sophisticated communicative interaction and hence increasingly sophisticated patterns of joint action. Mind here is fundamentally understood as the actions of bodies directed towards themselves, just as social is understood as actions directed towards other bodies. The second distinctive feature of human bodies produced by biological evolution are hands, which are the basis of the capacity to use and make tools, and so develop technologies. This capacity also enables more sophisticated ways of undertaking joint action, that is, more sophisticated social forms.

Furthermore, the physiological need to belong, as well as physiologically-based communicative interaction and tool use, cannot be understood as instinctual, that is, as automatic responses dictated by a genetic program. This is because the thrust of human evolution has been to sever the direct link between environmental stimuli and bodily responses. The human brain has evolved in a form that is largely plastic so that it is shaped by the body's experiences and those experiences are predominantly social experiences, that is, the patterning of attachment and separation interactions between bodies. This is reflected in the evolution of the human development process in which the human body takes a relatively long time to mature as evidenced by the long period of infancy and childhood. Another way of saying this is that human interactions are not instinctual but learned so that while the interaction of genes plays a significant part in forming the body, it does not directly form the actions of that body. The impact of genetic interactions on the actions of a body are only indirectly influential through the role they play in forming human physiology. Patterns of human action are learned, that is, they are evolving social processes. The brain does not represent a pre-given reality and it does not store anything in any straight-forward fashion. Instead, the brain simultaneously shapes and is shaped by actions patterned as relations between bodies, where those relations are iterative, nonlinear processes constantly reproducing patterns of interaction, always with the potential for transformation.

This is a completely different view of human evolution to neo-Darwinian theory, the basis of evolutionary psychology, in which genes are thought to code actions in the form of hard-wiring in the brain. The understanding of biological evolution presented in Part I of this book is also completely different to that underlying psychoanalytic theory in which the implicit understanding of biological evolution is very similar to that of evolutionary psychology. The view of brain functioning as iterative pattern forming processes presented in this book is also completely different to that under-lying both cognitivist and psychoanalytic psychology. The latter are both based on assumptions of mind as an internal model or world consisting of stored representations, notions that are completely different to the iterative patterning processes described in Part I of this book. The consequence of taking the perspective I am arguing for on evolution and brain functioning is a completely different view of the relationship between the individual and the social. The social is essential to human survival in every sense and cannot be regarded as primarily in conflict with, or destructive of, indi-vidual functioning.

On the basis of the above views of evolution and brain functioning, I have been suggesting a particular way of understanding human groups as processes of communicative interaction between bodies. Just as Foulkes argued, belonging and communicating are central to any understanding of individuals in groups. However, in their communicative interaction, people are both constraining and enabling each other. In other words, power is an irremovable aspect of human communicative interaction, which must be understood, at the same time, as power relating. This immediately leads to the recognition that patterns of inclusion and exclusion are inevitable aspects of communicative interaction and power relating simply because inclusion–exclusion is an irremovable aspect of power relating. Another way of talking about inclusion is to talk about attachment and another way of talking about exclusion is to talk about separation. This immediately establishes a link with human physiology so that the intimate connection between human social relating and human physiology is central to an understanding of individuals and groups.

This connection between the body and the social points to the importance of anxiety, a process of bodily arousal triggered by exclusion/separation, and the manner in which social processes of inclusion/attachment regulate the bodily experience of anxiety. The regulation of anxiety is then a social, not a purely individual, process. The importance of being included and avoiding exclusion as a means of regulating anxiety points to another aspect of human interaction. To be seen to be unworthy in any way is to risk exclusion and the affect of being seen to be unworthy and excluded is shame. Shame is also simultaneously social and individual in a physiological sense and it too plays a major role in the possibility of more and more sophisticated communicative interaction and joint action because of its importance in generating and reinforcing individual self-control. The social processes of shame, closely linked to the individual experiences of guilt, are thus very important aspects of human interaction. Any sense that one gets of being about to be exposed to shame and exclusion can quite easily trigger some form of panic, which is the fear of the fear of being exposed. And responses to shame and panic can very easily take the form of aggression and other destructive processes such as envy and jealousy. Human emotions, from loving to hating, from creative attachments to destructive exclusions are thus all social processes individually experienced as variations in body rhythms.

Furthermore, the capacity of mind enables fantasy and imaginative elaboration, which express the vicissitudes of attachment and separation patterns of behavior that are socially evolved rather than genetically pro-grammed. Linked to this are the unconscious aspects of communicative interaction and power relating. As people interact, much of the patterning of that interaction becomes habitual, or automatic, and this applies as much to the private, silent interaction of the body with itself, mind with its patterns of self-control, as it does to the public, vocal interaction between bodies, the social with its evolved norms. In these interactions, com-munities of individuals evolve social habits, which are largely unconscious, having individual and social aspects at the same time. Here there is no distinction between individual and social unconsciousness because by unconscious I mean aspects of the patterning of communicative interaction and power relating that people are not aware of and those aspects are simultaneously relevant to the patterning of individual and social processes. Some unconscious aspects are so because habit has made them automatic. Other aspects are unconscious in the sense that they have not been formulated. And the vicissitudes of attachment and separation generate other aspects, namely, unvalidated patterns of interaction. Here, patterns of interaction were once formulated but met either with apathy or some kind of hostility and so are never articulated again. All of these aspects reflect conflict and pathology but also the potential for novelty and transformation.

It is complex processes of the kind described in previous paragraphs that I have referred to throughout this book as complex responsive processes of relating. By analogy with the properties of abstract iterative, nonlinear interaction identified in the complexity sciences, I have argued that complex responsive processes of human relating have the intrinsic capacity to pattern themselves in coherent ways. I have argued that such patterning emerges in narrative forms, which can be described in terms of continually iterated themes patterning the experience of being together. Again by analogy with the complexity sciences, these self-organizing, iterated themes perpetually reconstruct the past in the process of constructing the future. And the future so constructed emerges as both continuity and potential transformation at the same time. The potential for transformation arises because iterative nonlinear interaction has the capacity to amplify small differences. Transformation is possible, then, only when interaction is characterized by difference. I have suggested that illness is patterning of interaction that is rigid or stuck, showing great continuity and very little difference. Health, on the other hand, is patterning of interaction characterized by difference and variability and thus the potential for transformation.

What I have been describing is a fundamentally paradoxical way of thinking. There is the paradox of individual minds forming and being formed by the social at the same time. There is the paradox of the patterning of mind and social emerging as continuity and potential transformation at the same time. There is the paradox of creative and destructive patterns of interaction emerging at the same time. There is the paradox of conscious and unconscious patterning at the same time. The complex responsive processes perspective is also one in which words are thoughts, are meaning, are experience. There is no notion of a flow of experience that people operate on, or give meaning to, in the form of words. The words and the feelings are the experience.

This paradoxical logic is completely different to the logic that is employed in psychoanalytic theorizing, systems thinking and group-analytic thought when it relies on these sources. The logic there is that of 'both . . . and' dualism, which eliminates paradox. This dualistic logic leads to very different ways of dealing with the relationship between the individual and the social. In the 'both . . . and' logic, one resolves the inside–outside problem by arguing that the social is in the individual in the form of representations of social relationships and the individual is in the social in the sense of being a part of the social system. There is no paradox because one deals sequentially with the individual and the social, linking them with communication understood as sending and receiving mental contents. The result is a theory facing considerable conceptual problems to do with doubtful spatial metaphors of inside and outside, the dubious sender–receiver mode of communication, and the notions of representations and storing of memories contested by recent research on the brain. I have also argued that an approach which regards the individual as part of a system has difficulty in explaining human free choice. Also, systemic theories locate the source of novelty and transformation in the individual without really explaining how they occur. The complex responsive processes perspective accounts for free choice, novelty and potential transformation in terms of the intrinsic property of iterative nonlinear interaction to pattern itself as continuity and potential transformation through the possibility of amplifying small differences in iteration.

Complex responsive processes of relating, then, take the forms of bodies directing their communicative actions toward themselves, the process of individual mind, and bodies directing their communicative interactions toward each other as social relations. Individual mind and social relations are thus two aspects of the same process of bodily interaction and it is in this sense that the individual is social to the core. Identity emerges in the human communicative interaction and power relating so far described and it does so simultaneously in individual and collective forms as 'I' and 'we' identities. The two are inextricably linked and for humans one is not possible without the other. And as soon as one recognizes 'I' and 'we' identities, one sees that identity is as an aspect of inclusion and exclusion and thus power relating. Identity is therefore closely interwoven with processes of anxiety, shame and panic.

A therapy group is fundamentally like any other group. Individual and collective identities are continually iterated in the group as continuity and potential transformation. The therapist's role is to participate in a carefully attentive manner in the complex responsive processes of relating that are a group. Immediately, one sees that the action of the group is prospective and that interaction is reproducing the past in constructing the future. The therapist, therefore, is not aiming at uncovering what is unconscious in the sense of wishes that were once experienced but now suppressed. There is no notion of uncovering a given, true past because this implies a memory state rather than social processes of iteration. As a therapist, one is not necessarily aiming for insight in terms of making the unconscious conscious. Indeed, healing may take place without insight as people talk differently to themselves and to each other without even being all that aware that they are doing so. The therapist implicitly focuses attention on the thematic patterning of interaction through his or her manner of participating, seeking to enrich or complexify the conversation and so escape from rigid, stuck patterns. The centre of the therapist's attention is 'habitus,' that is, the unconscious patterning of interactions. The central concern, therefore, is just the same as in psychoanalysis but the notion of what is unconscious is different. Indeed, the whole explanation of what one is doing in a group is different because one thinks in terms of process theory, a theory of bodily action, in which there is no inside and no outside.

The perspective I have been outlining differs in fundamental ways from that underlying psychoanalysis. Indeed it is a theory that stands in contradiction to psychoanalytic meta theory, although the central concern of the therapist is the same in both, namely, that which is unconscious. The basic reason for the difference is this. The theory of complex responsive processes is a process theory, an action theory, in which inside and outside have no meaning. Psychoanalytic thought is based on the basic assumption of mind inside a person as an internal world and the social outside of persons as a system. There have been very few attempts to get away from this assumption, the most notable being by Schafer. However, he develops an action theory based on the notion of individual agency rather than the notion of the social process. Notions of internal worlds and individual agency are not 'reality' and they feel natural and attractive to people in the West only because social evolution has made it so. What is taken for granted as psychic reality has in fact been developed by analogy with the camera obscura, reflecting a basically Leibnizian idea of monads. Psychoanalytic thinking is also in the tradition of Kant and his notion of the autonomous individual. Thinking in terms of complex responsive processes, on the other hand, is in Hegel's tradition in which we know through social processes. Another problematic feature of psychoanalytic thinking is its assumptions of representations and storing of memory. These ideas are fundamental to psychoanalysis and cannot be as easily dropped as outdated ideas of psychic energy. It is the reliance on notions of inside and outside, representation and storing, sender–receiver communication and the primacy accorded to the individual which is the basis of my argument that it is problematic to think in terms of psychoanalytic theory about human action and psychotherapy

Another major distinction between psychoanalytic and complex responsive process theory has to do with the view that the former so often takes of the group as a regressive phenomenon, while the autonomous individual is mature and creative. Psychoanalytic theory displays a deep suspicion of spontaneous group formation, while from the complex responsive processes perspective, grouping is understood as naturally creative and destructive processes of human relating. The psychoanalytic view of groups, it seems to me, is incompatible with the recognition that humans can only function in groups. Indeed it is a rather strange view of human activity when one bears in mind that individuals on their own can do nothing. Indeed they cannot even have minds in the absence of relationships with others.

I argue that the psychoanalytic and complex responsive processes perspectives are contradictory and incompatible with one another and the choice between them has significant implications for what one does as a therapist. From a psychoanalytic perspective, one is concerned with intrapsychic fantasy, defenses and repression. One thinks in terms of regression and uncovering the past. One thinks spatially in terms of containing anxiety. From a complex responsive processes perspective the therapist is a participant in the social process of the group and there are strong power implications in the position one takes. One is analyzing emerging themes patterning interaction rather than intrapsychic fantasy. I argue against retaining two contradictory theories of this kind, moving back and forth between them as Foulkes did, because it clouds thinking and eliminates the paradoxical logic that is essential to the complex responsive processes perspective.

However, in drawing attention to the differences between psychoanalysis and the complex responsive processes perspective and in drawing attention to what I regard as problematic about the fundamental assumptions upon which psychoanalytic theory is built, I am not arguing for any wholescale rejection of psychoanalysis. On the contrary, in developing a complex responsive processes approach in Part I, I drew on a great deal of psychoanalytic thought. The complex responsive processes approach takes attachment–separation as central, just as psychoanalytic attachment theory does. The vicissitudes of attachment and separation and the consequences of early failures in attachment are central to both psychoanalysis and complex responsive processes theory. Indeed, one of Freud's great insights, namely, the importance of early patterns of behavior and their repetition throughout life is also central to the history-dependent theory of complex responsive processes. Psychoanalysis' concern with unconscious process is also central to a complex responsive process approach and the theory of unconscious process it incorporates is drawn in significant respects from the work of relational and intersubjectivity psychoanalytic theories. The ideas of intersubjectivity theorists and psychoanalytically oriented developmental psychologists, with their notions of mind as organizing principles, are also taken up in complex responsive processes theory in the form of narrative themes patterning the experience of being together.

What I am arguing for is a move from psychoanalytic and systemic meta theories with their notions of internal worlds and social systems, representations, memory stores, sender–receiver modes of communication and dualistic 'both . . . and' thinking. I am arguing for a move to process thinking in which paradox is central and which understands human identities, with their simultaneous 'I' and 'we' aspects, emerging in self-organizing communicative interaction between human bodies, where identities emerge as continuity and transformation at the same time. The advantage of such a move, I suggest, is a way of thinking that is not characterized by the serious conceptual problems of psychoanalytic and systemic modes of thinking and is far closer to ordinary, everyday human experience.

Bibliography

Agazarian, Y. M. (1994) 'The phases of group development and the systems-centered group,' in Schermer, V. L. & Pines, M. (eds) *Ring of Fire: Primitive Affects and Object Relations in Group Psychotherapy*, London: Routledge.

Agnati, L. F., Bjelke, B. & Fuxe, K. (1992) 'Volume transmission in the brain,' *American Scientist*, 80, pp362–373.

Allen, P. M. (1998a) 'Evolving complexity in social science,' in Altman, G. & Koch, W. A. (eds) *Systems: New Paradigms for the Human Sciences*, New York: Walter de Gruyter.

Allen, P. M. (1998b) 'Modeling complex economic evolution,' in Schweitzer, F. & Silverberg, G. (eds) *Selbstorganization*, Berlin: Dunker and Humbolt.

Ameriks, K. (ed.) (2002) *The Cambridge Companion to German Idealism*, Cambridge: Cambridge University Press.

Ansbach, C. & Schermer, V. L. (1994) *Object Relations, the Self and the Group*, London: Routledge.

Anzieu, D. (1984) *The Group and the Unconscious*, London: Routledge and Kegan Paul.

Aram, E. (2001) 'The experience of complexity: learning as the potential transformation of identity,' unpublished thesis: University of Hertfordshire.

Aron, L. (1991) 'The patient's experience of the analyst's subjectivity,' reprinted in Mitchell, S. A. & Aron, L. (eds) (1999) *Relational Psychoanalysis: The Emergence of a Tradition*, Hillsdale, NJ: The Analytic Press.

Ashby, W. R. (1945) 'The effects of control on stability,' *Natura*, 155, pp242–243.

Ashby, W. R. (1952) *Design for a Brain*, New York: Wiley.

Ashby, W. R. (1956) *Introduction to Cybernetics*, New York: Wiley.

Atwood, G. E. & Stolorow, R. D. ([1979] 1993) *Faces in a Cloud: Intersubjectivity in Personality Theory*, Northvale, NJ: Jason Aronson Inc.

Atwood, G. E. & Stolorow, R. D. (1984) *Structures of Subjectivity: Explorations in Psychoanalytic Phenomenology*, Hillsdale, NJ: The Analytic Press.

Barrie, J. M., Freeman, W. J. & Lenhart, M. (1994) 'Cross modality cortical processing: spatiotemporal patterns in olfactory, visual, auditory and somatic EEGs in perception by trained rabbits,' *Society for Neuroscience Abstracts*, 414.10.

Bateson, G. (1973) *Steps to an Ecology of Mind*, St Albans: Paladin.

Bateson, G. & Bateson, M. C. (1987) *Angels Fear: Towards an Epistemology of the Sacred*, New York: Macmillan.

Bateson, G. & Ruesch, J. (1957) *Communication: The Social Matrix of Society*, New York: Norton.

Beer, S. (1966) *Decision and Control: The Meanings of Operational Research and Management Cybernetics*, London: Wiley.

Beer, S. (1979) *The Heart of the Enterprise*, Chichester: Wiley.

Beer, S. (1981) *The Brain of the Firm*, Chichester: Wiley.

Beiser, F. C. (ed.) (1993) *The Cambridge Companion to Hegel*, Cambridge: Cambridge University Press.

Beiser, F. C. (2000) 'The enlightenment and idealism,' reprinted in Ameriks, K. (ed.) (2002) *The Cambridge Companion to German Idealism*, Cambridge: Cambridge University Press.

Benjamin, J. (1990) 'Recognition and destruction: an outline of intersubjectivity,' reprinted in Mitchell, S. A. & Aron, L. (eds) (1999) *Relational Psychoanalysis: The Emergence of a Tradition*, Hillsdale, NJ: The Analytic Press.

Bion, W. (1961) *Experiences in Groups and Other Papers*, London: Tavistock Publications.

Boden, D. (1994) *The Business of Talk: Organizations in Action*, Cambridge: Polity Press.

Bortoft, H. (1985) 'Counterfeit and authentic wholes: finding a means for dwelling in nature,' in Seamon, D. & Mugerauer, R. (eds) *Dwelling, Place and Environment*, Dordrecht: Martinus Nijhof Publishers.

Bowlby, J. (1969) *Attachment and Loss Vol I: Attachment*, London: Penguin Books.

Bowlby, J. (1973) *Attachment and Loss Vol II: Separation*, London: Penguin Books.

Brown, D. (1994) 'Self development through subjective interaction: a fresh look at ego training in action,' in Brown, D. & Zinkin, L. (eds) (1994) *The Psyche and the Social World: Developments in Group-analytic Theory*, London: Routledge.

Brown, D. (1996) 'Discussion on article by Nicola Diamond I,' *Group Analysis*, 29, 3, pp317–320.

Brown, D. (1997) 'Conversation with Norbert Elias', *Group Analysis*, 30, 4, pp515–525.

Bruner, J. (1990) *Acts of Meaning*, Cambridge, MA: Harvard University Press.

Chamberlin, D. (1987) 'Consciousness at birth,' in Verny, T. (ed.) *Pre- and Perinatal Psychology: An Introduction*, New York: Human Sciences Press.

Chodorow, N. J. (1986) 'Reconstructing individualism: autonomy, individuality and the self in Western thought,' reprinted in Mitchell, S. A. & Aron, L. (eds) (1999) *Relational Psychoanalysis: The Emergence of a Tradition*, Hillsdale, NJ: The Analytic Press.

Churchman, C. West (1968) *The Systems Approach*, New York: Delacorte Press.

Churchman, C. West (1970) *The Systems Approach and its Enemies*, New York: Basic Books.

Cosmides, L. & Tooby, J. (1992) 'Cognitive adaptations for social change,' in Barkow, J. H., Cosmides, L. & Tooby, J. (eds) *The Adapted Mind: Evolutionary Psychology and the Generation of Culture*, (pp163–228), New York: Oxford University Press.

Cushman, P. (1991) 'Ideology obscured: political uses of the self in Daniel Stern's infant,' *American Psychologist*, 46, 3, pp206–219.

Dalal, F. (1998) *Taking the Group Seriously: Toward a Post-Foulkesian Group-analytic Theory*, London: Jessica Kingsley.

Dalal, F. (2001) 'The social unconscious: a post-Foulkesian perspective,' *Group Analysis*, 4, 34, pp539–557.

Damasio, A. R. (1994) *Descartes' Error: Emotion, Reason and the Human Brain*, London: Picador.

Damasio, A. R. (1999) *The Feeling of What Happens: Body and Emotion in the Making of Consciousness*, London: Heinemann.

Darwin, C. (1859) *The Origin of Species by Means of Natural Selection or, The Preservation of Favoured Races in the Struggle for Life*, London: John Murray.

Darwin, C. (1871) *The Descent of Man*, London: John Murray.

Dawkins, R. (1976) *The Selfish Gene*, New York: Oxford University Press.

Diamond, N. (1996) 'Can we speak of internal and external reality,' *Group Analysis*, 29, 3, pp303–317.

Durkin, H. E. ([1983] 2000) 'Some contributions of general systems theory to psychoanalytic group psychotherapy,' in Pines, M. (ed.) *The Evolution of Group Analysis*, London: Jessica Kingsley.

Eldridge, N. & Gould, J. (1972) 'Punctuated equilibria: an alternative to phyletic gradualism,' in Schopf, T. J. M. (ed.) *Models in Paleobiology*, San Francisco: Freeman, Cooper and Co.

Elias, N. ([1939] 2000) *The Civilizing Process*, Oxford: Blackwell.

Elias, N. ([1969] 1983) *The Court Society*, Oxford: Blackwell.

Elias, N. ([1970] 1978) *What is Sociology?*, Oxford: Blackwell.

Elias, N. (1987) *Involvement and Detachment*, Oxford: Blackwell.

Elias, N. (1989) *The Symbol Theory*, London: Sage Publications.

Elias, N. (1991) *The Society of Individuals*, Oxford: Blackwell.

Elias, N. (1994) *Reflections on a Life*, Oxford: Polity Press.

Elias, N. & Scotson, J. L. ([1965] 1994) *The Established and the Outsiders*, London: Sage.

Ezriel, H. (1952) 'Psychoanalytic group therapy: II interpretation and research,' *Journal for the Study of Interpersonal Processes*, 15, 2 (May).

Fisher, R. A. (1930) *The Genetic Theory of Natural Selection*, Oxford: Oxford University Press.

Fletcher, J. (1997) *Violence and Civilization: An Introduction to the Work of Norbert Elias*, Cambridge: Polity Press.

Fonseca, J. (2001) *Complexity and Innovation in Organizations*, London: Routledge.

Forrester, J. (1958) 'Industrial dynamics: a major breakthrough for decision-making,' *Harvard Business Review*, 36, 4, pp37–66.

Forrester, J. (1961) *Industrial Dynamics*, Cambridge, MA: MIT Press.

Forrester, J. (1969) *The Principles of Systems*, Cambridge, MA: Wright-Allen Press.

Forster, M. (1993) 'Hegel's dialectical method,' in Beiser, F. C. (ed.) *The Cambridge Companion to Hegel*, Cambridge: Cambridge University Press.

Foulkes, S. H. (1934) 'Biology in the light of the work of Kurt Goldstein,' reprinted in Foulkes, S. H. (1990) *Selected Papers: Psychoanalysis and Group Analysis*, London: Karnac.

Foulkes, S. H. (1948) *Introduction to Group Analytic Psychotherapy*, London: William Heinemann Medical Books Limited.

Foulkes, S. H. (1964) *Therapeutic Group Analysis*, London: George Allen & Unwin.

Foulkes, S. H. (1966) 'Some basic concepts in group psychotherapy,' reprinted in

Foulkes, S. H. (1990) *Selected Papers: Psychoanalysis and Group Analysis*, London: Karnac.

Foulkes, S. H. (1968) 'Group dynamic processes and group analysis,' reprinted in Foulkes, S. H. (1990) *Selected Papers*, London: Karnac.

Foulkes, S. H. (1971) 'Access to unconscious processes in the group-analytic group,' reprinted in Foulkes, S. H. (1990) *Selected Papers: Psychoanalysis and Group Analysis*, London: Karnac.

Foulkes, S. H. (1973) 'The group as matrix of the individual's mental life,' in Foulkes, S. H. (1990) *Selected Papers: Psychoanalysis and Group Analysis*, London: Karnac.

Foulkes, S. H. (1975a) 'The leader in the group,' reprinted in Foulkes, S. H. (1990) *Selected Papers: Psychoanalysis and Group Analysis*, London: Karnac.

Foulkes, S. H. (1975b) *Group Analytic Psychotherapy: Method and Principles*, London: Karnac.

Foulkes, S. H. (1977) 'Notes on the concept of resonance,' reprinted in Foulkes, S. H. (1990) *Selected Papers: Psychoanalysis and Group Analysis*, London: Karnac.

Foulkes, S. H. (1990) *Selected Papers: Psychoanalysis and Group Analysis*, London: Karnac.

Foulkes, S. H. & Anthony, E. J. ([1957] 1975) *Group Psychotherapy: The Psychoanalytic Approach*, London: Karnac.

Freeman, W. J. (1994) 'Role of chaotic dynamics in neural plasticity,' in van Pelt, J., Corner, M. A., Uylings, H. B. M. & Lopes da Silva, F. H. (eds) *Progress in Brain Research*, Vol 102, Amsterdam: Elsevier Science BV.

Freeman, W. J. (1995) *Societies of Brains: A Study in the Neuroscience of Love and Hate*, Hillsdale, NJ: Lawrence Erlbaum Associates Inc.

Freeman, W. J. & Barrie J. M. (1994) 'Chaotic oscillations and the genesis of meaning in cerebral cortex,' in Buzsaki, G., Llinas, R., Singer, W., Berthoz, A. & Christen, Y. (eds) *Temporal Coding in the Brain*, Berlin: Springer.

Freeman, W. J. & Schneider, W. (1982) 'Changes in the spatial patterns of rabbit olfactory EEG with conditioning to odors,' *Psychophysiology*, 19, pp45–56.

Freud, S. (1908) 'Civilized sexual morality and modern nervous illness,' in Freud, S. (1991) *Civilization, Society and Religion*, Vol 12, Penguin Freud Library, London: Penguin.

Freud, S. (1913) 'Totem and taboo,' in Freud, S. (1990) *The Origins of Religion*, Vol 13, Penguin Freud Library, London: Penguin.

Freud, S. (1921) 'Group psychology and the analysis of the ego,' in Freud, S. (1991) *Civilization, Society and Religion*, Vol 12, Penguin Freud Library, London: Penguin.

Freud, S. (1927) 'The future of an illusion,' in Freud, S. (1991) *Civilization, Society and Religion*, Vol 12, Penguin Freud Library, London: Penguin.

Freud, S. (1930) 'Civilization and its discontents,' in Freud, S. (1991) *Civilization, Society and Religion*, Vol 12, Penguin Freud Library, London: Penguin.

Freud, S. (1991) *Civilization, Society and Religion*, Vol. 12, Penguin Freud Library, London: Penguin.

Fromm, E. (1980) *The Chains of Illusion*, London: Sphere Books.

Ganzarain, R. (1989) *Object Relations Group Psychotherapy: Groups as an Object, a Toll and a Training Base*, Madison, CT: International University Press.

Gardner, H. (1985) *The Mind's New Science: A History of the Cognitive Revolution*, New York: Basic Books.

Garfinkel, H. (1967) *Studies in Ethnomethodology*, Englewood Cliffs, NJ: Prentice Hall.

Gilbert, P. & Bailey, K. G. (eds) (2000) *Genes on the Couch: Explorations in Evolutionary Psychotherapy*, Philadelphia, PA: Brunner-Routledge.

Gleick, J. (1988) *Chaos: The Making of a New Science*, London: William Heinemann Limited.

Goffman, E. (1981) *Forms of Talk*, Philadelphia, PA: University of Pennsylvania Press.

Goldberger, A. L. (1997) 'Fractal variability versus pathologic periodicity: complexity loss and stereotypy in disease,' *Perspectives in Biology and Medicine*, 40, 4, pp543–561.

Goldstein, K. (1939) *The Organism*, New York: American Book Co.

Goodwin, B. (1994) *How the Leopard Changed its Spots*, London: Weidenfeld and Nicholson.

Goodwin, R. M. (1951) 'Econometrics in business-style analysis,' in Hansen, A. H. (ed.) *Business Cycles and National Income*, New York: W. W. Norton.

Greenberg, J. R. (1986) 'Theoretical models and the analyst's neutrality,' reprinted in Mitchell, S. A. & Aron, L. (eds) (1999) *Relational Psychoanalysis: The Emergence of a Tradition*, Hillsdale, NJ: The Analytic Press.

Greenberg, J. R. & Mitchell, S. A. (1983) *Object Relations in Psychoanalytic Theory*, Cambridge, MA: Harvard University Press.

Griffin, D. (2001) *The Emergence of Leadership: Linking Self-organization and Ethics*, London: Routledge.

Haldane, J. B. S. (1932) *The Causes of Evolution*, New York: Harper Brothers.

Hebb, D. O. (1949) *The Organization of Behavior*, New York: Wiley.

Hegel, G. W. F. (1807) *The Phenomenology of the Spirit*, trans. A. V. Miller, Oxford: Oxford University Press.

Hodgson, G. M. (2001) 'Is social evolution Lamarckian or Darwinian?' in Laurent, J. & Nightingale J. (eds) *Darwinian and Evolutionary Economics*, Cheltenham: Edward Elgar.

Hopper, E. (2001) 'The social unconscious; theoretical considerations,' *Group Analysis*, 34, 1, pp9–27.

Huxley, T. (1863) *Man's Place in Nature*, New York: D. Appleton.

Jackson, M. C. (2000) *Systems Approaches to Management*, New York: Kluwer Academic.

Jefferson, G. (1978) 'Sequential aspects of storytelling in conversation,' in Schenkein, J. (ed.) *Studies in the Organization of Conversational Interaction*, New York: Academic Press.

Kant, I. ([1790] 1987) *Critique of Judgement*, trans. W. S. Pluhar, Indianapolis, IN: Hackett.

Kauffman, S. A. (1995) *At Home in the Universe*, New York: Oxford University Press.

Kelso, J. A. Scott (1995) *Dynamic Patterns: The Self-organization of Brain and Behavior*, Cambridge, MA: MIT Press.

Kernberg, O. D. (1976) *Object Relations Theory and Clinical Psychoanalysis*, New York: Jason Aronson.

Kernberg, O. D. (1998) *Ideology, Conflict and Leadership in Groups and Organizations*, New Haven, CT: Yale University Press.

Klein, M. (1988) *Envy, Gratitude and Other Works 1946–1963*, London: Virago Press.

Langer, S. K. (1967) *Mind: An Essay on Human Feeling, Vol 1*, Baltimore, MD: John Hopkins University Press.

Laplanche, J. & Pontalis, J.-B. (1967) *The Language of Psychoanlaysis*, New York: Norton.

Laszlo, E. (1972) *Introduction to Systems Philosophy*, New York: Gordon and Breach.

Leader, D. (2000) *Freud's Footnotes*, London: Faber and Faber.

Le Bon, G. (1895) *The Crowd: A Study of the Popular Mind*, New York: Ballantine.

Leibniz, G. W. (1992) *Discourse on Metaphysics and the Monadology*, Buffalo, NY: Prometheus Books.

Leowald, H. (1960) 'On the therapeutic action of psychoanalysis,' in (1980) *Papers on Psychoanalysis*, New Haven, CT: Yale University Press.

Leowald, H. (1972) 'Perspectives on memory,' in (1980) *Papers on Psychoanalysis*, New Haven, CT: Yale University Press.

Levy, S. (1992) *Artificial Life*, New York: First Vintage Books.

Lewin, R. (1993) *Complexity: Life at the Edge of Chaos*, London: J. M. Dent.

Lewontin, R. C. (1974) *The Genetic Basis of Evolutionary Change*, New York: Columbia University Press.

Lewontin, R. C. (2000) *It Ain't Necessarily So: The Dream of the Human Genome and Other Illusions*, London: Granta Books.

Lewontin, R. C. (2001) *Sunday Times*, 8 July 2001.

Lintot, B. (1983) 'Mind and matrix in the writings of S. H. Foulkes,' *Group Analysis*, 16, 3, pp242–248.

Lombardi, K. L. (1998) 'Subject relations as seen through prenatal observations,' in Rucker, N. G. & Lombardi, K. L. (eds) *Subject Relations: Unconscious Experiences and Relational Psychoanalysis*, London: Routledge.

McCulloch, W. S. & Pitts, W. (1943) 'A logical calculus of ideas imminent in nervous activity,' *Bulletin of Mathematical Biophysics*, 5, pp115–133.

McDougall, W. (1920) *The Group Mind*, London: Cambridge.

McGuire, M. T., Raleigh, M. J., & Brammer, G. T. (1984) 'Adaptation, selection, and benefit-cost balances,' *Ethology and Social Biology*, 5, pp269–277.

Marone, M. (1998) *Attachment and Interaction*, London: Jessica Kingsley.

Matte Blanco, I. (1975) *The Unconscious as Infinite Sets: An Essay in Bi-logic*, London: Duckworth.

Matte Blanco, I. (1988) *Thinking, Feeling and Being*, London: Routledge.

Maturana, H. & Varela, F. J. (1992) *The Tree of Knowledge: The Biological Roots of Human Understanding*, Boston: Shambhala.

Mead, G. H. (1932) *The Philosophy of the Present*, Chicago: University of Chicago.

Mead, G. H. (1934) *Mind Self and Society*, Chicago: Chicago University Press.

Mead, G. H. (1936) *Movements of Thought in the Nineteenth Century*, (ed.) M. H. Moore, Chicago: Chicago University Press.

Mead, G. H. (1938) *The Philosophy of the Act*, Chicago: University of Chicago.

Mead, G. H. (1977) *George Herbert Mead on Social Psychology*, (ed.) A. Strauss, Chicago: University of Chicago.

Meares, R. (1992) *The Metaphor of Play: On Self, the Secret and Borderline Experience*, Melbourne: Hill of Content Publishing.

Mennell, S. (1992) *Norbert Elias: An Introduction*, Dublin: University College Dublin Press.

Mennell, S. & Goudsblom, J. (1998) *Norbert Elias: On Civilization, Power and Knowledge*, Chicago: University of Chicago Press.

Menzies Lyth, I. (1975) 'A case study in the functioning of social systems as a defence against anxiety,' in Coleman, A. & Bexton, W. H. (eds) *Group Relations Reader*, Sausalito, CA: GREX.

Merleau Ponty, M. (1964) 'Indirect language and the voices of silence,' in *Signs*, Evanston, IL: Northwestern University Press.

Merleau Ponty, M. (1976) *The Phenomenology of Perception*, London: Routledge, Kegan & Paul.

Midgley, G. (2000) *Systemic Intervention: Philosophy, Methodology, and Practice*, New York: Kluwer Academic.

Mitchell, S. A. (1986) 'The wings of Icarus: illusion and the problem of narcissism,' reprinted in Mitchell, S. A. & Aron, L. (eds) (1999) *Relational Psychoanalysis: The Emergence of a Tradition*, Hillsdale, NJ: The Analytic Press.

Mitchell, S. A. (2000) *Relationality: From Attachment to Intersubjectivity*, Hillsdale, NJ: The Analytic Press.

Mitchell, S. A. & Aron, L. (eds) (1999) *Relational Psychoanalysis: The Emergence of a Tradition*, Hillsdale, NJ: The Analytic Press.

Nicolis, G. & Prigogine, I. (1989) *Exploring Complexity: An Introduction*, New York: W. H. Freeman and Company.

Nitsun, N. (1996) *The Anti-group: Destructive Forces in the Group and Their Creative Potential*, London: Routledge.

Ogden, T. H. (1994) *Subjects of Analysis*, London: Karnac.

Orange, D. M., Atwood, G. E. & Stolorow, R. D. (1997) *Working Intersubjectively: Contextualism in Psychoanalytic Practice*, Hillsdale, NJ: The Analytic Press.

Philips, A. W. (1950) 'Mechanical models in economic dynamics,' *Econometrica*, 17, pp283–305.

Pinkard, T. (2000a) *Hegel: A Biography*, Cambridge: University of Cambridge Press.

Pinkard, T. (2000b) 'Hegel's phenomenology and logic: an overview,' in Ameriks, K. (ed.) (2002) *The Cambridge Companion to German Idealism*, Cambridge: Cambridge University Press.

Pinker, S. (1994) *The Language Instinct: The New Science of Language and Mind*, New York: William Morrow.

Pinker, S. (1997) *How the Mind Works*, New York: Penguin Books.

Piontelli, A. (1989) 'A study in twins before and after birth,' *International Review of Psychoanalysis*, 16, 4, pp413–426.

Piontelli, A. (1992) *From Fetus to Child: An Observational Study*, New York: Routledge.

Pippin, R. (1993) 'You can't get there from here: transition problems in Hegel's phenomenology of spirit,' in Beiser, F. C. (2000) 'The enlightenment and idealism,' in Ameriks, K. (ed.) (2002) *The Cambridge Companion to German Idealism*, Cambridge: Cambridge University Press.

Prigogine, I. (1997) *The End of Certainty: Time, Chaos and the New Laws of Nature*, New York: The Free Press.

Prigogine, I. & Stengers, I. (1984) *Order Out of Chaos: Man's New Dialogue with Nature*, New York: Bantam Books.

Racker, H. (1968) *Transference and Countertransference*, New York: International Universities Press.

Ray, T. S. (1992) 'An approach to the synthesis of life,' in Langton, G. C., Taylor, C., Doyne-Farmer, J. & Rasmussen, S. (eds) *Artificial Life II, Santa Fe Institute, Studies in the Sciences of Complexity, Volume 10*, Reading, MA: Addison-Wesley.

Reite, N. & Field, T. (1985) *The Psychobiology of Attachment and Separation*, Orlando, FL: Academic Press.

Renik, O. (1999) 'Analytic interaction: conceptualizing technique in light of the analyst's irreducible subjectivity,' in Mitchell, S. A. & Aron, L. (eds) *Relational Psychoanalysis: The Emergence of a Tradition*, Hillsdale, NJ: The Analytic Press.

Rescher, N. (1991) *G. W. Leibniz's Monadology*, Pittsburgh: University of Pittsburgh Press.

Reynolds, C. W. (1987) 'Flocks, herds and schools: a distributed behavior model,' *Proceedings of SIGGRAPH '87, Computer Graphics*, 21, 4, pp25–34.

Ricoeur, P. (1970) *Freud and Philosophy: An Essay on Interpretation*, New Haven, CT: Yale University Press.

Ridley, M. (1997) *The Origins of Virtue*, London: Penguin Books.

Roberts, J. P. (1982) 'Foulkes' concept of the matrix,' *Group Analysis*, XV/2, pp111–126.

Rose, M. & Rose, S. (2000) *Alas, Poor Darwin: Arguments Against Evolutionary Psychology*, London: Jonathan Cape.

Rose, S. P. R. (1995) 'Memory formation: its molecular and cell biology,' *European Review*, 3, 3, pp243–256.

Rucker, N. G. (1998) 'The prenatal anlage of psychic life,' in Rucker, N. G. & Lombardi, K. L. (eds) *Subject Relations: Unconscious Experiences and Relational Psychoanalysis*, London: Routledge.

Sacks, H. (1992) *Lectures on Conversations*, Oxford: Blackwell.

Sara, S. J. (2000) 'Retrieval and reconsolidation: toward a neurobiology of remembering,' *Learning and Memory*, 7, pp73–84.

Schafer, R. (1976) *A New Language for Psychoanalysis*, Newhaven, CT: Yale University Press.

Schafer, R. (1983) *The Analytic Attitude*, NY: Basic Books.

Schafer, R. ([1983] 1993) *The Analytic Attitude*, London: Karnac.

Schore, A. N. (1994) *Affect Regulation and the Origin of the Self: The Neurobiology of Emotional Development*, Hillsdale, NJ: Lawrence Erlbaum Associates Inc.

Shaw, P. (2002) *Changing Conversations in Organizations: A Complexity Approach to Change*, London: Routledge.

Shegloff, E. A. (1991) 'Reflections on talk and social structures,' in Boden, D. & Zimmerman, D. H. (eds) *Talk and Social Structure*, Cambridge: Polity Press.

Shotter, J. (1993) *Conversational Realities: Constructing Life through Language*, Thousand Oaks, CA: Sage Publications.

Shotter, J. (2000) 'Wittgenstein and his philosophy of beginnings and beginnings and beginnings,' paper for Wittgenstein Conference in honor of Rom Harre, American University, Washington DC.

Shotter, J. & Katz, A. M. (1996) 'Hearing the patient's 'voice': towards a social poietics in diagnostic interviews,' *Social Science and Medicine*, 46, pp919–931.

Siegel, D. J. (1999) *The Developing Mind: Toward a Neurobiology of Interpersonal Experience*, New York: The Guilford Press.

Skarda, C. A. & Freeman, W. J. (1990) 'Chaos and the new science of the brain,' *Concepts in Neuroscience*, 1, 2, pp275–285.

Smith, D. (2001) *Norbert Elias and Modern Social Theory*, London: Sage.

Smith, T. S. (2001) 'Hyperstructures: strong interaction and the biological structure of social life,' unpublished manuscript.

Smith, T. S. & Franks, D. (1999) 'Emergence, reduction, and levels of analysis in the neurosociological paradigm,' in Franks, D. & Smith, T. S. (eds) *Mind, Brain, and Society* (Volume 5 of Social Perspectives on the Emotions), Stamford, CT: JAI Press.

Smith, T. S. & Stevens, G. T. (1996) 'Emergence, self-organization, and social interaction: arousal-dependent structure in social systems,' *Sociological Theory*, 14 (July), pp131–153.

Smith, T. S. & Stevens, G. T. (1997) 'Comfort-regulation as a morphogenetic principle,' in Markovsky, B. (ed.) *Advances in Group Processes*, Vol. 14, Stamford, CT: JAI Press.

Smith, T. S. & Stevens, G. T. (1999) 'The architecture of small networks: strong interaction and dynamic organization in small social systems,' *American Sociological Review*, 64, June, pp403–420.

Smith, T. S. & Stevens, G. T (2002) 'Hyperstructures and the biology of interpersonal dependence,' *Sociological Theory*. Forthcoming.

Sole, R. & Goodwin, B. (2000) *Signs of Life: How Complexity Pervades Biology*, New York: Basic Books.

Spezzano, C. (1999) 'A relational model of inquiry and truth: the place of psychoanalysis in human conversation,' in Mitchell, S. A. & Aron, L. (eds) *Relational Psychoanalysis: The Emergence of a Tradition*, Hillsdale, NJ: The Analytic Press.

Stacey, R. (2000) *Strategic Management and Organisational Dynamics: The Challenge of Complexity*, London: Pearson Education.

Stacey, R. (2001a) *Complex Responsive Processes in Organizations: Learning and Knowledge Creation*, London: Routledge.

Stacey, R. (2001b) 'Complexity and the group matrix,' *Group Analysis*, 34, 2, pp221–241.

Stacey, R. (2001c) 'What can it mean to say that the individual is social through and through,' *Group Analysis*, 34, 4, pp457–472.

Stacey, R., Griffin, D. & Shaw, P. (2000) *Complexity and Management: Fad or Radical Challenge to Systems Thinking?*, London: Routledge.

Stern, Donnel (1983) 'Unformulated experience: from familiar chaos to creative disorder,' *Contemporary Psychoanalysis*, 19, 1, pp71–99, reproduced in Mitchell, S. A. & Aron, L. (eds) (1999) *Relational Psychoanalysis: The Emergence of a Tradition*, Hillsdale, NJ: The Analytic Press.

Stern, Daniel N. (1985) *The Interpersonal World of the Infant*, New York: Basic Books.

Stern, Daniel N. (1995) *The Motherhood Constellation: A Unified View of Parent–Infant Psychotherapy*, New York: Basic Books.

Stewart, I. (1989) *Does God Play Dice*, Oxford: Blackwell.

Stolorow, R. D. & Atwood, G. E. (1992) *Contexts of Being: The Intersubjective Foundations of Psychological Life*, Hillsdale, NJ: The Analytic Press.

Stolorow, R. D. & Atwood, G. E. (1994) 'Toward a science of human experience,' in Stolorow, R. D., Atwood, G. E. & Brandchaft, B. (eds) *The Intersubjective Perspective*, Northvale, NJ: Jason Aronson Inc.

Stolorow, R., Atwood, G. & Brandchaft, B. (1994) *The Intersubjective Perspective*, Northvale, NJ: Jason Aaronson.

Stolorow, R. D., Brandchaft, B. & Atwood, G. E. (1987) *Psychoanalytic Treatment: An Intersubjective Approach*, Hillsdale, NJ: The Analytic Press.

Stolorow, R. D., Orange, D. M. & Atwood, G. E. (1998) 'Projective Identification Begone! Commentary on a paper by Susan H. Sands,' *Psychoanalytic Dialogue*, 8, 5, pp719–725.

Streatfield, P. (2001) *The Paradox of Control in Organizations*, London: Routledge.

Sucharov, M. (1994) 'Psychoanalysis, self psychology, and intersubjectivity,' in Stolorow, R. D., Atwood, G. E. & Brandchaft, B. (eds) *The Intersubjective Perspective*, Northvale, NJ: Jason Aronson Inc.

Thelen, E. & Smith, L. (1994) *A Dynamic Systems Approach to the Development of Cognition and Action*, Cambridge, MA: MIT Press.

Trotter, W. (1916) *Instincts of the Herd in Peace and War*, London: Fisher Unwin.

Tustin, A. (1953) *The Mechanism of Economic Systems*, Cambridge, MA: Harvard University Press.

Varela, F. J., Thompson, E. & Rosch, E. (1995) *The Embodied Mind: Cognitive Science and Human Experience*, Cambridge, MA: The MIT Press.

von Bertalanffy, L. (1968) *General Systems Theory: Foundations, Development, Applications*, New York: George Braziller.

von Foerster, H. (1984) 'On constructing reality,' in von Foerster, H. (ed.) *Observing Systems*, Seaside, CA: Intersystems.

von Glaserfeld, E. (1991) 'Knowing without metaphysics: aspects of the radical constructivist position,' in Steier, F. (ed.) *Research and Reflexivity*, London: Sage.

Waddington, C. H. (1962) *New Patterns in Genetics and Development*, New York: Columbia University Press.

Waldrop, M. M. (1992) *Complexity: The Emerging Science at the Edge of Chaos*, Englewood Cliffs, NJ: Simon & Schuster.

Watzlavick, P., Beavon, J. & Jackson, D. (1967) *Pragmatics of Human Communication*, New York: Norton.

Webster, G. & Goodwin, B. (1996) *Form and Transformation: Generative and Relational Principles in Biology*, Cambridge: Cambridge University Press.

Weick, K. ([1979] 1995) *Sensemaking in Organizations*, Thousand Oaks, CA: Sage.

Weissman, A. (1883) 'On heredity,' reprinted in Hall, T. S. (ed.) (1986) *A Sourcebook in Animal Biology*, New York: Hafner.

Westphal, K. (1993) 'The basic context and structure of Hegel's *Philosophy of Right*,' in Beiser, F. C. (ed.) *The Cambridge Companion to Hegel*, Cambridge: Cambridge University Press.

Whitaker, D. Stock (1985) *Using Groups to Help People*, London: Routledge, Kegan & Paul.

Wiener, N. (1948) *Cybernetics: Or Control and Communication in the Animal and the Machine*, Cambridge, MA: MIT Press.

Wilson, E. O. (1992) *The Diversity of Life*, New York: Norton.

Winnicott, D. W. (1965) *The Maturational Process and the Facilitating Environment*, London: Hogarth Press.

Wise, R. A. & Rompre, P. (1989) 'Brain dopamine and reward,' *Annual Review of Psychology*, 40, pp191–225.

Wood, A. W. (1993) 'Hegel and Marxism,' in Beiser, F. C. (ed.) *The Cambridge Companion to Hegel*, Cambridge: Cambridge University Press.

Wright, K. (1991) *Vision and Separation: Between Mother and Baby*, Northvale, NJ: Jason Aronson Inc.

Wright, S. (1940) 'Breeding structures of populations in relation to speciation,' *American Naturalist*, 74, pp232–248.

Index

Index compiled by Lewis N. Derrick